Writer's Guide to Hollywood Producers, Directors, and Screenwriter's Agents

2002–2003

Writer's Guide to Hollywood Producers, Directors, and Screenwriter's Agents

2002–2003

Who They Are! What They Want!
And How to Win Them Over!

SKIP PRESS

PRIMA PUBLISHING

Published by Prima Publishing, Roseville, California. Member of the Crown Publishing Group, a division of Random House, Inc., New York.

PRIMA PUBLISHING and colophon are trademarks of Random House, Inc., registered with the United States Patent and Trademark Office.

The *Writer's Guide* and cover design are trademarks of Random House, Inc.

All products mentioned are trademarks of their respective companies.

Every effort has been made to make this book complete and accurate as of the date of publication. In a time of rapid change, however, it is difficult to ensure that all information is entirely up-to-date. Although the publisher and author cannot be liable for any inaccuracies or omissions in this book, they are always grateful for corrections and suggestions for improvement.

ISBN 0-7615-3187-4
ISSN 1091-5850

02 03 04 DD 10 9 8 7 6 5 4 3 2
Printed in the United States of America

Third Edition

Visit us online at www.primapublishing.com

This book is dedicated to my readers and students everywhere, whose fine Hollywood dreams I hope come true, and Hollywood's most important people, the folks in the seats looking up at the silver screen.

Contents

Part One
Writer's Guide

Part Two
All About Agents, Lawyers, and Managers

Part Three
All About Producers and Directors

Preface

$\mathbf{A}$ lot has changed since I prepared the second edition of this book, both for me personally and within Hollywood. If you have either of the previous editions, you know that after the frustration of selling two feature scripts in a row but seeing neither film go into production, I quit screenwriting and turned to writing books. Preparing the first edition of this *Writer's Guide* brought me back to Hollywood and I've been firmly entrenched ever since, helping the Hollywood Film Festival get started, speaking about selling to Hollywood across the United States, and helping writers around the world.

In 2000, my biggest project was *The Complete Idiot's Guide to Screenwriting* (Alpha Books/Macmillan), a book I initially didn't want to write but am happy I did. From what other people are telling me about it, I actually do know something about screenwriting. For example, the book was Book of the Month at The Writers Store (see www.writersstore.com) in December of 2000.

I'm still amazed how many writers are attempting screenplays, looking to grab that Hollywood brass ring from all over the world. So I try even harder to help them, because I know how hard it can be. I know this—if you write a truly great screenplay, it's almost impossible to not succeed.

Since I started writing scripts again, I've had three feature films optioned and written two for hire. I've been a staff writer for a kids' TV show on the United Paramount Network. I wrote several episodes of a syndicated "reality" show. I created and sold an original Webshow which you might never see, due to the "dotcom" meltdown of the year 2000. And I've consulted writers around the world, both for free and for hire. Now I'm growing anxious. Although I always love meeting new friends and helping other writers, all I want to do now is tell my own stories, not co-write with someone else, flesh out another person's screen dreams, or be seen primarily as a central source of Hollywood information. I want to share my original stories with the world, write my own scripts and maybe film them, and publish some novels I've had in the hopper for years.

For all these reasons, this may be the very last *Writer's Guide* I will ever do, and so I've done my level best to make it the most complete and helpful one ever. I've gone beyond writing into digital filmmaking and other ideas that might help writers succeed. Anyone who's spent much time in Hollywood knows that the real powers are the writer/director in feature films and the writer/producer in television. That's the direction in which I'm headed, and if I can help you get there, great.

To veteran readers of this book, welcome back. To new readers, glad to meet you. To all of you, my very best wishes for silver screen success.

Acknowledgments

Through two previous editions of this *Writer's Guide* and well over a decade in the entertainment business, I continue my fondness for Hollywood, that high stakes, glamorous business to which people aspire worldwide.

Hollywood is a state of mind as much as it is a location. I know this because, on a daily basis, I hear from writers around the world who are writing screenplays or who want to sell their book or story to the movies.

You're one of those writers, no doubt, so first things first. This book is for *you*. Sometimes I cringe about the "now you've got a friend in the business" slogan of this book, but I really do try to be a friend to those needing advice, even when I deal with a couple hundred letters a day.

Now a little bit about my own influences, and the people who gave me inspiration and dreams at times when life looked a little bleak. I've been homeless more than once in my life, and poor most of my life, but many is the time I've found comfort in the products of Hollywood and been able to forget my troubles. So I give back, even though I'm not the most successful screenwriter who ever typed FADE IN.

In the last edition, I acknowledged cinematic influences who helped me see the best of the human family more clearly: Humphrey Bogart, Ray Bolger, Frank Capra, John Ford, Gene Kelly, Jimmy Stewart, and Orson Welles. I left off the magnificent Billy Wilder last time, so let me hastily add him to that list. I can't leave out Elvis Presley. After I saw the opening sequence to his *Kid Galahad*, I was thoroughly hooked on Hollywood. When I saw him dancing with Ann-Margaret in *Viva Las Vegas*, I was gone, man. Thank you, Hal Wallis, for all those Elvis movies.

And just in case you're wondering, Horton Foote's Oscar-winning screenplay for *To Kill a Mockingbird* remains my favorite.

I still love the cowboys: Hopalong Cassidy, Roy Rogers, Gene Autry, and John Wayne, and when I think about the passing of Ben Johnson, there's always a little sadness that he died before he could appear in that movie of mine he wanted to do.

I acknowledged a lot of personally influential women in the last edition, all actresses, but since writing *The Complete Idiot's Guide to Screenwriting*, my admiration skews more toward ladies like Frances Marion, the most successful screenwriter of all time. Donna Reed in *It's a Wonderful Life*, however, still knocks me out.

Although I continue to marvel at most things that Robert Bolt wrote, from *Lawrence of Arabia* to *A Man for All Seasons*, I'm encouraged by having writer/producer/directors like M. Night "Sixth Sense" Shamalayan and the Coen brothers on the scene. And when I see scripts as good as *Shakespeare in Love*, I'm thrilled, even though I had a variation of the same story optioned over a decade ago. While I still love Akira

Kurosawa for sheer power, George Lucas for vision, and Walt Disney for the joy he gave us all, I've gained great admiration recently for international filmmakers like Ang Lee, who gave us the magnificent *Crouching Tiger, Hidden Dragon*.

I continue to appreciate those who took my writing seriously early on: ICM agents Jeff Berg and Jack Gilardi; producer/director Richard Donner; producer Jennie Lew Tugend; producer Ron Hamady; screenwriters Robert Daley and Ernest Lehman; agent Joel Gotler; director Gus Trikonis; producer James Nelson; and multi-hatted actors Danny DeVito, Michael Douglas, Robert Redford, Robin Williams, and Michael York.

Newer Hollywood influences whose advice and assistance I value include: Carlos de Abreu, founder of the Hollywood Film Festival; attorney Bruce Grakal; Paul Mason, head of production at Viacom; producer Robert Katz; and Gary Shusett, founder of the Sherwood Oaks Experimental College.

I also deeply thank all those marvelous individuals who shared their own unique views and dreams by being interviewed for this book.

Information sources I thank are: Alex Amin, Ryan Williams and FilmTracker.com; Howard Meibach at HollywoodLitSales.com; Marc Hernandez at ShowBizData.com; the Academy of Motion Picture Arts and Sciences, CreativePlanet.com, *The Hollywood Reporter*, the Internet Movie Database, the *Los Angeles Times*, the *New York Times*, *Variety*, and the Writers Guild of America.

Then there are the non-Hollywood friends whose friendship and assistance I greatly appreciate: Julie Comins, Executive Director of the Aspen Writers Conference; Gregory Evans, UK screenwriter; FictionWorks.com publisher Ray Hoy; Randy Ladenheim-Gil, editor of my *Complete Idiot's Guide to Screenwriting*; Gabriele Meiringer, founder of The Writers Store; agent Craig Nelson; and Claire White, editor-in-chief of Writers Write.com.

I thank the people at Prima Publishing, both past and present, who have worked hard to help me get this book to the public.

I acknowledge authors Joseph Campbell and Napoleon Hill, whose inspiring works help me to make myself better and, hopefully, help me make the world better in turn. I thank all the writers of screenwriting advice whom I've never met, and most of the ones I have.

I thank fellow writer Bill Quick, who is always able to help me laugh at Hollywood when I most need to do so, and authors John Dalmas and Sol Stein for their shared wisdom. And Chris Patton for simply being a friend.

Last but not least, I cannot acknowledge enough my brothers Tim and Jay, who supported my writing through the years when others did not, and my wife (and fellow author) Debbie Press, who every day in every way makes everything possible. And our kids Haley and Holly, who give us hope for the future. I love you guys. You're the only Oscar winners in the movie of my life.

Introduction

Here's a scenario for you. It was in the first book, and it's just as relevant now as ever . . .

Imagine a cave. Down a long and steep incline, a group of people sit, staring fascinated, their faces illuminated by something projected on a wall before them. Listening intently, they react visibly to what they see and hear, but rarely comment openly, for to do so would violate the etiquette of the gathering. They are rapt in their attention, seeing little of themselves or each other, their impressions formed by shadows cast for their view.

They are not modern moviegoers. They are prisoners, as described in the "Allegory of the Cave" by Plato. If you don't know the story, and you want to write and sell screenplays, I suggest you read it. And while you're delving into the ancient Greeks, try to get through Aristotle's *Poetics* as well. He covers the principles of dramatic storytelling in a timeless, still applicable fashion.

Many beginning attempts at a Hollywood writing career closely resemble the plight of the prisoners in Plato's ancient tale. A clan gathered by the fire, listening to stories or wisdom passed down from elders, is an ancient tradition. Now, in urban centers around the world, our elders are often no longer our main source of wisdom. These days, the fire most people gather before is a flickering projection cast forth by an electric lamp. Our favorite storytellers may be young, old, or middle-aged. They may be male or female, of any race, from any country on the planet, yet each successful tale transfixes the crowd, gets them talking, moves them to tell their friends. If the story is told in a fascinating way, if it is particularly popular, our modern storytellers are invited back repeatedly. And their greatest accolade is a recognition their peers may offer, in another large "cave" filled with the greatest movie stars on Earth, where mankind's largest audience will watch in fascination to discover who is the greatest storyteller of the year. Best Screenplay, Best Adaption, Best Picture are announced at the Academy Awards.

That's where you come in, writer. Before you write your acceptance speech, you should probably know that the writer is not considered the author of a film. That's why the Writers Guild of America is on a collision course with the Directors Guild of America over the "possessory credit" we see onscreen as "A Film By." Writers are getting more active in Hollywood and may be on strike by the time you read this. If they are, one big reason will be doing away with possessory credits when the director did not also write the screenplay.

If a film is nominated for an Oscar, the award from the Academy of Motion Picture Arts and Sciences, the producer or director could become wealthy (or even wealthier) very quickly. Sadly enough, a writer dealing with Hollywood might labor in relative poverty for decades. Even after "making it," the writer might suffer. When *Forrest Gump* made $300 million at the box office, author Winston Groom publicly groused about not receiving any royalties. Paramount Pictures, already infamous over losing a lawsuit in a similar situation with columnist Art Buchwald over a story created for Eddie Murphy which eventually became *Coming to America*, did not admit that Groom had a case about *Forrest Gump*. They did, however, write him a check for $450,000 "in good faith" that he would eventually have some royalties due.

Every month it seems there is a story in "the trades" (*The Hollywood Reporter* or *Variety*) about some writer who, overnight, has sold a property for the kind of money most people can only dream about. Writers in Hollywood may have their gripes, but for those on the A-list, paydays aren't a problem.

But tell me this—how many screenwriting Oscar winners' names do you remember, compared to the beautiful faces of Best Actor or Best Actress?

When you understand how films are made, you understand why the writer has a sometimes forgotten place in the film business. A motion picture is a curious beast, put together by the collaboration of dozens, hundreds, even thousands of people. It may not survive long at the box office, yet go on to live forever, like 1939's *The Wizard of Oz*. The members of the "clan" who gather to create a film may not know one another and may never see each other again after filming; even more so the temporary clans in movie theaters worldwide. The artificial fire that flickers on faces and races through minds of movie watchers for two hours or so lives on only in their imaginations. If a movie creates an emotional impact with audience members, they will tell their friends. Reviewers in print, radio, TV and cyberspace will provide reviews. They will all talk about the stars, the special effects, the director. Will they discuss the writing? More often than not, only in negative terms.

Stars and directors will talk about making the film on talk shows. They might discuss their private lives. The screenwriter will only occasionally be mentioned. "It was a *great* script," they might say, if the writer is a personal friend, but the writer will almost never be invited to be a guest on the talk show, despite the fact the entire filmmaking process begins, and usually cannot commence without, a script.

Nevertheless, making a movie is the most collaborative creative process in all of the arts. A script is only a blueprint from which the building begins, and the architect who draws it up (the screenwriter) will most likely never be the person whose name they put on the building.

Let's turn back the clock a few thousand years. The aforementioned allegory by Plato was meant to illustrate the degrees in which our nature may be enlightened or unenlightened. He presented a scenario of men kept as prisoners in a cavernous under-ground chamber where a long passage led down into the cave, from an entrance open to light. A fire burned, and the light from the flames projected the shadows of puppets onto a wall in the back of the cave. The prisoners recognized as reality nothing but the shadows. When one of the prisoners was set free and shown the objects which have been making the shadows, he grew perplexed that the puppets, not the shadows he had seen for so long, were the true reality.

The freed prisoner had to learn to slowly grow accustomed to the real world, Plato told us. When the man ascended out of the cave and first saw the sun, his eyes were so suddenly filled with radiance that he was temporarily blinded to all the things he now found to be real. It was a long period of adjustment before the man truly realized the nature of even the simplest things in his new environment. Imagine then, said Plato, that our now free and enlightened man thought of his old companions in the cave. Enthusiastic with his newfound knowledge, he returned to the cave too quickly, and found his eyes clouded by darkness. The prisoners, acting on the shadow realities in their minds and having nothing with which to compare the tales of their returned companion, laugh at him. They say he has gone up and come back only to have his sight ruined.

Following this logic, they decide it is not worth anyone's time to even attempt an ascent from the cave. Furthermore, they have a violent reaction to their returned comrade. If they could lay their hands on the man who is trying to set them free and lead them up, says Plato, they would kill him.

When you've been around the business of Hollywood a while, you may discover that 90 percent of everyone you come in contact with has at least a notion that they, too, could write an award-winning screenplay. They can't, most likely, or they would. And because they can't and you, the writer, can, you may be subjected to any number of strange complaints and reactions, often stemming from the recipient's frustration over not being able to write a good script.

On the other hand, there are many successful people in the film business who realize that writing is not their particular best talent, who nevertheless have a great sense of what will work in a script and what will not. They range from script readers to studio executives, and the well-meaning (who predominate the business though it often seems otherwise) should not be confused with those who are jealous and overly critical.

Let's say you are a person who wants to write and sell screenplays, perhaps even make motion pictures. Watching moviegoers smile, laugh, cry or shudder at movie scenes you create might be the greatest professional reward you will experience. The first time such a reaction was seen, in fact, might have spurred you, as a young person or later in life, to become a screenwriter or filmmaker. The love of the audience might be your driving creative force for a lifetime. This is precisely what happened to the most successful filmmaker of all time, Steven Spielberg. The visual scribe of Boy Scout Troop 294 in Scottsdale, Arizona, young Spielberg filmed everything from cookouts to camping trips with his dad's movie camera. To earn his first merit badge, he made a movie and showed it to his troop. The applause of his fellow Scouts, Spielberg once told me in an interview, "felt real good on my heart" and spurred him to pursue a moviemaking career. And he's given back; the Boy Scout filmmaking badge came about due to Spielberg.

But here's the rub, as Shakespeare would say. Spielberg never graduated from film school. He made film after film after film, learning his craft. By the time he got to Hollywood, he was more than ready.

Similarly, most of the successful screenwriters I know write many, many scripts before they start to sell.

From ancient times, great storytellers have always relished the smiles of an audience and worked very hard to improve their craft. Keep working at it. When the word "rewrite" is your best friend, you'll understand what it takes to make it.

In Plato's allegory, the prisoner who was set free learned the necessity of a gradient approach. It was a steep and difficult ascent to the outside of the cave, and the brilliance of the new world was at first so dazzling it was overwhelming. Think of yourself as a released prisoner when you first approach Hollywood, because you might be treated like one, at first. When you arrive with bright new ideas designed to stun the world, remember Plato's freed man. When he returned to his comrades in the cave, he hurried too quickly and was noticeably affected by the darkness. When he tried to present a reality too different from the one long-accepted by the dwellers of the cave, they were ready to kill him.

If you approach Hollywood with bright new ideas, don't expect them to be taken seriously at first. The Hollywood community may be decidedly liberal, politically (even that is changing), but people writing checks in any major American business are generally conservative, when it comes time to let go of money. Tried and true methods and stories usually win out.

Hollywood is a town to be learned slowly and surely if you are to last, and persistence is one of the key elements of screenwriting success. You need to know what Hollywood has bought in the past, what they are buying in the present, and who is most likely to take a chance on your great new ideas.

The top screenwriters make only one-quarter what top film stars make, and rarely more than directors. Producers can make far more than stars, but the money to make films is not handed out to just anyone. Even if you are independently wealthy, it is generally a good idea to not try to produce a film until you know a good deal about the nuts and bolts of how films are made.

What you should never forget, though, is the great importance of writers in Hollywood. The essential nature of the writer in Tinseltown was perhaps best expressed by film studio executive Irving Thalberg, the model for F. Scott Fitzgerald's unfinished Hollywood novel *The Last Tycoon*. If the name rings a bell, it may be because Thalberg is the man the Academy of Motion Picture Arts and Sciences Irving G. Thalberg Memorial Award was named after—this is the award given at each Academy Awards for the most consistent high level of production achievement by an individual producer. Thalberg reportedly said: "The writer is the only absolutely essential element of Hollywood, and he must never find out."

Sorry, Irv, the cat's out of the bag, and it didn't like the confinement.

The only requirement for lasting success in Tinseltown is talent. If you have writing ability, there's room for you, though you might have to wait a while to get your chance. If you're not willing to stick it out, no matter how long it takes, you're in the wrong business. After all, Plato described only one person who escaped from the cave, and even he had a hard time.

The Hollywood landscape is constantly changing, the rules are rewritten with every weekend's box office results, but the business just keeps on going. Year after year, hundreds of films are made and distributed to eager audiences around the globe. No matter how it appears sometimes, someone has to write every single one of them. If you desire to be the one who draws up the blueprint, puts the show in motion, if you have the drive and talent to be the absolute essential element that Hollywood cannot do without, read on.

And don't let anyone deter you from your worthwhile dreams.

May you bring us light out of darkness, with some grand story that only you can tell. There's tons of room in Hollywood, but it's all at the top.

PART ONE

Writer's Guide

Hollywood Success in 25 Words or Less

Can you succinctly describe the property you're trying to sell? If you cannot, my guess is you don't have your story well-defined. These days, people you contact at production companies or agencies will ask you: "What's the logline?" If you can't rattle it off to them, you've probably blown a chance.

Where did that term come from? Think of a log on a desk in which notations are made. When a script, book, or other source material arrives, it is logged into a notebook manually or described in a computer file. Think of the short film and program descriptions in *TV Guide*. That's a logline.

The former catch phrase was "high concept," a phrase I first heard when I was trying to sell a TV miniseries idea to Barbara Hiser, an Emmy winner who at the time was head of TV miniseries development for Twentieth Century Fox. When she asked me what the high concept was, I sat there, stumped. "The high what?" I croaked. Barbara chuckled and explained that a high concept was a couple of sentences (preferably less) that describe the entire story. Yes, even a miniseries.

Hollywood still likes the idea of the high concept—for example, "*Die Hard* on a spaceship"—but the term most commonly used is *logline*.

To succeed in Hollywood, you need to speak Hollywood, or find someone to represent you in Hollywood who knows the latest slang. The idea of a logline or high concept may sound like crass commercialism—art reduced to 25 words or less—but consider this. A film distributor has to sell a film to the public, and if the concept is simple enough, his marketing department's job is half done. And when someone says they saw a great movie, don't you ask what it's about?

When you conceive a film story, you'll probably start with an idea. Maybe it's a simple "what if?" In my own experience and in interviewing dozens of other writers, I've learned that if you cannot clearly state the premise of your script in 25 words or less (at most, a couple of sentences), chances are you don't have your story focused and you will have trouble getting a good script written.

HOLLYWOOD SHORTHAND

About a year ago, I had the pleasure of getting to know Alex Amin, whom I had briefly met when he was working with agent-turned-producer, now turned back to agent Dave Phillips when I first interviewed Dave for the first *Writer's Guide to Hollywood*. Alex and some other extremely knowledgeable industry people had for some time been running a site known as scripttracker.com, which development executives and producers from several hundred of the very top companies in Hollywood logged on to every single day to trade information about available projects.

How did they first mention a property? With the shorthand of the logline. If the description sparked their interest, they inquired further. That's an industry standard.

Alex and his partners soon expanded their site into a new entity called Film-Tracker.com. Like similar sites on the Internet, they had in mind charging writers to "cover" submitted material and, if they found the property promising, to recommend it to one or more of the top companies already resident on their site. Billy Crystal's company is one. While the coverage was the standard 1.5- to 2-page format used by studios and production companies, each piece was first described by a logline.

Some veteran producers, however, still think in terms of high concept, which is slightly different than a logline. For example, Steven Segal's *Under Siege* was basically "*Die Hard* on a destroyer."

A HIGH-CONCEPT PRODUCER

No one understands high concepts better than the highly successful David Permut, whom I met when he was producing *Dragnet*. Consider how Permut sold the *Dragnet* film to Universal. While "channel surfing" one night, he saw an old rerun of Jack Webb's *Dragnet* TV show. Clicking farther along, he saw Dan Ackroyd in a rerun of *Saturday Night Live*. A brainstorm began. The next morning, Permut's first call was to Bernie Brillstein, who managed Ackroyd. Permut explained his concept of Ackroyd starring in a movie send-up of the old TV show, and Brillstein liked the idea. Permut immediately called Frank Price, who was running Universal Studios, and set up a pitch meeting.

What high concept did Permut pitch? "Dum, da, dum, dum!" It was the opening theme music to the old 1950s Jack Webb TV show, and instantly recognizable. When Price learned of Ackroyd's interest, he told Permut it was a deal—perhaps the quickest deal ever made from the pitch of a high concept. *Dragnet* was also one of the first TV shows to be adapted for the big screen. Of course, after he'd sold the studio on the project, he had to find a writer to do the script. The one he picked was an unknown screenwriter whom he felt had great promise. Amazingly, that writer turned him down, but a high-concept logline from that writer led to another deal.

"Early on in my career," Permut told me, "I wasn't in a position to go after the megastar writers, the established talent, and so I was left to my own devices, cultivating and finding new talent. One was Dale Launier, a young guy who was working at a Federated Stereo in the Valley. He had written a script that I had fallen in love with. Dale was a struggling screenwriter, but although I offered him numerous rewrite assignments on projects I had set up around town, he turned them down. Finally, I offered Dale a chance to collaborate with Dan Ackroyd when I had set up *Dragnet* in 1987. I said 'Look, I think you and Dan would hit it off. He's looking to collaborate with somebody.'" Launier turned him down, because he didn't want to write anybody else's ideas. Luckily for him, Permut remained impressed (which shows you how far good screenwriting can take you).

"He told me a true story the third time we got together," Permut said, "about a good friend of his who was set up on a date. He was told, 'She's blonde, she's hot, but whatever you do, don't let her drink because she gets out of control.' So what happened was, his friend went out on this date with this girl and she fit all of his qualifications, and the first thing he proceeded to do over dinner was order a bottle of champagne. He misinterpreted the warning, I guess. Everything that could go wrong on a blind date, did. I said to Dale, 'It's a great idea for a movie. Everybody's been on a blind date, and we can all relate to that experience. It's your idea. Let's see if we can pitch this around town and sell it.'"

Within a two-week period they met with "just about every studio executive in town," and by the end of the second week, they had three offers from three different studios. Amazingly, there was nothing in writing, story-wise.

"I had nothing but Dale's writing sample," Permut told me, "the script I met him through that was representative of his work. Jeff Sagansky had just been named president of Tristar, so Dale and I went over to Tristar and met with Sagansky and the other executives there. It was about seven o'clock at night, and Jeff was aware that three other studios were vying for the project and he loved the concept. Jeff was really able to grasp the concept and he bought the project, and a year later the film was released. It was Bruce Willis' first picture, *Blind Date* with Kim Basinger. It was one of the most successful movies at Tristar. Blake Edwards directed it. Later, Dale did *Dirty Rotten Scoundrels*, and more recently he did *My Cousin Vinny*."

Permut is still open to new writers. "The reality is," he told me, "I accept material through recommendations, and it doesn't need to be through an agent or through the formal chain of command. Many of the films that I've done evolved by those very experiences that are more unconventional than conventional. Of course, some movies I've made have come through agents. Screenplays certainly, spec (speculatively written) material. The more established writers will usually be represented by agents and attorneys and the like. But I'm always looking for good stories, an idea, an original idea I'll have once in awhile, a newspaper article, a true story where we have to track down the rights. It all starts there. The basis of any movie is a good story. If you start off with a story that isn't good or really doesn't have any merit theatrically, or a script that doesn't have any merit theatrically, it's hard to build a house without the foundation. The script is the blueprint and the foundation of any movie, and you see what happens."

So there you have it. If you can lay out a logline or a high concept, and you have a screenplay writing sample to show you can write well, you have what the majority of Hollywood executives want. Of course, it helps if the logline or high concept they want is *about* your screenplay sample, but a sale is a sale.

SELLING IDEAS TO HOLLYWOOD

How much can you make on a great high concept? In November 1997, Warner Brothers paid $400,000 against $1 million for Andrew Kurtzman's and Eliot Wald's high-concept spec script *Teething*. A couple unable to have children adopt a baby and discover it's a vampire. Do the scenes start playing in your head right away? The writers, however, were already known quantities, responsible for scripting films like *Down Periscope* and *Camp Nowhere*, and writing for the TV show *Saturday Night Live* in the 1980s.

What? You haven't seen the movie pitch described above? You didn't know *Down Periscope* was a box office failure? That's one reason the current emphasis in Hollywood is more on loglines, which convey the actual story, and less on high concepts.

Ultimately, it's all in the execution of the idea. Audiences don't pay to watch great ideas. Producer Robert Katz told me that there's a saying around town that he agrees with; he would rather have a mediocre concept with great writing than a great concept with mediocre writing.

In 2000, screenwriter David Ayer (see the "Lightning in a Bottle" chapter later in this book) sold his *Squids* idea, based on his real-life experiences in the United States Submarine Service, for $1.5 million to producer Art Linson. This followed, however, a rewrite credit on the successful *U–571* and several other sales and rewrite work. The people who sell concepts to Hollywood are, almost without exception, people already working in Hollywood, known quantities who can be trusted to deliver a screenplay suitable for filming.

Personally, unless I knew that a producer knew my work and would hire me to write a screenplay based on a concept I pitched, I would not pitch an idea unless I was describing a book or screenplay I had already written. And in the current (early 2001) atmosphere, with potential industry-crippling strikes threatened, producers, studios and television networks are only looking for scripts they can put into production with very little additional work needed.

SELLING IDEAS AS AN UNKNOWN

"Pitching" is usually a face-to-face meeting in which you describe your property to a producer or executive capable of giving you a deal. In the TV movie business, which offers a much faster turnaround between the time a project is "green-lighted" and the time it is seen by the public, high-concept pitches predominate. Think *Switched at Birth*. TV movies, though, are generally written by industry veterans.

My favorite successful high-concept pitch sale is from a producer who had a project about a genetically altered dog that goes berserk. He described it as "Jaws on Paws" and got the deal. That was Robert Kosberg, who will take a movie idea from anyone and, if he likes it, pitch it to major studios. Kosberg presents himself as the most successful pitchman in Tinseltown, with 50 or so sales, the most successful being *12 Monkeys* with Bruce Willis. You can see what he has to offer at his Web site, www.moviepitch.com, and decide whether or not you want to offer him a logline or high concept.

Sometimes a writer doesn't know what a story is really all about until they've rewritten it a few times. M. Night Shamalayan has said in interviews that he didn't know Bruce Willis' character in *Sixth Sense* was dead until the fifth draft. That was the great surprise at the end, of course, and it truly made the movie special. So if you don't have a beginning, middle, and end of a story spring into your mind fully formed, keep writing if you're onto a story you are passionate about. The essence of the tale might reveal itself in the process.

A GREAT CONCEPT FULLY REALIZED

No better example of a fully fleshed-out, great idea is a best-selling novel that led to a TV series on the Sci-Fi Network for writer Eric Garcia. When I first heard the title *Anonymous Rex*, I immediately understood and loved this film noirish detective romp based on the premise that dinosaurs have survived to modern day, living among us in secret. How Garcia's success story came about, though, is anything but an A to B tale.

"*Anonymous Rex* was originally called *The Tar Pit Exodus*," Garcia told me. "My agent got it and said we ought to change this title. I agreed. She would tell people about it and say we have this horrible title and finally, John Karp at Random House—who hadn't even seen the book—called her and said, 'How about *Anonymous Rex*?' He'd only heard about the basic concept of the story. She told him that if her client likes it, she'd give him a preview of the book before it was sent to every other publisher.

"I thought about the title, *Anonymous Rex* by Eric Garcia, and it seemed so perfect. I finished it on a Wednesday, my agent read it on a Thursday, she gave it to John on a Friday, and he made a preemptive bid on a Sunday so that no other publisher ever saw it. Since then I've done *Casual Rex* and *Hot & Sweaty Rex*, and I get a dozen e-mails a day from people suggesting other titles. I'd been writing since I was 12, but the first book I ever completed was *Rex*. During my senior year of high school we had a drama teacher who had studied film, and he said what you really want to write is scripts because that's where the money is. Then when you want to write the stuff you like, you can write books."

Garcia described to me a roundabout Hollywood career that began in Miami, Florida, moved through the film department at Cornell University in upstate New York, and then to the University of Southern California (USC). When he discovered that

USC's film department emphasis was toward directing and cinematography, he switched to the English department, where he took a class with novelist T. C. Boyle, whom he found "amazing."

"By the time I got to USC, I had written five or six scripts," he said. "By the time I sold *Rex*, I had probably written 25 or 30 scripts, but never sold anything."

His real Hollywood education came during an internship with the Ruddy-Morgan organization, where he got his first paid writing jobs while working with producers Al Ruddy, Andre Morgan, and Grey Fredericksen. Before being paid for screenwriting, he worked in development, reading scripts that came in. To his surprise, in the entire time he was there, he only read one script that he thought should be bought. Then, after graduating from college in the summer of 1995, he found his writing "wasn't really going anywhere." With the support of his wife and family, he kept at it, recruiting his wife as a coach who made sure he wrote at least 20 pages a day.

A breakthrough came in the summer of 1996. "We had a friend out from Miami and he wanted to go to Vegas. So we're supposed to take off and my wife said 'Did you write your pages today?' She wouldn't budge. So I sat down and started writing something new, which turned out to be the first line of the book, though it got changed later. I wrote: 'There are 16 of us huddled in Harold Johnson's basement, and the reek of sweat on leather is beginning to make my eyes water.' And I started doing this thing that became a council meeting with these dinosaurs sitting around in a basement yelling at each other. I didn't know where it was going. They were not in the human suits, but as they were leaving the council meeting and going out to the cars, my main character talked about how he put his suit back on. In Vegas, I ended up getting rear-ended on the strip, multi-car collision. When I came back, I forgot I'd written anything."

Fast-forward to mid-November 1996.

"Mid-November has been a theme of this book," Garcia observed. "I'm looking through my computer files and at this time everything was falling apart with a thing I'd written for Al and Andre, and another script I'd written for someone else. I looked at this file called Tar Pit. I reread it and I thought oh, kinda fun, but I didn't know what to do with it. An hour later, after I'd played racquetball, I took a shower and in the shower the rest of it came to me. The entire book, the plot, the twists at the end, everything. It was all there. Not in the format that it eventually ended up in, but the basic thing. So I sat down and I started writing and literally one month to the day later, I was done. Mid-December of '96 I gave it to my wife as a Hanukkah present. She read it and said 'What are you going to do with it?' I said 'I don't know, I don't know anybody in the book world.' It sat in my house from December '96 until mid-December '98. Just sat in my house. I didn't show it to anybody. I would ask my film agent 'Do you know any book people?' and he didn't. No one I knew did.

"Finally, in December of '98, two years after I wrote the very first page, my wife and a best friend of ours who had read the book finally convinced me to do something with it. I set goals for myself, and I said by August I would have an agent for it. I figured it was a weird book, so most agents who read it would just be confused. So I went to my bookcase and picked out books that I thought were cool and similar to mine. I called the publishers and pretended I was a Hollywood agent who was looking for the spoken word rights, which is a bizarre right that most publishers don't keep. They gave me these names, and one name came up three times, Barbara Zitwer. It turned out she's the most open agent in the world, who will read literally anything from anybody. I wrote her a letter and included the first chapter, and two weeks later I got a letter back from her apologizing about the delay.

"In Hollywood, two weeks is not a delay! So I thought, I like this woman! I sent her the rest of the book and the third day she called me from her hair salon while getting a permanent and she was on page 152 and loved it. She sent me 12 pages of ideas and prodded me in the direction of really parodying film noir. When I started to do that it all started to click. I did a lot of research, reading Raymond Chandler, Dashiel Hammett, stuff like that. I knew my hero had to have a vice but couldn't be an alcoholic, so I came up with the herb addiction. The rewrite took me about two weeks. Barbara started talking it up to the editors, and the next thing I know she's calling me at 5:00 in the morning, telling me she was selling my book for an ungodly sum of money, with publication scheduled for mid-November."

With a healthy six-figure-advance book sale, one might expect a huge rush of interest from Hollywood, particularly over a pop high concept like *Anonymous Rex*. There was massive interest from producers and studios, but in the end they were all (surprisingly enough) scared off by the estimated special effects budget. Finally, Robin Williams' company, Blue Wolf, got attached, but couldn't close the sale because Disney was in the process of making the all-digital animated *Dinosaur*. The studio didn't want another "dinosaur picture."

"Finally, in September the book was written up in *People* magazine," Garcia said. "After that, the Sci–Fi Network got interested. By then, I was already contracted to do more books in the franchise, so I didn't want to let it go and take a chance that some other writer would screw it up like had been done with the V. I. Warshawski novels. I fortunately had the luxury of saying no, if I couldn't write the screenplay. Then I wrote the novel *Matchstick Men*, which we sold very quickly to Warner Brothers, with Random House as publisher. So now I had four books with Random House set up and the first one published. I had a track record, so when I decided to get the movie interest going again, I began having meetings with interested companies and finally settled on Alliance Atlantis because they had a great reputation for treating people fairly. Mid-November we signed the contracts, and my film and TV agent at Endeavor convinced everyone that I should be co-producer and write the pilot. Basically, what the network realized was that I was going to do it that way or we weren't going to do it at all. Now we're talking about premiering the series in the winter of 2001 or 2002. Maybe November, whatever works. I'm in a good place."

A good place that started with a great idea, even if it took a while to incubate. But that's Hollywood. A truly great idea generates excitement that can lead to fame and fortune. So keep working on that concept, even if you have to write or rewrite the novel or screenplay to get that idea in tip-top shape.

Which brings us to the next chapter about selling to Hollywood. Eric Garcia gained a lot of respect in the entertainment industry by becoming the author of a book favorably reviewed in a prominent national magazine. He sold not just a novel, but a book franchise, then made money from the sale of the film rights. Now he's making money, both writing the scripts and producing the series from the same property.

Have you ever considered following a similar path? Turn the page, and let's discuss more reasons why, for some writers, a book might be the best pathway to screenplay success.

Maybe You Should Write a Book, or Even a Comic Book

There is a very simple reason why I advise new writers to attempt a novel instead of a screenplay—*pure money*.

You might have picked up on that in the first chapter with the discussion about *Anonymous Rex*. If you sell a novel, you get an advance against royalties. If a production company, studio, or network wants to make it into a movie, they have to buy the rights to do so. Often, they'll give a novelist a chance to write at least the first draft of the screenplay. If the book is published in hardcover, the author will also make money with a paperback sale, and if a movie is made, chances are, even more paperbacks will be sold. If the movie is highly successful, a television network might want to make it into a TV series. And you might end up with some kind of franchise, like *Star Trek*.

Contrast this to selling an original screenplay. You get paid for the script, but you might not get a chance to do the rewrite (there's almost always a rewrite) if they figure that what you sold is the best you can do. If the screenplay is made into a movie, there might be a paperback "novelization," but unless you've published a novel, you might not get the chance to write the book.

WHY BOOKS MAKE SENSE

There are other reasons I advise people to write a book if they're at all capable of turning out a competent one:

- Hollywood generally has a good deal of respect for published authors because a printed book shows someone took you seriously.
- Writing a novel often allows for deeper story development than a screenplay.
- The ratio of novels written to novels published is far higher than the amount of screenplays written to films made.
- In this day of relatively inexpensive software programs, electronic books, and Internet distribution, an author can publish a book and present it to potential buyers (including producers), bypassing middlemen altogether.

With regard to the latter point, I know a little bit about e-publishing. My book *How to Write What You Want & Sell What You Write* began as a class for UCLA Extension Writers Program, then became a print book from Career Press and did well. When it came time to do a revised version, I opted for an electronic book for Boson Books (see www.cmonline.com/boson/nonfiction/howto/howto.html). In 2000, the first electronic book awards, the Eppies, were held in the United States, and my book was a finalist in the nonfiction category. When she notified me of my finalist status, I opened a discussion with one of the board members, Patricia White. I learned that Pat had some e-novels, which had done very well. Partially as an experiment, I took a look at one of her books and thought enough of it to refer it to producer Robert Katz. To my surprise, he was willing to read it in electronic (Adobe Acrobat) format and entered into negotiations for the rights.

I've since learned that many readers, development executives, and producers are willing to read books in this format. So even if you can't get your book published, you can publish it yourself under a business name and create the impression that someone other than yourself has thought enough of your work to publish it. Having a book published is like a personal referral of worth, which is important in Hollywood.

IF HOLLYWOOD GOES TEMPORARILY OUT OF BUSINESS

There's another reason why writing a book might be a good idea, at least in 2001. *Strike*. Although I hope it doesn't happen, there has been a lot of buzz in the entertainment industry about the possibility of the Directors Guild, the Screen Actors Guild (SAG), and the Writers Guild of America (WGA) all going on strike simultaneously. The existing agreement the WGA has with its signatories (as of this writing) expired on May 1, 2001. Should they strike, no WGA member will write scripts for hire or deal with producers until the strike is settled. If a writer is not a WGA member and chooses to write for a producer during this time, they risk being branded a "scab" and banned from ever joining the Guild.

This is why the end of 2000 saw an increase of projects in development being put into production more quickly, as producers, networks and studios tried to get projects underway before a WGA strike in May or a SAG strike in June 2001.

So what will all those successful screenwriters be doing when they're not on the picket line? They'll be writing spec screenplays, which will flood the market when the strike is settled, provided it lasts long enough for them to write those scripts, like the last strike. Some of them might create new TV series to sell. Some might write novels, but my guess is that's a small percentage. The vast majority of WGA members make a living writing for TV. Therefore, if your spec screenplay arrives in Hollywood post-strike, it had better be amazingly good, even better than usual, to have a chance against the spec screenplays of all those successful writers with high-powered agents.

In New York, however, where publishing is concentrated in the United States, authors will not be on strike, nor will publishers. The same goes for Canada, and for publishers in England who seem increasingly favorable to the publication of books from non-U.K. residents. Approximately 55,000 books are published each year in the U.S. alone, over half of which are nonfiction. On the other coast, said the *Hollywood Reporter* in its December 26, 2000 edition, 266 literary properties (including screenplays, comic books, novels, plays, pitches, magazine articles, and teleplays) "were bought or optioned by entertainment companies from December 1, 1999 to November 30, compared with 247 in 1999 and 322 in 1998." Of those numbers, 101 were pitch sales.

In comparing book sales to movie sales, how do you like the odds?

HOLLYWOOD'S LITERARY APPETITE

This used to be the first chapter of this book, and I loved seeing people's faces at one of my talks when they saw the above headline. Some would puzzle over it, some would laugh, and one or two, inevitably, would look up and ask, "Why should I write a book? I want to know about screenplays!"

I always told them to read the chapter and see if they agreed with me. I also explained that after selling a couple of scripts I thought were going into production and ended up not getting filmed, I got disgusted with Hollywood and went back to journalism. Then I got into writing books and published almost two dozen titles before the first edition of this *Writer's Guide*. When preparing that book, I suddenly discovered that old Hollywood acquaintances (mostly producers) had a renewed, higher level of respect for me as a published author.

In the history of the world, filmmaking is a relatively new art form. At times, I've told audiences that I feel many Hollywood people consider movies to be a secondary art form, with not quite the cachet of a published book, which can survive thousands of years.

Does that explain the continuing allure of books in Hollywood? I don't know for sure, but it's as good an explanation as I've found. Although you can now curl up by the fireplace with your own personal DVD player and favorite movie, it just doesn't have quite the feeling and intimacy of a good book, does it?

But back to what matters, selling your stories. Here's how I opened up this chapter in the first edition.

"TV Networks Catch Book Fever from Movie Studios," read a headline in the March 4, 1996, issue of *Variety*. "Book Business Puts New York on Hollywood's Map," said another *Variety* article. "In the past few weeks," Michael Fleming reported in the first piece, "studios have been paying staggering sums for movie rights to books. Now television, considered a distant second for books, has emerged as a viable outlet for big best-sellers with sprawling storylines." The article went on to say that CBS was making a major deal with Julia Roberts' production company, Shoelace Productions, to do a miniseries based on the Helen Hooven Santmyer novel . . . *And the Ladies of the Club,* after spending $2.1 million for Mario Puzo's *The Last Don.* Although *Ladies* has not yet appeared on TV, Puzo's book became a 1997 miniseries.

Books remain a TV favorite, and with good reason. Even though a feature film had already been made from Frank Herbert's classic *Dune,* the Sci-Fi Channel thought it should be a miniseries. In the fall of 2000, *Dune* was a huge hit for this increasingly important network.

In the second edition of my *Writer's Guide,* I reported that New Line Cinema had purchased Rodney Barker's *And The Waters Turned To Blood* for a mid-six-figure sum, that first-time writer Patrick Robinson's HarperCollins novel *Nimitz Class* sold in the high-six-figures, and that Carl Hiassen sold his next novel to Jaffe Entertainment for $1 million even though they had only seen the first 76 pages! David Morell's novel, *Extreme Denial,* sold to Michael Douglas for $1 million. And an agent I interviewed at the time told me about selling an unpublished manuscript to Wendy Finerman (the producer who made *Forrest Gump* happen) for $400,000.

Still, none of them have been made into movies, and few of the big-buck book sales I commented on in the second edition became films, with the exception of the Civil War novel *Cold Mountain* from first-time novelist Charles Frazier, which won the National Book Award for fiction. That movie, written and directed by Anthony *"The English Patient"* Minghella, could be a winner.

Hollywood studios buy a lot of properties that never see the screen. Television networks, however, generally air most of the properties they buy, particularly bestselling books, which have a built-in audience. If you decide to write a book, you might ask yourself what type of story it is. If it was filmed, would it most likely appear on television, as a major studio feature, or as a low-budget, independent film? If your script could be shot on a low budget, in this day of inexpensive digital filmmaking, you might as well write a script. Just like Hollywood, publishers look to buy potential blockbusters, and "small" novels from first-time authors rarely promise that.

WHO BOUGHT WHAT

A large part of this book is the listing of agents, directors, and producers who might give you that big sale. The more you know about any potential customer, the better, which is one reason many people who bought the first edition of the book also bought the second. To that end, let's examine what studios bought books, and which didn't.

Artisan

Fueled by the amazing success of *The Blair Witch Project*, Artisan became a major player, but the properties they acquired in 2000 were mostly spec scripts, and mostly comedies. No books (nonfiction) or novels (fiction).

Disney

Walt Disney's studio picked up two novels, one book (a nonfiction true story), but one of the acquisitions was major indeed. Clive "Hellraiser" Barker signed a deal with Disney that could earn him as much as $8 million for the rights to four upcoming fantasy novels called, ugh, *The Arabat Quartet*. Disney called the novels, focused around a girl who enters another dimension, a mix of *Harry Potter* and *The Wizard of Oz*. Given Barker's past success, Disney made the deal without reading a word of the novels. Barker was already on a roll, with his *The Thief of Always* going into production. Other acquisitions included Don DeLillo's 1985 National Book Award winning novel *White Noise* for Barry Sonnenfeld to develop and direct; *Big Trouble*, the bestselling comedic novel by Dave Barry; and Gary Paulsen's 1994 book *Winterdance: The Fine Madness of Running the Iditarod*, about the author's participation in the 1,100-mile dogsled race from Anchorage to Nome, Alaska.

DreamWorks SKG

While Steven Spielberg flirted heavily with directing *Harry Potter*, the task ultimately went to director Christopher Columbus. There's a good deal of respect for books at DreamWorks. I first noticed it when I pitched a TV series once at Spielberg's production company, Amblin. The books under consideration were nicely placed on shelves, while scripts were piled against the wall. Spielberg was scheduled to direct the adaptation of the bestselling *Memoirs of a Geisha* for Red Wagon Productions, but he opted to rewrite and direct Stanley Kubrick's *A. I. (Artificial Intelligence)* instead. Spielberg also agreed to direct the feature adaptation of the adventure novel *Big Fish* for Columbia Pictures/DreamWorks after completing *A. I.* for Warner Brothers/DreamWorks and *Minority Report* for 20th Century Fox/DreamWorks.

The big DreamWorks book news came when, midyear, Spielberg paid $2 million for a first novel by Marc Levy, an unknown French architect. Based on bedtime stories he told his young son each night, Levy's *If Only It Were True* sold 230,000 copies and was translated into two dozen languages while perching atop bestseller lists in France at the time of the film sale. Why did Spielberg outbid other studios? Because it's a love story about an architect who moves into an apartment inhabited by the spirit of a young woman whose body is in a coma in a hospital. Spielberg has always wanted to direct a great love story.

Meanwhile, DreamWorks paid a reported mid-six-figures for the feature film rights to the unpublished first novel, *About the Author* by John Colapinto. Marc Platt, scheduled to produce the movie with Abby Wolf, is a producer who likes books. In the fall of 2000, his *Legally Blonde*, based on a comic novel by Amanda Brown about a homecoming queen who enrolls at Stanford Law School, was lensed for MGM. Platt also set up (via Universal, where DreamWorks is based) *Sex and the City* writer Candace Bushnell's "Snow Angels," one of four romantic comedy novellas that appear in Bushnell's novel *Four Blondes*. Following on the heels of *Saving Private Ryan*, they optioned bestseller *Flags of Our Fathers* (Bantam) by James Bradley with Ron Powers about the six men in the famous flag-raising photo during the World War II battle of Iwo Jima, one of whom was James Bradley's father. DreamWorks also bought *Tokyo Underworld* by Robert Whiting, a true story of a U.S. Marine up against the Japanese mafia in post-World War II Japan, for Martin Scorsese to direct.

One expects that there would be a love of books at a studio whose symbol is Huckleberry Finn, fishing off a crescent moon.

MGM/United Artists

In addition to the Marc Platt project previously mentioned, the combined studio that put movie musicals and James Bond on the map bought another novel in 2000. They also bought two comic books for adaptation.

Miramax

The company Harvey and Bob Weinstein named after their mother was awash with book buys in 2000—maybe she made early readers out of them. Almost half their acquisitions, in fact, came from a book or novel. Many of their buys were the usually eclectic Miramax fare like Charles Baxter's novel *The Feast of Love* (Pantheon Books), and the comedy-thriller *Fake Liar Cheat* (Pocket Books), a first novel from Tod Goldberg. Perhaps wanting to compete with the Harry Potter craze, they picked up *Artemis Fowl* (O'Brien, Ireland) by Irish schoolteacher Eoin Colfer. In a more serious vein, they rescued *The Shipping News*, the 1994 Pulitzer Prize–winning novel by Annie Proulx, from turnaround oblivion at Columbia Pictures. They also paid mid-six-figures against a purchase price close to seven figures for *The Brothers Bielski*, a book proposal by Peter Duffy about Jewish brothers who hid 1,250 Jews from the Nazis in a forest during World War II. The company also acquired feature film rights to F. Scott Fitzgerald's semi-autobiographical romantic first novel, *This Side of Paradise*. After the critical success of the movie adaptation of Joanne Harris' *Chocolat* (see the interview with Ms. Harris later in this chapter), Miramax acquired feature film rights to Jeff Shapiro's dramatic novel *Renato's Luck* (HarperCollins), for *Chocolat* producers, David Brown and Kit Golden. (Brown and Golden also produced the feature of Frank McCourt's Pulitzer-winning *Angela's Ashes*.)

One movie that you'll probably never see from the studio is an adaptation of *Insane Clown Posse*, a sex book supposedly exposing Clinton critics by John Connolly. According to Internet columnist Matt Drudge, Connolly for months had been labeling members of the Office of the Independent Counsel as "fags," "faggots," and "queers" during conversations with media figures and Washington insiders, after private investigators were hired to dig deep into the private sex lives and business dealings of major and minor Clinton critics. When the project was exposed by Drudge and others, it dropped off the radar.

On a lighter note was the acquisition of *Ella Enchanted* (HarperCollins), Gail Carson Levine's bestselling and 1998 Newberry Honor Book–winning update of the Cinderella legend. It's a fantasy about a young girl who is placed under a spell by a blundering fairy so that she must obey every command she receives.

New Line

Even the home of Freddy Kruger likes books. Nearly a third of this studio's acquisitions were books or novels, the most important being *A Heartbreaking Work of Staggering Genius* by David Eggers (Simon & Schuster) for over $2 million. The memoir details how both of Eggers' parents died of cancer within five weeks, leaving him the task of raising his 8-year-old sibling. The book was so well thought of, Eggers was given the right to approve a screenwriter, a director, a producer, and even elements of the screenplay. This type of author power is very rare in Hollywood. Only J. K. "Harry Potter" Rowling comes to mind as earning that kind of respect recently. New Line must like novelists; another of their acquisitions was a comedic novel about a woman-chaser who masquerades as an author by getting his picture on the cover of a book written by the school loser and becomes famous in the process.

Paramount

Over half a dozen books and novels were acquired by the only major studio actually resident in Hollywood. None of them, perhaps, had the literary pedigree of other tomes already mentioned, but the name recognition was high. Keanu Reeves committed to star in *Hardball,* a drama about an inner-city Little League baseball team from the Daniel Coyle book *Hardball: A Season in the Projects*. The thriller *Without Remorse* (adapted from Tom Clancey's novel) also looked very promising.

The same goes for projects controlled by veteran producer Mace Neufeld, who continued developing David Brin's Hugo and Nebula award-winning science fiction novel *Startide Rising*, along with three sequels to the book. Neufeld produces the Tom Clancy "Jack Ryan" series. Perhaps convinced that book franchises are definitely the way to go, Neufeld originally set up the Michael Connelly's books *Black Echo*, *Black Ice*, *The Concrete Blonde*, and *The Last Coyote* as a Paramount/Columbia coproduction.

The biggest book buy at Paramount, however, was the Michael Chabon novel *The Amazing Adventures of Kavalier & Clay*, which went for "north of $1 million" four years previously, after Chabon presented his one-page idea for the book to smart producer Scott Rudin. How smart and book-wise is Rudin? He bought *The First Wives Club* even though Olivia Goldsmith couldn't find a publisher.

Sony/Columbia

By far, Sony and all its subsidiaries bought more properties than any other entity in 2000. Seventeen of their acquisitions were either books or novels, and they bought four comic books as well. Production company Centropolis Entertainment got Bob Brier's action-adventure *The Murder of Tutankhamen: A True Story* (Berkley Publishing Group). The success of *The Mummy* might have had something to do with it, but then Centropolis tends to enjoy exotic fare. Columbia ordered a sequel to *Stuart Little* after the book-to-movie brought in $128.6 million domestically, a nice profit over the $100 million budget. By far, the genre preference on the Sony lot was for thrillers, both in books and novels acquired and screenplays, too. Former Disney honcho Joe Roth's Revolution Studios is housed at Sony; he has a close relationship with predominantly comedic Julia Roberts, for whom he acquired Jane Heller's comedic novel *Sis Boom Bah* (St. Martin's Press) for Roberts to star in and produce.

One of the thrillers bought is Nelson DeMille's novel *The Lion's Game*, about an ex-NYPD homicide detective investigating an Arab terrorist in the U.S. Another is Sony-based Phoenix Pictures' seven-figure deal for John Katzenbach's dark thriller, *Dr. Starks' Last Vacation* (Ballantine). Executives only had to read half of the manuscript before making the deal. Last, but not least, Columbia grabbed Robert Crais' novel *Demolition Angel*, for a healthy $525,000 against $1 million when the movie goes into production, with Crais also writing the script—a thrilling deal for any writer.

20th Century Fox

Not many literary properties found a home at Fox this go-around, and the major players in that area were producers Arnold and Anne Kopelson. While their tastes run to thrillers and science fiction, other Fox book buys were thematically all over the place. Fox 2000 made a deal for the feature film rights to Ralph "Sonny" Barger's bestselling autobiography, *Hell's Angel: The Life and Times of Sonny Barger and the Hell's Angels Motorcycle Club*, cowritten with Keith and Kent Zimmerman. New Regency Productions announced plans for the thriller *High Crimes*, based on the novel of the same name by Joseph Finder, and it looked like Fox 2000 was finally going ahead with *The Hardy Men*, a movie about the "Hardy Boys" grown up, to be produced by Ben Stiller and Stuart Cornfeld's Red Hour Films in conjunction with Robert Kosberg and "Hardy Boys" book series rights holders, Nelvana.

If you're not familiar with this popular old-young adult book series, take a look at http://members.aol.com/Hardyboy01 (Series Book Central), or www.geocities.com /Athens/Atlantis/3191 (the Hardy Boys Page).

Universal

After the killer box office taken in by *The Grinch* starring Jim Carrey (#1 for the year 2000), it's a Dr. Seussical cinch that we'll see another Seuss classic onscreen via Imagine and Universal, this time *The Cat in the Hat*. Producers at Universal didn't come in with many books, but some sound very interesting, like James Vanderbilt's fantasy thriller pitch based on the Isaac Asimov novel *The Caves of Steel*, which will be done by Vanderbilt's Wychwood Productions. *Steel* is the first book in Asimov's "The Robot Series" trilogy, so if it's a hit, we may see more of the same. And if richest-man-in-the-world Bill Gates didn't have enough problems, Universal acquired the rights to Regan-Books' *Microserfs* by Douglas Coupland, about misfit computer programmers at Microsoft.

At least when they do go for books at Universal, you can count on them being something big. Maybe it has to do with that theme park right next door, but what kind of ride can you fashion around Microsoft that doesn't crash at least once a week?

Warner Brothers

The most interesting studio with regard to books happens to be my favorite. Maybe it's because we both live in Burbank. Two of the book-based Warner movies in 2000 were major flops. First was the *Pay It Forward* heart-tugger starring two Oscars winners and the hottest kid actor on the scene: Kevin Spacey, Helen Hunt, and Haley Joel Osment. Warner only distributed the Franchise Pictures John Travolta-starrer *Battlefield Earth*, based on the mega-sized book from the mega-sized ego of Scientology founder L. Ron Hubbard. *Battlefield Earth* was so abysmal that when *Movieline* magazine did an article in its August 2000 issue offering reasons why Hollywood might really be crazy, the #1 item was a picture of Travolta in his "Terl" character outfit.

The good news (at least for book writers) is that over 25 percent of the properties acquired by Warner and its on-lot producers came from either books or novels. Most promising might be a joint project of Rob Reiner's Castle Rock Entertainment and Tom Hanks' Playtone Company, the Chris Van Allsburg children's book *The Polar Express*, with Hanks planning to star in the film. Van Allsburg's last book-to-movie was *Jumanji*, and this one looks to be just as big a hit with kids of all ages.

Warner Brothers-based Baltimore/Spring Creek brought in Nathaniel Philbrick's nonfiction bestseller *In the Heart of the Sea: The Tragedy of the Whaleship Essex* (Viking), a retelling of the true story on which Herman Melville's *Moby Dick* is based. If it has any success like the Baltimore/Spring Creek *The Perfect Storm* (#4 at the box office in 2000), based on the Sebastian Junger book, it looks like a whale of a hit.

Morgan Creek Productions not only inked bestselling author-screenwriter Caleb Carr (*The Alienist*) to a two-picture deal, they agreed to let him direct a short film as well. Morgan Creek also hired Carr to rewrite the next installment of its *Exorcist* franchise (the original's re-release in 2000 did amazing box office).

Along that horror-ible line, Gerber Pictures at the studio in 1999 bought *A&R*, an unpublished novel about the music industry, from first-time novelist Bill Flanagan. Another Gerber project was the supernatural comedy *Drake Diamond: Exorcist for Hire*. Then there was the ecological disaster novel *Dust*, acquired for Jan De Bont to direct and produce through his Blue Tulip Productions.

On a much calmer note was the buy with Gaylord Films of *A Walk to Remember*, the Nicholas Sparks tear-jerker novel of 1999, with Denise Di Novi to produce.

If you read the Eric Garcia interview in the first chapter, you might remember his mention of the option of his unpublished novel *The Matchstick Man* for producer Sean Bailey. That made Garcia an even happier camper, and Warner did even better for a lady British author named Robyn Sisman for her *Just Friends* (Penguin U.K.) a romantic comedy to be produced by David Heyman. The deal included bestseller bonuses that might push the ultimate payday well past $1 million.

You can't blame Warner for getting enthusiastic about a book from a British female. After all, all indications are that they'll do very well with their movies of books about some kid named Harry Potter.

BOOKS TO TELEVISION

As usual, television networks continue to love books because of the built-in audience. In conjunction with the BBC, A&E put the three-hour movie *Armadillo* into production, which William Boyd adapted from his novel of the same name. Dark novels from prolific novelists continued to thrive. Anne Rice's 1979 novel *The Feast of All Saints* was slated to air on ABC via Showtime, and author Dean Koontz struck a deal to produce a series of two-hour movies for the Fox Network based on the novella thriller *Black River*. Koontz also planned to turn the thrillers *Winter Moon* and *Dark Rivers of the Heart* into miniseries, and to create a TV series based on his novel *Twilight Eyes*. NBC planned a miniseries from the *First to Die* novel by James Patterson, the first book in the Alex Cross series (which gave us the Ashley Judd/Morgan Freeman *Kiss the Girls* feature from Paramount). At the time of the deal, the five Cross novels had sold 50 million copies worldwide. Like Koontz, Patterson's deal allowed him to be involved as a producer.

And ye olde scare-meister was back with "Stephen King's Rose Red," an original six-hour miniseries for ABC expected to air during the February 2002 sweeps period.

For television, the appealing element of book buys (at least for the adult audience) tends to be those with strong female characters in danger. Another example is the four-hour miniseries for ABC by Alliance Atlantis based on author Gregory Maguire's novel *Wicked: The Life and Times of the Wicked Witch of the West*, a fantasy adventure based on the Wicked Witch in *The Wizard of Oz*.

Books are also good as source material for TV series, particularly if they appeal to the teenage market. *The Black Book: Diary of a Teenage Stud* (HarperCollins), based on a series of young adult novels written under the pen name Jonah Black, described as a cross between *Sex and the City* (HBO, which came from a book) and *Malcolm in the Middle* (Fox series). Fox got the series over ABC because they seemed more compatible to the producers.

Book sales to networks require a lot more work than book sales to studios and production companies; so pay attention to network norms.

FROM COCOON TO BUTTERFLY

For a long time now, producers have been willing to read unpublished book or novel manuscripts and make a deal. When David Saperstein first came to Los Angeles, he had a completed manuscript under his arm, which got promptly turned down by over fifty producers.

"It was my first novel," David told me. "The first fiction I had ever written. I tried several New York agents and some publishers and got nowhere. I had some friends in L.A., so I thought I'd go out there and give it a try. Through some friends, I met some studio people and had four or five interviews with agencies in town. Every time, I would walk in with this thick manuscript under my arm. They would say, 'Don't you have a page or one paragraph or something?' I'd say 'No, just this book.' So they'd say 'Tell me about it.' (I found out that no one in power in Hollywood reads, or at least it seemed that way.) So I'd tell them my story and they would say, 'That really doesn't sound like a movie.' It took a year to make the rounds, and people kept telling me, 'Your story is about old people. No one cares about old people. It's got science fiction. Science fiction has been done. It's a wrinkle story!'

"I remember that one very well—'it's a wrinkle story!'

"'Young people go to the movies,' they'd say. 'Not old people.' So then I met David Field, who was a producer at Fox. We talked a little and David picked up the phone and called several agents. One was Melinda Jason, who wasn't frightened about having to read a manuscript. Well, by then I was moving back to New York. I met Melinda on a Friday and I was leaving on a Sunday. She read my book over the weekend, called me on Monday, and said it was wonderful. She wanted to show it to someone. 'Does this mean you're my agent?' I asked. 'Yeah,' she said. So the person she showed it to was Lili Fini, who gave it to Richard Zanuck, and they optioned the book. It took six years before the movie was made, but that's another story.

"So now I think, well now that I'm making a movie maybe I can get the book published. I met with a New York agent who told me, 'Well, they optioned *Cocoon*. That doesn't mean they're going to make the movie.' So nothing happened. Then I asked Zanuck-Brown (the production company) to write the screenplay, but I was told I was a nobody, so I couldn't write the script. Over the next five years they had several writers on the project. I saw a few of the manuscripts, and one or two were scary. Toward the end, I went out and met the last writer they got, and he basically went back to my original story. That was Tom Benedek.

"Then, when the movie got made and I had the 'Story By' credit, several of the writers who had been hired over the years to work on the screenplay tried to get story credit, but I won in the Writers Guild arbitration. When the movie was in pre-production, the New York agent made a publishing deal for me. The book was a bestseller and went into seven languages. The publishing contract came probably six to eight months before the movie was shot. Bob Zemeckis had been announced to direct the movie, but he was replaced by Ron Howard. That summer Zemeckis made the first *Back to the Future* movie, so I guess it came out all right for everyone."

Unlike many novelists who watch their work become a film, Saperstein ultimately loved what they did with his *Cocoon* story. It turned out to be very much like the book, he told me, upholding the spirit of the novel. Saperstein was also writing screenplays, and when they were shooting the movie of *Cocoon,* he was directing his first feature film, *A Killing Affair.* Saperstein had nothing to do with the second *Cocoon* movie, even though he first conceived *Cocoon* as a trilogy of three books. Part of Saperstein's writing success derived from a filmmaking background. Another part came from his intense desire to write what he wanted, no matter how unpopular it seemed at the time.

"When publishers asked me for another book, they wanted one about old people, but I don't write the same thing. I just write what I feel, whether it's commercial or not. You have to write from your heart and your gut." Saperstein's latest venture is an interactive novel called *Dark Again* that you can read all about at www.darkagain.com.

No Matter Where You Live

The great thing about a book is that you can sell it from anywhere. You don't have to come to Los Angeles like David Saperstein did, largely due to electronic communications. One of the best examples is *Chocolat*, a novel from 35-year-old British author Joanne Harris, whom I met via e-mail. A former schoolteacher, her charming tale set in France offered a scrumptious story that readers, actors, and critics loved, and the movie from Miramax is equally popular. The novel sold over a million copies and the movie received Oscar nominations. Here are some thoughts this hot *Chocolat* writer shared with me over the Internet. (She'll probably bake me for that pun.)

Skip: Miramax bought your book for six figures, and you say you feel like you've won the lottery. How has this changed your writing life?

Joanne: Well, given that I've now packed in my full-time teaching job, things should have changed a lot. In fact I'm not really conscious of many important changes. My writing ability tends to be cyclic, independently of how much time is available, so when I'm "In The Zone," as it were (which happens for about two months a year, not always consecutively), I write like crazy regardless of trivialities like food, sleep, housework, etc. The rest of the time I do what I can. Giving up the job now means that I have the luxury of far more time than I am used to having, and at first that panicked me a little; I'm used to timetables, the enforced discipline that working in a school gives you. I spent the first three months of my new freedom watching old Westerns and telling myself that I'd start work tomorrow. After a while I got out of that cycle, and began to impose a discipline on myself, and I find that serves quite well most of the time, though I still have an inexplicable need to stop work and make a cup of tea every day at 11:00 A.M. precisely.

Skip: Are you at all interested in writing films?

Joanne: I think I would be in the right circumstances. I adapted one of my earlier books for screen, and got a very good response, so I now feel more confident. Basically I'm willing to try anything if it works, and I have never been one to limit myself to doing one single thing.

Skip: You've always written only for yourself. Do you think that by doing that you've shaped your own success?

Joanne: I try not to think about the commercial possibilities (if any) of my writing. The few times I have tried to do so have resulted in spectacular failures, and I have since concluded that (a) I have no concept of what will sell and what won't, and (b) that if I try too hard to please other people I usually fail to please myself, and the project dies on me anyway. My own enjoyment has always been the principal motivating factor in my writing, and if I make too many concessions to what other people think I should be doing, I tend to lose the plot altogether. Besides, my experience is that success is very much a hit-and-miss affair; some apparently surefire successes have bombed dramatically, whereas some very unusual and unexpected things have done very well. Which is as it should be.

Skip: Do movies help or hurt the telling of great stories in books?

Joanne: It depends on the movie. Some are easier to adapt than others, and it takes an inspired script and a brilliant director to put across all the subtleties of a book into a movie. Plenty have tried, but there are only a handful that have succeeded. Basically I think the mistake sometimes arises in attempting to reproduce a book too faithfully; the films which really gain a life and individual identity are the ones which, while keeping the faith with the book, have also added dimensions of their own.

Sometimes I find that a movie, by giving concrete form to something which hitherto was essentially the property of the reader (and therefore shaped by the reader's imagination) does remove a dimension from the book, in that no two readers are likely to agree on precisely how a work is to be interpreted, and that interpretation is likely to be a matter of individual taste. Also, a poorly-written book with an engaging plot can sometimes make a very good movie, but a really rich and complex book is difficult to make into an 80-minute script. Too many things don't translate properly, and what you get—not counting some really wonderful exceptions—is often an oversimplified, cartoonish version of the original, with much of its charm lost. On the other hand, the reading public is very small in comparison to the film-going public, and anything which renews interest in books and makes them available to a wider audience has to be a good thing.

Skip: Now that you've had a smash success, do you feel any pressure to best yourself?

Joanne: Success has nothing to do with it; I'm always putting myself on the spot to do better. I'm never entirely satisfied with what I do, and I'm always looking for new directions. Now, of course, I feel much more under scrutiny by other people, so that increases the pressure. I'm not used to having a high profile in this area: I was confident in my former life because I knew exactly what was required of me as a teacher, and I knew I was good at it, but this is an entirely different game. There are no rules to follow that I can make out; and the stakes are much higher. I think it's going to take some getting used to.

Skip: You adapted one of your earlier books for screen, and got a very good response. With the success of the movie of *Chocolat*, have you gotten a green light on your script?

Joanne: Not on that one, although to be fair, I never submitted it to anyone (I only used it as an example of an adaptation I had done). The company to whom I showed it have optioned my next book, though, and have commissioned me to write the script for it. Plus there is now growing interest in my other books. Useful things, movies.

Skip: Are you now inclined to write a new idea as a screenplay?

Joanne: Possibly, although only if I thought it wouldn't work as a book.

Skip: Are you worried about any "sophomore jinx"?

Joanne: I take this to mean "second book syndrome." Thankfully, not anymore. My second book was published in the UK eight years ago (to a resounding silence), and the second book after *Chocolat* (which is in fact my fourth book) came out last spring. Any jinx I may have had is well out of the way by now . . . Although now that you mention it . . . Oh, don't get me started!

Skip: Was there anything about the book-to-movie experience that you've been through that caught you unawares? Were there things about the process that you'd like to share with other writers?

Joanne: Yes, well nearly all of it took me unawares, really. First, I'm profoundly grateful that I didn't accept to write the script. Technically I might have managed, but emotionally, professionally, etc., I really needed to see it done properly before I leaped in at the deep end. It's important to watch the process (as much of it as you can, including all the rewrites, the filming, the changes, etc.) before making these "I could have done that" assumptions.

I know that I have been very lucky in all this; no big problems, no unsympathetic scriptwriters making a hash of my book, no drama queens demanding the impossible, a very nice director [Lasse Hallstrom] who allowed me on set and gave me a lot of useful insights on how filming is done. It's all a question of getting the right personalities, and I'm aware that in this I have been luckier than most. Even so, I got a lot of help from William Goldman's *Adventures in the Screen Trade* books, which, as well as being immensely entertaining in their own right, gave me some idea of what to expect. Finally, the obvious, which still needs a mention: If you are unhappy with something in the script, or have notes or comments to contribute, then say something about it! I found that when I did, I was immediately much more involved in the process, and my opinions were taken into account.

It also helps enormously if you have the star of the movie on your side, as I did (and they have liked the book)!

Book Agents Can Live Anywhere

Another thing about writing books is that many literary agents have built successful careers without living where publishing is centralized, in New York City. So they don't care where you live, unlike Hollywood agents who advise you to spend some time living in southern California when building a screenwriting career. And if your book is published and picked up by Hollywood, you'll arrive here under a completely different set of circumstances.

Jim Hornfischer, the agent for the aforementioned *Flags of Our Fathers*, which sold to DreamWorks, had another project air as a CBS Hallmark Hall of Fame production in November 2000. *The Lost Child* was based on the memoir by Yvette Melanson, *Looking for Lost Bird*, about a woman raised Jewish in New York who discovered she was a Navajo stolen from the reservation as an infant. Hornfischer lives in Texas and finds that location does not hamper his agenting efforts in any way.

"This is a relationship/reputation business," Jim told me. "My effectiveness as an agent is based on the breadth and depth of my network of editors, and their level of confidence that by opening an envelope from me, they're not wasting their time. Film producers/rights purchasers often come to me, having read reviews of my clients' work in *Publishers Weekly*, but more often I coagent with West Coast talent agencies—William Morris, The Artists Agency, and Agency for the Performing Arts, typically."

You can find out more about the agency and the authors they represent by logging onto www.theliterarygroup.com or contacting Hornfischer at:

The Literary Group International

8202 Emberwood Drive
Austin, TX 78757

Another Reason to Write Books

If you are a good novelist, Hollywood might have need of your services, to turn a script into printed prose. But, like most things in Hollywood, there's a catch. William Quick, who wrote the novelization of *The X-Files* (the storyline was taken from three major scripts of the story arc of the show's first season), says it's simple—you have to know somebody. Quick got the *X-Files* job because he knew an editor at HarperCollins. A well-known name in science fiction, fantasy, and cyberpunk (he's one of the founders of the genre), while attending the Nebula awards Quick met with actor/director William Shatner, two editors, and his agent. Everyone got along famously, and before long Quick had a multi-book deal ghosting novels for Shatner. Because he was fascinated with the money being made by writers in Hollywood, Quick turned some spare time into a speculative cowritten script with Shatner based on the books. Next thing you know, he had a Hollywood agent and was writing a speculative (spec) *X-Files* script to use as a writing sample to get in to pitch to TV shows. He made a sale, and joined the Writers Guild of America, but he's still writing books.

"The people that publishers like to use for this are people they regard as having a certain level of quality and are utterly dependable," Quick said of his novelization work. "When the book is due, they want the manuscript, not excuses. Your talent isn't selling the book, anyway. It's the name on the cover."

Quick had no written credits on the first books he did with Shatner, and wanted none. He felt Shatner's name was what would sell the novels. Curiously, Shatner books written by another writer who share cover credit with the former captain of the starship *Enterprise* have not sold as well as the Quick books.

In the latest series, however, Quick receives a written acknowledgment inside each book, and Shatner has always taken pains to introduce Quick as his cowriter and mention him in interviews on "The Howard Stern Show" and other media appearances.

Maybe you should write a novelization? It might lead you to boldly go where you've never gone before, maybe even into the WGA.

THE COMIC BOOK CONNECTION

Less than a dozen comic books were picked up by the studios in 2000, but the success of the *X-Men* movie and the projected success of the forthcoming *Spiderman* movie might help increase that number. So should the sequel to Sony's *Men in Black*. Some comic stalwarts fell on hard times, however; *Spiderman* creator Stan Lee's company went bankrupt, and the comedy-adventure *Mystery Men* from Universal, based on Bob Burden's *Dark Horse* comic book, was simply awful.

One person who has slowly and steadily built a Hollywood career for himself based on his comic work is Dwayne McDuffie, who has been creating comics since about 1988, when he sold the comedy series *Damage Control*, about an engineering and insurance firm who cleans up the rubble created by the epic battles between Marvel superheroes. When I interviewed him in April 2000, *Damage Control* was in development by Village Roadshow.

"Since then," Dwayne told me, "I've written for just about every major comic book company. I've written *Spider-Man, The Avengers, Back To The Future, Prince,* and tons of other stuff you have no hope of ever having heard of. Although I prefer to write humor (and have done so whenever those kinds of assignments were available), there's almost none to be found in today's mainstream comics. Maybe we should find another name for them."

Although he's gotten notoriety for his ethnic characters, Dwayne started writing about black characters late in his career at Marvel. His success with *Deathlok*, a book about a pacifist who finds himself in control of a powerful military cyborg, was the first comic he ever worked on to sell over a million copies. It gave him the financial wherewithal to cofinance Milestone, his own company, in 1992.

"We called ourselves multicultural, by the way, and we took that very seriously. Both our product and our creative staff were representative of many different racial, religious, and ethnic groups. My hope was that we would find fresh water, if we looked in different wells. I think we succeeded."

Unfortunately, Dwayne's ethnic background hindered him in comics.

"In the comic business, it's been a major hindrance," he said. "In 1988 when I made my first sale, I became only the second black in history to write for one of the majors. There have been maybe a dozen since then, but only one currently has a regular assignment. The racial barriers in comics, particularly on the writer/editor side, have always been substantial, and the current downturn in the market has, of course, made things worse. I could tell you ugly stories but I prefer to look forward. The ugly stories are bad for my digestion."

He's still undecided about Hollywood, even though he has sold a feature script, *Chaos and Order*, to Fox.

"I haven't even really 'been' to Hollywood yet. The producer has met me (he's also the cowriter, he hired me), but nobody from the studio has. I'm not sure they know what color I am. Maybe they'd be pleased, maybe they don't care. I've got enough friends in the business to know that race is a limiting factor and I'm sensibly wary but frankly, I haven't had anything hit me in the face, as of yet.

Starting his own comic book company was relatively easy, Dwayne said. They copublished Milestone with DC Comics, whose president, Jenette Kahn, "was very fond of our titles. She sold several DC properties for media over the years and came very close for various Milestone characters on several occasions."

If you're thinking of the comic book-to-movie route, however, take heed. Dwayne found writing scripts easier than writing comics.

"In comics, you have to absolutely control time," he said. "The example I like to use is 'A man comes home from work, he's tired. As he enters his apartment, he absently tosses his coat across the back of a chair. He flips through his mail, sees one particular letter. Opens it. His face falls as he reads the news. He crumples the letter, that horrible thing, and allows it to fall to the ground.' Okay, in moving pictures, that sequence is a leisurely 20 seconds, tops. In a comic book, as written, it's two-and-a-half pages (or over 20 percent of your space in a standard, 22-page issue). That's too long. You can't do it that way. You have to find *specific moments in time* in that sequence to sell the action so you can cut it down to a page or less. It's much harder than just describing the entire action. As you might imagine, a sequence like a fight or a chase multiplies this problem considerably."

Skills learned in writing comics translate to screenplays.

"Comic books do force you to write visually. You can't give an artist a script full of great dialogue scenes. You have to give him something to draw. This skill travels well."

For more information, take a look at www.dwaynemcduffie.com. The site includes lots of samples of both professional comic book scripts and "Marvel-style plots" (a treatment that the director shoots from, then gives back to you to write dialogue to loop in after the fact). You can also reach him by e-mail at DwayneM595@aol.com.

SHOULD YOU WRITE A BOOK?

Allow me to reiterate the facts: Approximately 55,000 new books are published each year. Only 300 to 400 movies are put into production, yet 20,000 new stories and screenplays are registered with the Writers Guild of America. Calculate the number of people writing books versus the number of people writing screenplays, and you might get some idea of where the better odds are. Hardly anyone at a movie studio will read a new writer's screenplays except on the recommendation of a trusted friend, and though independent producers are more likely to read an unagented script, they'll also read un-published books and e-books. And if you sell your book, then sell it to Hollywood. You can make money off it several different times. You might also make money via ancil-lary rights, such as a video or computer game spin-off or a TV series. If your original manuscript is a screenplay, you might sell a novelization of the film (providing the film gets made), but it will normally be for a lot less money than if it were sold first as a book.

Hollywood bigwigs rarely read scripts, much less book manuscripts. It's still that way. Many executives only read what is called "coverage," a one- to three-page synop-sis of a project. Once your project has been "covered" by a reader, that review stays on file at a studio or production company in case it ever comes back after that executive has moved on to another position. In most offices you visit, you'll find scripts from major agencies piled on the floor, while the books under consideration will be placed on shelves. Books get respect.

I still believe that Hollywood subconsciously thinks of film as a secondary medium. Unlike the collaborative nature of film, an author of a book rarely shares the spotlight with another writer. Getting down to pure physical characteristics, celluloid does not last; it crumbles to dust after enough years. Videotapes do the same. Maybe with DVDs which last almost forever and offer a number of "extras" with a movie, that might help shift the perception of films to a loftier level.

WHAT KIND OF BOOK SHOULD YOU WRITE?

Study James Ellroy and Elmore Leonard. When Brian Helgeland accepted the Acad-emy Award for *L.A. Confidential*, he told the audience, "In my house this will be known as an Ellroy." Hot screenwriter Scott Frank has also claimed he lives "in the house Elmore Leonard built." Both authors are continually popular with Hollywood.

On the other hand, the success of *Harry Potter* has caused a Hollywood stampede toward young adult novels, particularly from actors with their own production compa-nies. Kelsey Grammer's Grammnet Productions went after Carol Plum-Ucci's novel

The Body of Christopher Creed, while John Malkovich's production company, Mr. Mudd, optioned Lucy Wadham's novel *Lost*. Meanwhile, Drew Barrymore's Flower Films made a deal on Daphne Athas' *Entering Ephesus*, a novel *Time* magazine called one of the "10 best works of fiction of 1971."

The great thing about a book is that it can sometimes create a booming market in niches that publishers and Hollywood didn't know existed. One example is the success of Jerry Jenkins' Christian thrillers, the *Left Behind* novels. The most recent book of this fundamentalist series about the Apocalypse entered the *New York Times* fiction bestseller list at No. 1. Jerry and his coauthor, retired evangelical minister Tim F. La-Haye, sold some 17 million books in the United States in five years, about three million less than the Harry Potter series. As I wrote, the authors made $10 million each from the series. When *Left Behind: The Movie* appeared in video stores in November 2000, it topped VideoScan's First Alert VHS chart for the week, beating out *Toy Story 2*. The money from the series enabled Jenkins to fund his son's feature film directorial debut (see www.americanleather.com). I've never met a screenwriter who did that. Check out Jerry's progress at www.jerryjenkins.com.

WHERE TO KEEP UP WITH THE BOOK BUSINESS

Studios are so attuned to being the first to learn of a hot new book, they hire book scouts. In spring 2000, Warner Brothers exclusively retained the services of New York–based Maria B. Campbell & Associates, a company previously associated with Amblin Entertainment and DreamWorks. While the literary consulting firm agreed to be exclusive to Warner, the studio remained open to getting material from others. Campbell, in her seventies, is one of the top international book scouts, with a roster of 16 clients including movie-crazy Germany's *Berlin Verlag*, *Blessing Verlag* and *Der Spiegel*.

If you know you're going to have a book published, you might try getting it mentioned in *The Village Voice Literary Supplement* and hope they select you to be one of their "Writers on the Verge," which has become an early warning system for anyone tracking promising new authors. To follow the type of first novels being published, take a look at www.first-novels.com, a site which tracks all first novels published during the year, with information on literary quotes, pseudonyms, publishers, reviews, and other items.

Better yet, subscribe to the free e-mail newsletter from Publisher's Lunch (www.publisherslunch.com) and keep track that way.

BOOKS ENGENDER RESPECT

There is something about a book that engenders respect for the writer. Books simply get taken more seriously. Plus, the writers I admire most write both books and screenplays. This has been going on in Hollywood since its earliest days. Did you know that

Mario Puzo (author of the *Godfather*) wrote the first draft of the first *Superman* film, directed by Richard Donner? Donner told me Puzo handed him a 500-page screenplay! Famed novelist William Faulkner worked on many Hollywood scripts, including (with screenwriter Jules Furthman) the great Humphrey Bogart/Lauren Bacall film *To Have and Have Not* (adapting a novel by Ernest Hemingway), and later with Furthman and Leigh Brackett on another Bogart/Bacall film, *The Big Sleep* (from the Raymond Chandler novel). From F. Scott Fitzgerald to Elmore Leonard, many fine writers have done time in Hollywood writing scripts. If you have a short story in mind, or a larger story and the expertise to turn it into a novel, I say write it. Let the screenplay follow. If you're convinced that a screenplay is the only thing to write, that's fine with me, but I'm lazier than you are. I like to make money off the same story more than once. And you know what? Even if the technology lets us do it, who wants to take a movie to the beach?

Lightning in a Bottle:
The Great Spec Script

Okay, so you're not interested in writing books. You're crazy about the movies, and you want to write that great script that sells for over a million dollars. You want to move to California, live near the beach, and mingle with the stars.

Hey, I can't blame you. I've done all that!

Okay, so I didn't sell that script for a million dollars yet. All things in time.

Sales of spec screenplays in 2000 were slightly less than sales of "pitches," which are almost always the province of proven screenwriters. According to the *Hollywood Reporter*, 82 specs sold to major and mini-major studios, while 90 pitches sold. Remember, however, that there are over 7,000 established production companies in the Los Angeles area alone, and the vast majority of them do not have offices on studio lots. When you consider Canadian production companies and other entities around the world, you'll see why I always advise most aspiring screenwriters to investigate the independent market first.

To give you some idea of what it takes to sell a script that puts you on the Hollywood map, and what can happen afterward, let's look at some writers I've come across who have been made career breakthroughs.

SOLD IN CYBERSPACE

Betsy Morris was someone I met on the Internet, when we were both regulars on the Usenet newsgroup misc.writing.screenplays. Betsy made the news in 2000 when one of her scripts was optioned by American Zoetrope via Francis Ford Coppola's Web site at www.zoetrope.com. She told me it was her first option. "I came very close once before on a different script," she said, "but it fell through at the last minute. I have done a paid rewrite, although 'paid' is a marginal term."

Here's an excerpt from the press release issued by Coppola's site:

REAL SCRIPTS OPTIONED OFF VIRTUAL STUDIO

August 28, 2000, San Francisco, CA: Francis Coppola announced that two scripts have been optioned from his virtual studio Web site, www.zoetrope.com. The five-time Oscar winner launched the virtual studio site in June 2000, fulfilling a 20-year ambition by reopening his legendary Zoetrope Studios on the Web. Over the past two years, Coppola has built three literary sites on the Web for short stories, novellas, and screenplays.

"We have always believed in the priority of finding new and excellent writers and stories. The advent of *Zoetrope: All-Story* magazine, and our new Zoetrope Studios virtual studio site is beginning to give us a real advantage, as well as helping writers whose work might not otherwise be seen," said Coppola.

The two scripts, "Brave New Word" by Steven Blair and "Christiana Claus" by **Betsy Morris** are being optioned by Alliance Atlantis for American Zoetrope Television. "I'm extremely excited about the innovative way we found these first two scripts," said Tara McCann, Senior Vice President and Head of Television at American Zoetrope. "Without a doubt, the quality of material I have read has consistently been worthy of cinematic consideration, and even if the concept isn't one that we would currently buy, I have now come to learn of several talented writers that I would have never known about, had it not been for the screenplay site. . . ."

"Christiana Claus" centers around an 11-year-old girl who hates Christmas because her father is Santa. The story centers around her adventures when she leaves the North Pole and travels to the shopping mall. She makes new friends and learns the real meaning of Christmas in this heartwarming story that will bring smiles to the whole family. Author **Betsy Morris** writes computer manuals and online help systems for a financial software company by day and pursues her screenwriting at night. "Christiana Claus" is Morris' fourth screenplay. "New Hope" was a Moondance finalist and "Access Denied" was a 1999 finalist at Austin. Her latest script is titled "No One of Consequence."

Before these options were announced, I saw a lot of idle chatter on newsgroups from various writers, mostly complaining about the Zoetrope process. I posted opinions that Coppola wouldn't put up a site unless he was serious about the process succeeding, and naturally I got "flamed" by the naysayers. As evidenced by Betsy's previous efforts, the willingness to persist and ignore negativity worked for her, along with great writing.

E-BOOK TO MOVIE

New Orleans resident Pauline Baird Jones made her own luck via Internet marketing. On November 9, 1999, Indiegal Productions announced plans to film Pauline's script "I Love Luci—When I Don't Want to Kill Her" on location in New Orleans. "Luci" was adapted from Pauline's novel of the same name, which might be the first electronic book to be adapted for the big screen.

"We were looking for a script with a New Orleans setting that would be suitable for the independent market," said Indiegal producer Angela P. Shapiro, "so we requested Pauline's script after receiving her pitch via e-mail. Her script had a nice mix of characters, but more importantly, it spoke to us."

At the time of the announcement, the script was a finalist in America's Best Screenwriting Competition; it had tied for first place in the First Draft Screenplay contest that summer. The book was released in June 2000 by electronic publisher Starlight Writer Publications (www.starlightwriterpublications.com) as the launch book for their new romantic-comedy line, Sunlight Romances. Pauline's first e-novel, *Pig in a Park*, was voted best e-book of 1998 by the Reviewers ListServ, and was the first e-book to receive a Romantic Times Reviewer's Choice award for best e-book, in 1999. Both were released in hardcover by Thorndyke Press (with *Pig in a Park* retitled *The Spy Who Kissed Me*).

Pauline's sale brought a smile to my face because her script was head and shoulders above the competition when I was a judge for the Script-L screenplay contest in early 1999. Although I knew who Pauline was due to her prominence in the e-book community, I didn't know who had written the script. After the contest was over I traded e-mails with Pauline and learned how she had made the sale. She told me she finds that writing both the book and script simultaneously helps both.

"When I need to know what is happening, I work on the script," she said. "When I need to know what the characters are feeling and thinking, I'll pull up the book and work on that. It's like I've finally found *my* way to write. I wrote stage plays first, many years ago, then quit that and started writing novels, but everyone always told me my books would make great movies. It took me a long time to really hit the mark with my books as far as the characters' inner worlds are concerned, so I consider myself a stage/screenwriter who went astray and learned how to write novels."

She wrote *Luci* as a script after agent Donald Maas told her it read like a movie script. She'd written stage plays, but didn't know how to write a script, so she let Maas' suggestion simmer until she "tapped into the online screenwriting community" and was finally inspired to write the screenplay. When it didn't place in the Austin "Heart of Film" competition, she stuck it in a drawer for a year until a friend called and told her about Sally Merlin, a former producer who was the East Coast editor for *Scr(i)pt* magazine. Sally worked on the script with her until they both felt good about it, then Pauline started e-pitching the script.

Pauline is screen-friendly, with most of her reading done on a computer screen and the rest on her Rocket Ebook. She says she now buys very few non-digital books.

The path she took to success wasn't a short one. This stay-at-home mom and writer started writing plays in 1984, had one produced in 1985 at a university, and then turned to writing short fiction and nonfiction. She made her first writing sale in 1987. After her first agent quit the business, Pauline started doing her own marketing of books and scripts. She recently signed with Writer's House agent Karen Solem.

For more information about Pauline B. Jones' works, see www.paulinebjones.com.

A MORE TRADITIONAL ROUTE

Screenwriter Dwayne A. Smith's first sale was his script *Joe's Last Chance*, which sold to Intermedia Films and Outlaw Productions in mid-year 2000. Dwayne signs his e-mails with "I Love the Internet" but he learned about the movie business in the very real world. Ambitiously, he began shooting a 35mm feature with his own money, but couldn't afford to finish it, so he decided, "rather naively, that I would write a spec to get the finishing money."

Title card: SIX YEARS LATER

Dwayne sells his script. Nevertheless, he "paid his dues," starting as a production assistant, working on locations and making a few short films. His first spec script got him "hip-pocketed" by United Talent Agency, meaning that while the agent didn't offi-cially sign him, Dwayne could refer interested parties to the agent about his script. Fol-lowing that, he had a lot of pitch meetings over the phone "that went nowhere."

"I got hired to write a comedy for almost no money a few years later," he told me. "Nothing came of that either, so I punched out a few more specs. Finally, with one titled *Dead Already*, I got the attention of Lawrence Mattis of Circle of Confusion. He left the door open for me to send him whatever I wrote. My very next script, *Joe's Last Chance*, was the one he took out. *Joe* was received very well."

Dwayne did what most writers do who find agents who make sales. He met another writer, Bill Massa, on the screenwriting newsgroup. "Bill was very serious about screenwriting and was already signed with Circle," Dwayne said. "He read my script and immediately passed it on to Lawrence, who hip-pocketed me for a year before I sold *Joe's Last Chance*."

Unlike Pauline Jones, Dwayne never entered any screenwriting contests. He planned to, but never got around to it. His work on music videos and a low-budget horror flick didn't help much, either. "None of that is really connected to writing a spec," he told me. "I studied the market and read a ton of specs. I was in a whole other world."

After the sale, he noticed that the phone rang a lot and he got many assignment op-portunities and "meet and greets" (the "get to know each other" meeting that often pre-cedes a screenwriting job).

When I last touched in with Dwayne he was rewriting *Joe's Last Chance*, then planned to revisit *Dead Already*, "which many feel is a better script than *Joe*. Then I'm going to write my million-dollar spec. Well. . .all my specs start off that way anyway."

His advice to aspiring screenwriters is to do a lot of reading.

"What helped me the most is reading lots of specs. Not scripts in general. I mean specifically specs. I can't emphasize this enough. Screenwriters have contacted me after the sale, asking for advice. First thing I ask is 'How many specs have you read?' Most have only read a few. Everyone I know who does this business seriously reads dozens, especially the specs that sell for the big money. You gotta study the market and know what studios are buying. That's my approach anyway."

MAKING HER OWN CHANCES

Heather Hale has enough energy to knock you down just walking in the room, and she's had her mind set on writing success for a long time. When she was four years old, someone asked her what she wanted to do when she grew up and she said, "I wanna do somethin' wid wurds." She went on to get a degree in creative writing and has written just about everything: infomercials, marketing videos, training CD-ROMs, newsletters, and newspaper and magazine articles.

Though she's always wanted to write "The Great American Novel," when she realized that people don't read as much as they watch television and movies, she got a screenwriting certificate at UCLA and has since worked on numerous television shows and writing assignments. Like Dwayne A. Smith, she read tons of specs ("more screenplays than you could move with a truck") and attended numerous seminars and workshops.

She's also got a bit lucky.

"It was a right place, right time kind of thing in that I met a woman who had an idea she wanted to develop into a screenplay," she said, "and she just happened to be friends with Vanessa L. Williams. She was the mother of Vanessa's music producer. It wasn't like I had an 'in'. Long story short: My aunt passed away and my father became the executor of her trust, making us sudden landlords of a property we couldn't sell for two years due to capital gains tax issues. We just happened to rent it out to this woman. It was synchronicity, and being in the right place at the right time. The association led to my first real Hollywood deal."

The script she sold was *The Courage to Love* (credited with Toni Ann Johnson), which aired on the Lifetime Network in 2000. Once the script was bought, however, she felt a bit abandoned.

"They pretty much forgot I even existed," she said, "unless they needed me to sign something or mailed me a check. I wasn't involved in the production, I never met the stars, I never stepped on the set. I even had to throw my own premiere party and make my own VHS copy of the movie. They did send me a movie poster, which hangs framed in my office now, and inspires me whenever I get down. I don't think I was treated badly or well—probably just normal for a neophyte. Everyone has this image that your career is made after your first deal. I haven't found that to be so true. Sure, I've had this produced credit as a Lifetime Original Movie, and I've worked on two PBS series (one of which won an Emmy). I've associate produced a talk show and written for a series of documentaries, but I still have to hustle my tail off every day.

"One way it changed me was that now I have more confidence. I don't feel like I'm just bluffing when I hand out a business card that says I'm a screenwriter. I really am. People are beginning to take me seriously. I've got some decent, legitimate blurbs to put in cover letters or work into conversations at Hollywood parties, so just for the boost to your own confidence, its invaluable.

"There was a point during the whole production process (I had to go through WGA arbitration) and I was like, 'Take all the money, treat me like shit, do whatever you feel you need to do—just don't take my name off that movie!' Because, ultimately, that's all that matters. If my name's not on it, my career hasn't started. Thankfully, I actually got bumped up to first position 'Written By,' so it turned out in my favor—difficult as it was to go through. The WGA really defended the original writer with the vision. I can't be thankful enough for that."

Now Heather's goal is "to get some big spec sales, get some writing assignments, and really make a career out of this." Meanwhile, she's helping other writers. She founded and coordinates the Screenwriters OnLine Cooperative (www.SOCscreenwriters.com), which is linked to the WGA site. It's a free (but invite-only) screenwriting craft and career development forum for writers based essentially on sweat equity. "It's you read our screenplays, we'll read yours," she explained. "I've worked really hard to create a nurturing, constructive culture. It used to be *huge*, but it became unwieldy—so now I do periodic housecleanings. I have no qualms about kicking people out who are mean-spirited or who come at us for a self-serving hit and run (where they get all these great critiques with no intention of ever reciprocating)."

She's also been involved with a number of "real world" screenwriting conferences and film festivals, including Selling to Hollywood. As anyone who's met Heather at one of these events will tell you, her first sale definitely won't be her last.

MILLION-DOLLAR MAN

Mid-April 2000, a notice in *Variety* announced that David Ayer had sold *Squids*, the first major buy of Art Linson and David Fincher's Indelible Pictures. If the movie got made, said the article, Ayer would be paid $1.5 million regardless of his credit on the picture. The company was the team behind Brad Pitt's *The Fight Club*. *Squids* was described as a "coming-of-age story set on a nuclear submarine during the waning days of the Cold War."

"David is one of the freshest and most daring young screenwriters in Hollywood and we are thrilled to be working with him," producer Linson said. And New Line president Michael De Luca added, "This is the kind of material we were hoping to develop when we made our production commitment to Indelible Pictures."

I grinned because I knew the true story behind *Squids*. In fact, I've known Dave since he was a teenager in high school. I remember when he joined the submarine service and when he first started writing. These days when he's working, he listens to The

Doors a lot, and the first time he ever heard the band was when I played a tape for him on our way to a convention in Reno, Nevada. Now Dave is an A-list writer in Hollywood, constantly in demand to rewrite existing projects and to come up with new projects, and I couldn't be happier for him. This process started after he wrote the script *Training Day*, made at Warner Brothers with Denzel Washington and Ethan Hawke starring. *Training Day* is about an LAPD veteran who shows a rookie narcotics cop the ropes during his first day. Set in the now somewhat infamous Ramparts division in midcity Los Angeles, it's based on interviews Dave did with locals and police while living in the area, and was written years before the L.A. Police scandal of 2000.

The screenplay that put Dave on the map was the rewrite he did on another submarine movie, Jonathan Mostow's *U-571*, which hit #1 at the box office ($19.6 million in its first weekend) and helped Universal achieve #1 studio status in 2000.

When I learned about Dave's million-dollar sale, I sat back and thought about the small world of Hollywood. I remembered having a script of mine rejected by Art Linson after being recommended by his wife. I was angry at the time, but in retrospect I realize the script had problems. And the week before *U-571* hit #1, my friend Jennie Lew Tugend's *Return to Me*, Bonnie Hunt's fine directorial debut, had been #1 at the box office.

Sometimes I think Hollywood is so small a town you can't sneeze without someone who knows you offering you a Kleenex. It really is a relationship town, and talent keeps those relationships alive.

When Dave and I sat down for an interview at his house in the Hollywood Hills, I explained to him that in the third edition of the *Writer's Guide to Hollywood*, I wanted to add a new chapter about how screenwriters got their first big break, to try to shed some light on what producers were looking for, and what it took to make that breakthrough. Dave stated flatly that they were looking for Lightning in a Bottle, giving me the title of this chapter. Lightning in a Bottle. Wild, marvelous energy. Captured magic, perhaps. In a town where they've been making movies for almost a century, to which audiences keep returning, I could think of no better term. Every producer I've ever met has told me they were looking for something great. Rarely has anyone done much to delineate exactly what they'd like, but always they will say, "I'll know it when I see it."

Frankly, I haven't met many writers whom I think are capable of being A-list writers. I read a lot of mediocre scripts. I hear the same thing from readers I know. Aspiring writers usually don't write commercial screenplays that stars want to be in. Dave seemed to have a natural knack for it, so I wanted to know how his A-list career had evolved. From what I knew, Wesley Strick (*Cape Fear* and many others), had encouraged him early on. Or should I say, provided the initial spark.

"I went to his house to do electrical work," Dave said, "and I ended up telling him some of my sea stories from the Navy. He said I should write some of them down, so I wrote four short stories about my life experiences in the Navy. Eventually, he read them and said I had a great ear for dialogue, whatever that meant, and a strong sense of character. Writing was never anything I'd considered, but when he reacted strongly, it convinced me that I should write a script about it. As we became friends, it got to the point where I realized that if a guy of this caliber in the business was prodding me to write, I'd be stupid not to at least give it a shot. So I wrote a script, typed it up on an electric typewriter, read all the screenwriting books and all that stuff, and eventually came up with a draft. Wesley gave it to a development guy who was on the lot at Disney and this guy went nuts. This guy reacted in a really positive way to my writing and characterizations. It was the original draft of *Squids*."

The script didn't get bought, however, but Dave had cultivated a fan on the Disney lot. So he wrote a second script, "a little saltier this time," and got a similar positive reaction. Wesley Strick gave the script to some producers that he was working with, which didn't result in a sale but opened more doors. Dave kept writing, a third script, and a fourth one, then finally he grew frustrated with getting close but not selling.

"I'd been trying to second guess what I thought they wanted and wasn't really getting anywhere," Dave told me. "I was starting to see a pattern. So I decided to write something for me, something so crazy and so out there that I didn't have to worry about people liking it because I knew there wasn't a chance in hell they were going to pick it up. Just totally for me. And that was *Training Day*. When I first wrote it, I was way ahead of the curve. I finished it in 1996 and it kind of sat around."

He did manage to get a paid assignment, though. In 1995, he was hired by Innerscope to rewrite a script called *Midnight Oil*, about some high school kids who steal the SAT test answers. He did a rewrite at scale, a polish at scale, but the movie didn't get made. He made the mistake of quitting his job while doing the rewrite, and quickly learned that beginning screenwriters can't always count on steady employment. When he wrote *Training Day* and began circulating the script, he found that people either loved it or hated it.

"It upset people. It would cause a strong reaction. I knew I had something because it would cause a strong reaction. It was a really good script but most folks weren't interested in something about law enforcement at the time. Then it became front-page news in the *L.A. Times*. Same guys, same division, Ramparts, that I wrote about."

One of the strong positive reactions came from two agents at International Creative Management. And as usual in Hollywood, interest in the right place changed everything.

"Somehow ICM got a copy of that script. As it started circulating around, people in the business would tell other people, hey you gotta read this. ICM calls me up one day. I was with this smaller agency that was mostly TV, and the only job I got out of there was a chance to write the Tupac Shakur bio. I started researching that and started going into this crazy nexus of street gangs and the police and the feds. The cops are shooting each other, the system, it was just insane. I started getting calls from prison. I realized, you know what? I don't need the money. My first big deal, a $100,000 gig. I was driving to the lawyer's office to sign the contracts and I'm thinking, wouldn't it be great if

I got in an accident so I wouldn't have to sign those contracts? And the second I thought that, a red flag goes off, and I'm thinking I shouldn't be doing this job. I had a good soldier mentality, just get the job done. But this was not going to be healthy. So I told the lawyer forget it. I walked away from it, and immediately after that I got a call from ICM and it was Todd Feldman and Amy Ferris calling me. They said, 'Hey, we're not supposed to be doing this, we know you have representation.' I was like, yeah, well, thanks very much but goodbye. And I hung up on them. They called me back after about five minutes. I picked up the phone and they gave me a really good spiel. They said look, you know this is business. This is your life and we understand your loyalty and everything but your first priority needs to be your career. Just take a meeting. Come in and talk to us. So I went and talked.

"I signed with them and based on *Training Day* they were able to get me some bookings, the first being a rewrite of a James Ellroy script, *Plague Season*. I did a pretty good job. [The film went into production in April 2001.] They were able to get me jobs. I did a rewrite on a Stephen Segal movie, *The Patriot*, which was my first hired-gun production rewrite. I ended up getting credit on it through Writer's Guild arbitration, which I didn't expect. It wasn't exactly the way I wanted to step out on the block as my first produced credit, so I used a pseudonym. Now if someone pulls up something on the computer and sees a list of credits, *The Patriot* isn't under my name. What I learned from that project was I could handle all the pressure of a production rewrite, which is a different kind of writing in the sense that you have to get it done immediately. There's no time to screw around. You have to write, do the work, just sit down and do it. It has to be usable material. The movie was in preproduction. They were scouting locations, looking for places. I had to listen to a lot of voices. Production design people, transportation people, the director, obviously the talent. So it was a lot of coordination, really complex. The big thing was the budget. I had to cut out the fancy stuff. The whole experience was a hard core lesson, and working on it established that I could do that kind of job."

More assignments followed. He did a book adaptation about a Marine boot camp called *Making the Corps* for Jersey Films. The word was out that Dave could do law enforcement and military projects. Then one day Tod Feldman called and asked if he was interested in doing a World War II submarine picture.

"Hell yeah!" Dave exclaimed. "So I went and had lunch with Jonathan Mostow, who read *Training Day* and *Plague Season* as samples. And he said that he'd already decided to hire me. We sat there at lunch, and I told him I had served on a submarine in the Navy. He said, 'Right on!' We sat there for three or four hours just talking about it, and I realized this was a tough assignment. They'd already spent $12 million on sets. Michael Douglas had originally been cast to star, but he pulled out of the project, so I had to rewrite it for a younger man, and we didn't know who yet. And I turned in a draft and it got green light without a star! Then they closed Matt McConaghey. Overall, it was a lot of fun, one of the best times I've had writing. Working with Mostow was super-collaborative. Most of the time in the business you get your marching orders, a set of notes, and then you lock yourself into a room all alone until you're done. In this case, he'd written some scripts and the original draft, so he and I cranked on it in Rome in a little room for a month, just going over the script. I got to work with McConaghey and Harvey Keitel and Bon Jovi, which was great. It was an amazing writing experience. Once I wrote a new scene, which entailed a different section of the submarine that would have to be used. I always walked down to the set in the morning where they were building and constructing the sets at Cinecitta Studios, and the next morning I arrived and bam! The set was halfway done already. Wow! It was weird to see my words impact the world, see them built up like that."

Another production rewrite followed *U-571*, and the project got greenlit by Universal, making Dave three-for-three on the production rewrites. Despite his growing reputation, however, he finds that with each project he is in some ways starting all over.

"The first thing is building your representation, getting people aware of who you are as a writer and what you can do. But you always have to audition for jobs. Always. You always have to go in there and have good ideas and knock the socks off of the producers. Go in there and give them some ideas. I've done that. I've read great scripts and had a take on them. And sometimes you just don't click. You might have a hard time communicating with some people. They don't understand what you want to do, especially in a production situation. There's this ironic situation that develops where they have a script that isn't up to par to go shoot yet, but it's still the basis of a project they're doing, so in a sense they don't want to change it because it's their blueprint. So I'll try and figure out what's special on this project that made them willing to spend the money to get it made. I try to retain that, and yet not be afraid to offer suggestions I think make sense."

I told Dave that Tom Schulman took the same approach with *Dead Poet's Society* that Dave did with *Training Day*, just writing something for himself. Dave said he thinks that will always work.

"When it comes from the heart, you can't beat it, when you're being honest to yourself as a writer. It's gonna outshine any clever construction."

Now, with *Squids* (which he's rewriting from scratch), he's in the best of both worlds.

"It's like writing on spec. I just have to get out a story from the heart that I enjoy writing. It's not like the heavy lifting of a production rewrite or the drudgery of a job where you're adapting someone else's work, fixing someone else's script. This is all me again. I think that every writer has one or two great scripts in them, and that's it. The rest of them are video games. This is going to be one of those scripts for me. It helps that I'm working with Art Linson on it. He's an old hand. It's a passion project that I'm getting paid for writing. You can't beat that. It's been 10 years since the original, during which I learned how to write. The story is a lot different now, and it's a lot more fun to write because instead of concentrating on the technical details of execution

I can concentrate on getting into my emotions at the time and with a perspective where I'm not so emotionally wrapped up in the events the story is based on. And I know what elements you need to have in a story to make it work. So it's a lot of fun."

For a long time now, Dave Ayer has had jobs backed up, even two or three projects going on at the same time. I sympathized with him, having had the same situation myself for a few years now. In my experience, aspiring screenwriters don't realize just how hard some people in Hollywood work. It's a lot less glamorous than most believe.

"I'll finish a job on a Friday and start a new one on Monday," Dave said. "I've been doing that for a few years now. And it gets pretty tiring. *Squids* has been, for the past few years, the light at the end of the tunnel, the brass ring for me. I'm finally able to do it, and I get to play a little bit. I'm trying to have that same *Training Day* attitude, where I'm pretending that no one's gonna read this but me. Otherwise, the big danger is getting institutionalized, because Hollywood wants a fresh voice to bring into the fold. After you go through the development process a few times and get some cuts and bruises, it can take the fight out of you and you can start internalizing all the rules of the road, which is kowtowing to the lowest common denominator of acceptability. Don't offend anybody. No sex, smoking, drugs. No foul language. If you write a PG-13 you can only use the F word once, so you have to pick that F word very carefully. I just think that my life experience is a little different from typical suburban upbringing. That's part of being a writer, I think. A responsibility or a curse. You have to go out into the world and experience it, see what's out there, and bring it back and write. I look at reading scripts like taking a college course. You're learning a new set of people, a new set of circumstances. There's always technical stuff to learn about that subject at hand. So that's what's one of the aspects, you're always learning. It just doesn't stop."

What keeps him grounded is a core of friends he's had a long time. Nevertheless, he had some problems moving into the million-dollar club.

"This society teaches that money is the do-all and be-all of human existence. With so many people living from paycheck to paycheck, the money was all I could talk about for a while. I was coping. Success is a difficult process. It's almost like death in the sense that your old life dies and you have this new life and things are different and you're not sure how. The message you grew up with is that money is the solution to all problems. I don't have to worry about rent and, theoretically, I should have some freedom, but the reality is that I work all the time. I really haven't had a chance to go out and enjoy the money. You get to the point where it becomes pretty abstract. You stare at your bank statement and feel great about it. That's natural. Then you get to the point where you know it's still you. You're still the same person. I'm just not into the Hollywood scene. If you go to a Hollywood party or you go to a mall it's the same thing. I have representation, so he's out there doing my legwork for me."

For other writers aspiring to capture lightning in a bottle and sell it to Hollywood, he suggests that success might be something that happens naturally, rather than something that is forced.

"I didn't grow up saying I wanted to be a writer. I failed high school. Writing found me. I didn't pursue it. It's a blessing because I had a set of skills I didn't know I had. Talent, that's what they're paying for. You can have all the studious dedication you want, learn the craft and write a zillion scripts but unless there's some intangible core talent there, it's not going to get anybody's attention. I really can't explain what it is I do. I think a lot of it is being able to write good characters. And it's ideas. Not necessarily the big commercial script idea, but little nuts and bolts about how things work in the real world that'll link up Rube Goldberg devices in your imagination. You're nothing without imagination. I was a big daydreamer growing up. I'd concoct these elaborate stories and scenarios in my head as kind of an escape. But however I got here, I learned that when you say yes to a job, it's a big, big, big, big deal. These people are hiring you for a purpose and if you say yes and you don't deliver what they expect, they're going to be angry. They're not going to hire you again. No smart producer in this town is going to hire somebody without calling the last five people they worked with to get the lowdown. My rule for saying yes to a project is if I read it and if it's something that I would work on spec, then I'll know it's the right project.

"It's a small town, a family business. It really is a handshake business, one of the last handshake businesses around. I've gone in and started a project and finished a project before the contract's been done, before the lawyers have ironed out the contract. That's the nature of it. I'm not going to screw them and they're not going to screw me. Because if either of us do much of that, we ain't gonna be in business much longer. It's about getting the work done. You don't have time to wait for the lawyers. I'm at the point now where I'm willing to get up and walk away from a negotiation. You have to have in your head a set of conditions that have to be met. If they're not met, you have to be willing to say, 'forget it'. The same thing overall in this business is that it's a lot tougher than I ever could have imagined. Had I known what I was getting myself into, I never would have had the courage to start it in the first place. A lot of picking a project is a guaranteed delivery on materials and something that's going to get you up in the morning to write, but the other thing is who you're working with, because it's as simple as do you like this person? Are you willing to spend a few months alone in a room with this person? Do you get along? I'm at the point now where I can pick who I work with. That's a real luxury, a very fortunate situation."

He's adamant about the hard work an A-list career requires.

"In L.A., the population is four million or something. I think two million of those people are writers. I can't tell you how many times I'll go out somewhere and meet somebody and go, 'What do you do, man?' And they'll tell me they're a writer. So I'll ask them, 'What have you written?' And it's just usually, 'Well, I got this screenwriting program. I have a really cool idea.' Rarely, they've written one script. That pisses me off. I bust my butt to do what I do, and with all this success and everything it took me a long time to get to the point where I'd actually call myself a writer. I didn't do that until after *U-571*. When I got that credit, I told myself, Okay, now it's official. There's this old cliché, writers write. And that's it. It's the loneliest job in the world. It's hard for years and years and years, but it pays off. I'd work full-time and then write in the evenings. I'd work for the man, and then I'd work for myself. I did that for years. You have to pay those dues. A screenplay is one of the most difficult forms to write. It takes a long time to learn how to get it right."

Obviously, Dave Ayer is someone who's learned how to get it right, repeatedly. In Hollywood, that's screenwriting gold. Which is why he's now a million-dollar man.

BOTTLING THE LIGHTNING

What can we learn from all these stories? If anything, that there is no one clear route to screenwriting success. One writer knew what she wanted to do at age four. The most successful one says that writing found him, not the other way around. One constant throughout all these stories is hard work. Every single successful writer I've ever known, in any discipline, puts in a lot of hours. Once they embark on their career, they don't turn back, despite discouragement that would deter less hardy individuals. If everyone ever tells you that Hollywood is easy, urge them to seek psychiatric help. It takes talent, hard work, and adaptability to make it. It also takes an ability to be flexible about the needs and desires of others because film is the most collaborative medium of all. Even if you think your script is perfect, it's probably not. The lightning that you are trying to bottle in a great script is, ultimately, a bit of yourself. Maybe a lot of yourself. If you make it as a screenwriter, there will be something about your own particular unique ability to create characters, dialogue and story that will set you apart from others and make producers want to film your written images for projection on a screen 30 feet high. Or, alternatively, on television screens in millions of homes.

How do you catch that lightning and put it in a bottle?

You'll know it when it's done. And I hope this chapter helped provide a spark of inspiration to let that current loose.

Getting Past
the Gates

Let's say you think you have something great, whether it's a book, a novel, a comic book, a screenplay, or even a magazine article to which you own the film rights. Whatever it is, you think you have lightning in a bottle. Good luck. Most likely, once you find someone who will read your material, if they have their own company, they'll give it to a reader to "cover." Readers come from all walks of life and are usually people who may themselves be writers. They work very hard, reading dozens of properties each week and writing one- to three-page descriptions of what they thought of each item. They will usually have three choices: Pass, Consider, or Recommend. Because they might get blamed if they recommend something be acquired which later turns out to be a flop, they rarely recommend a property.

Once a producer finds a reader whose opinion they can trust, they're loath to let them go. I've known of freelancers who live as far away as New England. They get scripts via Federal Express, then fax the coverage back to the producer, or e-mail it. And they all usually work 10 or more hours a day, usually being paid around $50 to $100 per covered script when working for respectable companies. What do I mean by "respectable company"? One that pays its staff. Some companies seek free labor—"Be an intern! Learn how Hollywood works!"—rather than paying people a living wage. Either way, assistants and readers are mostly underpaid. Union readers and people on staff get benefits, but not freelance readers. They don't get sick days or paid vacations; they're paid only for the "piece work" they complete.

So please keep that in mind the next time you feel like getting angry over having your project rejected. It could be for any number of reasons, and you just need to move on.

Usually, though, it's the writing. Having read a lot of scripts from beginning writers, I can tell you that a great number of screenplays, even those from reputable agencies, simply aren't that good. If you don't believe me, try cycling through some movies on cable channels on a Saturday night to find something you think is worth watching. As I told Eric Garcia, who only found one worthwhile property while reading for the Ruddy-Morgan Organization, many is the time my wife and I (we have small children at home) ended up watching that company's *Walker, Texas Ranger* on CBS simply because it was the best thing on television on Saturday night.

I've even read award-winning screenplays that I thought had little chance of getting made. These awards did not come from contests within Hollywood, though. That's why I don't recommend many contests at all. Only a few mean anything within the industry. But don't take my word about the general quality of screenplays. Here's what a professional reader told me.

THROUGH A READER'S EYES

Elizabeth Stevens read my *Writer's Guide* and sent me an e-mail. I had no idea what she did for a living, but I found out when I sent out an e-mail saying I had free passes to the Hollywood Film Festival 2000. Liz took one of the passes, and we met one day during the festival. One day, she hopes to become a producer, which I've found is true of the vast majority of readers. Keep that in mind when you submit your work. There's an old saying in Hollywood that you see the same people on that way up that you see on the way down, meaning you might want to try to be as nice as possible to others and not take the attitude that you're just dealing with a gatekeeper who should be tricked and bypassed. Liz told me it took a lot of effort and a lucky break to gain an inside footing in Hollywood. These days, Sandra Bullock's Fortis Films is a reading client, and she works for others who are equally successful. She finds the accomplished actress is anything but the type of quirky character she often plays.

"Sandra is an astute businesswoman and a powerful Hollywood player," Liz told me over lunch. We were at the Hamburger Hamlet on Hollywood Boulevard, across the street from Mann's Chinese Theater. "She's clear about the kind of material she seeks—exemplary work featuring exceptionally strong female protagonists. My advice to writers approaching anyone of her stature is to do their homework carefully before submitting: Know the actor's history, current standing and tastes, and be very cognizant of what the actor is seeking in new material. Don't offer someone a script that's just like the last three films they made—they've been there, done that."

The first thing I wanted to know was how many pages of a script or book Liz would read before she decided to pass, since the first few pages are crucial in getting a reader to read an entire screenplay.

"When I read for a contest or when I know feedback for the writer is important, I always read the entire screenplay," she said. "Otherwise, I can't comment intelligently about overall structure, themes, arcs, resolution, etc. When I read for a producer or star, I read the whole script unless I'm told it's okay to bail out after the first act if the writing is substandard.

"In forming an opinion, however, I can usually tell by a few pages whether the writer has real talent and skill. If, by about page 12, I don't want to keep turning the pages, I suspect a lack of skill or poor structure. If I find myself on page 20, still wondering where the story is going, the writer has an uphill battle in winning me back over."

I wondered how she handles it personally when people find out she reads for important stars, since getting past stars' agents is a particularly fond pursuit of some writers.

"Lots of people ask for favors," she said. "As everyone in Hollywood knows, it's part of the job to ask. It's my job to protect my clients—and my reputation—by making sure not to waste their attention on material that's not up their alley, and most people asking for favors respect that. Most clients are interested in hearing from me if I have something outstanding to refer to them, but I won't compromise my integrity by pushing a script that doesn't meet a particular client's interests and standards."

She read dozens of books: on the industry, on the players, and on the craft of screenwriting. With the help of information in my *Writers Guide*, she began cold-calling producers, asking for a chance to read for them. Some of those most receptive and helpful were Steve Longi at Permut Presentations and Rick Gough at Loreen Arbus Productions. She tries to keep this in mind as she considers the hard work that goes into any property that crosses her path.

"I try to be an objective reader, knowing that my clients' tastes don't necessarily match mine. For example, even though I'm not an action-flick aficionado, I enjoy reading action screenplays and critiquing their quality. I'm past the age when 'coming-of-age' stories resonate personally, but I still appreciate a well-crafted story on this theme. In general, a good story is a good story, no matter its genre or milieu. In particular cases, like science fiction, I know I won't do justice to the material, so I decline the assignment. One personal issue that I have big trouble ignoring is work that is misogynistic in nature. It's just really hard to endure the offensiveness."

As I suspected, even with professionally written screenplays, "recommends" from her are rare. Among screenplays written by newcomers or part-time writers, "recommends" are even more rare.

"Not only do producers need excellent material," she told me, "they need writers who are professional: Writers who are in this for the long haul, to write and write, and then rewrite and rewrite. Writing is really all about rewriting. If that sounds like a hassle, you're not a professional writer."

Liz offered the following personal tips to writers, based on her long experience as a reader:

1. Make me care about the characters at the same time you are intriguing me with their plight.

2. Describe your characters. Give names, ages, and some physical and personality traits to help a reader "see" them and distinguish between individuals. Try to make character names dissimilar so it's easier to tell the players apart. It may be cute to name an entire family with alliterations, but it makes for a confusing read. Also, for the same reason, don't overdo the use of Sr. and Jr., or daughters with the same name as mom.

3. Tell me a story that keeps me compelled to turn the pages.

4. Work hard on expositional scenes. Find ways, other than dialogue, to get the information across. Be creative!

5. If you don't understand terms like these, your screenplay will reflect your lack of knowledge and experience: back story, character arc, theme, plot point, planting, payoff, and ticking clock.

6. Take me somewhere new or show me something unusual. If it is germane to your story, set it in an intriguing industry, locale, or milieu. For me, the glimpses into air traffic control in *Pushing Tin* added immensely to the story of John Cusack's character's personal macho challenge. A reader/viewer can absorb lots of information at once, so there's room to engage the reader/viewer with insights while you regale them with your comedic, romantic, dramatic, or adventure tale.

You can reach Elizabeth Stevens at EAStevens@compuserve.com.

WRITER AND READER

A *Writer's Guide* reader, Ken Goodman, told me about Carolyn Carpenter, a writer and professional script reader who works with Hollywood companies, including Innovative Artists, StoryBay.com, the Sundance Institute, and Dreyfus/James Productions (Richard Dreyfuss). Ken said that although he got "a pretty average review" on his script, Carolyn's feedback was right on, both the negative and positive. She was encouraging and spent time with him on the phone afterward. This was a paid review, the kind of thing I personally charge $250 for to discourage people from asking me to do it. I didn't ask what Carolyn charges, but when a paying customer is happy, that tells me something.

Unlike Liz Stevens, Carolyn's emphasis on the business has always been writing. When she first moved to Los Angeles, she worked as an assistant for a writer/director at Columbia Pictures. Reading scripts was one of her favorite duties. With a Bachelor of Arts in Drama, she told me she has been obsessed with film and theater her entire life, writing her first screenplay at the age of 10.

"I've taken extension film classes and I've devoured books on the process," Carolyn said. "I'm a union actor, and I worked as a professional ballerina and musical theater dancer until a car accident changed my direction. In film, I've worked as a script supervisor, a director's assistant, a production assistant, a grip, a stage manager, and in wardrobe. I've also been the associate producer at a successful theater. I wrote and am set to direct a short film selected by Panavision's Young Filmmaker Program. I produced, wrote, and directed instructional videos that sold over a million copies in the retail market. As a writer, I have had several plays produced in Los Angeles and Orange counties."

Is this the typical "reader as gatekeeper one must evade" that you've had in mind before reading this? When Carolyn began contemplating reading full-time, she researched the necessary qualifications and approached companies about gaining experience. Now she knows what to expect, but she's always hoping for a great new property.

"I can usually tell if I'm going to pass within the first 10 pages," she told me. "But I never chunk it. I've tried. I've been ordered by agents and producers to read the first act and stop if it's a pass. But I'm just not able to do that. I'm compelled to read the entire thing. That's not to say I don't skim, especially if the script is predictable. It doesn't take a lot of investment to read a bad script as it's easy to stay one step ahead of the story. But I'm never able to toss it without having a clear idea of the overall story. I also have tremendous respect for writers and give them the best shot possible."

Since she reads for Constantin Films and the German market as well as the American/North America market, I asked if she had any tips for a writer who wants to sell to the German and/or European market.

"In my experience, crossover is the biggest key to the foreign market. Anything popular in Europe must also be saleable in the States. I never get a request for something strictly for the European market. It needs to at least do well in the American video market. I know there are companies that cater strictly to the European market, but I don't work for them. Usually, American themes are popular in the foreign market. Stories about the underdog prevailing as well as action movies and sports themes work well because they don't require a lot of complicated dialogue. Big event films also do well in the foreign market."

I've often wondered if a reader's own personal story preferences come into play when reading, particularly if they are also writers.

"I try very hard not to bring my personal preferences to the job. It's fortunate that I like all genres. I don't care if a script is a no-brainer comedy or an epic adventure. But by nature, this business is extremely subjective. The only time my personal preferences get in the way is when a script is ridiculously and unnecessarily violent. As filmmakers, we have the opportunity to help guide society in a positive direction. Useless violence is dull and pointless. I don't consider myself a moral judge, but I could live without the hundreds of Tarantino knockoffs that include the splattered brain matter without the engaging characters and unique structural storytelling."

Like almost every reader I've ever spoken with, she was disappointed over the same old writer blunders. She described them to me, and revealed how often she finds a truly memorable script.

"Laziness. Typos. Scripts that are 50 pages too long because an author isn't able to edit themselves. (Fifty extra pages of brilliance I don't mind. I wish it would happen more often.) Cliché characters, especially women. I also loathe being hit over the head with obvious dialogue and a blatant message. I believe audiences are smarter than a lot of writers (and producers) give them credit for. I recommended two scripts last year. A boxing story and a comedy about gargoyles taking over New York. I also recommended a manuscript about the relationship between two brothers, one of whom is a professional ballplayer. They were vastly different projects. But their common bond is a free spirit. The authors weren't afraid to let go and be ridiculous or emotional or honest, depending on what the story called for."

And so once again, we come back to writing from the heart.

"My most common note," Carolyn said, "especially to young writers, is to let go. Write what you know. Even if the characters are in unusual locations or unfamiliar situations, they are ultimately reflecting the human experience. Audiences count on writers to reveal deep issues in order to vicariously release their fears, joys, and dreams. Also, write something . . . anything . . . on a daily basis. Spew, dig, share, exclaim, release, unleash, purge, write, write, write, write. . . ."

THE READERS UNION

What readers are paid is entirely up to the producer if they're an independent, but studio producers work with union story analysts. Until May 2000, these 180 individuals belonged to IATSE Story Analysts Local 854, which was formed in 1954. That changed when they merged into IATSE Editors Local 700 "to give greater bargaining strength to all the members of Local 700." The editors local has 6,000-plus members.

WHO ARE DEVELOPMENT PEOPLE, ANYWAY?

Development people are staff in a company who read scripts looking for one to produce, know their bosses' tastes, and are usually aspiring producers. Very often, they're also writers. Many are "Trust Fund Babies" who have family money to support them, so they're only working the long hours to learn the business. The titles vary. No one on staff likes being called a reader; that's reserved for people they hire from outside, usually. You'll run across Director of Development, Vice President of Development, and Creative Executive. They all mean roughly the same thing. This person isn't the head of the company, but the primary person looking to find good material.

After the company makes a deal for your property, it goes into "development," meaning that it will be rewritten and polished until a director, stars, and financing are secured. You may do the rewriting, you might not. What will they rewrite? They might change the location, to take advantage of cofinancing opportunities in some foreign country. Then it's story, followed by dialogue. When shooting begins, actors may want to rewrite dialogue on the set, having put together enough background on their characters so that they feel comfortable saying, "He wouldn't say that." Directors will have their own ideas about the script, and sometimes they can hurt a script. For example, many people contend that Shane Black's *The Long Kiss Goodnight* would have been a smash hit if shot the way it was written. But that's showbiz.

Generally, the whole movie rides on the shoulders of the script. That's one of the reasons why, when millions are on the line, movie executives try to cover all the bases and get a number of writers to rewrite the screenplay. Carrie Fisher was reportedly paid $100,000 for a weekend's work, rewriting René Russo's dialogue for *In the Line of Fire* to make it more feminine. A lot of people must be happy with the script before the camera ever starts rolling. Sometimes the process takes so long that it is referred to as "development hell." Remember that phrase. If you spend any time at all trying to sell screenplays, you'll hear it far too often. I used to shudder at the phrase "development."

What was to develop, I thought? My script was perfect! What was wrong with those dumb producers? Couldn't they see my blood-soaked sweat, mixed with the ink on the page?

Eventually, I learned that no matter how passionate I was about my work, making movies is a collaborative business, and the first gatekeeper you must pass (other than an agent or representative) is the person designated to read scripts at a production company. I advise to you to befriend "D-people" rather than try to get around them. I was a wiser writer when I understood the hierarchy of production companies, and how invaluable readers and development people can be to producers. I learned that someone who is Director of Development one week may be the supervising producer of the company the next. D-people not only read scripts, they hire readers to read scripts, and they chat with other D-people about what properties are hot and which ones are not. They do this on the phone and online. That's why you shouldn't view D-people and readers as mere hurdles to be jumped over or evaded. Even if you get directly to a producer or director, they will probably give it to someone in their office to read first.

I had to learn not to violate the etiquette and hierarchy of Hollywood, whether I liked the system or not. Eventually, I saw that the structure was in place to keep busy producers from going completely nuts from trying to keep up with everything. I also discovered that a lot of producers don't trust their own counsel and always get a second opinion.

It can be a complex process, and in a way you can't knock it. If your script can't pass muster going up the ranks, maybe a film of your screenplay won't please the public, and the producer could lose the cushy housekeeping deal with the studio (the office, the staff, and the salaries paid by a studio betting the producer will come in with a winning project).

Screenwriters must learn to deal with the fear factor. Fear is one reason they call it Tinseltown, a facade masquerading as a community. Cheerfulness that masks terror is not uncommon in Hollywood. It's not like my home state of Texas, where people tell it like it is, at least as they see it.

Mel Brooks once said that Hollywood is a town that can "nice" you to death. When producers told me they loved my script, or my pitch, I figured I was one step away from paying cash for that house on a hill. When I was told, "We love it but don't think we can get it made," no one explained to me that I was probably getting a bum's rush on a red carpet. The reality is this: Few people in Hollywood will risk angering a writer by telling him or her flat-out how they feel about a project unless they are unqualifiedly nuts about it. They have an innate fear that the writer will write a blockbuster script that they might not get a chance to see if the doors are not kept open.

Once someone gets to know you and genuinely likes your material and keeps reading, you'll get more honest and helpful answers. And as you become more experienced in the business, you're more likely to take criticism easily. If people sense that you can take it, they might be more honest with you from the start.

Before you ever drive your script through the gates of development, I advise writers to do what Stephen King does. If 10 friends have the same comments about something he's written, he pays attention. If they all say different things, he's not likely to care much because it's probably just opinion. Stephen King has had more properties made into film than anyone, so his methods count with me.

THE BASICS: WHAT ANY D-PERSON EXPECTS OF YOU

The first D-person I interviewed for this book is out of the business now, but the complaints she had about the submissions she received are the kind I still hear. Let's take them up one by one:

Problem: Screenplays are not typed in proper screenplay format or have dialogue that runs all the way across the page (stage play).

Solution: Get a copy of *The Complete Guide to Standard Script Formats—Part I: The Screenplay* by Cole/Haag. It's available at The Writers Store (www.writersstore.com) or directly from CMC Publishing, 11642 Otsego Street, N. Hollywood, CA 91601.

Problem: The writer doesn't understand three-act structure or the commonly accepted story elements in use today.

Solutions: Read my *Complete Idiot's Guide to Screenwriting*, but first, read Aristotle's *Poetics*. Most importantly, read as many recently-sold professional scripts as you can.

Problem: Screenplays submitted are too long.

Solutions: For a long time, the norm has been 90 to 120 pages for feature films. These days they run shorter, up to about 115 pages. Comedies are generally shorter. Don't use a software program to "cheat" and squeeze your words into a shorter length; it will probably cause problems later. Keep rewriting until you excise all the unnecessary scenes. Learn to say more in dialogue with less, and learn to say with action what you're explaining via dialogue.

Problem: Anxious writers submit properties to producers who don't like their kind of material.

Solutions: Research the people you contact before you contact them. Try to meet people in the business personally, which is the best way to sell anything.

Problem: Screenplays and stories seem too contrived or too much like a copycat version of a recent hit. (Remember, it's usually only writers already working in the system who get paid to copycat.)

Solutions: Write something from the heart that you would really like to see. Write a lot; you'll gain confidence and an original voice.

Problem: Typographical errors, bad spelling, and a general disregard for the English language.

Solutions: A good education. Barring that, a thorough study of *The Elements of Style* by Strunk & White.

Problem: Ignored rules.

Solution: Some companies might pay to send your script back if you don't send them a self-addressed, stamped envelope (SASE). Most independent companies, however, expect to either have a SASE to return your script with or to be able to throw your script away.

Problem: Writer with an attitude.

Solution: Have patience. If you don't hear from them within six weeks, you might not hear from them. A short reminder phone call, e-mail, or even postcard might not hurt, but much more than that might send your script to the round file (trashcan).

Problem: Unrealistic expectations.

Reality: If an independent producer likes your script, they might only offer you a token $1 option until they can secure financing for the movie. They might pay you six figures at that time, but chances are good they'll pay you Writers Guild minimum purchase price for a low-budget film, with 10 percent added on to pay your agent (15 percent if it's a manager, but usually only "minimum plus 10").

Any film that is made from one of your scripts may change your career forever. You'll probably get a good agent if you don't already have one, and people in Hollywood will take you much more seriously. Have you always thought that getting a good Hollywood agent will solve all your problems? The problem with that idea is that most agents want writers who are easy to sell, and that means proven quantities (which means already sold and/or produced screenwriters).

In most cases, you need some sort of introduction to get a good agent, and that usually comes from another writer signed with the agent, or a producer or director or executive whose opinion the agent trusts. Development executives at independent production companies, however, usually don't insist on new writers having an agent, or expect them to have one. Sometimes, you can simply mail them the script if they like your query. Other times, they'll ask you to sign a release. Or they might be satisfied to have the property submitted by an attorney. It varies from producer to producer, even those housed on studio lots, but generally you have a better chance with an independent production company.

SCRIPT TRACKERS AND COVERAGE SERVICES

In the first edition of this book, I didn't interview a director of development for a major feature film company housed at a studio, even though I knew several such people. I left them out purposely because writers who are not represented in some way often find getting an audience with this type of development executive difficult at best. You usually need a great sample script to get their attention, and, in most cases, you'll need an agent to get it to them.

As I compiled the second edition of the *Writer's Guide to Hollywood*, I learned that more "on the lot" production companies than ever before were open to material from sources other than recognized agencies. To give readers an idea of what a studio production company wanted, I interviewed Matt Luber, then Vice President of Development for Diamond Heart Productions (*To Die For* with Nicole Kidman and other films) at 20th Century Fox. Matt was the first to show me a "tracking" Web site, where directors of development, VPs of development, creative executives, and story editors would congregate online to discuss available projects and available writers.

Via e-mail and online chats, trackers follow every property circulating at top production companies, TV networks, and studios. By cooperating amongst each other about what properties are out there, trackers can often get the jump on buying a hot property. Tracking became such an intense phenomenon that in the fall of 1997, producer Steve Stabler optioned the rights to Ben Queen's black comedy spec script *One Track Mind*, a story about a tracker who gets a hot script from a writer who is murdered and tries to pass it off as his own, since the writer has no friends or heirs.

One problem: The other trackers are onto him.

Though I have no idea what became of that script, I do know that tracking has now expanded into the broad public. Trackers quickly realized that they could make money prescreening material for producers, charging writers trying to break into Hollywood.

Hollywood hasn't gone completely online. Producers do many more phone calls than e-mails, and although everyone still reads tons of scripts, these pregatekeepers offer an interesting option to writers. But if they like your script, who do they recommend it to?

D-people get submissions from top agencies. They know what hierarchies are in place and how those relationships work. A development person who is plugged-in can tout a project around town and get it sold. They might also be able to kill a project, or at least hurt its chances of selling.

As Matt Luber told me that day over lunch: "Writers should try to understand. It's a small town, and when you're on the outside, sometimes you don't realize just how small it can be. It pays to make friends."

So how do you make friends if you don't know anyone? What if you don't live in southern California and have no plans to go there at any time in the foreseeable future? A coverage service might be an option.

Since the last edition of the book, I was approached by a number of script coverage services to work with them. They all:

- Charge a fee to read a property (script, novel, book, or other) and provide industry standard coverage.
- If they deem it worthy, recommend the property to an agent and/or producer who might want to take it on.
- Provide consultation services to improve the work.

All of this is in a "gray area" of Hollywood. Some purists will tell you to never pay anyone anything to comment on your work. More pragmatic and experienced hands know that many successful writers have paid editors and consultants to help their work reach a professional level, and that a number of well-known writers have "ghost" help.

If you think that you might need improvement, I list some possibilities below.

FILMTRACKER.COM

Two fellows, Alex Amin and Rafi Gordon, approached me one day and told me about their company. They had a site called ScriptTrackers.com that had been going for about a year. Paid subscribers included hundreds of the top production companies in Hollywood. They showed me the list, which I've kept confidential. I was impressed. The purpose of their service was to allow D-people to form groups onsite, according to their own likes and dislikes, and to have a general place to discuss available material and writers. Alex and Rafi explained that they also had a database of over 6,000 industry contacts, with the ability to search and correlate any contact with another. They wanted to open this up to writers all over the world on a subscription basis, along with the ability to have coverage done and recommendations (if warranted) made. Because they had hundreds of top companies already resident onsite (something no other online service of its kind could claim), I realized their renamed FilmTracker.com had more possibilities than most.

Given the nature of dotcoms, who knows what will be around by the time you read this, but I hope that FilmTracker will be one of the sites that makes it. If you sign up for any online script coverage service, your main question should be *who* they can get to read your material if you sign up. If they are evasive or vague about it, that might be a bad signal.

A CORNUCOPIA OF CONSULTANTS

Rather than weigh in too heavily on the companies below, I'll list them alphabetically, describe a bit about them, and let you decide.

The Complete Screenplay

When highly successful producer Kathleen Kennedy was President of Amblin Entertainment, she wrote a letter of introduction touting Sally B. Merlin's skills as an agent and described her as "a person who finds emerging talent, nurtures it, and finds it a home." That letter is posted at www.completescreenplay.com. Though Merlin is now based on the East Coast, I've heard her praises from several readers. She says her "personal passion is to be able to utilize my gifts as a communicator to inspire, illuminate, and educate to the greater good." Anyone with a Platonic reference like that gets my attention, and apparently her clients' screenplays get the attention of top people in Hollywood. Another of her goals is "to help you reach your authentic voice." If she can do that, you're way ahead of the screenwriting game. Coming from a family of show business veterans, Merlin once sang "Bye-Bye Blackbird" with the legendary Judy Garland and apparently grew up with a marvelous outlook on life. Contact her via e-mail at smerlin@bellatlantic.net or phone 301-847-1410.

Creative Script Services

Kathryn Knowlton's motto is "Get Your Script from the Outside in with CSS!" A 15-year film industry veteran, Knowlton has worked with Richard Dreyfuss and been VP of Production for Jon Voight at Columbia Pictures. She "provides clients with access to the industry's leading producers, directors and studios." Contact:

CREATIVE SCRIPT SERVICES
11738 "F" Moorpark Street, Studio City, CA 91604
818-754-4779, Fax: 818-762-8238
E-mail: info@thescript.com

Graham Flashner

This L.A.-based writer/producer has worked in the film industry for a dozen years "on every side of the desk, not only writing and producing, but as a development exec (at CBS and Alliance Atlantis) and a staff and freelance script reader." He offers "quality coverage, notes, phone consultation, agent recommendations (if warranted), and general practical advice on all aspects of the biz." He guarantees a one-week turnaround from the time your script arrives, and a free initial consultation. No Web site, but you can reach him at:

GRAHAM FLASHNER
10806 Lindbrook Drive #3, Los Angeles, CA 90024
310-470-4262, Fax: 310-470-7027
E-mail: scriptdoc81@hotmail.com

Hollywood Experts

A unique collection of experienced veterans and some online courses can be found at www.hollywoodexperts.com including:

- Filmmaker/writer Mollie Gregory on showbiz job hunting
- Completion guarantor Joan Stigliano on film completion bonds
- Entertainment banker Lewis Horwitz on banking arrangements
- Banker Larry Da Silva explaining the financing of independent films
- Entertainment attorney Judith Merians
- Writer-producer Jo Lamond on preparing you for pitch meetings
- Unit production manager Betsy Pollock on preparing and managing the production of a feature film

- Studio business executive Leon Brachman on profit participations
- Story analyst Peggy King on dissecting a script

Like I said, they also have courses. Visit their Web site or e-mail theo@hollywood experts.com.

Hollywood Script Consultants

Craig Kellem and Judy Kellem have a great site at www.Hollywoodscript.com where you can get a free mini-consultation, a free query letter read, and a contest. Their fee is very reasonable given their experience. Craig Kellem worked as a development executive at both Universal and 20th Century Fox and also as an agent. Judy Kellem was also a studio analyst and is RSA/CTEFLA–certified, so she can provide special attention to non-native English speakers. Craig produced Eric Idle's classic movie *The Rutles* and was an associate producer of *Saturday Night Live*. Contact:

CRAIG KELLEM
11 Dorchester Road, Lyme, NH 03768
603-795-9424, Fax: 603-795-4323
E-mail: Craig.Kellem@Valley.Net

JUDY KELLEM
61 East 8th Street, PMB # 318, New York, NY 10003
E-mail: Judykellem@earthlink.net

The Insiders System

Probably the original script consultant in modern Hollywood, Natalie Rothenberg published her first *Writers Showcase* magazine in July 1993. Since then, she's helped over 700 writers in 45 states and five countries improve their projects, hone their writing skills, and find contacts, representation, and deals. With experience on both the buying and selling sides of the film, TV and publishing, she saw a need and developed a two-step system to help writers and decisionmakers find each other. One of my readers, Ted Gasowski, seemed very pleased with being showcased in her quarterly publication, and it's an impressive one. Projects described in her magazine get read, and she is also available for consultations. Contact:

THE INSIDERS SYSTEM FOR WRITERS
1223 Wilshire Blvd., #336, Santa Monica, CA 90403
800-397-2615 or 310-899-9775
E-mail: insiderssystem@msn.com
Web site: www.insiderssystem.com

James P. Mercurio

With a master's degree from the University of Michigan in film and screenwriting, James Mercurio teaches screenwriting and film analysis in Los Angeles at the Learning Tree University. At the University of Michigan, he won a Hopwood Award in screenwriting, an award also won by Larry Kasdan and Arthur Miller. He has sold scripts and worked as director of development for Montage, a company whose producers' credits include *Gas Food Lodging*. I've found his posts on the newsgroup misc.writing.screenplays to be informed and insightful. You can reach him at:

JIM MERCURIO
5216 Corteen Place, #14, Valley Village, CA 91607
E-mail: ssjohny@aol.com

Peruse his Web site at http://members.aol.com/ssjohny. One thing you might like there is his analysis of the various story gurus on the seminar circuit.

Madeline DiMaggio

Voted best script analyst and consultant by the Freelance Screenwriters Forum, a national writers' group, Madeline regularly presents private workshops, and offers screenplay critiques and hourly private consultation. She's been called "The Goddess of TV Writing" and has credits longer than your arm. She's the author of the classic book *How to Write for Television*. She splits her time between California and Texas. Phone 831-373-2375 or 282-282-9431 or E-mail: Mdima93950@aol.com.

Movie Money

If you've heard the story of how *The Blair Witch Project* got extra financing and became a worldwide sensation, then you might be interested in the lady who wrote the business plan that made it possible. Louise Levison's company is:

BUSINESS STRATEGIES
4454 Ventura Canyon Avenue, Suite 305, Sherman Oaks, CA 91423
818-990-7774, Fax: 818-981-6857
E-mail: louisel@earthlink.net
Web site: www.moviemoney.com

RX4Scripts

With a Hollywood pedigree several generations long (his father was the great actor Keenan Wynn and his grandfather the fabulous Ed Wynn), Tracy Keenan Wynn now offers screenwriting consultations via the Web from his home in beautiful Aspen, Colorado. I won't even list the price here because this Emmy winner isn't charging anything near what he's worth. Get impressed by his extensive credits at www.imdb.com and then head over to www.rx4scripts.com and see what you think. You can e-mail Tracy at tracywynn@yahoo.com.

ScriptDoctor911

Aubrey M. Horton offers written script consultations only. If a phone or e-mail consultation is requested, then the writer will be billed an extra fee (including any long-distance charge). Horton has an MFA in screenwriting from UCLA film school and has consulted on projects for Dick Clark, HBO, Paramount and Warner Brothers. Contact:

AUBREY M. HORTON
P.O. Box 140977, Austin, TX 78714
E-mail: info@Guru-My-Screenplay.com
Web site: www.ScriptDoctor911.com

ScriptZone

Having personally met with Paul Young, I found him to be an affable, intelligent man with a long heritage in Hollywood (three generations of agents). His screenplays also have been acquired by Robert Redford/Wildwood Productions, Orion, Kings Road Entertainment, and others. He's an author and was once a Columbia Pictures story analyst. I haven't heard a bad report on his services. Contact:

LITERARY & SCREENPLAY CONSULTANTS
22647 Ventura Boulevard #524, Woodland Hills, CA 91364
818-887-6554, Fax: 818-887-6580
E-mail: scriptzone@aol.com
Web site: www.ScriptZone.com

StoryNotes

Rated as one of the top two screenplay evaluation services by *Creative Screenwriting* magazine in its March/April 1999 issue, Jeff Newman has written a column about screenwriting, had a number of his scripts optioned, and had one stage play produced professionally. While his prices seem a bit high compared to others with more experience, he's an active participant in the misc.writing.screenplays newsgroup and is more prone to give you more coverage than you expected. You can reach him at:

STORYNOTES
15721 Brighton Ave. D, Gardena, CA 90247
310-715-6455
E-mail: storynotes@aol.com
Web site: www.storynotes.net

The Screenwriters' Room

One of the first groups of script coverage consultants I met with was this company, and I found both the principals to be knowledgeable, connected, and great lunch partners. Kathleen Hannon was Vice President of Development for writer-director Andrew Bergman's company at both Castle Rock and Universal Pictures, working on films like the charming *It Could Happen To You*. She began her career at the prestigious Royal Court Theatre (London's theater for new writers). Ann Zald was a development executive for Interscope Communications and a creative executive for Universal-based Alphaville and was involved in the development of films like *Jumanji* and *Mr. Holland's Opus*. If they like what they see they can get it to people who count. Contact them at:

THE SCREENWRITERS' ROOM

12240 Venice Boulevard, Suite 11, Los Angeles, CA 90066
310-397-2970, Fax: 310-397-7277
E-mail: screenrm@earthlink.net
Web site: www.screenwritersroom.com

WELL-KNOWN COVERAGE SITES

Sites like ScriptShark.com get a lot of national publicity and have had results like a sale to Mel Gibson. The other major sites offering coverage and other services, in case you haven't already heard of them, are www.goodstory.com, www.inzide.com and www.storybay.com. I wish you the best with any you try.

BREAKING THROUGH WITH A QUERY

If you choose to go out on your own without dealing with a coverage service to advise you on the marketability of your work, you'd better know how to query effectively. Unlike the publishing industry, some people in Hollywood look upon the query letter as a crude country cousin. You can't reject it outright because very few people in Hollywood are comfortable with their position. There's always the possibility, however remote, that something great can be discovered in some unexpected place. Though short stories, or even novels, may be published thanks to introductory query letters I continually tell writers that if a query letter is their *only* way of contacting someone who can buy their work or sell it, that better be a *great* query.

Screenwriters basically need to take the POV (point of view) of a busy person who receives such a letter. Often, it's not the producer or agent but their assistant. That means (usually) a younger person than their boss with aspirations of their own. That's why you need to know:

- Who you're writing to, with their name spelled correctly
- Something about what they've done and what they like
- Where they're located or about to be located

It might not seem convenient or financially prudent to make a phone call, but it might help you sell. Also consider the following:

1. You might reach the person who would initially read your property and have a few words with them about it.

2. If you call late in the day, around 5:00 P.M. or later, you might get the head of the company, staying late, and be able to tell them about your work personally.

3. In either event, if the person you speak with likes what they hear, they'll be looking for your package when it arrives. You'll find out if their address is correct or if they're about to move (which happens a lot in Hollywood). You might even find out that they're willing to read something sent by e-mail (helpful if you're in New Zealand).

4. *Any* personal contact is almost always a better way to open a dialogue with anyone.

So let's say you make a phone call and explain who you are and who you're trying to reach and they don't hang up on you or say they don't accept unsolicited submissions. What if they say—

"What you got?"

(I wish the grammar was a bit better in Hollywood, but you're liable to hear that exact phrase.)

Your next step is to get right to the point. Tell them what your property is about and why you contacted their particular company. If you won any prizes with your work, or have any kind of track record as a writer, mention that later. Be prepared to state the logline of your work immediately. If they say something like: "That sounds interesting, let me take a look at it," that's about as good as you'll get. If you have the correct contact information at that point, get off the phone.

Then send the property that day; don't give them time to forget.

Hollywood people like to feel important. So if you aren't going to call and prefer to send a query, after telling them all of the above, also state:

- Reason for contacting them
- Name and logline of your property (and only one)
- Anything that sets you apart as a writer (awards etc.)

You might also add any information that could result in a meeting. If you plan to be in their area for a conference, for example, you might say you'd like to fit them into your schedule.

Make yourself easy to reach. Don't give someone an answering machine reason to hang up. Be as "reachable" as possible.

If you do write a letter out of the blue, it should on one page, certainly no more than two. For legal reasons, they generally need a "paper trail" that proves there is correspondence. So keep a copy of your letter, in print and/or electronically.

A sample query letter that I might send if I wrote query letters these days follows. The only letters I generally write these days are transmittal letters, which include the person's name and address and might say something like "Pursuant to our phone call [or e-mail] I'm enclosing   [Name of Property] . Thanks for taking a look, and I hope to speak with you soon."

Try to write any letter you send on personalized stationery, because it's much more professional. It's usually wise not to send in a script with a letter, but some agents don't mind.

(This query letter is about a real script of my own, which has been optioned but not yet made as a film.)

YOUR NAME [centered at top if you have no stationery]

Date

Paul Producer
Hollywood Movies, Inc.
555 Rodeo Drive
Beverly Hills, CA 90210

Dear Mr. Producer:

For many single women, turning 30 is traumatic. They begin taking stock of their lives, assessing their progress, and some who haven't found their great love think they are complete losers.

That's MIRABELLE FLOWERS, stuck in a small town in New Mexico, wondering if her Prince Charming will ever arrive. The night of her 30th birthday, she's waiting for her oddball collection of friends to throw her a surprise birthday party in the roadside diner she owns, when a stranger walks in who might just be the guy she's always wanted.

One slight problem—he might be an alien.

I know you've been particularly adept at selling romantic comedies like mine. My script, *Walking After Midnight*, was a finalist in two national competitions and a semifinalist in two others as a stage play. When two working Hollywood professionals told me that it should be a screenplay in the same week, I wrote the script.

I hope you'll take a look. You can reach me at the number or e-mail below, at your convenience.

Sincerely,

Me the Screenwriter

[centered at the bottom if you have no stationery]
Address
Phone Number
E-mail

Once you've sent the letter, forget about it. If you don't hear from them, you might not. If it's been six weeks or more, you can follow up politely with a phone call or e-mail, but after that let them contact you. If they don't, move on.

OTHER WAYS OF BREACHING THE GATES

With younger development execs, e-mail is a way of life, but that's not true of older veterans. When e-mail was relatively new, the novelty of it got a lot of people online, but now some guard their e-mail address as zealously as their unlisted phone number. So watch sending unsolicited e-mails just because you managed to snag someone's address. It might not get a reply. (I speak from copious personal experience.)

You're probably hip enough to the Net to know not to use ALL CAPS, which is considered shouting in cyberspace and rude. If you're smart enough to capsulize a logline in an e-mail header, even in one word (*Ghostbusters* comes to mind), you're more likely to get a response.

Follow general protocols of e-mail etiquette and use the same elements of a query letter mentioned above. Save copies of your e-mails with full headers, which give a unique signature to each e-mail. You might need them as evidence later.

Speaking of evidence, some companies will not receive faxes from people they don't know. I found that out once dealing with Howard Kazanjian, producer of *JAG*. Even though a mutual friend had mentioned a property of mine to him, because no one at the office knew me yet, they actually turned off the fax machine, saw my fax number and faxed me back saying they didn't know me and wouldn't take a fax from me. There's a legal reason for this kind of behavior, even if I find it to be rare. Fax machines keep records of sent and received faxes, which could be subpoenaed for court use to prove access. So don't send a fax unless you know they'll take it.

Will a producer read your script online? Not likely, but a reader or development exec might. If you have it posted on a Web page, you're probably out of luck. Some will read an electronic document, though, like an e-book or a screenplay formatted with Final Draft or similar software. If you have that available for download, it could work.

Should you send a synopsis? I don't, unless someone asks for one, and then I try to keep it to one page (single-spaced).

And then there's that odd animal called a treatment. What is a treatment? It's a double-spaced, scene-by-scene description of an entire movie, minus the dialogue (unless a particular line needs to be included). Although the very first Hollywood property I was ever paid for was a treatment, I *never* show them to a producer any more unless I know beforehand that this producer will hire me to write the movie if they like the treatment. Which is precisely what a treatment is for, anyway. It's a blueprint for writing a screenplay.

I've been told by a development executive I trust, however, that he would read a treatment to see if he wanted to read the script, but he's the only one who ever told me that. That's why I write treatments generally only for myself. If you think you're going to write a treatment and sell it without some proof that you're also a skilled screen-writer, then you know more than me, and I salute you.

To recap, you'll need the following to impress a gatekeeper and be invited into the castle:

1. A great property (preferably a spec screenplay)
2. Good people skills or an agent/manager with same
3. Thorough research on who you contact
4. Good phone etiquette
5. A clear statement (logline) of what you have to sell
6. Enough patience to not ruin your chances with neurotic follow-ups
7. The ability to persist until you do break through somewhere

I hope this chapter has given you some idea of the type of people you will run into in development, and the power they can wield toward helping your career take off. Rather than viewing them as gatekeepers to be outwitted with some shibboleth (secret pass-word) or ignored as you make an end-run directly to their boss, think of them for what they really are. Namely, very hard-working individuals who expect a certain standard and sophistication and who may soon go on to become successful producers.

Whether you submit your script or (better) get referred to someone in development to pitch your project, make sure you know the rules and something about the people you contact.

Be polite and patient throughout the process. They'll appreciate it, and so will you if they buy your project or recommend it to someone who will.

After all, if they acquire your project and work on it with you to get it in shape for filming, you'll be in "development hell" together until the script is ready, and you might as well start off on a cool note. Believe me, development hell is Heaven com-pared to no sale at all.

So now, let's say goodbye to development and move on up. Let's pay a visit to the kind of person most likely to buy your first script: an independent producer.

Someone's Gotta Love
It to Get It Made

One thing that has not changed, from the time I started in Hollywood through three editions of this book, is that producers don't spend a year or more of their lives getting a project filmed because they like it a lot or think it's pretty good.

They have to *love* it.

They have to be passionate about it, willing to do whatever it takes to get the project made. That holds true for all the key people involved in a movie, including the director and stars. If you're not personally passionate about your screenplay, how can you expect someone else to get excited about it?

It took director Sir Richard Attenborough 20 years to get *Gandhi* on the screen, and this was a biography of one of the great world leaders of the twentieth century.

If you've paid any attention to movie stories in the past few years, you've probably heard about how producer Wendy Finerman spent 10 years of dogged persistence before getting megahit *Forrest Gump* to the screen. She was hooked when she read, on the first page of Winston Groom's book, *It's not easy being an idiot.* Screenwriter Eric Roth had also been around for years with no breakthrough success. After reading only a portion of the book, he saw that the film would be a metaphor for the transition to adulthood of a generation of Americans, and he launched into writing the script with deep conviction. *Gump* was such a success, Roth ended up with a giant deal at Disney. For Wendy Finerman, conventional wisdom would have prescribed an easy success with *Forrest Gump*, because of her marriage to Mark Canton, who at the time ran a movie studio. Nepotism did not prevail; passion did.

And the prize for persistence goes to producer Mace Neufeld. At the Hollywood Film Festival 2000, he spoke of putting a film in production that he'd been working on for 22 years! In Hollywood, those who don't have patience shouldn't begin.

No matter how great a script you write, no matter how good your agent is, sooner or later someone will have to become as passionate about your script as you are, and that person will in all likelihood be an established movie producer. If you do not write something you are passionate about, your chances of finding someone else who is passionate about your work are greatly diminished. No script I have ever sold or had made was "just another script." I know many other writers (particularly TV writers) who have written many scripts only for money, but in every single case these writers are frustrated wannabe feature film screenwriters.

To find a champion of your work, you will need, first and foremost, a script someone feels they *must* champion, a script that *has* to be made, that they are willing to spend at least the next two years of their life with.

And that's if they get the film funded immediately.

Someone's gotta love it, or it won't get made. That's simply the way it is, no matter how small the production, or how large.

JENNIE'S PASSIONS

The most successful producer that I've known for the longest time is Jennie Lew Tugend, the person responsible for the 2000 hit *Return to Me*, and previously the surprise hit *Free Willy*. Why "surprise hit"? Because no one in Hollywood expected the film to make a lot of money, and certainly not over $150 million.

Jennie Lew began her film career by assisting producer/director Jerome Hellman for four years, developing projects that included *The Mosquito Coast*. From there, she went to work for director/producer Richard Donner at Warner Brothers. She became his president of production through the *Lethal Weapon* series and other films. She's been off that lot since 1997, and is now partnered with two other industry veterans to make small but meaningful independent films.

"I was blessed by having mentors who really were big guys," Jennie told me. "By that I mean big in spirit, who would allow you to learn, who'd say do this, learn it. Here, learn how to read, learn how to analyze, learn how to produce, learn how to go on the set, learn how to do a budget, read this. You know, who gave me the space and the freedom to learn. And boy, when you have that opportunity, you seize it! A lot of people aren't as lucky as I was. They are held back because the senior person is insecure. The insecure ones think: 'Well, I don't want to teach you too much because then you're going to have my job. So I'm going to keep you in your place.' But I was very lucky. I worked with people like Dick Donner who are bigger than life. He's so self-confident that he says, 'Here, kid, you do it.' And if he wants to let you run the show, you rise to the occasion. If you rise to the occasion, you can have it all. It's very important in this business to find a mentor."

Since leaving the lot and cutting down her overhead, Jennie will not accept projects sent in by writers she doesn't know. Unless she has spoken to a writer or the writer's representative about a project, she won't look at it unless you sign a release, and even then not unless she likes the high concept or logline you pitch her over the phone. Like most busy, successful producers, Tugend prefers to have projects referred to her via agents and other producers. She's flexible in how she gets a movie made, but not so when it comes to finding a project to produce. For her, it comes down to how she is approached, then how she likes what she hears. She also expects a writer to do some homework.

"If there's a writer out there who goes through the phone book and sends me the script with a cover letter, well, first of all, if that person hasn't called me personally, that's bad etiquette. We get stuff in the mail all the time, but if I don't know what it is, I don't know who it is, I don't know what it's about, I don't know anything about it, and it comes directly from the writer, it's immediately returned unread because it's unsolicited. That's one scenario. But let's say this writer has called me, and I take the call and the idea sounds interesting. And I say, 'Well, we can do this several ways, Mr. Writer. You can either send your script to me through an agent, if you have an agent, or you can send it to me through your lawyer. If you have neither, I'll send you my release form.' There has to be a paper trail because we all have to protect ourselves. So it behooves the writer on a cold submission to come through some other channel. Or if I say it sounds interesting and he says, 'Okay, I have a friend who's an agent,' I'll say, 'Fine, have your agent send it to me.' Then as a producer we'll look at. Well, let's see, who's the agent? Who is this? What did he say it was? It needs to be personalized in some way. Let's say the agent calls me and says, 'Hey, I have a script here, I know you spoke to the writer, I really believe in this.' You know, something to personalize it, some kind of a pitch. In other words, if I'm not going to have any idea what it's about, it'll go on the bottom of the pile."

Jennie's husband, James Tugend, is a successful screenwriter and producer who discovered a project she bought. James grew up in Hollywood. His father, Harry Tugend, was a legendary screenwriter who helped found the Writers Guild of America and hung out with friends like Billy Wilder and George Burns. James helps Jennie read scripts because their tastes are very similar, but if she and James don't agree on a project, she is not deterred.

What moves her to become convinced of the worthiness of a script? She estimates that she has rejected "maybe a thousand" scripts over the years. If there is a key element for rejection (other than the scripts just not being very good), it's because the story she is presented does not match her tastes.

"Often it's just the story itself, the kind of story. Every reader has his or her own sensibilities. For example, for me, if I got a script that was a raw slapstick comedy, I probably wouldn't get it. I wouldn't know how to produce that kind of a movie. It's individual tastes in terms of type of story. A good character-driven thriller would probably interest me more than a broad comedy of someone slipping on a banana peel, only because it's my own personal sensibility.

"Another reason scripts are often rejected is amateur writing. You can tell that the writer just doesn't understand cinema. When professional readers grade scripts—and they read at least two a day, every day—they have these categories that you check off. They grade them based on character, story, dialogue, content, and all that, and any one of those that fall into the poor or weak box usually is a reason to reject the script. When you look at the odds of how many movies get made and the ratio of scripts submitted to what gets bought or optioned for development, and then of those that actually get made, the percentage is very small. So when you are reading a script as a producer, you have to believe in the material. It's easily two years of your life. Am I going to fight for this material? Do I believe in it? Would I produce it? Would I spend my own money on this script? Because if I wouldn't, how can I ask someone else to? And so you do have to believe in it.

"It's always going to need work, because it's an evolving process. But if you feel connected to the material, or if it provokes certain emotions, it makes you cry and it makes you laugh, it scares you, it's a page-turner, then it's going to translate on film. It's going to make you cry. The first time I read *Free Willy* I cried at the end, right on the page, and that was the script's very first incarnation. When you read a script like that, you say 'Huh! There's something here.' And if by page 25 you're not involved in the story and you couldn't care less about the characters or whatever, well then, it's never going to translate to film. The audience is not going to care, either."

When the script that became *Return to Me* came across her desk it was known as *Distance Calls*, a spec screenplay Jennie sold to MGM. Actress Bonnie Hunt and her partner Don Lake rewrote the screenplay from page one, their main inspiration being the idea of the heart transplant in *Distance Calls*. The title came from a song that was Hunt's parents' favorite. Set around a family in Chicago, the rewrite was very personal for Hunt.

"Some romantic comedies sag because they have too much talking and don't go any-where," Jennie said. "You have to drive the story forward. Scripts shouldn't be over 120 pages, generally, but a story for kids, or a romantic comedy or other comedy should be 109 to 112 pages these days. Shorter scripts move faster onscreen. *Return to Me* was the shortest reading-to-film project I've been involved with. It took two years. The longest was eight years, and that was *Free Willy*, during which time we went through four writers. I started with *Return to Me* at MGM in May of 1997, and we started shooting in May of 1999. The movie was released in April of 2000. I don't want to spend two years of my life on something I don't love. These days it's a moment of decision, a turning point when I take on something new."

Jennie says she's happy if she can set up a picture one year after taking a project on. I asked her what her criteria was for selecting her next project.

"There are lots of reasons to reject scripts. Let's say I was looking for a thriller and I got one. Okay, now I'm predisposed to this genre, but it's poorly written, or it doesn't have a third act. A lot of scripts fizzle out in the middle. Unless there's a satisfying end-ing, then you can do one of two things. You can reject it, or if you really feel that there's something inherently workable in the material, then you can option it and roll up your sleeves and get into development. Scripts that I have bought to get made have elements of courage, moments of people changing. Not just your typical character arc, but something profound. We read so much, but some material I can tell you the whole story even though I read it 10 years ago. The script made an impression. Whether or not it actually got made, that's another thing, but if it's a good story, you're going to remember it.

"Scripts that don't work generally have a second act problem. I never took a class or went to lectures. I just read scripts, and I remember the good ones. I've found that by page 76 the stuff—the thing that makes the movie unique—is delivered, if anything's delivered at all. I can read a scene and know if we can shoot it or not. I don't want to read three-quarters of a page about having dinner. I want the story moved forward. If a writer feels a scene needs a tag and writes a page of dialogue about having dessert, that could mean half a day's work if we shoot it. That translates to $50,000 when a shoot costs $100/120K a day. So I know what to cut in a scene."

At the time of our most recent interview, Jennie had just taken a 122-pager down to 112. She told me she would examine each scene and say, "What is this about?" If the scene didn't really contribute, out it came.

"If a script's first pass is 130 pages, you need to get it down to 120. One-hundred fifteen if you can. When I'm reading I pay attention to characters, the size of the movie. The more I hear the characters speak, the more they take shape in my mind. If I can't sell it, I try to find ways to make the characters stronger before we show it. The writer can send me pages or do a whole new draft. It's a painful process. When the draft is okay, when we have 3D characters, when the story hangs together, then it can go into production. The whole process is based on relationships, trust, and desire to work together. Every script is different. In a year, with luck, if the script is right and a project has one piece of talent attached with third party financing, I can get it made.

"If I'm crazy about a script I might send it to an agency for packaging. But what writers have to understand is that I'm an independent producer. If there's no cash offer attached to a project, it might take the star months to read the script. I get hot specs to read because of my relationship with studios, but I'll look for a good story anywhere."

You have to be an optimist to be a movie producer, and you don't always have to work yourself to death, but Jennie feels it is imperative to constantly acquaint herself with new writers.

"It all starts with a script," she told me. "Unless it's a sequel or something. One of a producer's biggest assets is the writers that you know. I meet with writers as often as I can if I respond to their material. Let's say you sent me a script and I wasn't interested in that story, but I really liked your writing. You wrote great action, or great women characters, or whatever, or you had great dialogue for how children speak. I would call you or your agent and say, 'You know, I'm going to pass on this script, but your writer's really interesting, can we take a general meeting?' That's part of the game, you know? After that meeting I have a relationship with you, the writer, and maybe you've made me aware of some new idea of yours that interests me, and I want an early crack at it. A lot of people send me scripts but because I'm not a big machine, the odds are that, as a solo producer, I can only actively work on six projects, and I want to work real hard on all six. My operation is extremely small and personal. If we get involved in business together, you're part of what I'm doing every day. Every day."

In the years I've known Jennie Lew Tugend, she has continually made me realize that making a movie is rarely easy, even for a producer with her track record. When she sold Warner on *Free Willy,* for example, some executives wanted to rewrite the script to put an action-adventure grown-up male star in the lead. Jennie was finally able to convince them that this was different, that the *whale* was the star. $150 million later, they agreed. But even now, it's not easy selling new ideas.

"When you're a writer and you're sitting down with your agent and you say, okay, here's my new script. Who am I going to go to? The agent might go to the biggest, most active producer at a studio, because that's where the clout is. So sometimes you go with the clout, but sometimes it works better to, again, personalize it and let the script become this one person's passion project. The saving grace is that no one really wants to close doors. It's always in the back of an executive's mind that they might reject the next *E.T.*! I get hundreds of query letters, and I throw most of them in the trash because nothing sparks my interest. I read the queries on the weekend, despite the fact that I've never bought anything I learned about through the mail. Introductions are important, and so is the personal approach. I spoke at one of the Sherwood Oaks events put on by Gary Shusett, and one of the students there asked to call me later. He made an appointment, told me his story, and my assistant and I flipped over it. It wasn't the kid's personal story, but one he knew about. The kid read about it in a newspaper. I started trying to acquire the rights. If the project happens, the kid will be involved. When he asked if it was okay to make an appointment with me, I was impressed. He was very well-mannered and thoughtful."

Let me state again the title of this chapter: "Someone's Gotta Love It Enough to Get It Made." And let me add this caution: Even if someone does love your project, you can blow it by inflexibility. After the first edition of this book was written, I introduced Jennie to a project based on a bestselling novel whose sales were phenomenal. The project had been written up in the *New York Times* and the *Wall Street Journal*. Jennie was intrigued, and brought in a producer friend of hers who had a particular fondness for the type of material this project dealt with. After several meetings, though, it became clear to Jennie that the people in charge of the project had a different philosophy, so she politely abandoned the deal. The movie got made, but it was initially released on video.

Whether you like it or not, screenwriter, more often than not, someone will have to be in love with your project before it will ever have a chance of being bought, and they'll have to be completely enamored with it to get it made.

The Indie Route May or May Not Run Through Indiana

There are basically four ways you can go about building a Hollywood career as a screenwriter:

1. Write a spec screenplay so good that it wins awards in contests, gets instantly noticed by top agents and producers, thrills directors and stars, and gets green-lighted for production immediately.

I've never seen that happen.

2. Get noticed as a writer in some other way, by writing a book or building a career in theater, or by building a career in some other country first.

I've seen that happen a number of times.

3. Work your way up in a production company or studio in an administrative or production capacity until a writing opportunity presents itself.

This happens often enough, but seems to favor style over substance.

4. Do whatever it takes to get your script on film or tape, no matter how many times you're turned down, which usually requires becoming a filmmaker.

The people who become household names—the Coen Brothers, Spike Lee, Quentin Tarantino and others—do this.

In previous incarnations, this book has been about the marketing of properties to Hollywood, with an emphasis on independent producers. Now, due to (a) the possibility of industry-crippling strikes and (b) the affordability of digital filmmaking by anyone above the poverty level, this chapter about independent producers will look at some people who have believed enough in a project to make it themselves.

THE $800 MOVIE

I met Gavin Heffernan, a Canadian still in college at McGill University, over lunch in Burbank, California, after mentioning his digital movie *The Steaks* in one of my monthly e-mail newsletters. (See http://homepages.go.com/~thesteaks for a full look at the making of the film.) Gavin told me that he edited the movie (shot on a consumer model digital camera) on a Powerbook laptop with the addition of a 60-gigabyte external hard drive. Entire cost of filming? $800.

After doing some extra work on the feature film *Detroit Rock City* (New Line), Gavin was encouraged to create his own digital feature by Adam Rifkin and some other people in Adam's production company.

"Working on a movie set really pounded home the desire in my heart to make my own film," Gavin told me. "I learned that Hollywood wasn't Mount Olympus and that these weren't gods channeling their creative genius through a lightning flash into a $5-million camera with a halo floating around it. These were talented people pouring their hearts and souls into a sum that was simply bigger than its parts. I believed for the first time in my life that if I set my goal to becoming a filmmaker and never looked back, I could do it."

Like most successful filmmakers I've known, movies have always been Gavin's dream. When he was assigned a one-day job shadowing project for his high school class, he sent dozens of faxes to every company shooting in Toronto. Just when he thought no one would call, he was hired by Tim Sullivan, the associate producer of *Detroit Rock City*.

He kept in touch with Sullivan and Rifkin as he finished his fourth screenplay and was invited to the premiere of the film in Los Angeles. "It was another unreal experience and another rocket burst of desire to help drive me forward," Gavin said. While there, he told Rifkin about his concept for *The Steaks*. "He loved it and immediately offered to help. I asked if he thought I should try and shoot it. He gave me a definitive YES and explained that the best way to film it is to create a shooting schedule and treat it like its a $50 million production. He also told me that it could change my life. His enthusiasm instantly alleviated any doubts in my heart."

Everyone involved in the making of *The Steaks* was a volunteer. When searching for people to be part of the team, Gavin and his crew valued passion and determination "much higher" than skill or experience. "If the passion isn't there," he reasoned, "the crew will get tired, bored, and eventually they will give up. You need passion and the desire to ride that passion from beginning to end."

Before starting the script, he analyzed all the things he would have at his disposal. He aimed for a concept with 99 percent of the characters between the ages of 19 to 21. The story is about a promotional competition set up by a local radio station in which four students (two men, two women) live inside a Jeep for as long as they can. The last person remaining wins it. They get 45 minutes per day, and all day Sunday off. Food is provided by a local steak house, hence "The Steaks."

Having seen the film, I can honestly say that the story is very good. The lighting could have been better, and the sound. But it's a fine first product. It's an admirable start to what should be a long career. Take a look at his Web site, or contact Gavin Heffernan at thesteaks@hotmail.com .

A TRULY COMMERCIAL MOVIE

To get his script *Mulligan* made, Tim "Vandy" VandeSteeg convinced over 40 corporate sponsors that included Adidas, Lifetime Fitness, Radisson Hotels and Sun Country Airlines to chip in, with the anchor sponsor being Subway Restaurants. When VandeSteeg premiered *Mulligan* at the Minneapolis–St. Paul International Film Festival, it sold out every performance.

A "mulligan" is a golf term for another chance, another shot, after you blew it the first time. The movie is a relationship comedy centered on some buddies, á la *Swingers*, except they play golf instead of dance. VandeSteeg told me that wanted to make a funny and entertaining film that would showcase his talents and give him an opportunity to make more films. Like Gavin Heffernan, he loved movies since he was a boy, "raised by a single mother and father Hollywood." Thanks to the commercial sponsors, he was able to shoot on 35mm film, with cranes, dollies, and professional camera equipment that included a Steadycam. I was inspired when I read this on Tim's Web page: "The truth is, there's no better time to be a filmmaker than right now. If not now, when?" That's the kind of thing I'm always telling writers about finishing that book or script.

"Anybody can say they are going to make a movie and get all kinds of corporate sponsorship for the project," Tim told me, "but the types of businesses we have been able to attract are high profile, successful companies that aren't going to attach themselves to just anything. We had to sell them on the quality of the script, and in the process they were able to see how committed we were to getting it done. The big key is to find a way, how to creatively package your film, your idea, so it becomes so appealing to the potential sponsors that they cannot say no."

Having a core sponsor like Subway was the real breakthrough. It made a big difference in the production.

"When Fred DeLuca, the owner/founder of Subway, gave the okay to back a large percent of *Mulligan*, it gave us instant credibility," Tim said. "Outside of the monetary investment, the Subway name enabled my co-producers and I to go to other businesses and tell them that we were already aligned with the number two largest restaurant chain in the world. It wasn't like Subway just saw a good business investment and wrote us a check. Fred, along with many of their key executives, has supported us 100 percent throughout the whole process. They took a deep personal interest in the success of *Mulligan*."

To date, they have had over 50 sponsors. When I first saw Tim's Web site and Quick-Time trailer, I was impressed with the professionalism displayed. He's now planing an Internet broadcasting network, and a media database (theentertainmentdatabase.com) as a resource center "to help filmmakers, writers, actors, and musicians take it to the next level." For anyone who wants to make an indie feature, Tim offers the following tips:

"Get totally obsessed in what you are doing. LOVE it. Love what you're doing so much that there is nothing you rather be doing. Make mistakes, make lots of them, but learn from those mistakes and write them down. Those mistakes will help you build your new character, and if you build your character, you'll become stronger and more confident, and it will show. Remember: Filmmaking is a journey, not a destination."

If you'd like to read about Vandy Productions, check out: www.mulliganmovie.com or contact Tim VandeSteeg (vandy@spacestar.net) at:

VANDY PRODUCTIONS

7809 Southtown Center PMB #393, Bloomington, MN 55431
612-869-1525

When I last spoke with Tim, he was trying to get his film screened at the Sundance Film Festival. When he hit a brick wall, he and Subway set up the FreshFest special screenings. In essence, a festival within a festival. You can't stop that kind of determination.

WILLING TO WALK THROUGH CACTUS

One way to beat the unsold screenplay curse is to find an independent producer who believes in your script. Just don't expect to get rich until the movie is funded. Unless they get a feature-length film made, independents (also known as "indys" or "indies"; independent films also have the same nickname) rarely have funds available to option scripts (known as a "discretionary fund"). Development funds from investors or studios usually come after at least one success. One benefit to writers is that an indie producer will go out of his or her way to work with a writer to improve the script, and then do whatever it takes to get the movie made.

I've never found a better example of this than producers Don Ashley and Dan Wulkan, whose first feature film was a charming film called *The Cactus Kid*. The movie won Best Drama at the Telluride (Colorado) Independent Film Festival in 2000. Don founded their company, Delfino Entertainment, in 1995, after two years of searching for the right project to produce as his first feature. *The Cactus Kid* was written by Frank Renzulli, one of the head writers and supervising producer of HBO's *The Sopranos*. At the time Don made the deal on the script, though, Renzulli had not yet started working on the series.

"He gave it to me, literally gave it to me," Don told me over lunch at the Warner Hollywood Studios. "He said I could be involved in rewrites, produce it, direct it, whatever I wanted because I 'got' the story. Frank comes from TV. He wrote this script a year-and-a-half before he gave it to me. I loved the script, but had no money. He said go ahead, take the script, and we made a deal on the future profit. I raised the money, put together all the legal work, formed an LLC, sold units in it, the whole process. Frank allowed me to do the rewrites on location. If it was really an advanced rewrite, I would fax it to him. He'd rewrite it and fax it back to me."

Don was once a policeman, and the father of a young son, so the story of a police officer's love for his dying son struck a particular nerve. His only previous Hollywood credit, other than being a stand-up comic, was a punch-up writer for the TV series *Men Behaving Badly* for Carsey-Werner. When he started his production company, he chose an unusual (but clever) way to network with people who could help him succeed.

"I joined the Grand Havana Room," he said. "It's a private cigar club in Beverly Hills. I met an actor there named Mike Starr, who's been in 75 features. Ever see *Dumb and Dumber*? He's the guy that they killed with the chili pepper bit. I was talking to Mike at the club one night and he says, 'I gotta introduce you to Frank Renzulli because Frank's got the perfect script for you.' I meet with Frank over coffee, and a 15-minute meeting turns into a three-hour meeting. Frank tells me to follow him back to his house. So I do, and he opens up his safe and gives me the script. The story is about a 10-year-old son and his dad. His dad's a cop. The mom and dad are divorced but the dad lives and patrols in the area where the kid lives. At night when he's patrolling, he climbs into the kid's window to talk to him and hang out with him and they plan their weekends together. One night, he brings him a comic book called *The Cactus Kid* that his dad used to read to him when he was a kid. Well, at the beginning of act one you find out that Georgie has an inoperable brain tumor. He's gonna die. So one night the dad says, 'Georgie, if there's anything I can do, anything in the world, you name it'. And Georgie goes, 'Anything dad?' 'Yeah, anything.' He goes, 'I wanta rob a bank like the Cactus Kid.' So the dad, he says, 'Fine, let's rob a bank.' They rob the bank and now FBI's after them, they're going across the country, everybody's chasing them, bunch of stuff happens."

To keep from spoiling a touching story and a clever twist at the end, I'll end the story there. Because of his own background and young son, the script had great personal appeal to Don Ashley and he was passionate about getting it made. He didn't just like it, he loved it.

His partner, Dan Wulkan, came to Hollywood after being inspired by another independent filmmaker, Edward Burns.

"I was on Long Island and I saw *Brothers McMullen*. That literally made me come out here. I said this is a great independent film and if they can do it with the money they did it for I know I can do it. I came out here and produced my first couple of short films. I asked myself, Can you go rent a camera? Yeah. Can you call Kodak and get film from them? Yeah. Can you hold auditions and get actors that will work for free any day of the week? Yeah. Even on a short film. My attitude was, Just do it, even on digital video. Anything you can do on a smaller scale to bring you in on a larger scale."

Don calls Hollywood "the Business of a 1,000 no's. That's how many no's you gotta get before you get your project made. People aren't used to hitting one brick wall after another. Boom! No no no no no no. If you can't take the beating, you got no hope here."

I asked him if setting up a Limited Liability Corporation (LLC) and raise money by selling shares was a daunting task.

"It's easy," Don revealed. "It just costs money. I found a lawyer who handled that. Then I just kept looking for yeses. A hundred no's, then I got a yes. A cinematographer who had done something said he'd do it, and all of a sudden I had something easier to sell. My sales pitch kept getting better and better and I kept stacking up yeses. I got this actor attached, I got that actor attached. One guy would give me $20K if another would give me $20K, you know? I got the first guy, the second guy, the third guy. You just keep making the deal better and better."

"It's just believing in what you're doing," Dan added. "It's interesting how if you don't get worried about the money, the funding, if you show the energy without talking about it, if you literally physically show it, then it will pay off."

Meeting Don and Dan, I found their candor refreshing and their energy so ebullient I pitched them a script of mine that had been optioned in early 2000 for $5,000. I told them I had planned to do the movie with the great actor Ben Johnson, only he'd died before we could mount a production, but Ben had shown the script to Bill Paxton when they filmed *The Evening Star* together. Don and Dan told me their Delfino Entertainment was officed directly across the hall from Bill Paxton's production company at Warner Hollywood.

Wow, I thought. Small world Hollywood. What the heck, I decided. Maybe I could make that movie myself.

A PRODUCER ANYONE COULD LIKE

I interviewed Terence Michael for the first edition of this book, and his career has progressed steadily upward since. Like most successful indie producers, Terry has always displayed a willingness to do whatever it takes to make a project work while making it look easy. He started his career as a reader at Warner Brothers, interning for Lauren Shuler-Donner, producer wife of producer/director Richard Donner. Still in college, he offered to read and do coverage for free, and by doing so got exposed to what studios wanted, their formula. He maintains that even now, when he doesn't like a movie, it's always because it veers from that original formula he learned.

"I didn't know a thing about the business before then" he said, "but I grew up in the area, so I knew how to sneak on the studio lot. When I got the notion to get into the business, I put 120 pages of paper under my arm, with two brads through the paper so that it looked like a script. I put on a suit jacket and walked back in the gates after lunch, blending in with the rest of the studio people coming back. I went into the first door I found, which was Donner/Shuler-Donner Productions. I told them what I wanted to do, and Lauren interviewed me. She asked me what movies I liked. I said, 'Well, I guess I like Steven Spielberg.' I didn't get to see her much after that, but they let me read scripts."

In his senior year in college he met Bill Robinson at ICM, who had a reputation for helping young people and taught a class at Pepperdine called "How to Enter the Film Business."

"Bill taught us that it doesn't matter how you do it or what your educational background is. It's just all about dealing with people. That gave me the bug, but I didn't want to be an agent. So I sent out 200 resumes to names I got from the Hollywood

Creative Directory and got hired at Cinecore by John Hyde, a specialist in bankruptcy who went on to become the CFO at Orion, and I also worked for producer Gene Kirkwood. Together, they'd produced tons of movies, including *Das Boot*. When they split up, Gene hired me as Director of Development for Gene Kirkwood Productions. On my first day, he told me to get hold of Oliver Stone at his beach house and I did, even though Gene didn't have the phone number. Gene would say, 'I need to have lunch with this actress,' and I'd set it up. He also liked my taste in scripts. From him I learned what it's like to be an old-time, established studio producer. He'd get the studio to buy a property, set it up with agents, then not do much more. I learned development from him, but I got tired of it.

"From day one, I wanted to be a movie producer. Whenever there was a meeting I could go to, I was there. Using Gene's name got me in a lot of doors, but I was doing all the work. So using what I knew about business, I rounded up some investors and formed a corporation. I didn't know how hard it usually is; my naiveté drove me. The investors financed an office, allowed me to start buying scripts, and paid for lunches, meetings, and so on. The first couple of projects I put together never got made. At the time I was driven by a wonderful, potentially Oscar-winning script, which usually means it's the toughest sell in the world. But I got Stephen Baldwin and Mary-Louise Parker for the project, who, at the time, didn't mean anything to people. That project about four talking heads never got made. I slowly wised up by reading more and more books that I bought at the Samuel French bookstore, and by paying attention to the market. I went to the American Film Market and the Cannes Film Festival, and I began to realize that there are a lot of ways to get your movie made. I started playing devil's advocate with writers, telling them what I was hearing, being the bad guy producer. Now, I want a good script, but first and foremost I want people to go see it. That's what I focus on now. The script needs to be entertaining, not just a social statement. I laugh at myself now for my original naiveté."

He went the film festival route, raised money from foreign presales, put together budgets with a little from the studio, some from private investors, some from banks, and gap financing. He tried writing but realized his strength was in producing. He offered the following formula for taking a screenplay from option to feature film:

1. Find a great script.
2. Fix it until no one can pass on it.
3. Meet with as many directors as possible who can attract a cast of bankable actors.
4. Get the cast, which is difficult with no financing, but give them opportunities they don't usually have.
5. Get at least half the budget from foreign sales companies, who say "yes" with a check for video rights, etc.

His personal preference is romantic comedies.

"I don't do horror or erotic slashers, which makes it tough because foreign companies usually want B movies. When my formula is completed, I can get the rest of the money and go into production. When the picture is finished, I own it. And when I look at doing a project, I feel like I'm recruiting soldiers. If anyone is worried about money, I feel they aren't right for my team. The funny thing is, the ones who don't ask about it end up making the most money on my films. With one film, Eric Schaeffer [the director] put in over $500,000 of his own money, but he knew that *If Lucy Fell* had promise, and he thought we'd make a lot of money. As a result, we owned 100 percent of the film. We paid for everything."

This approach is the one used by old-time producer Joseph E. Levine, who gave the legendary William Goldman a leg up in Hollywood. The exit strategy Terry adopted was a worst-case scenario of making all the money back by selling it to foreign markets of cable channels. His investors have never lost money on any film.

"I think the climate changes every three or four years," he mused, "where everyone is chasing a certain formula to make this form of financing work. One year, it's comedies with gross-out humor, another it's thrillers with male protagonists. But overall, it's how 90 percent of the films (even studio-backed films) are being financed. Usually, no matter what your scenario is, you'll have to have collateral of some sort in order to get investors (i.e., the bank) to loan you money. Sales estimates from a legitimate foreign sales company is the simplest way to do this. And most banks have a list of which companies they prefer to do business with. We try to work with the same ones over and over again, but we're open to new collaborations."

He takes pains to make sure that talented beginning writers learn how the process works, and what to expect.

"Some good writers are ready to direct, and sometimes we can offer them that, so we pay them just a little bit up front for an option, WGA rates if we have to. Then we'll partner up with another producer, usually older guys. The way I figure it, everyone will get paid what they're worth, and by the time the cameras roll, my writers will get paid what they wanted. I like new writers because they have a fresh eye. Conceptually and tone-wise, they come up with things that need to be honed by established writers. Writers need to realize just how many scripts most indie producers get. I get a lot of material through directory submissions. Agents at ICM and the other agencies send me scripts. Some indie producers call, wanting to team up. Then there are all the directors I've worked with in the past, or any of the 60 people on the crew when I do a movie. A few managers regularly send me scripts. Scripts can come from the most weird, bizarre places. Parties, you name it.

If I had one piece of advice, I would tell a writer to have a great one-page pitch. Producers listed in the Hollywood Creative Directory and other books will read queries. A first-time producer will get a script around to a lot of places, like I did with the first script I packaged. By nature, we have to be persistent, get it read by someone who will say 'yes.' The pitch has to come from someone the person with the checkbook will listen to. Often enough, that's the director. That's how I've set up some projects."

Still, Terence's basic orientation has remained the same.

"We pride ourselves on always working with the original writer(s) and often first-time directors."

Good news for neophyte writers and directors. When I last talked with Terry, his company was posting three movies and only two weeks away from starting principal photography on two films that were starting on the exact same day. The three films in post-production were all financed differently. *Going Greek* starring Dylan Bruno (*Saving Private Ryan*), Laura Harris (*The Faculty*), Simon Rex (TV's *Jack and Jill*), Chris Owen (*American Pie*), and Charlie Talbert (*Angus*) was financed entirely with private funds from several individuals.

"No banks, no bond company," he said, smiling. "Total freedom."

I wanted to know whether he could still say his investors had not lost money.

"Yep, we can still confidently say this. We make all of our films for a price, knowing what budget will give us a profit in a worse case scenario if we just sold to limited territories. Certainly, some investors haven't done as well as they had hoped. On one case, it took them three years just to get their principal back. But they never lost."

Terry gets a steady stream of weekly submissions from writers reading the *Writers Guide to Hollywood*.

"The book has been a nice scout for us in areas we wouldn't normally look," he confided, "but the non-Hollywood submissions are often hard to wade through. Most non-mainstream sources are, to be honest, not that helpful for us. Submissions tend to come from first-timers with weakly-developed concepts. But you just never know, so we continue to search. Writers should realize that 90 percent of the time it isn't personal when they're rejected. The same goes for actors who audition daily. Depending on what our directors are looking for, or what our financiers are looking for, at any given moment we are searching for something specific. So if your script is a 'pass,' it doesn't mean your writing sucks and you should pack it up. Keep at it. If you've done your homework and written a solid screenplay that works on the page, you'll find your producer."

I've always been happy having Terence Michael as part of this book; such candor and wisdom are a benefit to screenwriters everywhere.

MASTER OF MANY WORLDS

With productions like the award-winning *Introducing Dorothy Dandridge* for HBO, *Price of Glory* starring Jimmy Smits, and *Selena* with Jennifer Lopez, it would seem that Robert Katz and his partner Moctesuma Esperza are the king of the ethnic films in Hollywood, or at least Hispanic-themed productions. The truth, though, is that they have simply followed their passions, which includes movies like *Gettysburg* and *The Roughriders* on TNT. I was first introduced to Bob by a mutual friend, thanks to a script of mine that Bob liked. Although we didn't make a deal on that screenplay, we became friends, and when I was asked to put together a couple of panels for the first Hollywood Film Festival, Robert Katz was one of the first calls I made. He graciously consented, and appeared with me on another panel I chaired at the last Book Expo held in Los Angeles.

Bob is one of the most accomplished producers I've known, able to set up projects on cable and network television as well as independent and studio features. The independent status his company maintains seems to be something that suits him well, and they find properties to move forward with based on simple criteria: great story, good writing, and compelling characters done in a unique and different way. With all their success, they remain accessible. Bob has always intrigued me because of his eagerness to welcome new media like the Internet and e-books.

"We get material from all sources," Bob told me, "whether it be a book, a pitch, a screenplay, something we see in a theater, or magazine article. We get anywhere from 10 to 30 screenplays a month. I guess we're more open about screenplays but we generally don't take them unsolicited unless there's something about them that intrigues us. I prefer to see a synopsis first to see if it's something we're even interested in reading. But in terms of where we get the material, because of the Internet now, I'll open up our e-mail and there will be a lot of requests. Most of them, 99 percent maybe, aren't for us, but every once in a while I'll find something interesting."

Many producers I know won't read e-mail, but I've found that Bob will read even an e-book if the premise intrigues him.

"I just need to see a synopsis that tells what the story is about," he said. "The majority of people who send us something via e-mail are from out of state. They might live in Spain or Yugoslavia. Unfortunately, they're sort of mundane stories, nothing of interest, but when there is interest I'll ask them to send me the screenplay. They have to pique my interest. Generally we get scripts from management companies, agencies, but most of them come in from individuals. They call or write and we request a synopsis. If we like that, we agree to read the script."

The company employs its own readers once scripts come in, and they don't take scripts from people they don't know, but if a writer manages to intrigue them, they'll listen. They stay open, he told me, because they've found that good projects "come from all different directions."

"We have a project now that was based on a magazine article," Bob said. "Somebody came in and said, 'hey, I own the rights to this magazine article.' We sent it to HBO. Another one was something that I saw on television, and Showtime is buying a script from us right now. On a more conventional route, we're mounting about four or five major feature films that came to us with directors like Simon Wincer attached. Another script came to me that I loved and I attached Harold Becker and I'm in the process of attaching Nic Cage. There's no scenario with which we can say, 'this is how it works.' It's about good material."

Although more pitches sold at a studio level in 2000, Bob isn't interested in hearing them unless a proven writer brings it in.

"Pitches are really impossible. There are so few people buying pitches from unknowns that I discourage hearing them."

The supposed feeding frenzy of studios and networks wanting to put things into production prior to an anticipated WGA and SAG strike hadn't done much to change Esperza-Katz's day-to-day operations when we spoke.

"We got calls over the last several weeks from networks saying what have you got that's ready to go?" Bob revealed. "If I have something ready to go, we get things set up, but we'd been working on it for months. More stuff is going to get made over the next six months, but if there is no strike, everybody's going to be sitting around in the summer and fall of next year, because all of the buyers will have spent all of their money!"

It's not just writers and actors who get put in a niche based on their past projects. When *Introducing Dorothy Dandridge* got a lot of Emmy nominations, following the success of *Selena*, I wondered if Katz and Esperza might have gotten typecast as biopic producers. Bob said they had some more in the works—rock promoter Bill Graham, singer/actor Bobby Darin, and composer Richard Wagner—but they had a lot of other things going on as well, including a *Gettysburg* sequel on TNT. With almost two decades of partnership behind them, they've learned to strike while the iron is hot, but to be judicious in what they pick. They spent a long time on the outside looking in.

"When I decided to get into the Hollywood feature business, I was doing documentaries in Europe," Bob said. "That was 1980, and for four years I toughed it out, only got one movie going in that period of time. I kept alive by hook or crook, went to all the kind of meetings that I now speak at. I don't know what magic happened that allowed me to succeed. It was just perseverance. I had the ability to keep going even when I was broke, I just didn't stop. I kept looking for new ideas. Moctesuma and I partnered in 1983 and we struggled for five or six years. We managed to eke it out and hang in there. How we did it? We always ask ourselves, how did we do that? I don't know. We did it. We persevered. We finally made our first movie, *The Ballad of Gregorio Cortez*, then *The Milagro Beanfield War* and very slowly we built. Over a 10-year period we did some TV, just kept ourselves alive, and then when *Gettysburg* hit, it sort of changed things. The film was monumental and people said 'Wow, these guys can produce,' and we did seven pictures in two or three years. When someone attaches themselves to this incredible piece of material, whatever it is, and ride the coattails of that piece of material and make their way through it, that's the smart way. In my case, I was just too stupid to quit. Making features was what I wanted to do and I never even thought about quitting. I just thought about how am I going to get through this next period until I can get something up and running."

Writers contact me from all over the world have repeatedly mentioned getting their "lucky break." I've always found that you make those breaks, and the way *Gettysburg* got made is a perfect example. When Katz and Esperza met Ron Maxwell, who had the screenplay adaptation of the book *Killer Angels*, it wasn't ready. The book was 1,000 pages, and the script was 400 pages.

"I read it and said this is great stuff, and told Ron, 'I'm sure you're going to edit it down.' He said he was. That was '83. So we ran into each other again in '85. He'd gotten it down to 260 pages but he couldn't sell it. I said, 'I love this piece, I'd love to get into business with you, let's stay in touch.' After *Milagro* came out, we worked to get the script down to a manageable size, at least 160 or 170 pages, and we went out to try to sell it as a feature. But Alan Sabenson at the time was running movies and miniseries at ABC, so we decided to pitch it as a potential miniseries. Alan loved it and bought it and said, 'okay, let's do this.'"

I know. You're thinking, but this came out on Turner Network Television. That's because ABC canceled the order.

"We immediately went down and prepped the movie at Gettysburg during the winter and it was snowing. I remember us marching around out there in the snow and we get a call from Alan because that Sunday night they'd aired a movie about Custer, a miniseries, and the ratings for Sunday night were so dismal that, even though it was still running on Monday, Alan called me and said, 'I'm going to pull the plug. I'm going to lose my job if I try to do this after last night.' So there we are up to our ass in snow in a field in Gettysburg on ancient cell phones with this happening, and we say, 'Now what do we do?' We sat around in this field, literally sunk in snow, freezing, then we came up with the idea to call Ted Turner. We got Ted on the line and guess what? *Killer Angels* was his favorite book! And he says, I want to do this, right over the phone to us. I'd never talked to the man in my life! We flew back to L.A. and met with the Turner people and that's how it got going."

While they were shooting *Gettysburg*, Turner kept coming down to the set, amazed at the tens of thousands of actors recreating the battle, "just mesmerized." One day he said to Bob, "You gave me my *Gone with the Wind* 10 years before I thought I would get it. So what do you want to do for an encore?"

Flabbergasted, Bob remembered the story of Teddy Roosevelt and the Rough Riders, and Turner agreed enthusiastically. The problem was, TNT wanted to do it based on a book.

"So we went around and looked at all these books and anything ever written about that period of the Spanish-American War, and there was nothing that applied. We knew that Teddy Roosevelt had written his memoirs and they were public domain. They were basically published diaries. But I wanted a story. Finally, we came back to the memoirs and just based it on that, but it took us a year to put that together, to get the green light."

If you look over movies made by Esperza-Katz, you'll find that the majority are based on true stories because the partners believe in real stories and characters. They find that other people in the business find a similar appeal in reality-driven stories. For anyone who finds a true story that they want to make into a movie, Bob insists they option the material before contacting him.

"Otherwise, what are you bringing to the table? You gotta control the material. Just because you alert a production company or studio to a great idea doesn't mean you're bringing anything. They don't need you for that. If you're passionate about it, have the passion to go out and control the material."

Like every other producer I've spoken with in the last decade, Bob has found beginning screenwriters woefully unschooled in what makes a great screenplay, one that will appeal to great actors.

"Most people really need to study their craft of writing," he said. "The problem we have with people trying to break in is that they just don't know their craft very well and it shows. By page 10, I'm ready to put it down, even if it's a great idea for a script. There's a saying at the studios these days—I'd rather have great writing and mediocre idea than a great idea with mediocre writing. Am I so compelled I can't wait to turn the page to see what happens, or am I having a hard time dredging through this thing page by page? It's the quality of the writer that turns us on. We've actually got a screenplay made, *Lorca*, which was a great screenplay but a mediocre idea. I've never been able to get a mediocre screenplay made based on a great idea.

"You have to think about the starring role. You have to make this really compelling piece of business because this is going to go to an actor, and most of these stars have done everything. They ask questions: What is it in this thing that I haven't done before? Do I get a chance to really emote? Most of the screenplays that come to me don't have this. People trying to break into the business don't think through that very well, but they'll send me something not particularly original and say it's perfect for Brad Pitt!"

The last thing I asked Bob was why they keep the door open when they read so many bad scripts.

"I think we're more open than some because we don't have deep pockets so that the agencies are always sending us the high-priced stuff. We have to scrounge. All the movies we've made, with a few exceptions, probably would have never gotten made if not for guys like us. We didn't have the latest hot script in Hollywood and had to make the best of what we happened to like a lot. Traditionally, we don't pay option money. If a writer is in the business of going for option money they should go to the big producers. Generally, if something comes in for us that's highly commercial and we like it, my approach with people which has been successful—I don't think we've lost one—when we loved it we said, 'Look it's not about option money here, it's about getting the movie made. Let us go get it set up with a studio or financing then you get your money.'"

We talked about writers terrifically eager for a million-dollar payday like they've read about in the trades, when the reality is, Hollywood is a long-term business.

"If this was easy, everybody would be doing it," Bob agreed. "This is the toughest business I know. I don't know of a tougher business because you're doing it by your wits. If you're living in Chicago or Pennsylvania or Florida and you've got a script, it's going to be very tough. It's not impossible, but you have to have a connection in L.A. Otherwise, you have to come to L.A. and work it. This is where movies get made. This is where movies get bought and sold. There are some minor markets in New York and other places, but L.A. is where 99 percent of all the movies we see in the theaters have their genesis. The actual transaction of saying yes, we want to make this movie happen here because the buyers are here. You gotta be where the buyers are. That doesn't mean you can't do it from those other places, and certainly the Internet has made things more accessible. I would advise people to log onto all these writer's databases and all of these places where you can get your scripts submitted, because people are starting to look at that. I don't do it myself but we have people who occasionally look things up there. We probably ought to be looking more. There's probably a movie or two in there. But if you're serious about wanting to make a career in the movie business, you have to be here, at least initially. If you're a writer, you have to be here to get yourself established. When you're established you can go live anywhere you want.

"Hollywood is a business of relationships. If they don't know you, you're not going to get their attention. It took us a long, long time to have the relationships that we now have. I would say to you that the most important thing in this town is relationships. If you don't have any, make some. Come out here, spend time, call people up. Tell people that you're looking to be in this business and ask for 20 minutes of their time just to get some advice. People in this town are generally very happy to give you advice. That's what I did. I called people up, I didn't say I wanted to pitch them a project. People are willing to see you if they know you're not going to be pitching them. I'm a sucker for it when people have asked me for advice. If I think it's appropriate and I have something to add, I'll give them 10 to 15 minutes of my time."

It wasn't just lip service. Esperza-Katz have made the majority of their films with first-time directors and have worked with many new writers. They give people several chances to provide them with the reason Bob Katz says he's in the business—to make good movies.

BEYOND INDIES

I'm glad there are independent producers out there like the ones mentioned in this chapter. To reach the people mentioned here, I didn't need an agent. You won't, either. I hear from writers all the time who want agents, and time and time again I tell them to contact producers directly, particularly the independents. More often than not, if you have a good query letter or pitch, you can get an indie to look at your script. To move up from the world of the free and small options, however, and to reach the major movers and shakers in both film and television, you will probably need a good agent or manager, or both. In the next chapter, we'll discuss them in detail, introduce you to some good ones, and take up other possibilities in this ever-changing mecca called Hollywood.

Agents, Managers, and Others

These days, beginning screenwriters might initially be better off with a manager than an agent, particularly a manager who also produces because agents rarely take the time to groom a writer any more. Most agents I know will give a writer about three month's worth of effort, and if no sale is made, they figure they're wasting their time. Also, most screenwriters who have been around a while know that the really big agents don't care about them until the writer has developed a track record or made a substantial sale. If you want to start with an agent, however, here's one way to possibly get around the closed doors.

CLIMB IN THEIR HIP POCKET

Agents are cagey. If they take on a new writer, tout a script around town, and no one wants it, that might diminish their credibility (they'll think it does, anyway). So an agent might offer to "hip-pocket" you. Think of them going to meetings wearing safari pants with big pockets. In that pocket, they just happen to have a copy of your screenplay, in case anyone mentions wanting something like it. What the term really means, though, is that they'll mostly leave it to you to tell people about your property, but if someone asks, "Who's your agent?" you can drop the hip-pocket agent's name and have the agent send it over. The agent might want you to pay mailing or messenger costs, or they might not. It varies from agency to agency. If you meet an agent or come in contact with one who shows some interest in your work, ask them if they'll hip-pocket you. I've seen that develop into a continuing relationship quite a number of times. You will, however, be expected to use reasonably decent etiquette with producers you contact because the hip pocket agent doesn't want to be embarrassed by someone who says they represent them.

DON'T JUST SETTLE FOR ANYONE

Agents, like producers and publishers, must be researched. Most writers starting out don't do this. They just blindly strike out looking for some agent, any agent. Don't rely on agents listed in this book to solve your script sales problem. Read other books as well. Go online, ask around, make phone calls. Find out who represents writers you admire. Just because an agent has a top thriller writer doesn't mean they won't take another—that agent knows who buys thrillers. If you don't do some research about agents, it's unlikely that you'll find one who's right for you.

In Hollywood, it's typical to have one agent until you sell a screenplay, then get approached by one of the large agencies for representation. As producer Ron Hamady once told me when I asked him to introduce me to his agent at Creative Artists, "They don't need you. They won't need you until you're already successful, and then you won't need them."

There are a number of very good agents at large agencies, but a beginning writer can get lost in that shuffle. One writer friend of mine wrote a hot script and got signed by United Talent Agency. The script was put on auction, with about 25 major production companies reading it on the same day, preparing to make a bid. Unfortunately, no one made a bid, frustrating and perhaps embarrassing the agent at UTA. From that point forward, my friend was for some reason always talking to the agent's assistant and not the agent. He was being "niced" as Mel Brooks might say. They didn't have the guts to tell him that they were no longer interested.

I've also seen it work the other way. Someone who lives in Los Angeles or New York (or another major world city where a big agency has an office) meets someone who is represented by a large agency and their new friend offers to introduce them to their agent, who takes them on and makes a sale. Just don't be surprised if your first script doesn't sell, if you get "back-burnered." Even if you don't live in L.A. or New York, you could still be represented by a major agency, but it's not likely. The big agencies have large staffs and large overhead. This means they need to represent established writers who sell regularly. They receive 10 percent (the legal limit in California) on what the writer makes. That means they have to sell a lot of scripts or get a lot of staff jobs writing for television. It's not very complicated.

When you do get an agent, be patient. It might take an agent a while to read your work, and then it might take a while for the agent to get a response once your work is sent out. If it's driving you crazy waiting, put that emotion into the new script you're writing.

A SHORT HISTORY OF AGENTING

To understand how Hollywood agencies work, let's start at the beginning. In 1898, Zelman Moses was a Jewish immigrant from Germany who was in love with New York show business. He changed his name to William Morris and founded an agency to represent vaudeville acts. He came into prominence when he made Mae West the number-one box office star, then did the same for some boys known as The Marx Brothers who were from his old East Side neighborhood. As a talent agent, Morris' only real competition was Music Corporation of America, or MCA, which became the parent company of Universal Studios. The William Morris Agency boomed in the early days of television, building shows around the talent on their roster.

The Morris agency remains the top television agency in the world and in recent years has made major strides toward becoming the major player in feature films. Most of the commonly accepted practices of agenting today began at William Morris, from employees starting in the mail room and working their way up (no matter what degree they brought to the job), to "packaging" (putting together an entire program or film with talent from one agency). William Morris is the model they copied.

How a Major Agency Operates

When I wrote the first edition of this book, there were three major agencies in Hollywood: CAA, International Creative Management (ICM), and William Morris. Now smart smaller agencies like UTA and (even smarter) Endeavor make a lot of deals. When first writing about how agencies work, I queried the top agents at one of the three majors mentioned above to see if I could put together a consensus on what they looked for in a script. The answers they gave me still apply. I'm fairly certain that the responses to my questions below would be the same if they came from other top agencies, and that goes for top foreign agents I've spoken with as well. Here are the questions, with answers distilled from several top agents:

Q: At what point in his or her career should an aspiring screenwriter expect to get an agent at a major agency?

A: At any point in your career. Signing with the right agency might be your one shot at the career break you need.

Q: If you are able to sell a script on your own, or make a film on your own, why do you then need an agent?

A: An agent will see you through the entire process of selling a script and getting it into production. A good agent provides career planning and connections and gets a writer to the next level of their career. Agents stay on top of what writers are getting paid. If you're already making money as a writer, the commission you pay an agent is a good investment in your career, particularly if you get an agent who shares your passion.

Q: Do you need an entertainment attorney as well as a good agent?

A: It depends on the agency. If an agency is big enough, it has a business affairs department stuffed with entertainment attorneys, so you won't need an outside attorney for entertainment matters.

Q: What are the components of a great, marketable script?

A: That never changes: good characters and a good story, told in a fresh way.

Q: Can a new writer get a script assignment via a great sample, or are those jobs reserved for seasoned writers? If so, how much does it pay?

A: Yes, a new writer can, but it's tough. If a new writer gets a script assignment through our agency, they'll get Writers Guild scale plus 10 percent.

Q: If a new writer only has a treatment, will you try to sell it?

A: We only sell completed screenplays.

Q: Is it easier to get started in TV, or in film?

A: It's actually possible to get a television staff writing position without a great script; the medium simply needs so many ideas. Some writers stimulate other writers. They're good in a room. So they make good story editors. Some are good at writing jokes, while others specialize in character development, or even in one character on a show. So day in, day out, getting started in television is easier if you live in L.A.

Q: What route would you suggest for a beginning writer?

A: It depends on your career goal, what you believe in, your passion. Focus on what you picture yourself being. Do you want to be the next Joe Ezsterhas? Callie Khouri? Or is David E. Kelley your role model? Also, you can get typecast as a TV writer and have difficulty breaking into feature writing, although that transition is far less difficult than it used to be.

Q: Do you see any current story trends that you feel will be sustained in the coming years?

A: You'd have to ask someone at a smaller agency. We look for talented writers, not trends. You can read *Variety* for the box office charts if you want to try to figure that out. They go back 10 years or more. We look for good writers and good projects, period.

POINTS TO PONDER

Leslie Kallen has been a mainstay in helping writers get started for years. In 2000, we both spoke at the same meeting of the California Writers Club and finally had a chance to compare notes. Leslie is well known for having a sure eye for writing talent. She represents screenwriters and fiction and nonfiction authors in association with The Literary Group International. Her screenwriting clients work in features and long-form television, on assignments in Hollywood and, internationally, for German and Canadian companies. Her authors are published by major companies like St. Martin's and Simon & Schuster. One day, an e-mail alerted me to an article Leslie had written that was so good I asked to include it here. Study "From Submission To $ale: Sixty Hot Tips For Screenwriters" well; it's a great list.

1. Don't send unsolicited scripts to agents or other industry professionals.

2. When people consider your work, their motivation to get it made and get you paid is more important than their credits.

3. When submitting, get a contact name for your submission, and mention "per our conversation," in your letter.

4. Don't follow-up call to see if your script arrived. If you follow-up call, it should be no sooner than 2 1/2 weeks after your submission.

5. Always have a clean, simple title page; avoid WGA Registration, copyright, date, draft, etc.

6. Title pages should have a centered title, in CAPS, the word "by" under title, and author's name.

7. Ask an agent if you may submit a rewrite, but don't interpret this to mean they'll represent you.

8. Communicate by mail with everyone you can. Letter writing is still a great tool.

9. Make out-of-state work for you. For example, sensibilities untarnished by Hollywood stereotypes are good for the work.

10. Don't oversurf the Web sites in lieu of human interaction.

11. When comparisons are communication tools, compare your work to hits, not good films that tanked at the box office.

12. Be able to describe your script in a brief logline, including the genre.

13. Avoid all camera angles in your work. Make it read clearly. You are writing for readers, not directing.

14. Avoid characters' feelings in narrative. Let it come through in story and dialogue.

15. Words like "remember," "realize," "thought," and "felt" are "feeling'" words. Save them for your novel.

16. Never have over 117 pages in your script; 107–112 is ideal.

17. Read a lot of scripts. You can find them online, or buy hard copies at Hollywood Book and Poster, Script City, Samuel French, or view them at the Academy Library. (All places mentioned are in L.A.)

18. Figure out a long-range plan to accomplish product output. For example, Ron Bass gets up at 3:00 A.M. to write.

19. Write them and finish them! How many scripts will you complete by the end of this year?

20. Don't guess trends; write your own story.

21. Be true to yourself in your writing.

22. Change "facts" if you're writing the "personal story."

23. Write a fictitious account of what really happened. Dramatic truth supersedes real truth.

24. Do one thing everyday to affirm your commitment to writing. Keep setting new goals.

25. Good screenwriters observe the interplay between people.

26. What are you writing about? Discovering your theme after you've finished gives you more insight for the next important step, which is the rewrite process.

27. What does your query letter say about you?

28. Your goal as a new screenwriter is to get your work read, as much as it is to get representation.

29. Read coverage/synopses of other peoples' scripts.

30. Work with other writers and do coverage on each other's work.

31. Use card stock covers, punched with two holes and two #5 brads (fasteners). Don't use term-paper style covers or folders. Color card stock is okay. Title on cover is okay.

32. Don't wait on responses to what you've submitted. Put your energy into another project.

33. Ask people you talk to for leads or other names.

34. Make rejection work for you. Look at it as being in the race, not as failing.

35. Avoid hostility about how the industry works, including the "unwritten rules." Laugh about it.

36. Query should be on 8 1/2 × 11-inch stationery.

37. Don't send scripts by registered mail, FedEx, U.P.S. etc. Regular U.S. mail is the recommended choice.

38. Generally, calls are returned after 5:45 P.M. Pacific Time. Don't call someone more than once a week. You're already on their call sheet.

39. Script consultants are reputable and can improve your work if you can afford them. Always have your script professionally typed and formatted. The more professionally presented, the better your chances.

40. Agents earn 10 percent commission. Some may ask you to make your own copies. Get an agents list from the WGA, west, (323) 951-4000.

41. Lawyers work with agents in deal-making. They are paid 5 percent of the deal, by the writer.

42. Agents make multiple submissions. Think about being "in the race" not about going against another client in the agency.

43. Agents work for free unless they close a deal.

44. Managers for writers are becoming increasingly popular. Because the laws are in flux, they can receive 15 percent or more in commission.

45. As screenwriters' cachet and currency increase, writers need a bigger team and will pay more commissions, like actors and musicians.

46. Have a sense of humor; it's the best tool in the business.

47. Read the trades, magazines, and online articles with a grain of salt. They include *Creative Screenwriting, Scr(i)pt, Screentalk, Hollywood Scriptwriter, Variety*, and the

Hollywood Reporter; and online, Done Deal, Hollywood Literary Sales, Inzide, Story-bay, and ScriptShark.

48. Evaluate the strengths and weaknesses of your screenplays. Do the first 10 pages grab the reader and suck him/her in? Do you have a catchy "inciting incident"? Are your acts structured well?

49. Don't ask to have your script returned. Don't include a SASE. The copy you send is the cost of doing business.

50. When placing calls, leave specific messages.

51. Paranoia about theft is wasted energy.

52. Avoid parentheticals under characters' names in the dialogue. Let actors act and directors direct.

53. Don't be married to your words. To paraphrase Faulkner, you must be prepared to give up your darlings. Be ready to cut your favorite lines of dialogue and scenes.

54. Find an ideal time to write your pages. Is it morning or night?

55. Know your goal when you contact someone. Is it to get read, get representation, say hello, or get a lead?

56. Write about what you know and what you're passionate about.

57. Originality is a pair of fresh eyes; a new take on an old plot.

58. Move your reader by crafting a great story. They'll remember your work even if they don't purchase it.

59. Have fun! If you know you want to write, that's what matters most.

60. An agent "contact" is good whether you're a client or not. (You'll find Leslie's company in the agents and managers section.)

AGENTS SOMETIMES DON'T STAY AGENTS, OR STAY PUT

When I interviewed David Phillips for the first edition of this book, it was in his production office in Century City, and he was also managing writers. His company, Corner of the Sky Entertainment, was housed at the top of a building you've seen before, the so-called "Nakatomi Tower" in *Die Hard*. Phillips was an agent in the motion picture department of the William Morris Agency when he had discovered an obscure documentary called *Hoop Dreams*. By the time he was done with it, *Hoop Dreams* had received international acclaim and been proclaimed by both Gene Siskel and Roger Ebert as their number-one favorite movie of 1994. At Fox-based Davis Entertainment, Phillips got a first-look deal, meaning Andrew Davis had a chance to finance a Phillips' project before anyone else. When I was preparing the second edition of the book, I learned that Phillips had gone back to agenting, two-and-a-half years after leaving the William Morris Agency to become a manager and producer. He signed with Innovative Artists to head the literary department there. It wasn't long before I got an e-mail from a reader saying Phillips had moved to Writers & Artists, and taken clients with him. A Hollywood job is like the weather in my home state of Texas—stick around an hour and watch the changes. This is why you should, if you find an agent you like, get to know them well. If they move to a better position, you'll go along. If you're troublesome, unhappy, or too demanding, you might get left behind with the furniture, and a chair can't flip through a Rolodex and make a call.

NOT AN AGENT, NOT A MANAGER

The Internet has made the world a much more interesting and smaller place. I first read about Alex Ross in an e-mail newsletter I receive every month from Lawrence Gray, a British writer living in Hong Kong who runs a group called Hong Kong Writers (see lawrencegray.com for details). Alex is a multilingual Hollywood veteran with a European background whose WriteMovies.com is billed as a Web site that is "Empowering Writers & Film Makers WorldWide!" From the site, he runs a Playwrights and Screenwriters Competition, whose purpose is "to find great new writers and get their projects produced."

"There is some amazing talent out there that cannot get a foot in the door," Alex explained. "It's hard even for people living in L.A. to get decent representation and meetings with people who can actually say yes. There are also a lot of writers in other countries who have grown up with Hollywood movies, know how to communicate visually, but again have no access to the industry, or/and hit the language barrier. This is our loss! We need new storytellers, we need new ideas on the screen. The system needs to be more of a meritocracy."

Previous to founding the site, Alex had been both an agent and manager. One of his more notable clients was Andrew Nicoll, whom he managed through several drafts of the marvelous *The Truman Show*. Prior to managing, Alex found that agenting was the closest thing he ever found to selling used cars.

"WriteMovies was a way to avoid that kind of disappointment. It gave me the ability to look at a lot of fresh material and choose the best without having to represent anyone. From there, submitting it to the right production companies with a view to producing is a lot of fun. Also, it allows me to be able to include non-English writing scribes. There is such a vast world of storytelling out there and Hollywood is so insular. We are definitely not in the agenting biz, which is important for writers to know. The winners of our contests get submitted to the studios and production companies. If there is an offer, the writers can ask for more, and we will try to get it, or they can turn it down. We do not commission the writers, nor do we act on their behalf. Unlike some other contests that immediately assume an option on the winning material, with our winners *all* rights remain with the author until he or she decides to sell them."

Alex told me that he's found it easiest to sell smart thrillers like *L.A. Confidential* and *The Usual Suspects*.

"We have years of training, experience, and a great track record in spotting talent. We go straight to the decision-makers. Simply put, if we don't turn your submissions into movies, we don't eat. You retain the rights to your material at all times, until some-one offers you a check and a contract. If you are one of the top five entries in one of our contests, we'll pitch your material to:

1. High-ranking execs at all the studios.
2. A minimum of 10 production companies like Castle Rock, Bruckheimer Films, Scott Rudin Productions.
3. The leading literary agencies."

For non-U.S. writers, they help develop material and provide them with contacts to get them noticed in Hollywood. They ask for three months to get the winning projects seen by people who can do something if they like the work. If this sounds interesting, see www.writemovies.com or contact them by e-mail at admin@writemovies.com. You can also reach Alex Ross at:

P.O. Box 7354, Beverly Hills, CA 90212
310-281-6213, Fax: 310-827-4887

A Manager/Producer Can Change Your Career

I was reintroduced to Rona Edwards in a Hollywood directory while researching the first edition of this book. I was happy to find her because she was one of the most cheerful and forthright development executives I encountered in my early screenwriting days. Rona is now a producer/manager, a hybrid occupation, which has grown increasingly prominent in recent years. Managers once had a bad name in Hollywood, particularly with agents, because agencies had to be certified by the state, yet anyone could call him or herself a manager.

When I asked Rona about the bad rap that some managers get, she emphasized that she was a producer who became a manager when she saw the need for writers to obtain more personal attention, more than they were getting from their agents in Hollywood today. She learned early on the types of mistakes that writers could make, and regretted that no one was coaching them into better writing.

Rona tells her writers that it only takes one person to like a script. One to buy it, two for a bidding war. Rona moved from development to running Port Street Films, TV star John Larroquette's company at Warner Brothers. She then became Vice President of Creative Affairs for Academy Award–winning producer Michael Phillips, and coproduced some television movies. When writers continued asking her opinions of managers despite having good agents, she realized that the industry had changed, and she started managing in addition to producing.

"Today agents don't have time to read," she said. "They don't have time to break in a new writer. A manager's not going to lose interest so quickly. They believe in the talent of the writer to sell eventually. Agents used to do that a lot more than they do today.

This isn't to say there aren't some fine agents out there, like Alan Gasmer at William Morris, who's a wonderful agent, or David O'Connor at CAA or David Lonner or Tom Strickler at Endeavor, but the writers I work with know they're going to get that extra special attention. They know they're going to get read when I go out with something because I know a lot of people and get answers fast. Getting it read at the right places is the main thing. Also, my writers have a ton of meetings with development execs at some of the top companies when they have a great spec."

Rona charges a 15 percent commission, the going rate for managers. What she doesn't do is "double dip." She has a clause in her contract that states that if she gets paid a producer's fee, she'll reimburse the writer any commissions paid on that particular project with the exception of option monies. Her management contracts tend to run for three years, with renewables every 90 days. So far, no one has walked. One thing that Rona doesn't recommend is tricks to get in the door. For example, from people who read this book!

"I hear from so many people because of your book," she told me at lunch, "and they all use your name like they're your best friend. And you know they don't know you!" She laughed.

I asked her about how she thinks things have changed since the first edition of the book and why agents seem to have even less time for new writers these days.

"The agent's job is to sell. There are a few agents who will assume responsibility for guiding a whole career. And if someone is not selling for you, they'll lose interest and you'll part ways. A manager, on the other hand, works on a project, and some of them are producers. In my case, they're also getting someone who was a development exec and who's produced movies. So we develop ideas, sometimes from one line into a full-fledged screenplay, and then I go out as a producer and try and sell it. Or I submit their material to agents and get an agent involved. I put the team together. A manager will take more care in the total career arena across the board, be a good listening ear, a good guidance counselor. Some agents will do that, a few really good ones who act like managers. If you have an agent like that, you don't need a manager."

Rona's most recent film was *Out of Sync*, which was one of VH–1's "Movies That Rock." Written by her client, Eric Williams, it was originally called *Lip Service*.

"It was the first script I read by him and I liked it. It was not the first script of his that I went out with, though. I went out with another script that I really liked that people were fighting for. They wanted to take it to a studio but it did not sell at a studio level. It was a huge feeding frenzy from the producer's point of view. Then I went out with *Lip Service* and it became *Out of Sync* because VH–1 renamed it. If VH–1 had not started doing movies with music, though, I may not have sold that script. There were very limited places to sell it. We had companies interested in it as a feature, but when we took it into studios, they didn't know what to do with a musical. Now I think they would. Times change. I don't lose interest in something and I don't wax and wane about when I believe in someone's talent. You want the screenplay bought, but if it doesn't work, you want them to at least like the writer. And that I seem to accomplish."

When she starts working on a script with a writer, she provides painstaking notes. She's worked through as many as 10 drafts on a screenplay, and she wishes that younger writers would work hard to improve their spelling and grammar, so she doesn't feel like she's grading their papers.

"I've told writers to never hand me a draft like that again. Get someone else to proof it; I'm too high-priced to be a proofreader. I have a theory about this. Spelling and grammatical errors don't mean that you're not a good writer, but when I see something that is grossly misspelled, I'm turned off. It turns me off, and it shouldn't because someone could be a really great writer, just not be able to spell. I know some good writers who are not really good with spelling, but at least they have someone proof it before giving it to me! I know an agent who sent back a query letter that was so badly constructed with so many errors, not just spelling but grammatical, punctuation, and so forth, she sent it back to the writer and said once you learn how to write, let me know. Some people it does bother."

When I brought up the argument over whether or not query letters are effective, Rona opined that managers are probably more prone to read a query than an agent. Little things like these, rules about people's likes and dislikes, are things she wishes beginners would take time to learn.

"Knowledge is it. The more you deal, the better, because the rules rewrite themselves all the time."

She feels the best way to break into Hollywood is still a good spec script.

"I always believe you start with the written word and that's the way to begin. No writer should bank on only one script, and I know writers who have done that. Then when the script doesn't sell, they're left flat broke, or they're left with nothing and wonder why everyone told them it was going to sell. There's nothing guaranteed in this business. All bets are off, and the minute I tell you a rule, you can discount everything I say, because it doesn't matter and rules are made to be broken. All I can tell you is from my own personal experience, but tomorrow a new experience is going to happen. There are no rules. Would you bank everything on anything in your life?"

So what can a new writer do to give themselves the best start?

"It's like gambling. There are no rules. Just start hopefully with a good story and something that you think is commercial and salable. Marketable. I have a thing, when I sell something, that I call a gotcha page. It's my own little invention. It tells you why the picture should be made, puts you in the general arena without giving all the story beats. It's a PR page. You see what's going to be on the poster and Hollywood is all about marketing. Generally, I don't accept unsolicited material, but if someone's sending a query letter with a line or two and has something that interests me, I might be interested in reading it. Again, you never know where the good material is going to come from. When

I've done development seminars, a lot of good stuff has come out of them. I've optioned a number of things. Most of the stuff that I have, though, comes from referrals."

Since Rona has produced in television, I wanted to know how that affected the options she took on scripts. Did she ask for a free option for six months like independent feature producers do?

"It depends. A year is what I try to get because it takes so damned long for people to read things, especially in television. In TV you can't double-submit like you can in feature films. I can't option for money. I'd rather put my money into photocopying, messengering, schmoozing people at lunches. Any time I go out with a script, it costs a minimum of $200 just for photocopies. What you're going to get from me as a producer and/or a manager is total honesty. If someone wants to pay $3,000 to $7,500 to option a writer's material, I say that's very good. In this day and age where money's tight and option monies are really hard, you should be glad to get anything, really." She looked at me and grinned. "But like I said, no one's left me yet."

A Veteran Television Agent's Words of Wisdom

Shortly after I met Marc Pariser, he became head of literary talent at the Metropolitan agency after spending a year-and-a-half as the Executive Vice President of Creative Affairs for Shukovsky English Entertainment, the people responsible for the TV series *Murphy Brown*. After Metropolitan, Marc had his own agency for a while, then moved to the Agency for the Performing Arts, an excellent boutique agency. Since he'd worked at all the major agencies, had been a producer and a TV executive, I asked Marc what he now thought about big agencies, with regard to writers wanting to break into television or film.

"The first thing I would say is that those places aren't the only game in town," he said. "For brand-new writers, they're not necessarily the best place to be. What they do best, they do for established writers and producers and actors. The business of packaging television and features happens on behalf of people who are established. Not that they don't take on new people from time to time, but when they do, they don't necessarily give them the same attention. They have larger overheads and have to make bigger money. I would suggest to new writers that small agents who have an appetite for building writing careers have more passion and work harder on their behalf. There are any number of good smaller agencies that represent not only new writers and producers but also established people. New writers should look at the shows and the movies they like, and find out who represents the people doing the work they like. I think they'll discover that, although a lot of them are represented by the big agencies, there are a lot of others who are represented by the small places."

I wanted to know if Pariser would look at new writers. He will, but he wasn't optimistic about the possibilities.

"It's always difficult to answer that because, as a general rule, I don't like to look at new people. For 20 years, I've found that when I read people who are unsolicited, I've had no success finding anybody viable to represent. I will read new people who are recommended to me by people I know. Recommendations are really the way to get into all of the places in Hollywood, so the key is still having somebody in the business read your script and like it. Or you can get read at a lower level and have your script work its way up through the ranks. I've yet to find something that's come in unsolicited that I've responded to strongly, and I've been, over the years, much more open than other agents to reading things that come in over the transom. So as a rule I tend not to want to do that, because it's very time-consuming. It takes time to sit down and read a screenplay and evaluate it."

Marc offered some advice about the seemingly overnight successes we read about in the trades.

"If you go around town and talk to people in television, executives working at networks, and ask them about Diane English, whom I represented for years and who is obviously very successful, if you ask them about her background, most of them don't know. Diane came to Los Angeles in 1981 and wrote television movies before she wrote series. All they know about her is *Murphy Brown*. She made very little money her first few years, but she was a very, very good writer. She wrote series episodes, then a pilot, got it made, 14 episodes were produced, and then it got canceled. Then she executive-produced a show that she didn't create. *Murphy Brown* happened seven or eight years after she started in the business, and that's pretty fast."

He said the chances of a new writer getting hired on an existing show doesn't happen very often, because executive producers are too busy during the season to read new writers.

"A lot of them don't want to read things that don't come from agents, so writers without agents are out of luck. Every so often, there's somebody who will read them. When Tom Pachett and his group were doing *St. Elsewhere*, they were renowned for not wanting to deal with agents. Everybody they read was not represented. The people they hired didn't have agents. But that was a very unusual situation."

I asked him whether a good new writer might get a job on a new show based on a great spec episode of a well-known show.

"When you're putting a staff together, you have different jobs to fill," he said. "On some of the jobs you need experienced people, like producer, executive producer, supervising producer. For other positions like staff writer or story editor, sometimes you're willing to take people who are green and can be trained. You end up picking from both categories, the experienced and the new people, when you're putting a staff together. At Shukovsky English, we loved finding new people who we could train in our own style and use for an extended period of time."

One thing Marc was sure about was the agent system. He didn't think it was apt to vanish any time soon. He considered the agency scene a slightly more level playing field than it was a few years ago, and conceded there are more managers than before, but he also understands the trend, which he says isn't new.

"There have always been agents who have become managers," he said. "There seem to be more veteran agents who are becoming managers these days. More unusual than anything else, there are members of the talent community signing up for management who didn't use managers before. A lot more writers and directors are signing up with managers, which has been fairly unpopular traditionally. It's for a number of reasons, but basically I think they're becoming dissatisfied with the kind of representation they get in the agency business. That doesn't need to be. I think you can still get good representation. I'm out to prove that. If you have an agent and a lawyer and a manager, you end up spending a lot of money for representation. If you have an agent who does the job correctly, you shouldn't need all that representation."

I asked Marc if he was starting out as a writer, knowing everything that he knows now, would he try to get into TV or features?

"I think it's a matter of personal taste whether you want to write series or features. The nature of the product is different in the two areas. The amount of work that's available is different in the two areas. The pace and the style of working is different. Features is a much more relaxed area. You get to spend a lot more time writing a screenplay than you do writing television, and the money is very different. By that, I mean you have a greater chance of success and a greater chance to make more money in television than in features, although most people on the outside probably believe the opposite. You can count on your fingers the number of writers who are gross participants in the profits of a feature film. If you hit with a series on television, you make a lot more money than you will in a whole career of writing features. So the two careers are very different, but there's much more crossover these days. If you're a good writer, you can become successful in one area and work in the other area as well. If you're starting out in the business, you have to decide where you want to spend your time. Having made that decision doesn't mean you have to spend your whole career only in that area."

After talking with Marc Pariser, some of the ideas I'd developed over the years for TV series started looking a lot more attractive. And even though I spelled his name wrong in the first edition of the book, he'll still read my work. What a guy.

AN INDEPENDENT AGENT

Often enough, if a screenwriter can impress an agent who has his or her own small agency, often called a "boutique" agency, they'll have the best of both worlds—an agent who grooms their career while touting their work with the top people in town. Among the many impressive things Ken Sherman has done over the years is to find funding for John Huston's last film, *The Dead*, plus being involved in the packaging of the feature film version of *Amadeus*, not to mention helping start the careers of many writers who are now showrunning television series and writing major feature films.

Sherman started his career as a reader at Columbia Pictures, then entered the William Morris training program where he became an agent in the film/television department and represented actors and directors. He then left the agency to form his own literary agency. His first film sale was the screenplay for the Richard Donner film *Ladyhawke*, a deal that immediately put him in a bind because actor/producer Dustin Hoffman and director/producer Richard Donner both wanted it.

"With *Ladyhawke*, I had taken the first-draft screenplay to the head of Warner Brothers," he told me, "who in turn gave it to Richard Donner. About the same time I took it to Dustin Hoffman's attorney. I didn't anticipate it, but both simultaneously made offers. The deciding factor was that Mr. Hoffman would only guarantee the screenwriter two weeks of his time within the next year to supervise on the script, while Mr. Donner was ready to go full force. The choice was the right one."

About a year later, Sherman's first agency was absorbed by the New York–based Lantz office. He stayed on, handling writers, directors, actors, producers, etc. It was with the Lantz office that he became involved in the packaging of *Amadeus* and other projects. Four years later, he moved to the literary department at the Paul Kohner Agency here in L.A., and it was there he found the financing for John Huston's *The Dead*. In two more years, he reopened his own agency in Beverly Hills, where it's been for a decade.

Some of the recent projects that bring him great pride are the selling of David Guterson's *Snow Falling on Cedars* and John Updike's musical of *The Witches of Eastwick*. Sherman told me that he feels agenting has completely changed since he began his career, that today an agent acts as a producer and packager, finding many actor/director elements when submitting to mainstream and independent Hollywood production companies. I asked him if this held true with every property he went out with.

"No, but it helps in today's market. Producers are overwhelmed with their own daily responsibilities, so anything I can do to help them with their process gives my client a leg up."

One of the few agents in Los Angeles who also represents top book authors as well as writer/producers and directors for film and TV, I asked him how he juggled it all successfully.

"Very carefully!" He laughed. "What I do is not very common in Los Angeles. Usually the title 'literary agent' means a traditional book agent like those based mostly in New York. I consider book agenting an open field here in L.A. The truth is, I like having an international reach with and for my clients. Therefore, I'll often represent multiple clients for different international agencies from London, Paris, New York, Chicago, San Francisco, and even for other agencies in L.A. in terms of film and TV rights."

When I told him the story of how Eric Garcia had managed to get a showrunner deal due to the success of his *Anonymous Rex* books, Sherman wasn't terribly surprised.

"If a writer has a successful book or series of books—and of course this also depends on who the producer who wants the project is—the writer has a much stronger chance for creative control. An added bonus is when the writer can prove to a studio or a network that they can write a fine screenplay. With this killer writing sample they might be given a shot at writing the first draft of the screenplay or series pilot. At the very least, they might go onboard as a functioning executive or coproducer on a series and thus be able to keep their unique vision of the project in focus while learning the business from the inside. I'll always ask for the right for my client to write the first draft screenplay, but we'll have a much better chance if the writer can demonstrate that they can write in the form in which the buyer wants the writer to perform."

I asked him what other tools a writer should bring to the mix to better their chances of staying on the project.

"They should have an open mind and be thoughtful and discrete in meetings, learn to bend with the big Hollywood egos, and be able to show a fine screenplay writing sample that will convince a producer they can handle the translation from book to big screen or television, including Internet possibilities if that's part of the picture."

As for his own agency, only about one out of a hundred of the projects from first-time writers is considered for representation. Two-thirds of the submissions they receive are scripts, one-third are books, and they only accept referrals from an existing client, producer, studio executive, production executive, editor, or someone they know.

It's probably not too heartening to read about this type of qualification, but I generally find that even small agencies these days have much the same policy.

MANAGER OR AGENT?

Some beginning writers are not able to get an agent, but do manage to get a manager. Since anyone can call themselves a manager, agents have to be licensed under California law. That should explain why there seem to be more managers out there these days. Just so you fully understand the roles of a manager and an agent, here are some basic differences.

- Managers charge a 15 percent commission or more.
- Agents are limited to 10 percent by law.
- Managers who are also producers (meaning they actually are capable of producing a movie) may attach themselves to a project yet not hinder it because financiers know the manager/producer can get the movie made. Managers who ask for an executive producer or other credit, yet do nothing to earn it, may hinder a project.
- Agents are prohibited by law from producing.
- Legally, managers can only advise clients about offers. Even though they do it all the time, it's illegal for them to solicit work for clients or negotiate or make deals. If you don't have an agent in addition to a manager, you need a lawyer to look over contracts.

- Large agencies have lawyers on the premises known as "business affairs." Smaller agencies have lawyers they work with.
- Managers provide more personal attention and may work harder to develop your career.
- Since agents work on a smaller commission and may not make money by producing your project like managers can, an agent's life is a numbers game. If they can't make a sale for you after a certain amount of time, you're liable to be out the door.
- When a manager relationship works, it may last a long time.
- An agent relationship that works may also last a long time, but sometimes when a writer gets hot they are wooed by larger agencies; writers are not as often wooed away by larger management companies.

It is not uncommon for top writers to have a manager (15 percent), an agent (10 percent), and a lawyer (5 percent) just like top actors. That's 30 percent out of each paycheck, not to mention the income tax bite. Choose your representation well, and go for long-term relationships. If you get your name in the trade papers regularly, producers and studios will find you.

Most of the top writers and actors I've come in contact with who have sustained careers have had the same representation for a long time. The basic question is this: *Whom can you trust?* Like a marriage, without trust, it won't last long.

SOMEONE TO GET YOU THROUGH THE DOORS

Most of the time, a breakthrough in Hollywood comes from meeting someone who "knows the town." Meaning, they can get people on the phone when they call because their opinion is respected. They know how show business works, and that matters more than their current position. Whether it's an agent, a lawyer, a manager, or anything in between, as a writer you owe it to yourself to find someone who can get you through the doors and get you treated right once you're inside. You'll have to prove you belong there with your talent, but remember this—connected people don't make introductions unless they think you have the necessary talent, in spades. In this town, the game is played on the inside.

One last caution. If an script agent or manager is not in southern California, preferably in Los Angeles proper, chances are very, very good they are worthless to you as a writer, at least with regard to selling to Hollywood production companies, studios, and networks. In previous books I included representatives in places like Ohio because of the novelty of it. As far as I know, none of these agents ever sold a thing for readers of my books, and I got complaints about some of them. In this edition, I list representatives out of the country, but these are people who are firmly involved in the film and television industries where they live.

Good luck, and I hope you find a marriage made in Heaven.

Gonna Get a Guru?

What if you can't find a manager or agent to represent you? What if you keep hearing that your screenplay needs work, but no one will take the time to tell you specifically what you need to improve?

A screenwriter trying to break in can get very disheartened, both from hearing criticism and in trying to find help. There are dozens of people who teach screenwriting, tons of books on the subject (including my own *Complete Idiots Guide to Screenwriting*), and a million screenwriters with theories that may or may not be valid. To sort through them and find the best and most reliable information seems like a project for a doctoral thesis, not a mere chapter in a book. So who can you trust?

Shortly before rewriting this chapter, I was at a meeting of screenwriters to comment on a screenplay we had all studied. The film from New Line had not yet been released. Many of them were aghast that a script that they thought still needed work had actually been filmed. I told them that in my opinion the script only fell apart in the third act, something Billy "Some Like It Hot" Wilder used to worry about a lot. I pointed out a better ending (using elements and scenes already present) and suggested a "chain lightning twist" at the end, meaning a scene where the protagonist would triumph unexpectedly, causing the viewer to flash back immediately to various points in the screenplay, mentally adding up all the clues that had been planted. The example I gave of a chain lightning twist was the ending of *The Usual Suspects* where the police interrogator realizes Kevin Spacey has been making up the entire story, or the point at the end of *The Sixth Sense* where you realize Bruce Willis' psychiatrist character has been dead all along.

I got feedback the next day from one member of the group, saying how much he appreciated my insight. He told me that other members had said they felt the same. Some of them had expressed their appreciation that night, and bought copies of my books. I'd brought them a new point of view, and they expressed their gratitude.

Which brings us to the world of screenwriting gurus. If a screenplay gets made, someone has to love it enough to shepherd it through production and get it distributed. If you can't write a script like that without coaching, it makes sense to find someone to help improve the way you go at it. So where do you look?

My criterion for effective teachers is simple: Have they personally achieved what they are telling you to do? If they haven't, have their students done so? Having sold many scripts and won an award for one, I still do not consider myself an expert on screenwriting. I can only report on what I've seen work, repeatedly.

In putting together a report on screenwriting teachers, I had to cover a lot of territory, because there are many these days. My map in this chapter might not be perfect, and you shouldn't expect it to be. It must be weighed against your own particular ambition and desires. So no matter how much you like or trust what I say, I advise you to do your own investigation. Any great life pursuit involves a lifetime of learning, and that was never more true than in the film business.

THE BASIC BOOK

Before you read any books on screenwriting, read Aristotle's *Poetics*. It's a short book, and though you might have to look up some terms having to do with poetry, I believe you'll find that the basic principles in this small book will come in handy over and over. For example, many screenwriting gurus will stress the importance of reversals in the plot, a place where progress made is lost. Over 2000 years ago, Aristotle referred to that exact thing as "perepetia."

THE SCREENPLAY MAN

The man who started the rash of screenplay theory books in recent years was Syd Field, with *Screenplay* (Dell). It's not *Poetics*, but it's basic Hollywood script knowledge, and it should be second on your list, right after Lajos Egri's *The Art of Dramatic Writing*. Field's second book, *Selling a Screenplay* (Dell), is much more complete in its discussion of how Hollywood works. Fields says that when you write a script, you create the marketplace. Along that line, he tells you how to methodically go about marketing your work, without depending solely on an agent. He also observes that 60 percent of new movies do not follow an established trend. While I advise educating yourself on what trends have developed in Hollywood, your script might sell because it does not follow an established trend, but you'd better know what those trends are. The uninformed in Hollywood generally are not the successful. *Selling a Screenplay* covers agents, attorneys, executives, markets, producers (studio and independents), and readers; it is as much a guided tour of how the business works as it is about elements of successful screenplays. Perhaps one of the best points Field makes is that movies are about life, not about old movies.

In 1998, he published his fifth book, *The Screenwriter's Problem Solver: How to Recognize, Identify, and Define Screenwriting Problems* (Dell). Calling this his "ultimate troubleshooting handbook," in *The Screenwriter's Problem Solver*, Field covers things like the best ways to tighten up a screenplay scene by scene, how to move a story with action instead of dialogue (a major downfall of many beginning screenwriters), and (very important) give producers the endings they need. Other Field books are *The Screenwriter's Workbook* and *Four Screenplays*.

Shortly after I wrote the second edition of this book, Field allied with the makers of the Final Draft software to offer an annual "Seminar at Sea." Also along on the four-day cruises are major producers and agents, so if you want an intensive interaction, contact Syd Field via www.finaldraft.com or call the company at 800-231-4055.

If you can't make the cruise, an alternative might be the video workshop Field and Final Draft offer entitled, "Writing a Screenplay that Sells to Hollywood." At the time the video course was shot, Field limited the class size of his screenwriting course to a dozen students. By putting it on tape, he provided the personable wisdom that students have grown to love, available whenever you're ready to watch. Having viewed the course myself and benefited, I highly recommend it.

OTHER ESSENTIAL BOOKS

Perhaps the original how-to-write Hollywood author, Lajos Egri asserts in *The Art of Dramatic Writing* (Touchstone/Simon & Schuster) that without a clear-cut premise, you can never take any script to a logical conclusion. Emotion is life is drama is emotion, Egri believes. Your premise must be the motivating factor behind everything in the story, and the story must contain high emotion. Egri examines three aspects of human existence: psychological, physiological, and sociological. The emotional growth of the protagonist, commonly known as the "character arc," is a series of conflicts that reveal the true nature of the hero.

Irwin R. Blacker's *The Elements of Screenwriting* takes a similar approach, but declares that conflict is the driving factor behind any good movie. Blacker breaks down a 100-minute dramatic film into 24 to 26 scenes in which each scene is approximately five pages long and advances the plot. He also offers five types of exposition (revealing information to the audience about characters and the story) you can use in a film:

1. Newspaper, radio, or TV
2. Song lyrics
3. Visual dramatization
4. Voice-over narration
5. Written presentation onscreen

Some of these devices are rarely used in modern cinema and may even be spoofed, as when Ron Howard cut from a youthful incident with a girl mermaid to modern-day New York City, and we read on the screen "New York City, this morning." Still, Blacker's book remains a staple.

Another good resource is William Miller's *Screenwriting for Narrative Film and Television*. Miller at times can seem as much a personal counselor as a screenwriting coach.

He advises writers to let the screenwriting process incubate, so as to stimulate the hypnagogic state or theta brain waves that occur between waking and sleeping. Tune out the conscious so that the unconscious can proceed, he says. "Three acts, premise, and conflict" also rate high attention. For Miller, there are three kinds of story line:

1. External
2. Internal
3. Interpersonal

All of these story lines may be present in the same script, according to Miller, but one will predominate if the script is to work.

When I got back into screenwriting after an absence of several years, I found William Froug's *Screenwriting Tricks of the Trade* (Silman–James Press) to be one of the best things I read. Lew Hunter (see interview later in this chapter) called Bill Froug "THE premier screenwriting teacher in the history of motion pictures." The great screenwriter Jeffrey Boam called Froug (in the foreword to the book) "the screenwriter's best friend and advocate." I won't do this great man a disservice by trying to describe his book. Rather, I insist you read it. But, to give you some example of his wisdom, let me simply say that more than any other screenwriting guru, he exhorts students to learn about writing movies by *watching movies*, whenever possible.

At this point, you may be wondering, "Okay, so which one is valid?" The honest answer is: maybe all of them. There are over 50 books applicable to screenwriting and writing for television, and some have a more specific focus than others do. For example, if rewriting is your weak point, the best reference is probably Linda Seger's *Making a Good Script Great* (Dodd Mead). Seger is one of the 80 consultants at Carlos de Abreu's Hollywood Entertainment Network Web site, and has written several books on improving scripts, but she's not a screenwriter.

William Goldman wrote two books any new screenwriter *must* read in order to understand how Hollywood really works: *Adventures in the Screen Trade* (Warner Books). Its follow-up, *What Lies Did I Tell: More Adventures in the Screen Trade* (Pantheon Books), is more of the same good stuff, with the added bonus of an unfinished screenplay that Goldman has several other top screenwriters comment on. This exercise alone is worth the price of the book. Goldman doesn't give seminars; he's too busy writing things like *Mission: Impossible 2* for Tom Cruise.

A VERY GOOD PRIMER

If you want a print list of almost all of the books available on screenwriting, as well as a thorough discussion of formats and other useful resources, you might try David Trottier's *The Screenwriter's Bible* (Silman–James Press). The book, a *Writer's Digest* Book Club Featured Selection, is available from Amazon.com. You can contact Trottier at www.davetrottier.com or by calling 800-264-4900. He updates his book frequently and also offers seminars. Many beginning writers swear by this book, and two of his students have won Nicholl Fellowships from the Academy of Motion Picture Arts & Sciences.

Books and Talkers

Getting your money's worth is a major concern. If you spend $195 for a two-day seminar and learn that movies elicit an emotional response from the audience or reader and that novels make people think while movies make people feel, have you gotten your money's worth? If you pay $5,000 to have your screenplay analyzed by the one of the major screenwriting gurus, is it worth it when the Writers Guild minimum (the price paid for the majority of screenplays) is only around $30,000? I suppose it is if they improve your script to the point that you get $50,000 or more for it. It's a matter of judgment. I teach and consult, but I try to keep things reasonably priced.

Truly Truby

There's a reason why Larry Wilson, screenwriter of *Beetlejuice* and *The Addams' Family*, describes John Truby as "the best of all the teachers." Take a look at my review of Truby's multilevel story organization and instructional software, "Write a Blockbuster," in the software chapter. Truby is the author of *The Great Movies: Why They Work*, an analysis of a dozen classic films (self-published, $24.95, see below for ordering information), and knows movies as well as anyone. His main writing credit was as story editor on the TV series *21 Jump Street* for the 1989–90 season, and as this book was written he had completed writing, directing, and producing a film.

Truby developed his theories by comparing and analyzing "literally hundreds of films after college." (He was a philosophy major.) He decided that there were seven major steps in a story: problem/need, desire, opponent, plan, battle, self-revelation, and new equilibrium, with the hero now at a higher or lower level. Not satisfied with the seven steps, he broke the structure down further into "Twenty-Two Building Blocks." The purpose was "to create a hero-driven, step-by-step plot in which all scenes are organically linked and motivated by the hero's need." The key to Truby's method was that he felt that under the normal three-act structure, you only got a few revelations, or in Hollywood-ese, "reveals." Truby believes in compressing a story to get as much plot as possible, instead of stretching a story to fit the three-act structure. According to Truby, recent Hollywood films average six to 10 major plot points or "reveals," so if you use the "old" three-act structure, you're out of the game.

One of Truby's competitors, Linda Seger, was once quoted in a *Writer's Guild Journal* as saying Truby's claims were basically semantics and that she wouldn't be surprised if his 22 points were much of what she was doing and simply called something totally different. Although I still prefer Aristotle and some variation of Joseph Campbell myth structure for some stories, Truby has a lot to offer. The main cities where he teaches are Los Angeles, New York, Toronto, and Vancouver, but in recent years he's spent a good bit of time in Europe. Truby has a great number of students who have been successful in Hollywood.

Truby has been spent a good bit of time with European clients recently. Jim Woodson, vice president of Truby's Writers Studio, told me that they have repeating consulting clients there, often working on a European show for a year.

Learn more by perusing the Web site at www.screenwriting.org or by contacting:

TRUBY'S WRITERS STUDIO
751 Hartzell Street, Pacific Palisades, CA 90272
800-338-7829
E-mail: johntruby@aol.com

Mr. "Story"

Robert McKee is an animated, sometimes gruff but effective Ph.D. in philosophy from the University of Michigan; his creative writing teacher there was Kenneth Rowe, whose other students included playwright Arthur Miller (*The Crucible*) and writer/director Lawrence Kasdan (*The Big Chill*). McKee began as a child actor and appeared on Broadway with the legendary Helen Hayes. He has been a story analyst for United Artists and NBC, written for the TV shows *Columbo* and *Quincy*, been on the faculty of the USC School of Cinema and Television, and hosted the series *Reel Secrets* for British television.

McKee feels that a writer must study the principles of the masters to gain an understanding of the craft and elements of the writing art. McKee does weekend seminars only, in major cities like Los Angeles and New York. He reportedly averages 250 students per class and has made upward of a million dollars a year with his classes, which might explain why he originally would not let students tape his lectures. In 1998, he finally published *Story* (HarperCollins), the long-awaited book based on his course, despite the fact that he had been quoted as saying the majority of screenwriting books are "appallingly shallow." McKee offers "The Classic Five-Part Narrative Structure":

1. Inciting incident
2. Progressive complications
3. Crisis
4. Climax
5. Resolution

Obviously, none of the above are revolutionary, but McKee strives to present "a practical course, putting a new light and perspective on the craft of storytelling from the basics through advanced concepts and techniques." At the end of the seminar I'm familiar with, he did a thorough analysis of *Casablanca*. Now, in his three-day course, he covers up to 100 films. Producers and development people all over Hollywood are grooved into the McKee philosophy. One screenwriter told me that when he started "talking McKee" in pitch meetings, he felt like he was speaking the native language. On his Web site, McKee claims that graduates of his "intensive three-day course" have earned 17 Academy Awards, 104 Emmy Awards, 19 Writer's Guild Awards, 16 Directors Guild Awards, and hundreds of nominations. What he *doesn't* say is how many of those came *after* the graduates took his classes. He claims over 35,000 attendees to his classes and workshops.

What do they learn? "The principles involved in the art and craft of screenwriting and story design, [which] proves the essence of good story is unchanging and universal."

One endorsement that impressed me about McKee (and I've also read his book) came from two-time Oscar winning screenwriter William Goldman: "I am more convinced than ever that [screenplays are] only about story. [McKee] is a tireless speaker, knowledgeable and passionate—it's three full days over a single weekend and no one feels cheated when he's done . . . I wish he'd been around when I started writing CUT TO for a living."

If you'd like to find out more about McKee, I suggest that you read *Story*. If you're interested in a seminar, visit www.mckeestory.com or contact:

TWO ARTS, INC.

P.O. Box 452930, Los Angeles, CA 90045
888-676-2533, Fax: 310-645-6928
E-mail: contact@McKeeStory.com

The Fix-It Lady

Once you have a script written, you need to rewrite it. That's where Linda Seger, author of *Making a Good Script Great* (Samuel French) comes in. Also the author of *Making a Good Writer Great* (Silman–James Press) Seger is one of Hollywood's top script consultants. She travels across the U.S. and to Europe discussing screenwriting in workshops like "Creating Unforgettable Characters: A 1-day seminar or workshop on creating dimensional characters." Many writers swear by what they've learned about fixing scripts from Linda. Visit www.lindaseger.com or contact her at:

LINDA SEGER/SCRIPT CONSULTANT

2038 Louella Avenue
Venice, CA 90291
310-390-1951, Fax: 310-398-7541
E-mail: cotlanza@ix.netcom.com

A Seminar to Help You Sell

One prominent screenwriting teacher will probably come to a city near you soon. Michael Hauge is the author of *Writing Screenplays That Sell* (HarperPerennial

Library). His seminar, "Screenwriting for Hollywood: From Concept to Sale," is delivered throughout the United States. Like McKee, Hauge is big on numbers.

- One essential objective every successful screenplay must achieve
- Five elements common to all successful movies
- Three methods of ensuring audience identification with characters
- Four primary character types
- Five major turning points of a screenplay
- Fifteen most effective principles of plot structure
- Seven steps to screenwriting success

People respond to numbered checklists, so you can't really fault Hauge for using this method. To his credit, he goes into detail about the business of Hollywood in his seminars, offering methods of getting scripts into the right hands and insight into how film deals work (which many screenwriting teachers rarely touch on). Coming from a development, story editor, and producer background, he also offers script consultation and evaluation. Philip Noyce, the Australian director of *Patriot Games* and *A Clear and Present Danger* said, "Michael Hauge's principles and methods are so well argued that the mysteries of effective screenwriting can be understood, even by directors."

Upon listening to Hauge at a "Selling to Hollywood" conference, I realized he'd improved his approach over the years and that experienced writers could learn something from his as well. My favorite item he put forth was that major characters have a "wound" (others call it a "ghost") that they need to heal during the process of the story.

To find out more about his workshops, contact:

HILLTOP PRODUCTIONS
P.O. Box 55728, Sherman Oaks, CA 91413
818-995-4209, Fax: 818-986-1504
E-mail: mhauge@juno.com

Seminar Central

If you read the agents chapter, you might remember the 60 tips for beginning screenwriters from Leslie Kallen. In addition to representing writers, Kallen teaches seminars ("How to Write the New American Screenplay and Get an Agent to Sell It for You") and arranges seminars for some of the top experts in the business. One of these seminars is "Screenwriting: Beyond the Basics" by UCLA Film and Television writing program chairman Richard Walter, who is the author of books like *The Whole Picture: Strategies for Screenwriting Success in the New Hollywood* (Plume). Structured like Walter's Master's Class at UCLA, participants in this seminar sit at a conference table and Professor Walter comments on their actual script pages. It's pretty much the same class (albeit abbreviated) where successful screenwriters like David Koepp learned the craft. (As this book was going to press, Koepp, who also wrote *Jurassic Park*, sold a comedy spec called "The Superconducting Supercollider of Sparkle Creek, Wisconsin" cowritten with John Kamps (*The Borrowers*) for $2.5 million against $3 million if produced.) Walter's class includes table readings, which staff writers and Hollywood veterans know well.

Kallen also works with Robert "King of the Pitch" Kosberg to promote his "How to Sell Your Idea to Hollywood" seminar. In case you've missed what a pitch is, it's basically selling your movie in person to someone who can write you a check or who can get someone else to write one. Kosberg talks about selling, critiques, pitching techniques and (here's the catch) "participants get a chance to pitch their own ideas to Mr. Kosberg for possible coproduction." Sometimes, Kosberg brings in people from production companies, but I've mostly seen him work alone. The real truth about his workshops and his own Web site, www.moviepitch.com, is that they are vehicles for Kosberg to acquire ideas that he can sell to studios. He doesn't write, he doesn't even do e-mail, but he's an ebullient salesman.

Having seen both Richard Walter and Leslie Kallen in action, I can personally recommend both. If you want a college-level workshop from one of the top professors in Los Angeles, Walter delivers that. Leslie Kallen provides good basic information that can save aspiring screenwriters from amateur mistakes. For more information, see the Leslie Kallen listing in the agent section.

BOOKS OF DIFFERENT COLORS

If you want a cheerleader to kick-start your scriptwriting, have a look at Viki King's *Write a Movie in 21 Days: The Inner Movie Method* (Perennial Library). King has written for television, including *Three's Company*, but the focus of her teaching is on feature films. Her method includes pounding out a somewhat structured, seen-in-the-head, written-from-the-heart draft of a script.

If you want a one-stop shopping screenwriting reference that covers all types of scriptwriting (including radio), written by a person who has been successful in all mediums, get *The Complete Book of Scriptwriting* by J. Michael Straczynski (Writer's Digest Books). You might know him from his long-running, Emmy award-winning television series *Babylon 5*. He's the creator, executive producer, and headwriter. I sold my first script to the nationally-syndicated science fiction radio show "*Alien Worlds*", and Joe Straczysnki was one of the show's writers. The first section of Straczynski's book is on television, an arena where he's had his greatest success and which offers more high-paying opportunities for writers than any other medium. Motion pictures are covered next, followed by animation, radio, the stage play, and ending with "The Business of Scriptwriting." This well-thought-out volume of over 400 pages offers definitions, sample scripts, contract examples, and a chapter called "Warning Signs" that should be required reading for any aspiring scriptwriter.

Gene Perret's *Comedy Writing Step by Step* (Samuel French Trade) is hard to beat if you think you're funny or want to be. Granted, it was published in 1982, but this long-time writer for Bob Hope knows more about comedy than three generations of today's comics. If you like the book, check out the annual Round Table Comedy Convention by contacting Linda Perret (WritComedy@aol.com), which takes place on a summer weekend in southern California. Also call 818-865-7833 for information.

A promising new edition to the flood of books about screenwriting (and writing in general) is *A Story Is a Promise* (Blue Heron Publishing) by Bill Johnson. Applicable to novels and plays as well as screenplays, this book offers as much as any other tome in how to craft the essence of the story that forms the basis of any large creative work. Johnson's "Story Director" method offers an easily understood way to "help writers check whether or not every story event, character action, and plot device serves to dramatically advance a story toward resolution and fulfillment of its promise." Contact:

BLUE HERON PUBLISHING

1234 SW Stark Street, Suite 1, Portland, OR 97205
503-223-8098, Fax: 503-223-9474
E-mail: info@blueheronpublishing.com
Web sites: www.blueheronpublishing.com and
     www.storyispromise.com

If you're a rebel and/or an experimental filmmaker at heart, someone who wants to try new things, I recommend *Alternative Scriptwriting: Writing Beyond the Rules* (Focal Press) by Ken Dancyger and Jeff Rush. They offer an intellectual dissection of film that offers new ideas like the "Working Against Genre" chapter.

The Mighty Martell

If you want to write action scripts, there is no better book on the market than *The Secrets of Action Screenwriting* by William C. Martell (First Strike Productions). Roger Avary (*Pulp Fiction*), said, "This book is dangerous. I feel threatened by it." Bill Martell is one of those always busy screenwriters who may not make the broad public radar like a Joe Ezsterhas but whose name appears on more movie credits than any other writer I know. He had 20 or so onscreen feature credits, which cannot be said by any other how-to screenwriting author. And he sold all those scripts on his own, or by referral that did *not* come from an agent!

Some statements clear up things beginning screenwriters might take years to learn. For example: "The bigger the villain's plan, the bigger the movie." Other tips are not so obvious, like: "The longer you 'hold' a plot twist, the more powerful it becomes."

If you've read many screenwriting magazines, particularly *Scr(i)pt*, you may have seen some of his articles; they're always enlightening. Pick up the book or booklets by getting in touch with:

FIRST STRIKE PRODUCTIONS

11012 Ventura Boulevard, PMB 103, Studio City, CA 91604-3546
E-mail: wcmartell@scriptsecrets.com
Web site: www.scriptsecrets.com

Men of Myth

The influence of Joseph Campbell's *The Hero with a Thousand Faces* (Bollingen Series/Princeton) has become very well-known in Hollywood in the last few years. If you haven't read the book, you should, as well as any number of other books by Campbell, including *The Hero's Journey* (Harper & Row). You'll find out why George Lucas said he couldn't have finished writing *Star Wars* if not for Campbell's work.

Two other writers have done screenwriters a favor by showing the applicability of Campbell's work to movies, the most notable being Christopher Vogler with his *The Writers Journey* (Michael Wiese Productions). Vogler discovered Campbell's work while studying at the University of Southern California, the school George Lucas attended. While working as a story analyst for Disney, he wrote the memo "A Practical Guide to *The Hero with a Thousand Faces*." The memo so impressed then studio movie honcho Jeffrey Katzenberg, he made it required reading for anyone running a project through the studio. This led to Vogler's book, which is now in its second edition. "The Comparisons of Outlines and Terminology" of Campbell's "myth structure" to Vogler's filmic applicability on page 12 is alone worth the price of the book. Find out more by surfing over to www.writersjourney.com.

Another book from Michael Wiese Productions is *Myth and the Movies: Discovering the Mythic Structure of 50 Unforgettable Films* by Stuart Voytilla. This fine book covers five films in each of the following genres: action adventure, western, horror, thriller, war, drama, romance, romantic comedy, comedy and science fiction, and fantasy. Of particular interest is the chart on The Character Arc on page 7 (with illustrations). No other book I know so clearly depicts on a single page the heroic transformation that takes place in the main character of great stories. I know of one top screenwriter/director who, upon contemplating a Hollywood career, sat down with videos of the top 50 movies of all time and their scripts. He watched the movies and read along from the scripts, and this is how he learned storytelling. By covering 50 very successful movies from all lands and decades, Voytilla has provided the essence of the above-described process.

For information on both these books and many more, see the Michael Wiese Productions Web site at www.mwp.com/pages/books.html or contact:

11288 Ventura Boulevard, Suite 821, Studio City, CA 91604
818-379-8799, Fax: 818-986-3408
E-mail: wiese@earthlink.net

Books on the Business of the Biz

If, by now, you're wondering why the heck I'm recommending all these books and that you can't ever possibly read all of them, remember what screenwriter Lawrence Kasdan said, "Being a writer means having homework for the rest of your life." I can hear you groan from here. In most cases, I've met and interacted with the authors mentioned herein as well as having read the books. And nobody pays for these reviews.

Although it's a bit dated (the author passed away some years ago), Carl Sautter's *How to Sell Your Screenplay: The Real Rules of Film and Television* (New Chapter Press) is still a fine book of advice. Sautter's "It's a Wonderful Job" episode of the TV series *Moonlighting* won the 1987 Writer's Guild Award for Best TV Drama. He was also nominated for an Emmy in 1986. I met Sautter at a seminar he gave, but he wasn't interested in only doing seminars; he was too busy making a very good living as a writer. He was a giving, enthusiastic person and teacher, and his passing was Hollywood's loss.

No book covers both the film and television business for writers as well as *Opening the Doors to Hollywood* by Carlos de Abreu and Howard Jay Smith (Custos Morum, Beverly Hills). de Abreu is the founder of the Hollywood Network and the Hollywood Film Festival, which goes into its fifth year as this book is written. I'm often asked for examples of treatments; you can find one here, but you can also find examples of a pitch outline, a step outline, and every type of printed material seen by not only film companies, but television companies as well. You can learn the basics of the entire industry in this volume, and you can find other answers at www.hollywood-network.com.

Want to sell a million-dollar spec script? Thought so. Read Thom Taylor's *The Big Deal: Hollywood's Million-Dollar Spec Script Market* (Quill/William Morrow) and find out how *While You Were Sleeping*, *Seven*, *In the Line of Fire*, *The Player*, and other scripts were sold. After a tour through *The Big Deal* you'll feel like you've lived in Hollywood for a decade. Is that good or bad? See www.bigdealnews.com.

If you head into a big deal, or even a tiny one, you'll probably need a lawyer. So you'll know what you're talking about, read *The Writer Got Screwed (but didn't have to): A Guide to the Legal and Business Practices of Writing for the Entertainment Industry* (HarperCollins) by Brooke A. Wharton. Repeatedly on newsgroups and in chat rooms, I saw this book recommended, so I finally picked it up. The instructor of a law class at the USC Graduate School of Screenwriting, Wharton covers everything in this book, even writing for soap operas. Has a producer asked you to send in a release with your script? You'll find one here. You'll also learn about copyrights, contracts, the Writers Guild of America and the protections it affords, and a thorough discussion of what the various representatives—agents, managers, lawyers—can and cannot do for you. There's even a chapter on competitions and fellowships. Read this book and feel secure as you swim with sharks. This is a highly-regarded entertainment attorney who advises, "Don't make your lawyers rich."

Just when I think there's a book for every single aspect of the business of Holly-wood, along comes a new one that fills another niche. *Hollywood 101: The Film Indus-try—How to Succeed in Hollywood Without Connections* (Renaissance Books) by Frederick Levy is much too long a title, but it's a worthwhile read for anyone planning to move to Los Angeles and/or pursue not just selling a script but a full-fledged career in the business. Levy covers the function of every single major player in the production process, from the writer all the way to the public relations firm that promotes the fin-ished film. Read Brooke Wharton's book to keep you from getting screwed; read this one to keep yourself from getting embarrassed.

If you ever consider producing your own film, I highly recommend *Producing for Hollywood: A Guide for Independent Producers* by Paul Mason and Don Gold (All-worth Press). It's a career-building, crash course on the independent production scene by people who have "been there, done that" in all aspects of film and television. It cov-ers everything from first pitch to final cut, including how to develop a prospectus, draft a budget, raise money, and take your project through three phases of production, then how to distribute and market the finished film. Gold was the production manager of *Diagnosis: Murder* at the time this book was sold, and Mason the senior vice president of production at Viacom. If you can't find it in your local bookstore, order it from the publisher at www.allworth.com/Catalog/PA171.htm.

BREAK IN AS A PRODUCTION ASSISTANT (P.A.)

If you want to know the basics of day-to-day operations on a movie set (and you should), take a look at Sandy Curry's 45-page P.A. booklet. If more screenwriters had a clue about the shooting of a movie or TV show, they would understand how a script can get mangled from script to screen (and possibly how to prevent it). Also, you can probably get a job as a production assistant if you study this booklet. Curry is a New York–based producer. A sampling of the contents:

- Everything that has to happen on a shoot day
- 10 things to check for when renting a vehicle
- The most important things to remember on set
- An 81-item glossary covering everything from AD kit to Zip cord

To get her booklet, contact:

SANDY CURRY
217 North Henry Street, Brooklyn, NY 11222
718-398-6610, Fax: 718-389-5507
E-mail: sbcurry@aol.com
Web site: www.paguidelines.com

TO SCHOOL OR NOT TO SCHOOL?

If at all possible, I highly advise you to spend a year in Los Angeles if you're serious about a Hollywood screenwriting career because some week-long or even weekend events might make all the difference in your career and provide that legendary "lucky break." One place to get started is in one of the screenwriting programs in the city where the film and TV business of the world is centered. There are three major programs in Tinseltown: the American Film Institute; the University of California at Los Angeles (UCLA); and the University of Southern California (USC). While there are many fine smaller programs both here and in other parts of the country, the emphasis of this book is on Hollywood resources. I've found that a great number of the writers of the most successful recent screenplays have been graduates of Los Angeles schools, so here are some brief descriptions of what the main ones may have to offer for your particular needs.

American Film Institute

For the advanced screenwriting student, the American Film Institute (AFI) is highly recommended. AFI offers a two-year graduate program training students in seven disciplines: directing, producing, screenwriting, cinematography, editing, production design, and digital media studies. If you want to write for television (where the bulk of Writers Guild of America members make their living) and can come to Los Angeles during the summer, AFI has a couple of options. The first is the AFI/Sloan TV Writing Workshop, an intensive three-week workshop offering participants a chance to work directly with Hollywood's top writers and producers, developing scripts for current one-hour dramatic television series. This workshop is designed for writers pursuing narrative writing for television. In addition to meeting working professionals in television, you also get to meet leading figures in the science and technology industry. No more than a dozen people are chosen to attend the workshop, and you must reside in the Los Angeles area during the workshop. There are a number of full-tuition scholarships available, which include money for living expenses.

AFI also offers the Television Writers Summer Workshop: Writing the Television Movie. This workshop is "an intensive, hands-on workshop designed to train writers in the creation and development of television movie scripts." Participants work directly with major working writers, directors, and producers to develop television movie scripts and have staged readings of their work, among other things. Since TV movies are a unique type of scriptwriting, if you have a burning desire to write them, this is the workshop for you. Up to 12 writers are selected for the workshop, and you must reside in the Los Angeles area during the workshop. Scholarships including tuition and a stipend for living expenses are available, based on ability and financial need.

Another yearly event is the AFI Fest, where films are debuted and panels are held on the subject of filmmaking. The highlight of the 2000 Fest was the Coen Brothers' *O Brother, Where Art Thou?* You can read about it online at www.afifest.com.

For more information on AFI programs, contact:

THE AMERICAN FILM INSTITUTE, EDUCATION AND TRAINING PROGRAMS

2021 North Western Avenue, Los Angeles, CA 90027
323-856-7600, Fax: 323-467-4578
E-mail: info@afionline.org

If you're interested in their East Coast program, contact:

THE AMERICAN FILM INSTITUTE

The John F. Kennedy Center for the Performing Arts,
    Washington, D.C. 20566
202-833-AFIT (2348), Fax: 202-659-1970
Web site: www.afionline.org /home.html

University of Southern California (USC)

USC students do very well, continually winning top awards. Nearly all the teachers at the big programs have written books. In the past, the USC Graduate Professional Writing Program has featured nationally-known authors like Betty Friedan (*The Feminine Mystique*) teaching nonfiction; Aram Saroyan, author of *The Romantic*, son of William Saroyan (and one of my former agents), teaching story structure; Jerome Lawrence, who wrote *Inherit the Wind*, teaching playwriting; and Ehrich Van Lowe, a writer for *The Cosby Show*, teaching screenwriting. Norman Hollyn, author of *The Film Editing Room Handbook: How to Manage the Near Chaos of the Cutting Room* (Lone Eagle), who is interviewed in the digital chapter of this book, teaches at USC. For information about USC programs, contact:

THE GRADUATE PROFESSIONAL WRITING PROGRAM

University of Southern California, Wait Phillips Hall, Room 404,
    Los Angeles, CA 90089-4034
213-740-3252

If you're primarily interested in screenwriting, contact:

JOHN FURIA JR., CHAIR

USC School of Cinema–Television, Los Angeles, CA 90089-2211
213-740-3303
Web site: www.usc.edu/schools/cntv/

The University of California at Los Angeles (UCLA)

Boasting alumni like Allison Anders, Francis Ford Coppola, David Koepp, Gregory Nava, and Tim Robbins, The UCLA School of Theater, Film and Television brings together the arts of theater, film, and television in one academic institution. The innovation of this mixing of the arts is one of the reasons the school is consistently ranked among the leading institutions in the nation. Another is the UCLA Film and Television Archive, the largest university-based archive in the world, second in size and scope only to the Library of Congress. Film and television historian and preservationist Robert Rosen is the dean.

The UCLA Master of Fine Arts Screenwriting program was designated "the Harvard of film-writing schools" by *The London Times* in 1992. Whether that's true or not, screenwriting students at UCLA work as hard as students at Harvard; they write a lot. By graduation time, a student will have written at least three feature-length screenplays "for either the commercial or experimental media" and they are based in the reality of what Hollywood buys. UCLA screenwriting professor Richard Walter tells students that movies must be violent, and that rational, reasonable behavior is good for neighborhoods, but boring in movies. "Beginning, middle, and end" is Walter's structure (acknowledging Aristotle), with intimate detail in each. With beginnings and endings, he advises you to start late and finish early for a better script. If a film ends too soon, you leave audiences wanting more, which is always healthy for the next script you write. Walter believes in the cathartic effect of movies on the population, saying film allows us to rehearse our emotions.

Other screenwriting instructors include Daniel Pyne, whose first produced feature film was *Pacific Heights*, and Mike Werb, a graduate of the Master Program in Screenwriting with credits like *The Mask* and *Face/Off*, cowritten with fellow UCLA alum Michael Colleray.

You might also be interested in the Professional Program in Screenwriting, a graduate-level, non-degree program modeled after the MFA Screenwriting Program. Students who complete the one-year program receive a certificate in screenwriting. For information about any of the screenwriting programs, contact:

UCLA School of Theater, Film and Television

405 Hilgard Avenue, Los Angeles, CA 90024
310-825-8787
E-mail: webmaster@emelnitz.ucla.edu
Web site: www.tft.ucla.edu/tfthome.htm

UCLA Extension Writers Program is the largest of its kind in the world. It offers a huge list of industry-related courses taught by working professionals. I taught there for a year. For information, start looking at www.unex.ucla.edu—some of the courses are offered online—or inquire about classes at their several Los Angeles-area locations at:

UCLA EXTENSION

P.O. Box 24901, Los Angeles, CA 90024-0901
310-825-9971 or 818-784-7006, Fax: 310-206-3223

Sherwood Oaks

One school for aspiring screenwriters stands head and shoulders above all others for continued excellence over the years, and more graduates that have gone on to large careers. Sherwood Oaks has no fixed classroom at all; rather, its students meet in hotels and often share lunch around a table with someone who can buy their work or sell it for them starting that very day. Here's an example. On August 15, 2000, I went to a "Pitch Day" Sherwood Oaks event at the Bel Age Hotel in West Hollywood. It was part of an entire week costing $750, so one day was $150. In a group of less than 10 people, I met: the story editor for Nicolas Cage's Saturn Productions; Kent Kubena, the director of development for Matt Damon and Ben Affleck's company and the man who dreamed up their "Project Greenlight" Internet-driven feature film production contest; and Rob Carliner, the producer/manager of Butchers Run Films, actor Robert Duvall's company. How does that sound?

Schoolteacher Gary Shusett started Sherwood Oaks to help people break into Hollywood. His brother Ron is a very successful screenwriter (*Total Recall* and others). I first came across Sherwood Oaks in the 1980s, and so did people like James "Titanic" Cameron. That's why you can meet people like him at Sherwood Oaks events. Contact:

GARY SHUSETT, SHERWOOD OAKS
EXPERIMENTAL COLLEGE

7095 Hollywood Boulevard, #876, Los Angeles, CA 90028
Phone 323-851-1769, Fax: 323-850-5302, Service 323-850-4444
Web site: www.sherwoodoakscollege.com

The Write Idea

A similar approach is taken by Paul Crockett of Write Idea Productions, who puts on quarterly "Let's Do Lunch" events at various venues around the Los Angeles area. Guest speakers address assembled writers in a banquet room and speak on various topics, with a vice president of development, creative executive, or story editor from a major production company sitting positioned at each table. Over lunch, writers introduce themselves and pitch an idea to the development execs, and as each course is served, the execs switch tables. On the day I attended, the speaker was Frederick Levy, author of *Hollywood 101*. The following companies were represented: Marty Katz Productions (*Reindeer Games*, the company where Frederick Levy works); Jaret Entertainment (*10 Things I Hate About You*); Fountain Productions (*The Santa Clause*);

Longbow Productions (*A League of Their Own*); Independent Pictures (*Swingers*); Cosgrove–Meurer (Independent films); Alex Rose (*Overboard*); Boz Productions (*Scary Movie*); Bridget Johnson Films (*As Good As It Gets*); and Mace Neufeld Productions (*Patriot Games*). Does that sound interesting? There were so many execs, I didn't know where to start pitching. If this makes you hungry, contact:

Paul Crockett, Write Idea Productions

21755 Ventura Boulevard, #145, Woodland Hills, CA 91364
818-594-4144, Fax: 818-591-7577
E-mail: info@awriteidea.com
Web site: www.awriteidea.com

Flashing Forward

If you'd like more than just lunch, check out the Flash Forward seminars put on by Suzanne Lyons and Heidi Wall. Wall has executive-produced and produced several movies for television, including Michael Dare's *The Bachelor's Baby* on CBS. Lyons was a writer/producer in Canada before moving to Los Angeles to start Snowfall Films. They offer master classes and course weekends with working lunches. Also, a Flash Forward workshop may be coming to a city near you if you live in a film-friendly town like Vancouver, New York, or Austin. Flash Forward teaches long-term career vision, cultivation of Hollywood contacts, and prompts you to arrange for a working Hollywood professional to mentor you. Contact:

Suzanne Lyons

2321 W. Olive Avenue, Suite A, Burbank, CA 91506
323-850-7392, Fax: 323-850-0392
E-mail: ffinst@aol.com
Web site: www.flashforwardinstitute.com

Scriptwriters Network

If you are in the Los Angeles area on a regular basis, or if you would like to keep up with current trends and events, have a look at The Scriptwriters Network, which meets at venues like Universal Studios on a monthly basis. To become a member you must:

- Submit a completed application form.
- Submit appropriate fees.
- Submit a completed script for evaluation and have it accepted by the Membership Committee.

There is a one-time, nonrefundable $15 application fee. Yearly membership is $75, which also entitles you to the monthly newsletter. Monthly newsletter subscription only is available for $40. Writers who live outside Southern California pay $50 for annual membership, but affiliate membership does not allow you to vote in the annual Network elections. If a person's membership is not accepted, annual membership fees are refunded.

Their Producers Outreach Program gets your unagented script read by specifically interested producers who have filled out a questionnaire detailing their specific areas of interest. The last time I checked, they had over 100 producers on the list. Each script submitted must get a "Recommended" by two readers, plus a third "Recommend" by a Committee Reader before notification is sent to the appropriate producers on the list. To qualify to be a reader, a person must have: (a) won a contest; (b) be a professional reader in the industry; (c) have sold a script; (d) be a person of long professional standing in the industry; or (e) have taken the free one-day class in reading for the Network. Members pay $20 to submit a script, and receive no less than two written critiques of the work. If a script receives two "Not Recommendeds," the author may choose to do a rewrite and resubmit (one time only) for free.

It's a good group, and many members are working screenwriters. To inquire, send a SASE for an application to:

SCRIPTWRITERS NETWORK

Attn: Membership Director
11684 Ventura Boulevard, #508, Studio City CA 91604
323-848-9477
Web site: www.scriptwritersnetwork.com

StoryBoard Development Group

I attended this writers group as a guest and we discussed the script of *The Prime Gig*, a New Line film starring Vince Vaughn, Julia Ormond, and Ed Harris. The screenplay was by William Wheeler (his first "written by" credit). I was invited there by the estimable Donie Nelson and thoroughly enjoyed our meeting on the Sony lot in Culver City to discuss this screenplay about the seamy side of telemarketing. They meet the second Monday of the month, always with a guest moderator, and may have upward of 80 participants, depending on the script being read, the weather, etc. Some of the writers drive two hours to reach the meeting. If this sounds interesting to you, contact StoryBoard Chairman Scott Burnell at 323-936-0672 or e-mail sburnell@earthlink.net.

Kitchen Master Course

Jeffrey Kitchen offers a 10-week course that many veterans say is the best. Jennifer Grisanti, Director of Current Programming at Spelling Television, said the class was "the most comprehensive one offered as far as making people understand how to apply the tools and make them work." It's a hands-on, results-oriented class covering sequence, proposition, plot, principles of dramatic action, dramatic logic, and the 36 Universal Dramatic Situations. Contact him at:

JEFF KITCHEN

849 N. McCadden Place #6, Los Angeles, CA 90038
213-243-3817
E-mail: jeffkitchen@earthlink.net
Web site: www.developmentheaven.com

Mistress of the Enneagram

For something a little different that could help you create more complex characters, you might want to study the Enneagram of Personality, a nine-pointed diagram with ancient roots used to describe nine basic personality styles and their interrelationships. Is your main character a Critic, a Lover, an Achiever, an Aesthete, an Analyst, a Pessimist, an Optimist, a Trail-Blazer, or a Connector? Shakespeare's Hamlet is, according to author and teacher Judith Searle, a Six (Pessimist), "preoccupied with worst-case scenarios, mistrustful, continually testing the loyalties of friends and family, often immobilized by his fears."

Actress/writer Searle, with a Master of Education degree from Harvard University, is the author of *The Literary Enneagram: Characters from the Inside Out.* Holding her Character Development workshops in New York and Los Angeles, she claims that "by understanding behavior you will create credible character arcs and character-driven plot twists that seem both inevitable and surprising." She uses film clips and excerpts from 18 novels to illustrate her points, including the interior process for both male and a female characters. For more information, contact Judith Searle at:

855 10th Street
Santa Monica, CA 90403
L.A. phone 310-393-5372, N.Y. phone 212-799-5254
E-mail: JSearle479@aol.com
Web site: http://members.aol.com/jsearle479/bio.html

Spec Script Marketplace & Pitchmart

Spec Script Marketplace is a bi-monthly publication listing screenplays for sale by genre, in short, synopses of 50 words or less. It is mailed every two months to 1,300-plus potential buyers. The cost to list one script for two months is $39. In four years it has produced nearly 50 option contracts, and one of those projects was producedin 2000.

The quarterly pitch sessions offer writers the opportunity to pitch their script(s) in person, in five-minute-long, one-on-one private appointments with development executives from production companies and producers. The events take place at a hotel in Santa Monica, California, from 6:30 to 9:30 P.M., and cost $99 per person. There are at least 20 companies represented each time. In two years, the sessions have resulted in 13 people finding representation (one of whom closed a six-figure sale in 2000) and writers who got their scripts optioned. Writers attending have come from as far away as Australia. Peel is a former television executive and screenwriter who has built this operation from the ground up. In addition to the Pitchmart results mentioned, she reports getting a steady, healthy request for scripts via the publication. Contact Eva Peel at:

> P.O. Box 1365
> Santa Monica, CA 90406
> 310-396-1662, Fax: 310-399-6196
> E-mail: scriptmarketplace@compuserve.com
> Web site: www.scriptmarketplace.com

The Career Strategist

If you're not ready for a class or pitching session, you might need someone like Donie Nelson, who can tell writers more about inside tips to the Hollywood game than any other person I know. With two decades of experience, in 1991, Donie began sharing her knowledge and industry contacts with a dozen screenwriters who had experienced frustration in marketing to Hollywood producers and agents. Donie reads every script, takes every phone call, and over 700 screenwriters from around the world have benefited from her unique approach to planning their screenwriting career. If you've ever felt overwhelmed at the prospect of choosing among all the potential mentors, out there, Donie is someone who can help you sort it out and formulate workable strategies for reaching your goals. She knows feature films, prime-time network, first-run syndication, and cable television (long form, comedy, and drama), and has extensive relationships with literary agents. She has participated in the development of over 50 feature films, developed numerous network television movies, supervised the production of almost 50 situation comedy episodes for first-run syndication and cable television, developed and sold network pilot scripts and supervised their production, and developed and sold projects to pay cable. She was a story editor for an NBC-TV dramatic series, supervised the novelization of a television movie, and was responsible for the operation of several story departments.

Her memberships include just about every organization in Hollywood that matters. I get dizzy just reading everything she's done. Contact:

DONIE A. NELSON

Career Strategies for Writers
10736 Jefferson Boulevard, #508, Culver City, CA 90230-4969
310-204-6808, Fax: 310-839-3985
E-mail: wrtrconsult@earthlink.net

SELLING TO HOLLYWOOD

Steve and Meera Lester sold their annual "Selling to Hollywood" scriptwriting conference to the American Screenwriters Association in 2000, and the show went on without a hitch in August. Top Hollywood speakers appeared, as well as writer/filmmakers like Gary Ross (*Pleasantville*), who was interviewed by screenplay guru Michael Hauge. (I also spoke following Ross and Hauge, about how to get on Hollywood's radar screen.) Representatives from production companies speak to attendees, and attendees with full conference registrations get a 10-minute consultation with a working Hollywood professional.

Perennial returnee Tom Wodniak had this to say about the conference, "It's a virtual Who's Who of the Film Industry. There are no attitudes or closed doors—opportunities abound around the clock! Over the last seven years, I've been able to introduce myself to a large network of VIPs. What amazes me is that they continue to make themselves available to my new ideas and projects."

In 2001, they are adding an advanced track session for seasoned screenwriters, along with the special workshops for previous attendees. Contact:

AMERICAN SCREENWRITERS ASSOCIATION

269 S. Beverly Drive, Beverly Hills, CA 90212-3807
866-265-9091, Fax: 513-731-9212
E-mail: sth@sellingtohollywood.com
Web site: www.asascreenwriters.com

Hollywood Film Conference

Let me guess. You're working a job and trying to find time to write. You might not live in Los Angeles. You can only afford to take one vacation a year, so you have to choose wisely within your budget. Here's the most comprehensive deal in town. What started as the Hollywood Film Festival is now the Hollywood Film Conference. In 2001, it takes place August 3–5 at the historical Hollywood Roosevelt Hotel, where it began five years before. The Conference Pass costs $495 and gives you access to over 100 established Hollywood professionals in four days of intensive networking. Agents, producers, directors, executives, and financiers from top Hollywood companies are all there. If you opt for the VIP Pass ($695) you also get access to all the film screenings, parties (in 2000 at the rocking Sunset Room), the Hollywood Internet Awards, and the prestigious Hollywood Movie Awards Gala Ceremony at the Beverly Hilton Hotel. At the 2000 Awards, VIP attendees dined in the same ballroom as these Hollywood names: Anne Archer, Halle Berry, Jeff Bridges, Russell Crowe, Richard and Lauren Donner, Richard Dreyfuss, Hector Elizondo, Frances Fisher, Morgan Freeman, Ray Liotta, Kenny Loggins (who performed), Michael Mann, Kelly Preston, Lynn Redgrave, John Travolta, James Woods, and many others.

I helped get the first conference started and have been the emcee at the Hollywood Pitch Fest the past couple of years. Here's a sample of one person from each of the panels I had time to watch: story analyst Andy Dobay from Warner Brothers, who teaches a class for UCLA Extension; Teddy Zee, President of Davis Entertainment; agent Neal Stevens of Neal Stevens & Associates (who teaches at USC); producer Mace Neufeld;

Kevin Wendle, CEO of iFilm and cofounder of CNet; Trevor Macy, COO of Propaganda Films; Steve Nemeth, head of production at Rhino Films; Paul Speaker of The Shooting Gallery in New York; and Barbara Mandel of the Motion Picture Literary Department at ICM. One of the many companies represented at the Pitchmart was Sean Connery's company, Fountainbridge, with Lynette Ramirez representing the Sony-based prodco.

When Carlos de Abreu was contemplating where to hold the first festival, he asked me where he should hold it. I suggested the Roosevelt because of its Hollywood tradition (the first Academy Awards were held in its Blossom Room), and because I thought Hollywood would welcome the festival with open arms, which it has done. Since that first year, Hollywood has undergone major renovations, with the new Academy of Motion Pictures Arts & Sciences complex almost completed across Hollywood Boulevard. It won't be long before the Hollywood of reality matches the Hollywood of people's imagination.

In 2000, the Best Digital Film winner, *The Poor & Hungry*, was one of the best films I've seen in a decade, made for $20,000 total. I saw it at Paramount Studios, which was the main venue for festival screenings. (See www.hollywooddigital.com.)

All in all, it's a marvelous week and well worth the money. Contact:

HOLLYWOOD FILM FESTIVAL

433 N. Camden Drive, Suite 600, Beverly Hills, CA 90210
310-288-1882, Fax: 310-475-0193
E-mail: awards@hollywoodawards.com
Web site: www.hollywoodconference.com/conference

Online Class from Industry Veterans

David W. Hagan has more produced, released, consulting, and ghostwriting credits than any other guru I've found. Those listed on his Web site include: *Miss Congeniality*, *What Women Want*, *The Grinch Who Stole Christmas*, *Meet the Parents*, *Gone in 60 Seconds*, *Austin Powers: The Spy Who Shagged Me*, *Armegeddon*, and *Ransom*. Amazingly, he only charges $60.00 for a screenplay evaluation, and $80.00 for rush service (within 24 hours) plus courier or mail charges. The company's Professional Writer's Workshop was begun in 1998 by David W. Hagan and David C. Calloway, both of whom are professional screenwriters and literary consultants with 20 years' experience.

They offer a number of courses and give a free copy of Michael Hauge's book *Writing Screenplays That Sell* to students. Hagan contends that if you make a list of your favorite films, *all* of them will have the elements of screenwriting that you will learn in The Creative Writing Course and The Screenwriting Basics Course. Contact:

HOLLYWOOD SCREENPLAY CONSULTANTS

17216 Saticoy Street #303, Van Nuys, CA 91406
E-mail: Dhagan1393@aol.com
Web site: www.SwiftSite.com/Cine-Vision2000

MY FIRST SCREENWRITING MENTOR

The first book I ever read on screenwriting must have been effective. I sold the first script I wrote (for a science-fiction radio series), and my first movie "treatment" garnered the admiration of Richard Donner, Robert Redford, and Michael Douglas. My next treatment was optioned for a feature film. The book was *Magic Methods of Screenwriting: A Practical Handbook of TV and Movie Scriptwriting* by Donna Lee, who founded the Hollywood Scriptwriting Institute in 1976.

Lee advises writers to create stories they really believe in—tales that move and inspire them—but she also says writers should spend part of their writing time being crassly commercial. When she put up a Web site, Lee added a monthly screenplay contest. The winning script is sent to a literary agent who sold a script for $400,000 in 2000, to be submitted to an appropriate producer. The winner also receives a one-year subscription to Creative ScreenWriting magazine. The entry fee is $50.00. Lee also offers a bonus: when you complete a script using the guidelines and assignments in her textbook, she is so confident you'll have a good script that she will personally submit it to a recognized Hollywood literary agent, at no charge. She also administers a correspondence course, which can be completed in 12 lessons, and submission of the completed script to an agent. Contact Donna Lee at:

HOLLYWOOD SCRIPTWRITING INSTITUTE

1605 Cahuenga Boulevard, Suite 216, Hollywood, CA 90028-6201
1-800-SCRIPTS (1-800-727-4787)
E-mail: info@moviewriting.com
Web site: www.moviewriting.com

THE FULL PERSPECTIVE—A CHAT WITH LEW HUNTER

Director Richard Donner called *Lew Hunter's Screenwriting 434* (Perigee) "the final word on screenwriting." Julius Epstein, the screenwriter of a little film called *Casablanca*, said, "To young, aspiring screenwriters: If it is not possible for you to enroll in Professor Hunter's class at UCLA, then immerse yourself in his book. It can be the quickest, surest path to a screenwriting career." TV producer and billionaire Aaron Spelling said, "If you want to learn about screenwriting, this is the book for you."

Hunter's book has sold better than any other screenwriting book. The funny thing is, he didn't want to write a book until someone suggested that he simply put his graduate course in book form. Hunter was a TV and film executive before he began screenwriting. His first screenplay, *If Tomorrow Comes*, appeared on Disney in 1971. It was a reworking of *Romeo & Juliet*. He overlaid the Capulets and Montagues, with whites and Japanese. His *Fallen Angel*, about child pornography, was the highest-rated TV movie of 1980 and won a Writers Guild award. Then he got a teaching offer.

"In 1979, Bill Froug called me. He was chair of the screenwriting department at UCLA and had a really fine career. He wrote for the original *Gunsmoke* on radio and was a producer and writer on *Playhouse 90*, and also wrote and produced on the original *Twilight Zone*. He and Rod Serling were very good friends. I taught for the first quarter and I liked it so much I went in to the man who was then chair of the department, John Young, and I said 'John, this is so wonderful, I hope I get invited back.'"

After becoming the cochair of the UCLA screenwriting department with Richard Walter, Hunter became "sort of the designer Godfather" of screenwriting programs. He helped design the European Conservatory for Screenwriting based at the Sorbonne and began teaching all over the world at places like Equinoxe, which is the European equivalent of the Sundance Film Festival. All the while, he continued making money as a screenwriter, but found it very exciting to be part of a program that turned out writers who wrote films like *River's Edge*, *Backdraft*, *Highlander*, and *Forrest Gump*, while other graduates were the showrunners (writers and producers) on TV shows like *Cheers* and *L.A. Law*.

In regard to talent, Hunter says, "I can tell you about craft. I can encourage you, and that's predominantly what a teacher can do. I can't make you be any better in terms of the talent aspect than what you came into that room with. But in terms of craft, specifically in motion pictures there is so much craft involved that the quicker you can understand it and assimilate it, and the further you learn the rules, the quicker you can either break or bend. It's funny, even the most experimental pieces have the Aristotelian beginning, middle, and end. *Smoke* has a very clear structure, but on the surface of it, it seems like it's a bit formless, you know. *Forrest Gump* was more of a traditional structure. It all has to do with the oral tradition of storytelling, and storytelling has a beginning, middle, and end.

"The very successful screenwriters have what I call 'the burn.' They all have an obsession to write. Writers write. All are writing, writing. They've all worked at it and they're not off drinking cappuccino at Hugo's (a popular west side L.A. eatery).

"The most common mistake I find that screenwriters make is to start before the story begins. I always think that you start on a event, or start, as Egri says, with 'rising conflict.' But they'll give you about 10 or 15 pages or scenes that happen before the story begins. Another error they make is that they're simply not being aware of the 'beginning, middle, and end' process, and they'll take too long. That ties in to what I just said. I really feel that you pretty well know what the movie's about on page 17. Around then, you have an idea that E.T. wants to go home, or that Butch says to Sundance, 'What about Bolivia?' You know on page 17. That's exactly the time when Humphrey Bogart slips the envelope in Dooley Wilson's piano (in *Casablanca*). On page 17 of *Citizen Kane*, you see this man, the William Randolph Hearst parallel.

"All seminal motion pictures are really based not only on Aristotle, but are tied into Joseph Campbell's *The Hero with a Thousand Faces*, where in the first act, the hero hears the calls to adventure and in the middle of the movie——the middle of the story,

the middle of the legend—the hero accepts the call to adventure, which means the protagonist in the middle of the piece decides to stop reacting and become actively involved in the story. He or she may have that forced upon them, sort of like Humphrey
Bogart has the decision forced upon him whether he will or won't help Elsa get out of
the country, but still they will then take an active part. The first half is reactive and the
second half is active. The third act is not necessarily so stringent in terms of middle. I
generally say it's anywhere from page 60 or 65 to 100 or 110 where the third act begins. It can be a rather short third act or it can be a longer third act.

"I asked Billy Wilder, who spoke to my class, to tell me about third acts. When I first
came to Hollywood and would run into Billy, I kept saying, 'How are you doing?' He'd
say, 'I can't find the third act, I can't get a third act, I can't get the third act.' People
don't say that too much any more, so when he came to my class I said, 'Tell me what
you think about a third act.' And Billy says, 'Well, if you don't have a third act, you do
not have a movie.'

"Yet most people get in trouble in the second act, in the confrontations, in the cause-
and-effects, the plot and things. They've got the first act pretty well done, if not great.
Your ending generally works fairly well, if not great, but it's that middle where we say,
'Oh, gee, I don't know whether this script is going to work or not.' Steven Spielberg
one time said, 'You know, we loved Diane Thomas (writer of *Romancing the Stone*) so
much because she would always say, "You don't like it? Let me fix it. It's the second
act. Let me fix it.'

"I think that as a writer you have to really deal with that second act, because it's the
most time-consuming. There's another reason, too. You want it simple because it's such
a short period of time. The 110-page scripts and the movies are so short. They're not
like books, where you can put them down and come back to them again. That train is
on that track and it's going all the way to the conclusion, and all of a sudden, holy cow!
You've still got a whole bunch of story left to tell, and I'm sitting here on page 110 and
I'm not even close to being done. In all the seminal pictures we've seen, they are not
complicated. You can go to the bathroom and come back and Rick is still trying to figure out what to do with the letters of transit, E.T. is still trying to get home, Butch and
Sundance are still trying to get to a life and a land that were simpler back in the days
when they were starting out as outlaws. The *El Norte* woman is still trying to go El
Norte, and with *Citizen Kane*, we're still trying to find out what Rosebud's about. The
simplicity of it all really represents power."

In addition to urging screenwriters to be in the game for the long run, Hunter insists
that they study in supportive workshops or groups.

"My own success as a writer would have come five years earlier if I hadn't been so
intimidated by the students at the time who told me I was a shitty writer," he told me.
"Students were so hostile and angry back then. If you called yourself a writer, they'd
say 'You're just an asshole, why don't you go back to the farm?' I was just blown away.
We do not have that at UCLA at all. We did have it when I started, but we don't have it

any more. Back then, the students were somehow encouraged to be openly adversarial to each other's material instead of collegial. It was just terrible."

For anyone studying screenwriting in a graduate program, Lew Hunter advises against making it their entire major. He felt that to do so would not provide enough of an educational background. For example, his student John Sweet's script *L'affaire du Collier (The Affair of the Necklace)* came from a real-life event. Had Sweet known little of the French Revolution, the script might never have been written.

"If I had it to do all over again, I would definitely go to NYU or UCLA." he told me. "At UCLA there's more of an emphasis on graduate screenwriting. At USC and NYU, it's more on the undergraduates because that's where the money is, the cash cow. I would encourage undergraduates to major in English, history, or a combination thereof rather than majoring in screenwriting. Most people under the age of 22 simply don't have the life experience to give you that kind of dimension that you can pick up on reading the first two pages of a great script. With UCLA grads, you can pick up an adult human being with life experiences, with knowledge of the human spirit that is really good, on the first page."

Lew Hunter structured his book, *Screenwriting 434*, like a script. It's not written in screenplay format, but the feeling is as though you are in a screenplay, from the FADE IN at the beginning to the FADE OUT at the end. He starts with getting the idea, then tells you how to refine it and fully describe your story in his "Two Minute Movie" exercise, which is guaranteed to change the way you go about writing scripts. Next is how to build characters, followed by the difference between writing an outline meant for you, the writer, and an outline meant for others to see. Then Hunter has a chapter for each of the three acts, and the last chapter is all about rewriting, a skill which all writers have to learn before they become successful. Here's an example:

"Don't risk damaging the fragility of your writer's id until you've written four to six scripts. Premature exposure to the world can be very hard on the heart in your chest or palm if you've got but one or two drafts in the marketplace. Four to six scripts diffuse the potential pain, so a single rejection isn't as devastating. You just know one of the others will strike fire. Also, the experience of writing 400 to 600 pages strengthens your confidence."

Although Lew Hunter may no longer cochair the UCLA program, the results of his work will be seen for decades to come, via the screenplays written by his students and the screenwriting programs all over the world he has helped. For details about his Superior Screenwriting Workshop, see LewHunter.com or screenwriting434.com.

THE LAST WORD: BE PATIENT

If you learn anything in preparing yourself for a career in Tinseltown, learn patience. You'll need it. I've observed that a high percentage of "overnight successes" take around 15 years. Very successful screenwriter Terry Rossio once said that he stopped being anxious about making it when he realized that just about anyone seriously dedicated to their profession made it within a decade.

All the people and places mentioned in this chapter come from my own personal experience. In times past, I would do the best research possible and report my opinions to my readers. Since finding someone to mentor you toward a deeply-cherished dream can be so personal to my readers, I tried to be more comprehensive with this edition.

Remember this: Just as there are definite shortcuts to writing a good screenplay, oftentimes as much work is put into selling script as went into writing it. And once it's bought, the work *really* begins. The key to Hollywood success is in finding someone who will share your vision and do whatever it takes to help you bring it to the world.

It's a people business, no matter what anyone tells you. When you reach your success, try to remember the Hollywood industry maxim of "giving back." You'll find that practiced by many more people than you would expect.

The Hollywood Library:
How to Research Tinseltown

There really is a Hollywood library, and I've been there many times, but that's the real world. This chapter is about digging the information you need out of a mythical place. Once you're ready to market a screenplay, you need to pay close attention to the periodicals that are read regularly by people working in the business and the books written by industry veterans that purport to hand you the keys to the kingdom. Hollywood is now a state of mind with no fixed country, and this "world film" attitude keeps getting stronger. First and foremost, Hollywood is about business. When you realize that box office revenue generally comes first, the whole environment starts making sense. Hollywood is a game of putting entertainment onto plastic, celluloid, and videotape in the most exciting manner possible, to get more people participating so as to make more money than the competitor. Those who succeed at this game have the most influence, own the biggest houses, and drive the nicest cars. Unless you're determined to write only what you want to write, no matter what anyone thinks about it, no matter how much or how little commercial potential it might have, you would probably be wise to keep up with everyday changes in the industry.

Times and tastes change, but the same story themes keep working. Just as Joseph Campbell noticed that the same monomyth kept getting told in religions and cultures around the world, in Hollywood, no matter what stories are being told, the dominant theme at the studios will probably always be "box office receipts." Keeping up with the publications of Hollywood (the worldwide version) will keep you plugged in to the people and properties that are causing the money to flow.

YOU MUST KNOW WHAT'S GOING ON IN HOLLYWOOD

To succeed as a screenwriter, it helps to keep up with what is going on in the world. To succeed in the business of Hollywood, you need to keep up with what's going on in Hollywood. If you want to write commercial scripts, write them with major stars in mind. It's not hard to know who the major stars are, but you should also keep track of who the rising stars are, such as TV stars who have not yet done a feature film. Let's say you've written a wild comedy script and you want Jim Carrey to star or Jay Roach to direct. The problem is, every comedy screenwriter and every working producer in Hollywood has the same idea. Once again in 2000, Carrey was the number-one comedic actor in the world, and Jay Roach gets offer after offer. It wasn't always that way for Mr. Rubber Face or the director of *Meet the Parents*. Carrey's first big break was in a long-forgotten TV situation comedy called *The Duck Factory* but few people remember that now. Jay Roach, via a mutual friend, read one of my scripts and liked it just before he launched into the stratosphere, successwise. Now I doubt I could get through to him. Find an up-and-coming Jim Carrey or Jay Roach, and you might be on your way. Unless you live in Los Angeles and regularly keep up with "the biz," you'd never know who those people might be.

Sometimes it's not difficult to gain access to people who will become major film stars. If you can honestly tell them "I wrote this with you in mind," and get to them in person at an event or (better) through a friend, they might help you get your project off the ground. Remember, though, A-list actors get money offers all the time. B-list actors can rarely get a film funded.

If your script gets some "heat" (word about it gets around town), and you are invited to have a meeting with a producer, director, or owner of a production company, the first question you might be asked is: "So who do you see starring in this?" This means you should write your script with "A-list" stars in mind, and have another, less expensive possible star list as well. To find out who these people might be——and not just the ones starring at the local cineplex——you need to read the publications called "the trades" (*Daily Variety* and the *Hollywood Reporter*). No matter where you live in the world, you can access both these publications in full on the Web. Some of the content is free, but the really important information costs money. Remember, you're trying to sell a screenplay for a Writers Guild minimum of around $30,000. If an A-list actor, director or producer gets involved, you can multiply that figure by a factor of 10. Is that worth a small investment? Here's a short description of Hollywood's major publications.

"I Read it in the Trades"

The Hollywood Reporter

Publisher Robert Dowling made the *Hollywood Reporter* Web site a fantastic resource for anyone wanting to keep up with Hollywood by initiating instant Web updates from reporters around the world. He came to his job after *Billboard* bought the *Reporter* in April 1988. His publishing background involved major sports and media promotions and several years at a high-tech magazine. He feels the trades offer Hollywood neophytes an intense education.

"They're essential," he told me in an interview. "If you come to town cold, the trades will tell you off the bat who the players are. For example, we are always talking about what scripts are bought, who's attached to what, who's changing jobs, who the players are on the field. At the *Reporter*, we cover Hollywood news in a very extensive manner. Our Special Issues department gives you a rundown of all films in production. Our Literary Hollywood covers scripts bought. We do a breakdown of the films produced in any given year, the shows going on TV, etc. If you're a novice to the business, you can learn the business. If you're already in the business, you'll keep yourself current."

When Dowling came to the *Reporter*, its reporting was generally not on a par with that of its competitor, *Daily Variety*. Now Dowling feels that they have surpassed *Daily Variety*, and he isn't afraid to say so.

"I've said to people in editorial that news is like an ante in a poker game. You have to have it to get in the game, but nobody applauds when you do. If you don't have it, you don't play. We now have as many exclusives as *Variety*, and our service areas, the chart information, results, and analysis far exceed *Variety*. We cover everything about movies in media, where the $3 billion spent by the studios goes. We have Oscar screening guides for people who are screening films under Oscar consideration. Our Literary Hollywood capsulizes everything bought in the last 30 days. If you want to know about the 6,500 films in the production charts, pre, pro, or post, we'll tell you. Our special issues cover pilot charts, network show pickups, women in entertainment, and some things *Variety* does not do. Our end-of-the-year value is considerably more."

Dowling had a reason for being so aggressive with the *Reporter*'s Web presence. "I believe that this is an information-driven business," he opined. "The key to information is speed. I want the *Reporter* to be thought of as *the* source of information on the entertainment community. Being on the Internet gives me a chance to put daily information out everywhere in the world instantly. We'll print each issue by 11:00 or 12:00 at night. Europe will have it at 8:00 in the morning on the Net, their time, before Los Angeles goes to bed. If news takes place at 9:00 in the morning, we will have a paragraph on the Net about that very quickly. That means that I'm giving people the one thing they want and I have: news. Tomorrow that information is worth a lot less. After every story each month, subscribers have the ability to get the full story. I am now an instantaneous publisher of entertainment information. The Hollywood Hyperlink on our Web site links the user to hundreds of sites. You don't have to remember anyone's Web address. I want people, when they think about Hollywood, to go to the *Reporter*."

The *Reporter*'s weekly International Edition covers film "festivals, markets, location surveys, deals, and dealmakers." The *Reporter* publishes over 100 special issues each year on subjects like their 12-part New Media Series, Independent Producers and Distributors, Women in Entertainment, Animation, Finance, etc. Both the print and Web editions of the *Reporter* offer weekly listings of all U.S. movies in production around the world. The special industry event issues such as those on the American Film Market and the Cannes Film Festival list all the movies available for sale to theaters. If you're not a film distributor, you might think this doesn't apply to you, but many of the production companies in these issues are independent filmmakers who buy scripts from new writers and you'll find personnel, addresses, phone numbers, and other information listed.

Subscribers of The Hollywood Reporter Online premium service get a lot of great extras, like the searchable archives, the Star Power listings to tell you who's hot (and one for directors), and Script Sales. For the latest prices, contact:

THE HOLLYWOOD REPORTER

5055 Wilshire Boulevard, 6th Floor, Los Angeles, CA 90036-4396
323-525-2000, Editorial fax: 323-525-2377
Web site: www.hollywoodreporter.com

Variety

Variety bills itself as "the daily newspaper of the entertainment industry." *Daily Variety*'s listed circulation is almost 30,000. It is published Monday through Friday, and there is also a weekly version. While the *Reporter* is an 8.5 x 11-page format, *Variety* is a larger and slicker tabloid size. Their special issues are comprehensive and far-reaching, and there's a bit more of a fun feel to them than the *Reporter*. They've also made great strides with their Web site in recent years, although the pop-up ads drive me nuts. A *Variety* online subscription is now $59 per year. You can't read much on the site but the articles are sometimes free at Yahoo! I particularly like *Variety*'s "Ten to Watch" Web site feature, which tells you 10 actors, directors, Euro directors, comics, screenwriters, and other rising stars to follow. They also feature photos of people on the Web site, which the *Reporter* does not. If you are in town and think you might have occasion to spot a hot producer around town, chances are good you can find out what she looks like from this Web site.

During the 2000 winter holidays, *Variety* let anyone be an online subscriber for free—handy for anyone planning a post–New Year marketing blitz. For the latest prices and information, contact:

VARIETY

5700 Wilshire Boulevard, Suite 120, Los Angeles, CA 90036
323-857-6600, Editorial fax: 323-857-0742
Web site: www.variety.com

OTHER MAJOR PUBLICATIONS

Academy Players Directory

Should you be serious about trying to make a film of your script, and want to know where to find the top stars and other actors, you might want to peruse the *Academy Players Directory*, published by the Academy of Motion Picture Arts & Sciences. It contains pictures and pertinent information on all the actors in the actors' unions. If you're on a budget, don't buy the books new. Three months after initial publication, the price goes down. In fact, the price drops every three months. The *Academy Players Directory* is published three times a year: January, May, and September. Each set is divided into four parts: (I) female Academy award nominees and winners, leading women, and ingenues; (II) male Academy award nominees and winners, leading men, and younger leading men; (III) character actors—comediennes and comedians; and (IV) stunt performers (women and men), children, and a Master Index. Actors wishing to be included in the *Directory* pay $75 per year. For information on prices and ordering, contact:

ACADEMY OF MOTION PICTURE ARTS AND SCIENCES

Academy Players Directory
8949 Wilshire Boulevard, Beverly Hills, CA 90211
310-247-3058
Web site: www.oscars.org (you can sign up for the online
    version as well.)

American Cinematographer

This magazine has been around since 1928, and there is none better if you want to know how great directors of photography get the looks they do in feature films you love. They now offer a six-month only subscription (as well as longer ones) so you can try it and see what you think. Contact:

AMERICAN CINEMATOGRAPHER

P.O. Box 2230, Hollywood, CA 90078
323-969-4333, Fax: 323-882-6391
Web site: www.cinematographer.com

BackStage West

Once upon a time there was a great little theater magazine in Los Angeles called *DramaLogue* where new writers could meet with other industry rookies. *DramaLogue* was bought out by *BackStage West*, the West Coast version of *BackStage*, both subsidiaries of BPI Communications like *the Hollywood Reporter*. If you're also a playwright, the mag is great. Contact:

BACKSTAGE WEST

5055 Wilshire Boulevard, Los Angeles, CA 90036
800-458-7541, Fax: 323-525-2226
Web site: www.backstage.com (you'll have to look for the
    West Coast items)

Black Talent News

Covering subjects of interest to African Americans in show business, this mag is also a networking tool and offers a free weekly e-mail newsletter. It features interviews with prominent African American entertainers, articles about issues, and film and television production charts. Published and edited by Tanya Kersey–Henley, it's available at bookstores and newsstands around the country, or you can contact:

BLACK TALENT NEWS LLC

1620 Centinela Avenue, Suite 204, Inglewood, CA 90302
310-348-3944, Fax: 310-348-3949
E-mail: info@blacktalentnews.com
Web site: www.blacktalentnews.com

Breakdown Services

Actors in major U.S. cities and Vancouver, Canada, are familiar with the Breakdown Services, which distributes information about films and TV show casting. Every casting director receives it. I met owner Gary Marsh years ago and was tickled to discover that he played the boy at the end of the movie *Camelot* whom Richard Harris as King Arthur exhorts to "Run, boy, run!" For what it's worth, many later successful writers have worked there writing the breakdowns of projects. In the April 2000 issue of *Written By*, Lynn Kadish recalls that "Just about every project that is being produced, from feature films to epic miniseries to half-hour comedies, comes through Breakdown and is read by the writers." If you need the service, or if you simply want a job, contact:

BREAKDOWN SERVICES, LTD.

310-276-9166
E-mail: gamarsh@ix.netcom.com
Web site: www.breakdownservices.com

Broadcasting & Cable

Variety is published by Cahners Publishing Company, which produces several other publications including *Broadcasting & Cable*, which covers broadcast and cable television, radio, satellite, and interactive television. Now a part of a large Web site called TVInsite, this is the magazine to read if you want to follow the television industry.

BROADCASTING & CABLE

Cahners Business Information
275 Washington Street, Newton, MA 02458
Subscription 800-554-5729
Web site: www.tvinsite.com/broadcastingcable

The Daily News

When reporter Jesse Hiestand contacted me about an article on aspiring screenwriters mid-2000, I knew the *Daily News* was getting more serious about entertainment biz reporting. I've enjoyed their *L.A. Life* section for a long time. The Daily News advertises itself as "California's best community newspaper." Contact:

DAILY NEWS

21221 Oxnard Street, Woodland Hills, CA 91367
818-713-3000
E-mail: subscribe@dailynews.com
Web site: www.dailynews.com.

Los Angeles Times

Though the *Daily News* keeps getting better, the main newspaper for Hollywood movers and shakers is the *Times*. Probably everyone in showbiz reads the "Calendar" section of the *Times*, even if only in the Sunday paper. People often talk about what they read in the *Times* on an equal par with "trades" information, and the daily edition is still only 25¢ per copy. Contact:

LOS ANGELES TIMES

P.O. Box 60164, Los Angeles, CA 90060-0164
800-252-9141
E-mail: customer.service@latimes.com
Web site: www.latimes.com

Written By

You don't have to be a Writers Guild member to subscribe to "the magazine of America's Storytellers." The official publication of the WGAw, there's no better magazine for screenwriters. Each month, you can log onto www.wga.org and read many articles for free, but the full magazine is better. To subscribe, contact:

WRITTEN BY

Writers Guild of America, west
7000 W. Third Street, Los Angeles, CA 90048
888-WRITNBY (974-8629)
E-mail: writtenby@wga.org

OTHER SCREENWRITING MAGAZINES AND DIRECTORIES

Canadian Screenwriter

Published on a quarterly basis, this magazine will tell you everything you need to know about writing movies for "Hollywood North." In 2000, over 50 movies were shot in Toronto, if that gives you some idea of the massive production in Canada. Although it's available from the Writers Guild of Canada office and at selected bookstores across Canada, you can also read selected, abridged articles and columns from the magazine at www.ericshawn.com/screenwriting.html. Go online at www.writersguildofcanada .com/magazine/subscribe.html and fill out the fields on this form and print it out for mailing to subscribe. (Hey, it's Canada.) Or pay $20.00 per year ($16.00 student rate), cheque (Canadian spelling) or money order only to:

WRITERS GUILD OF CANADA

123 Edward Street, Suite 1225, Toronto, Ontario, M5G 1E2

Creative Screenwriting

Packed with great interviews, screenplay excerpts, script reviews, and feature articles, this one's published six times a year and costs $29.95. Paid subscribers receive a CD-ROM called WriteWare, which is a compilation of every major screenwriting software package available. Contact:

CREATIVE SCREENWRITING

Erik Bauer, Editor
6404 Hollywood Boulevard, Suite 415, Los Angeles, CA 90028
800-SCRN-WRT (727-6978) or 323-957-1405, Fax: 323-957-1406
E-mail: ErikPSC@aol.com
Web site: www.creativescreenwriting.com

DGA

Published bi-monthly, the magazine of the Directors Guild of America is "what directors read." More important to writers is their annual *DGA Directory of Members*. which goes out free to DGA members. The Directory contains listings for DGA members in all categories for $25.00. See www.dga.org/magazine/magazine_index.htm or contact:

DIRECTORS GUILD OF AMERICA

7920 Sunset Boulevard, Los Angeles, CA 90046
310-289-2000, Fax: 310-289-2029

Fade In

This is a decent magazine, if a bit pretentious ("The First Word in Film"). The editor tends to "diss" anyone she feels is remotely competitive like . . . er, this book. Advertising their annual agency directory, she says, "The most complete directory of Hollywood literary agents, managers, and entertainment lawyers. Sure, you could buy that 'other' directory but then you wouldn't know . . ." (and then lists a number of things about various agents that anyone could discover). In February 2000, she came up with a stunt to pass a script idea between 40 writers and have a completed script. I sent her the following e-mail: "In 1990 the Independent Writers of Southern California put on a 'many writers' scriptwriting marathon that lasted 48 hours. We got on Showtime with it and TV coverage as far away as West Germany. I ran the event at the same time I was putting on a convention for 2,000 people, so it was a bit hectic, and I mentioned it in my book." And you know, I never heard from Audrey Kelly. Contact:

FADE IN MAGAZINE

289 S. Robertson Boulevard, Suite 465, Beverly Hills, CA 90211
800-646-3896
E-mail: grannystone@earthlink.net
Web site: www.fadeinmag.com

Film & Video

This magazine is free and will give you a fine understanding of what goes into making movies, all over the world. I highly recommend it mainly because beginning screenwriters don't have an adequate idea about how difficult it can be to make a film or all the people involved. You can reach the editor, Carolyn Giardina, at cgiardina @kipi.com or contact:

FILM & VIDEO

701 Westchester Avenue, White Plains, NY 10604-3098
914-328-9157, Fax: 914-328-9093
Web site: www.filmandvideomagazine.com

Hollywood Scriptwriter

A newsletter for over a decade, this now glossy magazine has an "Annual Agency Survey" in August, which lists Writers Guild of America–approved agents who will accept submissions. Every new subscriber gets a free bonus pack, which includes information on queries, a sample release form (you're often asked to supply your own by production companies or agents), and "How to Write a Treatment." Their articles and interviews are top-notch, particularly those by Adrian Loudermilk and Bill Martell, and the reviews by Montgomery Burt. The "Markets For Your Work" listings tend to be repeated and not from top companies. Contact:

HOLLYWOOD SCRIPTWRITER

P.O. Box 10277, Burbank, CA 91510
818-845-5525, Fax: 818-709-7540, toll-free 866-HSWRITER
   (866-479-7483)
E-mail: editor@hollywoodscriptwriter.com
Web site: www.hollywoodscriptwriter.com

MovieMaker

A magazine for anyone enthusiastic about making films, I'd recommend this one to anyone. You'll find things like an article by Eric Nazarian, the founding director of the Graduate Screenwriting Program at USC, discussing the fundamentals of translating a work of literature into a screenplay. Contact:

MOVIEMAKER MAGAZINE

2265 Westwood Boulevard, #479 Los Angeles, CA 90064
310-234-9234, Fax: 310-234-9293
E-mail: webmaster@moviemaker.com
Web site: www.moviemaker.com

Pacific Coast Studio Directory

There are thousands of production companies listed in this book, albeit few actual contact names. A subscription also gets you a Wall Chart and Index & Supplement Book. Individual copies are $16.00 each, and they've added a Technicians section to the Web site with a place for writers. If you want to locate a film commission, take a look at www.studio–directory.com/filmcomm.htm. Otherwise, contact:

PACIFIC COAST STUDIO DIRECTORY

P.O. Box V, Pine Mountain, CA 93222-0022
661-242-2722, Fax: 661-242-2724
E-mail: sd@studio-directory.com
Web site: www.studio-directory.com

Point of View

If you want to be a producer, this is your magazine. In publication since 1990, and endorsed by the Producers Guild of America, this is an excellent bi-monthly publication. You'll learn about producing teams like Mel Gibson and Bruce Davey, and tons more. Surf over to www.empire-pov.com/info.html or contact:

EMPIRE PRODUCTION & PUBLISHING

9313 'A' Burton Way, Beverly Hills CA 90210-3605
310-777-8867, Fax: 310-777-0167

Scene4

If you're into theater as well as film, have a look at the "International Magazine of Contemporary Theatre and Film" at www.scene4.com. Edited by Arthur Meiselman and published by Danin Adler, it offers "short, little reviews of theatre and film from people with an opinion, like you!" You'll also find "personal notebooks logged by actors, directors, playwrights, screenwriter . . ." *Scene4* also publishes new plays and scripts, and plays and scripts with production history, "formatted according to each author's expressed style." If you're not on the Web, inquire about print possibilities at:

SCENE4 MAGAZINE

6920 Roosevelt Way NE, Suite 117, Seattle, WA 98115
206-361-3863

Scenario

One of the best magazines for screenwriters who want to learn how the top writers ply their craft, this quarterly publication offers complete scripts and conversations with the people who wrote them. Some examples from past issues: *Bowfinger* by Steve Martin, *Being John Malkovich* by Charlie Kaufman, and *Midnight Run* by George Gallo. Take a look at www.scenariomag.com/index_current.html for info or contact:

SCENARIO

3200 Tower Oaks Boulevard, Rockville, MD 20852
800-222-2654 weekdays, Fax: 301-984-3203

Screentalk

This magazine was begun online by Eric Lilleor, who recruited his writers from all over the world via e-mail and published in color in electronic Adobe pdf format. By the time he moved into print, he was able to get people like Tim Robbins on the cover simply because he truly had created "The International Voice of Screenwriting" that he advertised. I had an article in the initial print issue. Contact:

SCREENTALK

Kornvej 6, Give DK-7323, Denmark
Phone/Fax: 45-7670-1020
E-mail: editor-in-chief@screentalk.org,
Web site: www.screentalk.org

Scr(i)pt

I was puzzled when I first saw this magazine advertised as "The Screenwriter's Magazine" despite being published on the East Coast. I've grown to like it due to the great articles. Editor-in-Chief Shelly Mellott told me that the mag reaches over 60,000 screenwriters with each issue and the advertisers are loyal because the readers consistently respond to the advertising. In the past, their coverage of contests, festivals, and conferences was particularly good, and now they've expanded into online classes and other things. Contact:

SCR(I)PT

5638 Sweet Air Road, Baldwin, MD 21013
888-245-2229, Fax: 410-592-8062
E-mail: info@scriptmag.com
Web site: www.scriptmag.com

Videomaker

This is becoming my favorite magazine, and it's one I read avidly with each issue, but then I'm into making digital movies. If you're not, this one might not interest you. If you're undecided, the magazine puts on expositions in the U.S. Read some sample articles or find out about the expos at www.videomaker.com. You can subscribe online or by e-mailing sales@videomaker.com. They also offer a free monthly e-mail newsletter. Not on the Web? You can still get a free trial issue by contacting:

VIDEOMAKER MAGAZINE

P.O. Box 4591, Chico, CA 95927
800-284-3226, 530-891-8410, Fax: 530-891-8443

Zoetrope: All-Story

This magazine, started by writer/director/producer Francis Ford Coppola, is a great read if you like short stories. As noted on the site, "in the past it was common for a short story to be adapted into a successful film (*Psycho*, *Rear Window*, *High Noon*)." Coppola says he started the magazine to "form a bridge to storytellers at large, encouraging them to work in the natural format of a short story." That's the kind of thing I want to support. They also have a competition that might interest you. Subscribe on-line, or by mail or fax at:

ZOETROPE: ALL-STORY

1350 Avenue of the Americas, 24th Floor, New York, NY 10019
Fax: 212-708-0475
Web site: www.zoetrope-stories.com

NEWSLETTERS

Just about every major publication with a Web site now offers free newsletters. Some of them are only come-ons to get you to visit the site and eventually subscribe to the print or online publication. Other "delivered by the postman" kind, are mentioned below. Feel free to e-mail me if you know of any good ones I've omitted, or if you start one.

Auteur

A free filmmaker's newsletter delivered to you via e-mail. Subscribe by sending an e-mail to: auteur-request@iList.net with the word "subscribe" in the body or see www.tk-productions.com/auteur.

Cinezine

"A totally free weekly e-zine dedicated to delivering movie news, reviews, and interviews with an attitude," this one is sent to e-mailboxes every Monday in two sections, one with news (mostly funny gossip) and the other reviews of movies. See www.cinezine.com.

Entertainment Directory

You can subscribe to a free newsletter at www.edweb.com . Just about everything in the business is covered.

Film Threat

Billing itself as "Hollywood's Indie Voice," this weekly newsletter offers "brutally honest reviews," and more coverage on film festivals than you can eat (or read). See www.filmthreat.com.

Hollywood Lit Sales

Surf over to www.hollywoodlitsales.com and sign up for the great monthly e-mail put out by Howard Meibach. Here's a sample, about the types of movies the major studios planned to release in 2001: Action Adventure—26; Animated—8; Comedy—71; Romantic Comedy—16; Documentary—4; Drama—91; Fantasy—4; Musical—2; Romance—15; Sci-Fi/Horror—22; Suspense/Thriller—19; Westerns—3.

IfilmPro

Although this newsletter is structured to draw you to the site and sell you services, it's free and full of useful information on things like contests, copyright and registration, and selling and pitching. The job information is very good and so is the Hollywood Creative Directory Online's "Movers & Shakers," which tells you about executive moves within the industry. What's surprising is that they make it so tough to sign up. Surf to www.ifilmpro.com and click on "Join" at the bottom. You'll have to fill out some information, and at the bottom of the form is a little box already checked to send you the newsletter.

Inside Dope

No, it's not about the U.S. drug war. It's a free e-mail delivery from Inside magazine offering pertinent articles from the inside.com site and elsewhere, covering any or all of the following: books, digital, film, media, music, and television. It details the convergence of the various media, perhaps better than any other.

Media Professional

This free e-mail newsletter is always jammed with great information and some interesting jobs. Send a message to MediaProfl@aol.com. The body of the message should read: subscribe Firstname Lastname (your first and last name).

Now Playing

This free e-mail newsletter comes from wga.org, the official site of the Writers Guild of America, west. Sign up by visiting the Web site or send an e-mail from the e-mail address to which you want the newsletter delivered to: join–wga@laser.sparklist.com.

Reel, Tape & Ink News

Though it's published in Northern California, the information about Hollywood writing opportunities in this $25 per year monthly newsletter is always good. It has a section on markets, another on attorneys and managers in the news, and is jam-packed with information. It's particularly helpful to people new to screenwriting. Sample issues are available. For more information, contact the editor:

MARY C. VARLEY

P.O. Box 4331, Santa Rosa, CA 95402-4331
707-583-2064 ext. 1462
E-mail: reelmaryrti@icqmail.com

ShowBIZ Data Weekly Update

Every week a free e-mail gives me showbiz news, box office receipts, the top 10 movie openings for the year to date, the top five distributors to date, upcoming film releases, and new movie sites, among other things. To receive this newsletter, register with ShowBIZ Data at www.showbizdata.com/register.htm and be sure to click "yes" after the line that reads "I would also like to receive e-Mail." The job listings are free, but you can get the weekly Jobmail Newsletter at www.showbizdata.com/contacts/job-board.cfm?act=n. ShowBIZ Data is always doing something amazing.

Spec Script Marketplace

Writer Eva Peel put in 10 years at CBS before she wrote her first screenplay and learned that finding buyers was difficult even for working writers with good agents. She started *Spec Script Marketplace* to help, and it now offers two script-marketing services: a bi-monthly publication and live pitch sessions. The publication lists movie scripts available for sale by genre, in short synopses of 50 words or less. It is mailed every two months to 1300-plus movie buyers—producers, development executives, and studio executives. The cost to list one script for two months is $39. In four years it has produced close to 50 option contracts, and one of the projects has been produced. For more information call Eva Peel at 310-396-1662, fax her at 310-399-6196, or e-mail her at scriptmarketplace@compuserve.com. The address is P.O. Box 1365, Santa Monica, CA 90406 and the Web site is at www.scriptmarketplace.com.

Writers Store eZine

Offering articles from top industry pros, reviews of software and books, and other useful items, this newsletter is always interesting. They also post information about events for writers, like the annual Los Angeles Writers Conference put on by UCLA Extension Writers' Program. I write reviews for them, too. To subscribe, visit the site and enter your e-mail address. E-mail news@writersstore.com to contribute. And to reach them by phone, call 800-272-8927 from the U.S. or Canada. International callers should dial 310-441-5151.

My advice is to read, in print or online, everything you can about what it takes to get a script onscreen. Should you also read magazines like *Movieline, Entertainment Weekly, Premiere,* and other "showbiz" monthlies that are geared toward fans? Having served as an editor of a Los Angeles entertainment magazine (*Entertainment Weekly,* no relation to the current publication), I can safely say that none of these magazines will assist you much in getting ahead as a screenwriter. Why? Because any movie news in such magazines is old news with regard to what Hollywood is buying today.

BOOKS, BOOKS, BOOKS

Other than the books already mentioned in the chapter on gurus, there are many helpful books for screenwriters. The following list contains books that might meet your particular needs. I cover a lot more books in my *The Complete Idiot's Guide to Screenwriting*, and Hollywood history not covered in this book, but many of the ones below are some of my all-time Hollywood favorites.

500 Ways to Beat the Hollywood Script Reader: Writing the Screenplay the Reader Will Recommend by Jennifer M. Lerch

A Friend in the Business by Robert Massello (TV writing)

The Art of Dramatic Writing by Lajos Egri

Broadcast Writing: Principles and Practice by Roger L. Walters

Good Scripts, Bad Scripts by Thomas Pope

Hollywood's Latinos, Then and Now by Luis Reyes and Peter Rubie

Making a Good Writer Great: a Creativity Workbook for Screenwriters by Linda Seger

Screenwriting: The Art, Craft, and Business of Film and Television Writing by Richard Walter

The Script Is Finished, Now What Do I Do? by K. Callan

The Scriptwriter's Handbook by William Van Nostran

Scriptwriting for High-Impact Videos by John Morley

Shooting to Kill by indie producer Christine Vachon with David Edelstein

Story Sense by Paul Lucey

Television Writing: From Concept to Contract by Richard A. Blum

The Tools of Screenwriting: A Writer's Guide to the Craft and the Elements of a Screenplay by David Howard and Edward Mabley

The Understructure of Writing for Film and Television by Ben Brady and Lance Lee

Without Lying Down: Frances Marion and the Powerful Women of Early Hollywood by Cari Beauchamp

Writing for Television and Radio by Robert L. Hilliard

Writing for the Broadcast Media by Peter E. Mayeau

Writing for the Media: Film, Television, Video, and Radio by Martin Maloney and Paul Max Rubenstein

Writing Treatments That Sell: How to Create and Market Your Story Ideas to the Motion Picture and TV Industry by Kenneth Atchity and Chi-Li Wong

Once you've learned your craft, you might want to enter a contest or try to sell your work directly. Perhaps you want to know which stars have the most "clout," or you'd like to figure out which directors and/or stars to approach. The following references might help.

The Bare Facts Video Guide by Craig Hosoda

For details, see the Web site at www.barefacts.com. Some producers and directors use the book in casting decisions; if an actress says she has never done nudity, they'll look her up in the book to see if she's lying.

Director Power and *Star Power*

Publications by the *Hollywood Reporter* that include scores (perceived worth to a project) and alphabetical listings for more than 800 directors and more than 500 actors and actresses, respectively. For information on the survey and prices, contact:

THE HOLLYWOOD REPORTER

5055 Wilshire Boulevard, 6th Floor, Los Angeles, CA. 90036-4396
866-525-2150 (toll free, 9 A.M. to 5 P.M. PST)
E-mail: subscriptions@hollywoodreporter.com

Spec Screenplay Sales

Howard Meibach's first book was the *Spec Screenplay Sales Directory 1994–1997*, which covered over 300 spec script sales. The information is primarily as an online database now, the *Spec Screenplay Sales Directory Online* at www.hollywoodlitsales .com. It offers 10 years of searchable information updated daily. You'll find an address/phone list database of agencies, production companies, guilds, law firms, and organizations. Meibach has also added comments about many of the companies, particularly in the agency category. Contact:

HOLLYWOODLITSALES.COM, INC.

2118 Wilshire Boulevard, #934, Santa Monica, CA 90403
310-828-4946
E-mail: webmaster@hollywoodlitsales.com

The World's Biggest Book of Writing Contests by Terry Kyle

The world's largest reference book of writing contest and writing competition information in virtually all English-language countries across all writing genres, including screenwriting, playwriting, and writing for television. Only available in electronic form, which allows live hyperlinking to more than 700 sites across the Web from within the book. Full details at www.ult-media.com or e-mail ultimate@ult–media.com.

SCRIPT SOURCES

You can read all the books, magazines, and newsletters you want, but probably the best education you can get about screenplays is to *read as many great ones as you can find*. It's not always wise to settle for screenplays you can download on the Web. Some are transcriptions of the completed movie and don't give you the proper perspective on the screenplay that *sold* and convinced people to make the movie.

One good script reference is *Motion Picture Scripts: A Union List–1998 Edition*, a large paperback available from the Margaret Herrick Library of the Academy of Motion Pictures Arts & Sciences. It covers the script holdings from six Southern California libraries, over 25,000 scripts. The staff of the Margaret Herrick Library put the book together, which you can obtain by contacting: J. Giancoli at jgiancoli@oscars.org or calling 310-247-3000 ext. 185. You can also write:

A.M.P.A.S.

8949 Wilshire Boulevard, Beverly Hills, CA 90211
Web site: www.oscars.org/publications/other/index.html

If I want a script that I know I can count on for credibility, I have several other sources that I might use:

BOOK CITY

308 N. San Fernando Boulevard, Burbank, CA 91502
818-848-4417, Fax: 818-848-5615
E-mail: burbbookcity@earthlink.net

LARRY EDMUNDS BOOKSHOP

6644 Hollywood Boulevard, Hollywood, CA 90028
323-463-3273, Fax: 323-463-4245
E-mail: edmunds@artnet.net

SAMUEL FRENCH BOOKSHOP

7623 Sunset Boulevard, Hollywood, CA 90046,
323-876-0570, Fax: 323-876-6822
E-mail: samuelfrench@earthlink.net
www.samuelfrench.com

SCRIPT CITY

8033 Sunset Boulevard, Suite 1500, Los Angeles, CA 90046
818-764-4120, toll free in U.S. (orders only) 800-676-2522,
     Fax: 818-764-4132 (24 hours)
E-mail: dan@scriptcity.net

If you'd like to help other writers, check out the Harvest Moon Publishing "writer's edition" copies of film and television scripts, featuring biographical information and forewords by the writers. A portion of all royalties is donated to the Writers Guild Foundation. The scripts are marketed through leading bookstores and via:

HARVEST MOON

P.O. Box 3332, Santa Monica, CA 90408

323-461-6981 (Monday through Friday 10 A.M. to 5 P.M. PST),
    Fax: 310-868-2727. Voice orders can also be placed at any time,
    day or night, via fax.

E-mail: online@harvestmoon.com

Web site: www.harvestmoon.com

REACHING THE STARS

It's not advisable to simply mail your script unannounced to a star. Nine times out of 10, they won't read it, and they or their assistant might remember your unfamiliarity with Hollywood etiquette if you ever contact them again. If, however, you somehow get an actor of note to ask to read your script via your agent, you can then simply call an agent and say "Mel Gibson (or whomever) said he wants to see my script. Will you send it to him for me?" What do you think the answer will be? The agent will "hip-pocket" you and send the script over. You're doing the work, and if you scare up a deal, they'll close it for you and get at least enough extra money to pay for their commission.

Of the online databases, I've found that FilmTracker.com provides the best information on actors' production companies. If that doesn't work, you might be able to find an actor with a few phone calls. First, call the Screen Actors Guild at 323-954-1600. You'll get a recorded message with several choices. The one you want is "press 3." Then press 1 ("to contact a performer with an offer of work"), which puts you through to an operator who will give you the number of the performer's agent. (They'll only give you three actors' contact information in one phone call.) When you call the actor's representative, ask the name of the performer's production company and where it is located. If they don't have a production company, ask for their agent and give them your best pitch to read the script. You probably won't have much luck, but you might as well try.

If the SAG approach gives you no joy, try the Producers Guild at 323-960-2590 to locate an actor's production company. If you get a recording, it may say that they will call you back only if they have the answer to your question. If you get a live person, however, and they have a listing for an actor who is also a producer, they'll give you the number—so you might want to call the Producers Guild first.

Remember, actors who are "bankable" are getting financial offers all the time, but if you strike a personal nerve with a script, or if you simply have a great script that's perfect for an actor, you might get them interested, and be well on your way to production.

And don't assume that they're always busy. In June 2000, separate articles in the trades pointed out that George Clooney, Matt Damon, and Harrison Ford could not find projects that they thought were suitable. I've seen similar notices about top actresses. Bruce Willis' former development person once told me from the audience at a seminar I was giving that Willis got so frustrated about it, he finally instructed him to simply find him something where he had something cool to say! It really does all come down to the script.

THE INDUSTRY'S BEST LIBRARY

The best bet for researching just about any film industry information, whether you're in southern California or not, is the Margaret Herrick Library at the Academy of Motion Picture Arts and Sciences in Beverly Hills. Call them at 310-247-3020. Telephone reference hours are 9 A.M. to 3:00 P.M. Monday, Tuesday, Thursday, and Friday. Walk-in hours begin at 10:00 A.M. the same days. The Academy Library phone reference service is such a great source of information that everyone in the entertainment business uses it. For information on what's in the library, see www.oscars.org/cmps /mhl/index.html, but this isn't the Library of Congress and everything isn't online at the site.

WRITTEN ABOVE THE LIBRARY DOOR: TRUST YOUR INSTINCTS

All the sources of information mentioned in this chapter might help you in selling your screenplay, but it will ultimately come down to you. Can you anticipate what the public will want solely by what they've wanted in the past? If it were that simple, film executives would not continually make mistakes. All writers can do is to get as much education about the business as possible, wherever they can. In the end, however, you have to trust your instincts. Dean Devlin of *Independence Day* fame has said that if you try to second-guess the public, you're in trouble. Devlin believes in making a script that excites him. Tom Cruise picks films he wants to make if he thinks they're cool (his exact words). Director Richard Donner told me that the ultimate index of any film he makes is if he reads a script and wants to see the movie. Nora Ephron feels the same way.

Making movies is the most collaborative of all the arts. It will take a team of people to film your project, and that team will have a leader. The team leader could be you, but only if you are determined to be a filmmaker, not just a screenwriter. Once your script is done—written from the heart, market analysis, or all of the above—someone will have to love your script as passionately as you do to get it onto the screen. So do a lot of reading at the Hollywood library. Your education will be reflected in your words.

Working the Hollywood Web: You Can Get There from Here

Hollywood tries to be on the cutting edge of media technology. Surprisingly enough, it doesn't always make it. Every Web venture put up by Time-Warner in the past has turned into a dud. We'll see what happens now that America Online (AOL) is a part of that mix. Executives at many major companies are shockingly tech-ignorant, and major media companies are no exception. I saw a top exec for Warner Brothers recommend to an audience at the Hollywood Film Festival that everyone have at least a 56K modem. Oh, really? How prescient.

If you are not using e-mail or surfing the Web, this chapter will probably not help you. In my view as a professional writer, if you're not online, you're falling behind. These days, if a studio executive or movie producer does not have an e-mail address on his or her business card, it is the exception rather than the rule. So if you're not already cyber-savvy, screenwriter, get wired. When you start dealing with producers, directors, and agents, don't be surprised if they expect you to be plugged in. There's a lot of ground to cover in this chapter, and the geography of cyberspace changes by the nanosecond. If you find a Web address herein that doesn't work, you can reach me at skip_press@excite.com or skippress@earthlink.net. And I'd be happy to hear from you about any you think I should have included.

ONLINE SERVICES

Most people I know started their Web journeys by subscribing to an online service like AOL, CompuServe, Genie, and Prodigy. There are plenty of Hollywood people with AOL addresses, but they don't bother to fill out a Member Profile. When putting together the first edition of this book, I searched through the Member Directory with the keyword "producer" and found legitimate film and TV producers like Gale Ann Hurd and writer/director Dan Petrie Jr. (now vice president of the Writers Guild of America).

Also, by searching with the keywords "book publisher," I found editor Jennifer Basye Sander at Prima Publishing, the publisher of this book, and I had a contract to write it two weeks after we first communicated via e-mail.

The AOL Writers Club area is interesting if you want to chat, but don't expect to find someone there who will buy your script. One good thing AOL offers for nothing is a listing of sites related to screenwriting. Head over to www.aol.com and do a free search with the word "screenwriting"—you'll come up with almost 3,000 sites.

My first online experience was CompuServe, and I always found it more conservative and serious in tone than AOL. Although AOL bought CompuServe, it's still maintained as basically separate. The Screenwriting Forum on CompuServe was once cohosted by John Hill, the writer of *Quigley Down Under* and other films, but it seems to have fallen off in interest lately and I hear he's no longer there.

Basically, there are simply too many other places to interact with other writers these days, and the online services that started it all have little to offer to the technologically-savvy.

ONLINE MAILING LISTS

Perhaps the longest-running screenwriting list is the one maintained by Jack R. Stanley (Jacks@panam.edu), who is the Chair of the Communication Department at the University of Texas-Pan American in Edinburg, Texas. To Join the SCRNWRiT e-mail list, send a totally BLANK e-mail to SCRNWRiT@listserv.techrscs.panam.edu and put "sub scrnwrit" (without quotes) in the body of the message. First, though, you might want to browse through the Web site at www.panam.edu/scrnwrit/ and read the 16 chapters of information about the group. Stanley offers this admonition: "Beware; this is an active list. You'll get 50 or more messages a day—sometimes more."

If you're interested in mailing lists, you can search the archives of many lists at maelstrom.stjohns.edu/archives/index.html, but you probably won't find any on screenwriting. You have to find those in other ways.

NEWSGROUPS

There are several Usenet newsgroups that pertain to filmmaking and movies. You'll need a newsgroup reader to get to them. You can use one of the Netscape or Microsoft products if you want, but I prefer a stand-alone newsreader. I use Macs and Multi-threaded NewsWatcher by Simon Fraser, which is built on the NewsWatcher code by John Norstad. It has great multi-threading capabilities, which refers to the ability of the application to perform several concurrent tasks like downloading articles from several newsgroups simultaneously. You can find NewsWatcher and most other Web programs for Mac at www.macorchard.com.

The most popular Windows application for newsgroups seems to be Free Agent, which is freeware available in both 16-bit and 32-bit versions. You can configure Free Agent for online or offline operation. In offline mode, the program briefly connects to the server to retrieve article headers, then lets you browse them offline and mark the interesting ones, and then goes online to retrieve them. Like NewsWatcher, it does internal multi-tasking, allowing you to browse articles in one newsgroup while retrieving headers for another. Read all about it at www.forteinc.com/agent/freagent.htm.

My favorite newsgroup remains misc.writing.screenplays. Oh sure, you'll find threads there like "Skip Press is a Complete Idiot" and there are flames galore, but I often laugh out loud at posts there from industry pros and those who want to be. That's where I met Rich Wilson, who occasionally updates the Frequently Asked Questions (FAQs) for the group at www.communicator.com. M.W.S. is a lively group, not always civil, but almost always entertaining, and many of the people who regularly post are working writers in Hollywood. One caution I have is to spend some time reading what others have to say before throwing your two cents in. It's called "lurking." To check out the Frequently Asked Questions (FAQs) of any newsgroup, try www.faqs.org.

To keep a post from ever being archived on a newsgroup, use the following line at the top of the message body—x-no-archive: yes.

In the "do what I say, not what I do" department, here's this: Before you react and fire off a "flame" (angry e-mail), count to 10 before hitting send. If you're really mad, take Mark Twain's advice and swear instead of hitting send.

A Cornucopia of Resources

No one online service or newsgroup offers you, as a future Hollywood success story, anywhere near the resources you will find on the World Wide Web. There are a great many sites on the Web that provide useful research tools for screenwriting. If you want to find out what movies a director has done, search the Web with the director's name and you might find a fan page that someone has put together. At one time, directors and producers didn't bother putting together their own pages, but that's changed. Now some of the top directors, like Barry Levinson, have their own Web sites and tons of information about what they're doing. Just don't expect too many to answer your e-mails from their site.

If you want a free reference shortcut, check out the Writers Guild of America site at www.wga.org and click on "Research Links" on the left. The links are compiled by WGA member Craig Schiller, and he has done an amazing job.

Now here's another update of Web site resources I've found while surfing in cyberspace. I list the most major sites alphabetically, with an emphasis on those that can help you the most in your Hollywood journey. Then I describe others I like for various reasons.

THE 500-POUND GORILLAS

Ain't It Cool News

Harry Jay Knowles is a guy who in his own words once described what he covers as "scripts, casting, preproduction, production, postproduction, test screenings, marketing, and the release of the films." Running a Web site from his apartment in Austin, Texas, Harry somehow manages to get hordes of people sending him inside information on reactions to movie screenings and other things. His site at www.aint-it-cool-news.com influences studio executives, many of whom regularly check the site to see what's being said.

Baseline

In 2002, www.Baseline.Hollywood.com will be 20 years old. In short, they were providing film and television information before anyone. They now advertise "over 1.5 million database records on projects tracked from development to release, cast and crew credits, box office grosses, celebrity biographies, talent contact information, company directories, and industry news. All easily searchable online and updated daily."

Copyright and Registration Sites

At some point in a screenwriting career, you'll hear that you should register your script or film property with the Writers Guild of America. What you don't usually hear until you're a little further down the road, careerwise, is that when a property is purchased, attorneys look for the "chain of title" to see who owns the original copyright on the work you're selling. If you don't know how to copyright your work, federal copyright in the U.S. can be registered by going to www.loc.gov/copyright. You can register a script (or any other property, including files with pictures) at one of the electronic registration sites that have become prominent. I recommend www.protectrite .com and www.writesafe.com. Both are cheaper than U.S. Copyright or WGA registration, and immediate. Will electronic registration hold up in court? Decide for yourself by reading the FAQs at each site. And for United Kingdom registration, see www.creation-bank.com.

Creative Planet

From www.creativePLANET.com you can explore the entire Hollywood industry. I particularly enjoy the free communities for animators, cinematographers, digital film-makers, directors, editors, motion designers, postproduction people, and visual effects artists (with free e-mail newsletters). Their contact database, www.inhollywood.com at $29.95 a month, is exceptionally good and offers a free trial.

The Hollywood Network

You can meet a lot of top Hollywood people online, and post questions they will answer, at Carlos de Abreu's very successful Hollywood Network. You'll find it at www.hollywoodnetwork.com. As mentioned previously, de Abreu is now the proprietor of the Hollywood Film Festival. In 1989, he enrolled in UCLA's film school at night and was promptly told that because he had a foreign background he could not become a writer in America. Ever ambitious and a master of marketing, de Abreu saw a distinct need in Hollywood. People wanted to break into the film business, but few knew how, and not everyone could move to Los Angeles. The Internet, on the other hand, was usually only a local phone call away to anyone around the world. If the world could not come to Hollywood, de Abreu could take it to them. Here's how he did it:

"Our philosophy is: Bridge the gap between Hollywood and the talent out there. We started with the Christopher Columbus Discovery Awards to find new writers around the world because we have access to the entertainment industry, to producers, directors, and so on. We bridged the gap for people who are talented but don't have access to the real Hollywood, not the fringe Hollywood. New Line bought one of our scripts; an independent producer bought several of our scripts. Several of our writers have made money, from $500 up to $60,000, five- and six-figure contracts. We get over 1,000 screenplays a year.

"Then we established Custos Morum Publishers, to create books that once again tell the reader how to access Hollywood in a professional manner. *Opening the Doors to Hollywood* came out in March of 1995 and has sold over 10,000 copies. Meantime, the Internet/World Wide Web sort of became a buzz at the beginning of 1995. So we decided to go a step farther, to establish the Hollywood Network. It's the number-one independent industry [Hollywood entertainment business] site in the World Wide Web. We have the Hollywood Actors Network, the Hollywood Directors Network, the Hollywood Producers Network. We have the Internet Screenwriters Network. We have the Internet Crime Writing Network. We have the Hollywood Access Directory, with over 30,000 entries. We're providing entertainment, services, and products.

"We established a faculty of professionals in the Hollywood Network, dozens of professionals, from established producers to script consultants to entertainment attorneys. We established all this real talent in interactive areas where people from any area in the world can come and ask questions live in chat lounges from our professionals."

The Hollywood Network worked for me. By browsing over the Producers Needs bulletin board, I found Perfectly Round Productions of Wichita, Kansas and became a staff writer for their show *Algo's Factory*, broadcast on the United Paramount Network. It's great.

The Hollywood Reporter

I read the *Reporter* online at www.hollywoodreporter.com every day. You can't read the entire daily magazine there, but you'll find news briefs, which are updated throughout the day from around the globe. Martin Grove's "Filmmaker Focus," a look at current movies and their creators, is posted exclusively on the Web site. They've also added a message board open to all, and even information on Web site ratings. It remains the best "trade" site for screenwriters and filmmakers.

iFilm & iFilmPro

Kevin Wendle was a Silicon Valley entrepreneur before starting www.iFilm.com, which is geared to the film lover more than the professional. If you love to watch short films on the Web, iFilm is the place for you (its main competitor being www.atomfilms.com), but don't overlook all the links at the bottom of the page. iFilmPro, billing itself as "The Industry Desktop," is the one serious screenwriters want. iFilm made a lot of noise in Hollywood when they acquired existing Hollywood resources like FilmFinders, the Hollywood Creative Directory, and ScriptShark (a coverage site that got more initial national press than any similar service) to start iFilmPro. A lot of iFilmPro is free, and the job board is particularly good. They also have free e-mail newsletters and the Hollywood Creative Directory at www.hcdonline.com.

INSIDE

If you surf to www.inside.com and click on the Film tab, you'll find one of the hippest online sites available. Based in New York and supported by a print magazine (described in the publications chapter), the coverage available for free from this Web site instantly makes it a 500-pound gorilla. I see media dots connected by *Inside* that few others are put together.

Internet Movie Database

Here's the pitch from www.imdb.com: "the biggest, best, most award-winning movie site on the planet." Maybe, but who cares about any awards? It's the first place most people look when they want to find movie credits on someone. Their listings aren't perfect, but they're good enough. Check out the "Movie/TV News" tab at the top of the site; you'll be treated to several choices, including the Daily Studio Briefing, which is always good. The rest of the "news" is the same old celebrity crap. Since it's been owned by Amazon.com, the site has been more geared to the standard consumer, but it's free!

ShowBizDATA

Oliver Eberle started programming computers in elementary school, in Stuttgart, Germany. Later in life he teamed up with director Roland Emmerich and made a couple of forceful movies, *Universal Soldier* and *Stargate*. Thus the Web site he developed is one of the best for Hollywood information. You'll it find at www.showbizdata.com. Eberle is the only working producer who is also a whiz at computing that I've come across. He's become affiliated with the Sundance Film Festival, and also offers discounted *Hollywood Reporter* subscriptions if you pay to access the site. With top people like Marc Hernandez now onboard, it offers an excellent job board and other free resources.

Variety

Variety came a long way with its Web site in recent years. It took the company a long time to finally get www.variety.com online, and they had snafus like trademark infringement trouble over using a name for one area that was already in use by a well-established site. Just before press time, *Variety* lowered its online yearly subscription price to $59. *Variety* provides online pictures of people with stories, while the *Reporter* does not, but here's the catch: If you're not a subscriber you can't read the articles at all. Big mistake because you can find many of the same articles for free on sites like Excite and Yahoo under "entertainment."

WRITERS GUILD OF AMERICA SITES

Writers Guild of America, west

The Writers Guild of America (WGA), west site at www.wga.org is a work of art, not only for its beautiful, simple design, but also for content. You won't be able to access the "WGA Members Only" area, perhaps, but that will come if you learn your screenwriting craft. You can now join the prestigious Writers Guild of America with both interactive writing and Web writing credits. Need a mentor? Sign up on the site to work with a pro. Need an agent? See www.wga.org/agency.html for their Guild signatory agents and agencies listings. To qualify as a Guild signatory agency, they must promise the Guild not to charge any fee other than a commission to any writer. Agents all over the United States as well as foreign agents are listed. By the time you read this, www.wga.org may also offer online electronic registration of your work.

Writers Guild of America, East

In case you didn't know, in 1997, the Writers Guild of America almost split into West and East factions over a disagreement. The crisis was averted, but the separate entities have different Web sites. You'll find the East site at www.wgaeast.org. I've always appreciated WGAE's Online Script Registration Service at wgareg.org/online.htm. The site also has a friendly feel and better sense of humor than the WGAw site, and a whole section for new writers that is excellent. Like the WGAw, they offer a free newsletter (bimonthly), only this one comes as a pdf (Adobe) document or in html (Web) format, not the e-mail of their western counterpart. Their Web links (the "Other Resources" tab on the opening page) have a lot more links to other unions. You'll also find their publication *On Writing* here.

OTHER AWESOME LINKS

In the last edition, I said you could never sleep, browsing the Web. It's gotten worse, as the sites listed below illustrate.

Absolute Screenplay—A bulletin board for aspiring screenwriters. All advice is free at www.thechronicles.com/absolute_screenplay.html.

Allexperts Writing Plays/Screenwriting Q&A—The oldest free Q&A service on the Net at www.allexperts.com/getExpert.asp?Category=677.

All-Movie Guide—At allmovie.com is sort of a compact version of imdb.com. You can also access allmusic.com and allgame.com from here. I like the "Worked With" you get with a search for someone's name.

AtomFilms: Get Into Our Shorts—If you want to get yourself known by making short films, www.atomfilms.com is the place to start.

Baretta—If you liked this old TV show like I did, check out www.jcn1.com /hose/Baretta.htm; you'll be amazed.

BlackScreenplays—A resource site on writing screenplays about the African American community at (you guessed) www.blackscreenplays.com.

Books 'n Stuff from Skip Press—After getting complaints over the many Web addresses in my e-mail "signature," I became the "Duke of URL" just to thumb my nose at the critics. I now have my own site at www.home.earthlink.net /~skippress with a news page.

BookWire—If you want to keep up with the book world, head over to www.bookwire.com, the 500-pound gorilla publishing site.

Terry Borst and Deborah Todd—At www.altscreen.cjb.net you'll find articles from the monthly interactive column of the WGA's *Written By*.

California Movie Maps—Want to know where certain scenes and movies were shot? gocalif.ca.gov/cgi-bin/cmm/moviescript will tell you.

Celebrities—For e-mail addresses, try www.thezone.pair.com/celeb. Insatiable? Surf by countingdown.com or www.seeing-stars.com.

Character Names for Specific Ages—For free info on what names were popular in specific years, see www.dfcreations.com/Nameandage.html.

CineStory—A nonprofit screenwriter's organization that works with emerging screenwriters to hone their craft is at www.cinestory.com.

Coming Attractions—Similar to "Ain't It Cool News" but less goofy, a great Vancouver-based site at corona.bc.ca/films/main.html.

Custom Search—Want your own specific Google? See www.sandybay.com.

Dark Horizons—At www.darkhorizons.com we find Australia's answer to Harry Knowles, regularly updated and equally interesting.

DirectorsNet—At the Directors Guild of America Links Page you'll find a lot of member sites, but most of them default to www.directorsnet.com.

Entertainment Directory—At www.edweb .com/movies, movies are explained step by step as well as ratings and other things.

EuroScreenwriters—A complete education on screenwriting on the Continent at www.euroscreenwriters.com, including communities, financing, organizations, and much more.

The Estrogen Files—A cute cyber-sitcom at www.theestrogenfiles.net.

Done Deal—At www.scriptsales.com, you can keep up with the scripts being sold and compare your own works to what Hollywood is buying.

Film Festivals Server—If you're looking to take a film to a film festival or meet filmmakers there, start at filmfestivals.com.

FilmFilm—This brainchild of Nora Ephron, G. Mac Brown, and Ron Brown at www.filmfilm.com attempts to be all things to aspiring screenwriters and filmmakers. Take a look, they might option your script.

Foreign Favorites—Have a look at: Australian film and TV at www.b4bfilmtv.com /home.asp; the BBC Online at www.bbc.co.uk (with information on writing for "the Beeb" at www.bbc.co.uk/writersroom); the European Film Academy at www.europeanfilmacademy.org; India's "Bollywood" covered by Nyay Bhushan at www.connectmagazine.com; the Irish Film Board at www.film-board.ie; German Entertainment News at www.mediabiz.de/gem/gem.afp; Peeping Tom's Film Club at www.geocities.com/SoHo/Studios/8451 (London site); SARTeC (Société des Auteurs de Radio, Télévision et Cinéma) in Quebec, at www.sartec.qc.ca; South African Independent Film at www .safilm.org.z a/main.html; UK Screenwriters' Workshop (formerly London Screenwriters' Workshop) at www.lsw.org.uk; UK Scriptwriters at www.darkin .demon.co.uk; The Wild East (Hong Kong-based site) at www.lawrencegray .com; and the Victoria Screenwriters (Canada) at members.home.net/ vscreenwriter/member.html.

From Query To Sale—"One screenwriter's gauntlet through the Hollywood slog" at www.mindspring.com/~spacklebeast/querytosale.

Greatest Films—I *love* this examination of the greatest Hollywood and American films at www.filmsite.org, and I'm not the only one.

Independent Feature Project West—Without question the best organization for independent filmmakers in L.A. See ifpwest.org.

Internet Fraud Complaint Center—Ripped off by a Web-based consultant? See www.ifccfbi.gov, a partnership between the FBI and the National White Collar Crime Center. The "s" means it's a secure site.

Inzide.com—Offering a free newsletter and access to a top management company, www.inzide.com has an amazing amount of industry information.

Joseph Campbell Foundation—If you liked *The Hero with a Thousand Faces* by Joseph Campbell, see his site at www.jcf.org.

Legal Advice—There are three Web sites I recommend to screenwriters: www .medialawyer.com, www.lawgirl.com, and Christine Valada in the "Ask a Hollywood Pro" section of www.hollywoodlitsales.com.

Los Angeles Times—"Calendar" in the Sunday *Los Angeles Times* is probably the paper's most popular weekly read, and you can get a lot of it for free at www .calendarlive.com. It's searchable, too.

Mandalay—Probably the best Web site of a mini-major, at www.Mandalay.com with offshoots to affiliates.

Mandy's International—Locate worldwide film folk at www.mandy .com. Search the jobs or have job openings e-mailed to you.

Megahit Movies—A site about films, which have generated more than $250 million in North American box office receipts, at www.megahitmovies.com.

Motion Picture Association of America—See www.mpaa.org to find out why that guy Jack Valenti was always appearing on television.

MovieBytes: Screenwriting Contests—There's a lot here, and no better information about contests than at www.moviebytes.com/mb_contests.cfm.

Movie Clichés List—You'll have a lot of fun at www.moviecliches.com, and you might even get some plot ideas.

Moving To Hollywood—At www.io.com/~dbrown/index.html is a great article about making the big move, and a sales pitch for a video.

Muse of Fire—At www.loop.com/~musofire is excellent information for beginning screenwriters from screenwriter-producer Alex Epstein.

Online Screenwriters' Workshop—Designed for screenwriters to join one or more e-groups (based on genre) to preview and provide feedback on one another's screenplays, at www.venicearts.com/workshopframe.htm.

Organization of Black Screenwriters—This site at www.obswriter.com features information for African American scriptwriters, as well as networking and research links.

Page BBS: For Professionals Only—A number of WGA writers started www .pagebbs.com. It's an intelligent discussion group.

Plot-o-matic—A very entertaining "automatic movie plot generator" at www .maddogproductions.com/plotomatic.htm.

Post-It Theater—Full-length flipbook feature films? See www.bigempire.com /postittheater/credits.html for great fun.

PR Newswire—To read the press releases put out by major entertainment and other companies, surf over to www.prnewswire.com.

Press Kits Plus—Only Hollywood could give birth to a site that sells things normally read once then thrown away. See www.presskitsplus.com.

Profnet—At www.profnet.com you'll find a collaborative of information officers that give free, convenient access to expert sources. You can also search their Experts Database and contact experts directly.

qwertyuiop.net—An excellent site at www.qwertyuiop.net. Have a look.

Reverse Info—Got a phone number but not a location, or vice versa? See http://in-132.infospace.com/_1_237060496__info/reverse.htm.

Rightsworld—A place where you can trade any subsidiary right imaginable at www.rightsworld.com. What do you have to sell?

Screaming in the Celluloid Jungle—A whole lot of information from someone born into the business at www.celluloidjungle.com.

Screenplay Junkyard—Roy Ashton's site at home.att.net/~whats-up-doc.

Screenscape—A U.K. resource for screenwriters and movie producers with free screenwriting templates at www.screenscape.fsnet.co.uk.

ScreenSite—See www.tcf.ua.edu/screensite/intro.htm for this site, which stresses the teaching and research of film and television.

ScreenStyle—Based in Minneapolis, home of a thriving film and screenwriting community, an online store at screenstyle.com.

Screenwriters & Playwrights—Charles Deemer's site offers his e-book ScreenWright and much more at www.screenwright.com.

Screenwriters Bootcamp—At www.screenwritersbootcamp.com, this site details the workshops given by screenwriter/story editor Robert Jordan.

Screenwriters Cyberia—Over 1,000 links at members.aol.com/swcyberia will keep you surfing as long as you can stand it.

Screenwriters Resource Center—This site at www.screenwriting.com is a collection of links and more, worth a long look.

Screenwriters Utopia—I've been impressed from the beginning by www.screenwritersutopia.com, created by Christopher Wehner.

Screenwriter's Workshop—"A group of writers in the same situation as yourself" at members.nbci.com/Noctivagus/screenwriter.html.

Screenwriting—There are two with that title; one from Jenna Glatzer at www.absolutewrite.com/screenwriting/screenwriting.htm and another from Allen White at screenwriting.about.com/arts/screenwriting.

Scripts Onscreen—This site at www.scripts-onscreen.com sells classic scripts, provides a list of screenwriting contests, and more.

Script Secrets—Bill Martell's marvelous www.scriptsecrets.com.

Sell Your Movie Idea to Hollywood — www.moviepitch.com is a site constructed to funnel ideas to "Pitch King" Robert Kosberg.

Sources for Screenplays—Try Alex Knowles' Script Wherehouse at members.nbci.com/scriptsplus/index.html, MovieScript.org at users.skynet.be/wvc/scripts.htm, Drew's *Script-O-Rama* (most popular)—At www.scripto-rama.com, or Simply Scripts "hundreds screenplays and transcripts of current, classic and soon-to-be-released movies, television, anime and radio shows" at simplyscripts.com/index.html.

Spec Screenplay Sales Directory Online Database—If you want to thoroughly research who sold and bought a screenplay like the one you're selling try the free demo at nt.hollywoodlitsales.com/specscript/index.cfm.

Stars & Their Agents—A lot of screenwriters try to get their scripts to stars. A good place to start is www.moviepartners.com/starsagent.cfm.

Technical Support—Fast and free technical support (both PCs and Macs) at www.protonic.com. All the techs there are volunteers.

Third Millennium Entertainment—One of the most unbelievable collections of screenwriting links you'll find is at www.teako170.com.

Tilting Windmills: An Exercise in Futility—An "almost-daily journal" at www .desensitized.org/wind about one writer's struggles.

Trailervision—Trailers for movies that don't exist at www.trailervision.com, and some of the best entertainment on the Web.

Undergroundfilm—If you consider yourself part of the avant-garde, check out www.undergroundfilm.com.

Viacom—To get an idea of the enormity of a media giant, visit www.viacom.com and click on "Businesses." You can also do a job search (as you can with most major studios online). I've worked on a project with the head of production of Viacom and like this company a lot.

Vincent's Casablanca—If you want to read the script of one of the most classic movies of all time, or find out anything else about Casablanca, see www .vincasa.com. Here's looking at you, kid.

The Virtual Script Workshop—A U.K. site providing information on Internet-based screenwriting courses for over six years, at www.xerif.com.

Webcinema—A nonprofit organization dedicated to the independent filmmaker at www.webcinema.org.

Wide Angle/CLOSEUP—Excellent "Conversations with Filmmakers" by David Morgan at members.aol.com/morgands1/closeup.

WireBreak—I hope this Webshow site is still up and running if you visit www .wirebreak.com. You might find a very entertaining show there called "Office Monkey" about a dot-com rebel created by . . . Skip Press.

Wordplay—This site at www.wordplayer.com is the brainchild of Terry Rossio and Ted Elliott, the writers of *Aladdin* and some other top films.

Worldwide Film Schools—At www.temple.edu/ufva/dirs/text52.htm is an amazing Temple University attempt to create a comprehensive list of online film/ video/communication schools and programs around the planet.

writernet—A U.K. "service which provides information, advice and guidance on all aspects of the live and recorded performing industry to writers . . . from the Arts Council of England and Regional Arts Boards" at www.writernet.co.uk.

Writers Script Network—writersscriptnetwork.com is probably the most effective free service linking up writers, producers, agents, and managers; it is put together by Jerrol LeBaron. Truly commendable.

The Writers Store—Hands-down the most comprehensive and successful outfitter to the creative screenwriting community. Established in 1982, The Writers Store provides the best software, classes, books, and information available, and a Webstore at www.writersstore.com.

Every time I try to do this Web site roundup, I inevitably get e-mails asking why I left this one out, or that some site is no longer working. Where did it go? Beats me. There are such things as search engines, and for Mac users, please do a Sherlock search on your own before firing off that e-mail to me.

Meanwhile, I hope all these links and descriptions help. See you in Hollywood, virtual or otherwise.

Converge Yourself

When the Writers Guild began allowing writers to join the Guild if they had enough Web and/or interactive credits, also known as "new media," I was very pleased. The Guild's benefits package is tremendous and there are a lot of reasons to join. Membership in the Guild is set up on a point system, with 24 points needed to join. To find out if you have new media credits from interactive or Web work that count toward membership, contact the Industry Alliances department at (323) 782-4790 or see that section at www.wga.org.

Like most full-time writers, I'm an entrepreneur. I write anything that pays a decent rate and embrace new ideas. I've written CD-ROMs for kids, and in 2000, I created an original Webshow called "Office Monkey" for WireBreak.com, a company headed by David Wertheimer, formerly the head of Paramount Digital. The latter experience was an eye-opener. I spent a good bit of time with the artists and executives at the company working on the show. I noticed that, with some improvement of my artistic skills and expertise with the Macromedia Flash software program, I could have put that show on the Web myself. So the next time I do such a project, I'll probably put it on my own Web site and then promote it. In this chapter I offer some thoughts along that line.

EVOLVING WITH MR. AUSTIN

To find out more about new media in the first edition of this book, I spoke to Charles Austin, who was the first interactive agent at the Agency for the Performing Arts. At our first meeting, Chaz felt that new media and Hollywood had not figured out how to make money with it yet. At the time, there were agents at ICM representing people who write computer games, with occasional breakthrough hits like *Myst*. Everyone felt there was plenty of money to be made on the Internet, but no one had worked out just how. The demise of so many dotcoms in 2000 was evidence that they still hadn't figured it out. The prevailing idea that all hit CD-ROMs would be turned into movies didn't materialize, but the gaming world is going strong. If the *Tomb Raider* movie (starring Angelina Jolie) turns out to be a hit, you'll see more game-to-movie projects.

One thing Chaz Austin impressed on me at our first meeting was the relative disconnection between Hollywood, New York, and Silicon Valley. He told me of a friend who understood New York publishing, Hollywood filmmaking, and Silicon Valley computing. She made a very good living as a consultant, "translating" projects to people in the different areas, flying around the country to coordinate the releases of books, movies, and CD-ROM or Web products on the same project. I've been inspired about this ever since because I understand all three like Chaz' friend.

For now, writing for new media isn't that lucrative, but I feel it is imperative that screenwriters learn to be more than simple scribes. I think they should learn to make films and also develop Web skills. Once broadband Web access is widespread and most people have cable modem access to the Internet, so that Web surfing is as fast as clicking through cable channels, the playing field might be leveled even further if you're already able to draw attention to yourself and your work via the Web.

Chaz Austin is now the President of Los Angeles–based Austin Digital Media Consulting (www.chazaustin.com), which expands market share for companies involved in new media and the Internet and represents out-of-area clients in the Los Angeles market and in Hollywood. He's a consultant on the Hollywood Screenwriters Network (hollywoodnet.com/Austin/index.html) where he posts his "Ask the CyberPro" column and answers questions.

Which brings us to the subjects of this chapter. Should you put up your own Web site for marketing your work? Should you post your screenplays at sites on the Web for potential buyers to read?

I sat down with Austin for another interview as I prepared this edition of the book. The first thing I asked him was what he felt had changed since last time.

"The main thing is how the Net is now part of a larger media mix," he said. "I received my masters in radio and TV and wrote my thesis on Marshall McLuhan, who sort of predicted all this. What some people don't realize is that each time the media changes, it doesn't get rid of the existing media. It just offers another way to reach the audience and use the new medium in conjunction with the other media. Traditional agencies are slow to understand the changes that the Net has brought. Hollywood took a long time to get the Net because it is the first truly interactive medium. It pitted Hollywood's basic greed versus the Net attitude that things are basically free. For Hollywood, dealing with that idea is like jumping in quicksand with both feet."

So how can an aspiring screenwriter or filmmaker use this contrast to get Hollywood to take notice?

"Well, the Net isn't an answer to everyone's prayers, but let's take the MP3 situation as an example. It has its good and bad points, but it leveled the playing field in music. Traditionally, agents and managers are a filtering process. You can use the same paradigm with the Net. If you're creative in the way you show your work. . .let's say you give people a little bit at a time, in the way short series are easy to read. Well, people might notice (exactly what Francis Ford Coppola does with his All Story site). You should think of a Web site as a way you can showcase yourself and begin to get attention. If you do a series of shorts or a Web show you can self-create a relatively inexpensive body of work as a sample of what you can do on a larger scale. It's not so much about money as it is being true to your vision. Once you've done something and people start asking about it, talking about it, it sells itself from that point on."

We talked about how movie stars get "thrown a bone" by studios who allow them to do personally-important projects that might not make much money, like Mel Gibson getting to film his version of *Hamlet*.

"Those projects give them a chance to show who they are," Austin said, "to do their own thing. With the Web, you can do much the same thing, have a good time and show who you are, use your own originality, without spending much money. What's great is that there was no showcase like this before. The Net is like a comedy club for visually creative people through electronics."

Austin told me that although he thought it might be several years before portal downloads of feature films would be widespread, broadband access will inevitably be as common as cable television. He suggested that creative people should start planning for that now, build a following, like some of the Web sites I've mentioned in this book.

"Then Hollywood will come after you," he said "The existing paradigm is already in place—Icebox.com. They're one of the few who have managed to port their Webshows to television." Austin teaches a course at UCLA Extension called "Making the Transition," where he elaborates on his observations and brings in top guest speakers from all areas of Hollywood. One thing that he tells his students is to think of building what he calls a "calling card portal."

"It can just be a small thing. Maybe you can make some money via ads on your site, but you can use it as a place to audition for studios and talent agencies."

WANT TO BE AN INSTANT "SHOWRUNNER"?

I knew a little about new media when I first put together this book but didn't consider myself an expert. So I went to someone who had made a lot of money writing for new media. Terry Borst was a successful screenwriter, a Writers Guild member, and coauthor of two very popular CD-ROMs, *Wing Commander III* and *Wing Commander IV*, which became the movie *Wing Commander*.

It's a small world in Hollywood. When I called Terry to tell him about the book I was doing he said, "Oh, I remember you, Skip. We ran into each other back when we both did word processing for law firms."

So much for impressing him with my journalistic genius. Terry works in TV and film much more than new media, and he expects that to remain true for most Guild members, although he knows several people in the WGA who had gained membership purely from CD-ROM credits. When Terry and I spoke, he was in the middle of writing an episode for the BBC TV show *Bugs*. I learned that he also taught a business communications class at the College of the Canyons in Valencia, California. I remarked that sounded like a curious part-time job for a screenwriter. It turned out the college had hired him shortly before his first studio project and he liked teaching, so he kept it up.

"The way I look at it, you take every job you can," he said. "I look at interactive as just one more market. I got into it accidentally. I didn't seek it out; I was just in the right place at the right time. The idea is to maintain all avenues."

I regularly read the monthly Alt.Screenwriters column he writes with Deborah Todd, covering "new media developments and strategies . . . on the digital frontier" for the WGA's *Written By* magazine. As mentioned in the Web chapter, these articles are also archived at altscreen.cjb.net. In their September 2000 article, "Don't Close the Icebox Door Behind You: A Showrunner's Short Sitcom for a Web Site Leads to . . . Where?" they tell the story of how Mike Reiss created the three-minute Webshow "Hard Drinkin' Lincoln" that Reiss described as "simultaneously adult and juvenile, smart and stupid." Reiss pointed out that "one advantage of online entertainment is that shows do not have to fit into neat time-boxes of 30 or 60 minutes."

How hard would it be to create such a show? Well, you'd need an artist if you couldn't do the drawing yourself. But it's not too difficult—Reiss had never used a computer before creating his show!

Take a look at *The Pretty Girl*, a 5:56 film by Gorman Bechard, at www .newvenue.com. Warning—it's not animation but a series of classy photographs with a single subject, backed by a narrative soundtrack. You'll need a Flash 5 viewer (free download from Macromedia.com) on your computer to view it. This "movie" (basically a slide show) is an example of how the length of a show on the Web can vary, and doesn't need to hew to the established standards of television and film.

So let's say you're a little ahead of Mike Reiss and know your way around a computer before starting, but don't know how to put up your own Web site, much less establish a show on a site. Allow me to mention a few tools that might help get you started toward creating a presence for yourself on the Web that people will notice and mention to others.

A WEBSHOW TOOLBOX

One of my "other" jobs for three years was writing the "Business Edge" column for *ComputorEdge* magazine, the largest free regional computing magazine in the U.S. The column was intended for small office/home office computer users, and I got to review a great deal of books and software. My favorite book about building Web sites during that time was Peter Kent's *Poor Richard's Web Site: Geek-Free, Commonsense Advice on Building a Low-Cost Web Site* (Top Floor Publishing). You can probably find it in your local bookstore or on Amazon.com, but if you can't, have a look at TopFloor.com. As well as being able to order the book, you'll find a great deal of information there, including a free newsletter of advice on maintaining and promoting a Web site.

You could take an easier route with your first site, and use something like the Click-n-Build templates I used to put up my first site at Earthlink.net. It won't be the kind of site you need to put up Webshows, but you can at least provide basic information about yourself with such a site. (If you want a reliable Internet Service Provider (ISP), I've been with Earthlink for years. If you mention me when signing up, they'll give me a free month.)

The easiest way to build a site is to get one program, Microsoft's FrontPage. It's the one that Peter Kent recommends, and I do, too. It's dual platform, it's the one most easily understood by ISPs, and you can manage and edit the same Web site and have it work for either Windows or Mac users. With "Wizards" that walk you through each process, it's unlikely you'll have any trouble with this software. One note—as you get more advanced with HTML (HyperText Markup Language), you'll learn about META tags and how they help you get noticed by search engines. FrontPage has a lot of self-aggrandizing Microsoft METAs built-in, which you might not want to promote.

Go see the Monkey at hotwired.lycos.com/webmonkey for more complex Web sites. There's more information there than you can shake out of a tree in Silicon Valley, and they even have lessons and projects for kids.

Other great tutorials can be found at the *Computer Arts* site at www.computer arts.co.uk/tutorials/web. This English magazine will walk you through the basics on most popular programs.

If you're a Mac lover like I am, get VSE Be Found at vse-online.com. It's an award-winning Web site promotion tool that features a META tag manager, a URL submission tool, a "watcher" that determines where your site is being ranked, and a link popularity checker. You might also take a look at the company's VSE Link Tester if you plan on including a lot of Web links on your site; it will help you quickly fix links and located resources you think you've lost. Then there's the Metagenerator freeware software for Mac at www.chez.com/renaud. It checks the META tag in your HTML files, and you can use it to modify, create or duplicate the META tag on one or more files simultaneously.

For anyone with a Mac, I also highly recommend BBEdit from Bare Bones Software at web.barebones.com. You can freewheel with this program and not be locked into a fixed set of options as with other software. The simpler version, BBEdit Lite, is a free download, and the company offers free technical support.

If Flash animations (like "Hard Drinkin' Lincoln") appeal to you, you'll probably want to spend a few hundred dollars for Macromedia's Dreamweaver. (Remember, you have to spend money to make money.) As advertised, Dreamweaver offers everything you need to develop a professional Web site. It lets you build Macromedia Flash graphics, has extensive visual layout tools, and a text-editing interface equivalent to BBEdit. Unlike BBEdit, however, it is available for both Windows and Mac platforms.

As far as planning the use of your Web site, you might take a look at Web Strategy Pro, which guides you through the process of "setting objectives, target markets, Web site strategy, detailed implementation, budgets, milestones, and forecast." It's described in detail at www.paloalto.com/webstrategypro.

Last but not least is a fabulous, low-cost program that's one of the best deals I've seen, particularly if you plan to make much use of video or animation on your site. I saw MovieWorks demoed at a video expo and had to have one. It's available for Windows and Mac at www.movieworks.com. You can do just about anything with this program. It's like having "lite" versions of Flash, Macromedia Director (multimedia), Photoshop (photo editor), Premiere (video editor), and Sound Edit Pro (sound editor) all in one under-$100 package that lets you create short- to medium-length (30 minutes or less) multimedia productions. I watched as five PowerPoint presentations were dragged and dropped into a MovieWorks file and posted to a Web site about as quickly as I could follow with my eyes. It's a stunning program that you can learn in under two hours, with step-by-step tutorials, and you also get over 300MB of royalty-free clips to use. Based on Apple's QuickTime, it is unlike similar programs in that it supports both analog video (AV) and digital video (DV). You can even create CD-ROMs with it. This one's a big wow.

Someone to Talk To

To subscribe to my free e-mail newsletter, e-mail me at skip_press@excite.com or skippress@earthlink.net. I'll keep you updated on my own Web site and Webshow plans. Meanwhile, if you want to participate in an ongoing discussion, take a look at the Intertainment Online Lounge at hollywoodnet.com/Novak/index.html. Host Jeannie Novak and her partner, Pete Markiewicz, are the authors of *Creating Internet Entertainment: A Complete Guide for Web Developers and Entertainment Professionals* (Wiley). They also have a Web hosting site called Kaleidospace at www.kspace.com.

Web TV with a Whole New Meaning

If you intend to build any kind of a business with a Web site, do yourself a favor and register your own Web domain. It used to be that people only thought in terms of "dot-com" if they wanted to have a commercial site, .net for a network, and .org for non-profits, but that has expanded. In November 2000, several new international domain names were added by the Internet Corporation for Assigned Names and Numbers (ICANN): .biz for businesses, .name for individuals, .pro for professionals, .museum for museums, .coop for business cooperatives, and .aero for the aviation industry. For more information on how this works, surf to the following sites: ICANN at www.icann.org; www.gtld-mou.org to read about the 1997 proposal; or cyber.law.harvard.edu for a Webcast of the meetings. Once you have your Web site ready, copyright it. How do you do that? Get an education at Benedict O'Mahoney's copyright Web site at www.benedict.com.

Here's a domain name alternative you might consider. As of this writing, you can register your own URL (Uniform Resource Locator) at networksolutions.com (which also offers a great Web site creation service at www.imagecafe.com), or at register.com. But consider this—what is a computer screen but a type of television? Take a look at www.tv. As they say on the site, "TV is the most widely recognized two-letter symbol in the world." The suffix was originally assigned to Tuvalu, a small Pacific Island nation, until some entrepreneurs got smart and made a deal. You can register a .tv domain for about half the price as other domains, and it'll be a bit more hip, too.

PRODUCERS, DEVELOPMENT PEOPLE, SPEC SCRIPTS AND WEB SITES

I get letters, lots of letters, mostly the e-mail variety, but many with the same question: "Would you advise posting my spec screenplay on _____ Web site?" And then they'll name one of the more popular sites, like Spec Script Library at www.screenplayers.net, The Spec Script Library at www.thesource.com.au, or The Writer's Spec Market at www.writerswebsite.com/ww/wmarket.

And inevitably I'll say (unfortunately), "No."

I really wish that producers, or even development people, would surf the Web, read a logline or synopsis, and download a spec script to read, but I've yet to encounter anyone who can buy a script who says they've done that.

In mid-November 2000, I gave a cowritten script of mine to someone I know at Drew Carey's management company. In the past, they'd liked another script of mine enough to pass it on to Drew. I let another producer I know read the script first, knowing it wasn't her type of material, and she told me that it was a "home run" if Drew Carey got involved. Toward the end of January 2001, I phoned my friend at Drew's management company and inquired about the status. She told me she liked the new script and had passed it on to her boss. Sorry she hadn't gotten back to me sooner, but over the holiday season she'd read almost 150 screenplays. How prone do you think she might be to find a Web site, read a logline, wait through a download, then read a script on a computer screen?

If you put up a Web site, do *not* post your screenplay there. You don't know who might download it (unless you're a very savvy computer person and can track such things), and probably no one important will download it, anyway. On the other hand, if your site has a short film or show you've put together that is truly entertaining, people actually will take a look at that, and they'll download it and pass it on to a friend or e-mail them about it. That's how many people have made breakthroughs in recent years, particularly Bruce Branit and Jeremy Hunt, who put together the hilarious "405" (see www.405themovie.com).

If you're not up to putting your own show on the Web, just put up some basic information about yourself, maybe even a short description of one or two projects that you have available. If you can get someone to look at your Web site and a logline intrigues them, they'll request the script. Make sure you have a clickable e-mail address on the site as well as a phone number, because they might pick up the phone and call. Do *not* put your home address there because you never know who might be reading your site, and besides, no development person or producer will send you a postal letter asking to see your work.

I've learned that producers will read a property onscreen—they just won't go to a Web site and read it onscreen. Unless you can put up short shows on your site, it should only be your billboard in cyberspace. Direct people there by e-mail, business cards, phone calls, or anything legal. Just don't expect them to stay there all afternoon, reading.

Happy surfing!

Television: Hollywood's Golden Goose

The majority of the working writers who are members of the Writers Guild of America, west, write for television. TV is the golden goose of the Hollywood industry. Stories of screenwriter mistreatment in the film world are rampant, even legendary, but in television the good writers rule. Writer/producers who can write a script, polish it as necessary, work with actors and directors and get a show delivered on time, are the kings and queens of the industry. To become one of them, you have a few options:

1. Get a staff job on an existing series, move up to coproducer, and eventually take over when the show creator moves on to other projects;
2. Work as a staff writer on a hit like *Seinfeld* and field offers when the show ends;
3. Write and/or produce a hit feature film and field offers from networks to bring the lightning over to their place;
4. Do something unusual like Eric Garcia did with his *Anonymous Rex* books and come in with a power position on a cable network with your own series based on your existing property;
5. Do something even more unusual like creating a hit short (animated or otherwise) that airs on the Web and get noticed like the creators of *405* and *South Park*;
6. Come up with some entree that amazes everyone (and please tell me how you did it); and
7. Live in Los Angeles or another television center.

Do you have to really have to live in Los Angeles or London or New York or Toronto? Maybe not, but you'll only sell something here and there if you're good, and you will probably not write for an ongoing television show, unless you're also able to produce it on location. Naturally, there are exceptions. I know a writer living in Maine who sold a screenplay to the Disney Channel via an agent she found in my *Writer's Guide*. I know another writer living in New Mexico who sold a screenplay to a German company after seeing a post on a newsgroup. Both of them used e-mail to set up the deals initially.

Many writers who aren't around the industry on a day-to-day basis get a little bit of knowledge about how television works, usually just enough to hurt them. For example, many screenwriters think that if their feature-length script is made as a movie for television, it might serve as a "back door pilot," meaning that if the ratings are good the network will turn it into an ongoing series. That sort of thing is rare these days. It used to be that the prevailing logic was to make a two-hour film that could also be sold to foreign markets, thus allaying the licensing fee (costs, usually around $3 million for a TV movie). Now, most networks will simply pay for the cost of a 30-minute or one-hour pilot and if it flies, great. If not, bye-bye bucks.

If a company has a number of divisions, however, that could still happen. *Sabrina the Teenage Witch* was a Viacom Production, and aired on Showtime. This was before Viacom owned CBS, or the popular show might have landed on the Tiffany Network. Instead, it went to ABC and then moved on to the WB Network. I have a full chapter on writing TV movies in my *Complete Idiot's Guide to Screenwriting* to show how different that type of writing can be, but here are some tips. Do you know what a "teaser" or a "tag" is? Do you have any idea what it means to "button" a scene? How about a "beat sheet"? See the Glossary in the back of the book. These are all terms that came from television writing.

There are, however, ways to get a long-distance education about how television works.

TVWRITER.COM

Larry Brody is a novelist, a screenwriter, a showrunner, and a producer, with a long track record in animation as well as "normal" shows. I've been recommending his "Better Stories Make Better TV! TV Writer Home Page" at www.tvwriter.com for years. I won't tell you about his site because I don't have room. Go take a look around. Meanwhile, here's some insight from Larry.

Skip: You've been in TV a long time. How has the medium changed for writers since you began?

Larry: When I started, in 1968, there were only about 4,000 members in the WGA, and less than half of them considered themselves TV writers. Also, shows did 26 episodes a season, almost every one of those episodes written by freelance writers under the direction of a kind of "all-purpose" producer who knew every facet of production from the nuts and bolts to script to the care and feeding of actors, and a story editor whose job was to guide and rewrite. What this meant, of course, is that although breaking in was difficult, it wasn't nearly as hard as it is today. There were more opportunities and less competition. There was also a great feeling of camaraderie. We were all in it together, trying not only to get work, but to do really good work. When writers got together in those days, we talked about literature and of how we wanted to reshape the world by bringing the elements of great literature to the small screen. I don't see much of that today.

On the other hand, age discrimination was rampant in those days—directed against writers who were too young. I was the youngest member of the Guild in those days, and although I worked occasionally, my real breakthrough came because Harlan Ellison saw my work and started recommending me to everyone he knew, and because "relevancy" became a saleable commodity on TV, as in issue-oriented stories featuring young heroes. I had more work than I could handle because I was the only writer in the WGA who knew current slang!

Skip: If you were starting in television today and moving to Los Angeles to get started, what would you advise a writer to do?

Larry: If I were starting out and moving to L.A., I'd advise every other writer to stay away so I wouldn't have so much competition. Ah, but seriously, I would try to get an agent before I came out here. That means that I'd prepare a portfolio with at least four scripts—one feature in which I wrote from my heart and soul, and three spec episodes for current series in the genres in which I felt comfortable. Then I'd call and call and call—not just agents but anyone who might know an agent because the best way to get one is to be referred by a current client . . . or the agent's best friend, lover, or mate.

Once I got to L.A., I'd try to live and work in "showbiz" areas, so I could make friends with other people who are starting out in various areas of entertainment. The truth about networking is that you don't succeed because you make contacts, you succeed because you make friends. As you and your friends succeed, you turn to each other for help, and you bring each other along. That's the way it's always been, and certainly the way it is now.

Skip: How true is it that writers over 30 pretty much can't work on sitcoms?

Larry: What I've heard is that if you're over 30, you should forget ever getting a break on a sitcom. However, I know people of all ages working in TV comedy—and drama as well.

Skip: You have a TV pilot contest. Along that line, how much attention do you think the industry pays to writers who win contests?

Larry: The thing to remember is that the Biz isn't a unified, solid front. It's composed of individuals, and of segments that those individuals congregate in. Which means that it's been my experience that working writers and writer-producers are left cold by contests because they think that those who judge them aren't using the same practical get-the-job-done criteria that writer-producers use when judging scripts. Senior development executives are a little more interested, but the real fans of contest winners are junior development people, who often cruise the contest circuit, including the Internet, to search for new talent. I think this is for a couple of reasons. The junior executives are younger and more interested in working with their contemporaries, i.e., "new" people. And the junior executives need ammo, which a contest victory provides, when they propose a writer or a writer's work for a deal. Interestingly—to me anyway—the importance of contests has increased greatly in the past few years, as the new generation moves onward and upward. I think that's a good, healthy sign because it means that new execs are genuinely seeking new talent and not just paying lip service to the hunt.

Skip: To really get noticed, does it still boil down to the great spec script?

Larry: What else can you go by? If I'm hiring a new writer, I have to know that he or she writes in a way that I like. In a way that'll make my life as a producer or story editor easier. So I have to base my decision on the writer's work . . . that, and on his or her attitude. You have to be a get-along-guy, someone that the buyer/employer wants to work with, otherwise no matter how great your spec is, you're out.

Skip: Do you think TV is a better medium for writers because it makes so much product, compared to film?

Larry: Let's face it, the best medium for writers is prose—books, stories. On the printed page the words stand out. Style means something in and of itself. The next best medium is the stage because it too is about words, because the dialog must tell the story, convey characterization, and be fascinating as hell to hold the audience. If you're interested in writing scripts, I don't think it's volume that gives TV writing the edge over films so much as control. There's a lot of philosophical freedom in writing screenplays, but ultimately the director is in charge and writers are quickly disposed of if their work doesn't convey the director's point of view. A dozen writers for a feature can happen these days. In television, the writer-producer is the boss.

I started TV Writer.Com because I wanted to give back to the medium I love—television. I'm hooked on TV. I'm moved by TV. And I've been very fortunate in my relationship with TV. I've had a lot of success, but have never forgotten how rough it can be out there for a beginner. So I'm trying to give back the help I got from people like Harlan Ellison and Gene Roddenberry and other, lesser-known writer-producers like Bill Blinn and Phil Saltzman, who saw a young man with potential and believed in him enough to teach him and give him a break. I want to teach others and give them their breaks. It's the right thing to do.

ANIMATED WRITERS

When I first embarked upon a Hollywood career, I knew a guy named Paul Haggis, who got together with me to form a writers group that met monthly, based on a list of contacts that I put together and mailed to everyone. Paul was smart enough to head into television, while I hewed to the "purity" of film and books. He's gone on to win an Emmy (for an episode of *thirtysomething*), buy a lot of real estate in the Los Angeles area, and create and help create shows like *Due South* and *Walker, Texas Ranger* and *Family Law*. He took the traditional, step-by-step route, beginning with animation writing, moving on to sitcoms, and moved steadily upward from there. I never tried writing animation much, but it can be a back door to prime television. Another person I met in those early years was Christy Marx, who went on to great success in animation. Christy is now one of the online mentors for the WGAw (see the Mentor section at www.wga.org), and on October 5, 2000, the WGA's Animation Writers Caucus presented its 3rd Annual Writing Award to her at its Annual Meeting and Reception. The honorary award is given to "that member of the Animation Writers Caucus and/or the Guild who, in the opinion of the Board of Directors, has advanced the literature of animation in film and/or television through the years, and who has made outstanding contributions to the profession of the animation writer."

Christy has written both animation and live action for television, feature films, and interactive, and has written comics as well. She allowed me to borrow from her Web site at www.sierratel.com/moonfire to share with you because all my readers don't have access to the Web.

Unlike many writers, she didn't always want to write. She was "about 26 before the little light bulb went off in my head, the one that said, 'You're a writer, stupid! Do something about it.'" A comic book fanatic as a child, she reached the point where her parents forbid her buying more comics. That didn't stop her, and she still collects the books. She says she was generally a tomboy, and "wanted to be Batman." When she discovered science fiction and fantasy with the works of Isaac Asimov, Ray Bradbury, Arthur Clark, Harlan Ellison, L. Sprague de Camp, J. R. R. Tolkien, she was hooked. She was also heavily influenced by the first-person, female protagonist novels of Mary Stewart. While a script reader for several movie companies, she began working on writing scripts and making friends among writers. Her first sale was a Conan story to Roy Thomas for *Savage Sword of Conan*. She sold several stories to Thomas, including one for a *Fantastic Four*.

"One day, a friend who wrote animation called and said the DePatie-Freleng Studio was making a *Fantastic Four* animation series and was looking for writers who knew the comic. I called and on the basis of the one comic book story, I got an interview with David DePatie. It was a very funny interview because I knew nothing about writing animation and I was boxed in by these two enormous dogs he had, trying to make a good impression. At any rate, he gave me an assignment and handed me a sample of an animation script to use as a template. And that's how I came to write 'The Diamond of Doom,' the first of many animation shows. My first live-action credit came years later. Once again, it happened by making contacts. In this case, I got to know J. Michael Straczynski through a private BBS. He gave me a chance to write for *Captain Power*. In short, a great deal of getting anywhere in this business is contacts, contacts, contacts. Much of what happens in this business is luck (being in the right place at the right time), but more than that it's about who you know and how determined and persistent you are. Of course, one of the key elements is having scripts for people to read. If you're looking to break into writing for television, you need a spec script for each type of show. An hour-long action spec for those types of shows, or a half-hour comedy script if you want to do sitcoms. It's generally agreed amongst pros that you should not write a script for the show you're submitting to. Choose a well-known show, but try to avoid shows that everybody else in the universe is writing spec scripts for."

[Note to reader: In the past year, shows have begun taking an interest in completely original show scripts. Go figure.]

Christy won't read unsolicited material, and that includes e-mail containing unsolicited ideas or attached files. But there's a lot to learn at her Web site, so drop in when you get a chance.

PEOPLE TO HELP YOU BREAK IN

If you want the official word on animation writers and unionization, the WGA's Animation Writers Caucus Chair is Craig Miller. If you want to receive information about future meetings about the caucus, contact the Industry Alliances Department at (323) 782-4511 or e-mail industryalliances@wga.org. The meetings are meant for theatrical animation writers (meaning already working) but it can't hurt to ask.

One group that will certainly welcome your presence is the Women in Animation Writers Roundtable that meets on Thursday evenings once a month. Meetings are free to members, $5 for guests. You can e-mail Sybil Baker at scrybble@juno.com for more information or call the WIA hotline at 310-535-3838. At the meetings, you can get feedback on your scene, treatment, pitch, or script in a warm, supportive group. Voice-over actors often do the readings. They also have a script competition, and seminars.

Also, in "The Way to Toontown" chapter of my book *How to Write What You Want & Sell What You Write* (see www.cmonline.com/boson/howto.html), you'll find basic information about what an animation script looks like, pay structure, and some advice from another master of the genre, Michael Maurer.

Where do you find an animation agent? The answer is usually "from a writer already writing animation," but one agent that I've come across is Jim Strader of Strader Entertainment. His roster is about 50 percent feature writers. Contact:

STRADER ENTERTAINMENT
71 Pier Avenue, Suite 328, Santa Monica, CA 90405
310-226-6166
E-mail: straderent@aol.com

That's animation, or at least a rough sketch. So how about the people that do prime-time television? Here's a couple.

VIEWS FROM AN INDEPENDENT PRODUCER

Stacy Codikow's first feature, produced at age 24, won the American Film Institute's Award for Best Feature. She hosts "The Insider Scoop to Getting Your Film Produced" for the Hollywood Indie Network at www.indienetwork.com/codikow. She cowrote the made-for-cable thriller *Victim of Desire*, wrote "Cycle of Violence" for the NBC series *Profiler*, and "Doppelganger" for the Paxnet series *Twice in a Lifetime*. She was also selected to participate in Chris "X-Files" Carter's AFI Writers Workshop.

"The first thing writers should know is a definition," Stacy told me. "Independent means 'not studio financed.' My company is not restricted by a deal to develop a particular type of project. We create our own guidelines about selecting and finding good material. We create a situation where the works of writers and/or directors can be developed and eventually produced, and we always have many projects in different stages of development, on our own or in collaboration. Development is a long and challenging process for any company, but we are in a position to create a haven for new writers to develop their work with the guidance of people who believe in their work and ultimate vision.

"To find the material from these first-time writers, we often read incredible amounts of scripts and treatments. We search for material via writing competitions and universities but we also accept many scripts directly. For the story department to run successfully, we insist that writers submit a treatment or synopsis, most preferably through our Web page. This should be no longer than one page, containing creative descriptions of the main story points. All scripts are logged, recorded, and are read in order of submission date. So don't panic if you don't hear from us. We haven't lost your script because it wasn't covered within the first two weeks. All material is discussed in a story meeting once a week, where decisions are made on whether to pass or to consider. If one reader recommends it, it will be covered by another. So your script may go through several meetings before you will be contacted about its consideration, and this can take time. If we are passionate about a project, we will explore every possibility to get it made because the only way an independent company gets paid is to make movies."

Stacy's Web site is at www.codikowfilms.com.

TVMOVIES@AOL.COM

I met Marc Lorber through America Online, where I was amazed to find him actively looking for scripts. After arriving in Los Angeles, he networked and made friends, and began selling TV and cable movies (as a producer) to companies like Jaffe/Braunstein, Hearst, Atlantis, Alliance, the Konigsberg Company, and Disney Television. When the TV movie business began to consolidate, he joined Mesmerize Studios, then moved to Hallmark Productions, followed by being head of television development at Phoenix Pictures. He is now the VP of Development for Carlton America, the Hollywood office of a major British company.

One of the first things he explained to me was that while the film world fluctuates wildly, television's needs are pretty much the same year to year, contentwise, which is why TV companies don't often get wildly creative. Conservative television networks like to use "approved" writers (meaning they have already written for television), so that makes it easy for a TV producer to say no to a "new" writer. The only way an independent TV producer can survive is to align with one of the major distributors or be part of one of the major networks or studios.

"Other than that," Marc said, "you have to have deep pockets from somewhere else to get through the good and the bad times. Some years you might make four to 10 movies, some years you might make two. Not many production companies make TV movies regularly."

The good news is the expansion of cable channels in recent years, but even if more TV movies and programs get made, there are limitations as to the kind of material someone like Marc will buy.

"First of all," Marc said, "what I tell people is that I probably pass fairly easily and quickly on three-fourths of the material that crosses my desk. It's two questions, and I write this in my e-mail to people. One question is, 'Does it personally interest me?' We want to be commercial, but projects take a lot of time and energy and passion, and if it doesn't interest you, life is just too short. If it is just a knockout project and I think, 'It's not everything I want, but we can sell it,' I might consider it. If it doesn't interest you, it will get boring real quick.

"The second and more important question is, 'Do I think I can sell it somewhere in the current marketplace?' There are some great stories I am personally interested in. I think they're great movies, I love them, I would love to do something with them, but there's nowhere I can sell them today. So you know you can either pass on those, you can put them in your file, put them on the shelf, revisit them later, it just depends.

"People e-mail me and want to know how they'll know I'm legitimate or how to protect their material. I tell them that not everybody is in the Hollywood Creative Directory, and not everybody has to be in Hollywood. If a producer is in some place other than New York or Hollywood or maybe Orlando, and they're not represented by a legitimate large agency or have a deal with a large company that is a deficit financier and network-approved, if they are not a network-approved producer who can pitch the story to a network, or they don't have legitimate things in production or in development, or movies that have produced, forget them.

"I don't try to bypass the agent. If a writer writes me that he has an agent, I want him to send the material through his agent. I want him to send the synopsis to me. I don't want to deal with all the calls and stuff from the agent, but on the other hand, if he's more comfortable sending the synopsis through the agent, fine. I say, 'Have the agent fax it or e-mail it or mail it to me.' It's just one greater step of protection for us."

I asked Marc what his criteria would be for hiring a writer who wasn't on a network "approved" list.

"It's easier to get somebody approved if they've written a script and brought it to you and they've created something original. Then it's easy to say, well, he's already created it, it's already come out of his head, so it's natural that he should at least have a crack at the first revision or the first draft or whatever. You need to do everything you can, not only providing their credits and references and resumes, but any sample of your work from articles to screenplays to whatever might be good for the project. They don't have to be a Writers Guild member. We're going to pay people at least scale, and more likely scale plus 10 percent, whether they're Guild or not.

"To be successful here, especially in TV movies, you must know that at some point there's a limited pie of money. A TV movie producer can only put up a certain amount of money, or he can go above that and take it out of his own pocket. It's hard for smaller companies to compete with a Carlton. What the writer should ask about a producer, even in a large company, is 'Does this person have passion for my project? Are they going to do their damnedest to get it made? Do they have the capability to do that? For a lot of people at a certain level, it's not about the money, and those are the people I'd much rather work with. It's really about, 'Do we connect? Do we have a common vision about things?'

"Television is a fantastic training ground because you can get your credits and your money and your involvement faster than you can in features. More people will see a television movie or cable movie, even a poorly-rated one, in one night than will see everything but 10 top features in a year. If we had 10 movies last year that made over $100 million and the average cost of a ticket is $5, that's 20 million people who have seen that movie, and some of those are repeat customers. A TV movie, let's say does an 8, which is a pretty poor rating. That's 954,000 homes per point, so that's almost 8 million homes. And let's say there are two-and-one-half viewers per home. That's over 20 million, and that's just the first time it aired. If you want your message or your entertainment to reach the largest number of people, it's television. That's the widest medium. Records, books, features, newspapers—nothing reaches more people than television."

Marc also offered good advice on the revision process. Unfortunately, he said, the majority of writers who contact him haven't done their homework and don't know the basic structure.

"People ask me, 'How do you respond to notes?' I say, 'Well, if you give the script to five people and five people generally say the same thing, then that's probably a note that you should respond to. On the other hand, if three people out of the five say the same thing, you ought to consider that note. If one or two did, then you have to say, 'Hmm, how does that play with me?' You don't have to take what they say for sure. I tell people to take my general notes with a grain of salt. I'm willing to passionately argue and discuss the merits of a character or a plot point. A producer's job is to play devil's advocate before taking a project forward, to anticipate what concerns the network might have and address those. So I try to come out with all the good devil's advocate questions so that we can address and answer those. If we still decide to do it X way, we have an answer when the network says, 'Yeah, but why doesn't he kill her?' I'm able to say, 'Well, here's why.' Everybody's job, from development people to executives, is to evaluate things. In one case in my whole life has somebody basically taken something outright and said, 'Great, I'll buy it.' They're always going to have notes and changes, thoughts and concerns."

Marc's still open for e-mail queries first. If he's intrigued by an e-mail he'll ask to see more. "And I always reply," he insisted, "even if it takes a few days or week depending on where I am and what I'm in the midst of. And I'm happy to explain my position on a query, as much as I can, dependent upon my time constraints."

Marc Lorber's definition of the perfect writer is one who takes notes easily "but fights to a point for what they're passionate about, writes as quickly as possible dependent upon the project and its needs, is flexible, and knows good coffee houses."

The perfect property, he feels, is one "the network will buy, that I can afford to option and purchase reasonably, and that I can thereafter afford to produce well for the budget I'm given."

Though he's never found anything he first learned about via e-mail that actually made it onto the screen, he has optioned a number of projects initially sent to him over the Net, and has met many writers via e-mail. Contact:

> Marc Lorber
> VP TV Development of Carlton America
> 12711 Ventura Boulevard, Suite 300, Studio City, CA 91604
> 818-753-6363
> E-mail: TVMovies@aol.com

TELEVISION NEEDS TO GROW UP

As I write this, negotiations are ongoing between the Writers Guild of America and the other major entities in Hollywood over new contracts. One sticking point is the auteur theory (a.k.a. the possessory credit). Lew Hunter told me that when he spoke with Jean-Luc Godard, the French director who started the "A Film by" agitation, Godard said he'd done it as a joke, and journalists proliferated it. Of course, people will argue with me that Andrew Sarris, with a magazine article in the 1960s, really started the "A Film by" thing. I just know what Lew told me, and he helped start the screenwriting school at the Sorbonne in Paris. Whatever the truth is about the idea, here's a question for you posed to me by a very successful member of both the Writers Guild *and* the Directors Guild.

You're a producer with just enough money to make one film. You have a choice of hiring a writer who has never directed or a director who has never written. Which would you choose?

The last time I spoke at the Aspen Summer Words writers' festival, I was introduced to Ashley Anderson, the granddaughter of Irving Thalberg (look him up at www.imdb.com if you don't know who he was). I asked her if it was true that Grandpa Thalberg had really said, "The writer is the only absolutely essential element in this town, and he must never find out." Since her mother (who owns a popular bookstore in Aspen) was only one year old at the time of her grandfather's death, Ashley said she couldn't be sure, but she'd heard that he really did say something like that.

In television, the writer/producers may be kings and queens, but not after a certain age. There's an age bias in Hollywood that doesn't show up much in the feature film world, but it does in television, and it's just as troubling as the possessory credit.

So troubling, in fact, that mid-November 2000, 28 television writers filed a class-action lawsuit against more than 50 TV networks, studios, production companies and talent agencies, alleging that they had been "graylisted" after age 40. Lisa Girion of the *L.A. Times* reported that one sitcom veteran goes to a salon to have her eyebrows plucked, her makeup applied, and her hair blown out before she attends a meeting. Her friends get collagen injections to deal with wrinkles.

Some of the writers had Emmys; all had a long list of credits. The 81-page complaint filed in federal court in Los Angeles sought unspecified damages and court supervision of network and studio hiring for five years or longer, until the alleged ageist exclusion ended. The lead law firm, Sprenger & Lang, had just won an $8 million settlement from CBS Inc. on behalf of more than 200 women television technicians who were victims of sexual discrimination in pay and promotions; the court put CBS under court supervision for four years. The firm also won two other multimillion dollar judgments on age discrimination, against First Union Bank and Ceridian Corp.

Of the WGA's 9,500 writers, the suit noted, two-thirds were over 40, "yet a third or fewer over-40 writers worked on 62 of the 122 night-time TV series for which records were available."

What caught my attention about the article was the fact that the lead plaintiff was Tracy Keenan Wynn, 55, a winner of Emmys for TV movies I loved, *The Autobiography of Miss Jane Pittman* and *Tribes*, and a feature I relished, *The Longest Yard*. I'd shared a panel with Tracy at a 1999 Aspen writers conference and was shocked to learn how his television writing income had virtually dried up, starting in 1997. A father of three, he'd lost his home and been forced into bankruptcy

Granted, the article pointed out that in 1999, *JAG* writer Paul Levine had signed on at age 51, but the CBS show had a generally older writing staff and was about a much more mature subject than most network programs. And Levine was a lawyer, too. *JAG* is about Navy lawyers.

So, naturally, I called Tracy and asked him to comment on the case. Here's what he was able to clear with his legal team.

"My professional career began in 1970 with *Tribes*, an original film for TV that garnered me an Emmy Award as well as a WGA Award. During these first few years, it was always understood that the more seasoned, 'veteran' writers would be getting the most desirable assignments. This was expected, as the younger writers such as myself needed to gain more experience to be able to master the craft of screenwriting.

"While the art of screenwriting is not something that can be learned, the craft can be. And like any craft, such as working with elegant jewelry or fine watches or intricate watercolors, it takes many years of experience for the artist to achieve the level of skill and competence necessary to be considered as having 'mastered' the requisite techniques.

"Never, at any time from 1970 until 1995, did I ever consider the possibility that as I matured as a screenwriter, I would not be gaining the concomitant respect and prestige enjoyed by my predecessors throughout the history of both film and television. It was my firm conviction that writers, perhaps more than any other craftsmen except for actors, were looked upon as honing their craft ever better with age. I also believed that from one generation to the next, younger writers would, as I and countless others have done, learn the craft and likewise hone their skills over time.

"It's as if the present obsession with 'the youth market' has blinded the network executives as well as many agents and producers. Somehow, the concept has evolved that older writers cannot write about young people. This, of course, is completely false; was Shakespeare only 15 when he wrote *Romeo and Juliet*? Was I a former pro football star thrown into prison when I wrote *The Longest Yard*? Was I a cowboy when I wrote the pilot for *The Quest*? And what can I say about myself and *The Autobiography of Miss Jane Pittman*? [Editor's note: Starring Cicely Tyson in an Emmy-winning appearance, this work is about a black woman in the South who was born into slavery in the 1850s and lives to become a part of the civil rights movement in the 1960s; it was adapted from the novel by Ernest A. Gaines.]

"Good, experienced writers are capable of writing about anything and from any perspective. A writer does not have to be a doctor to write a medical show. Nor does he or she have to be a cop, a lawyer, or anything else except a writer. If I need to learn the newest 'kidspeak' or 'mall rat' vernacular, I can ask my own children or their friends. Or, I can go to a mall and just listen. I can also update a lot of my own experiences; after all, we were all children once.

"If I need information on a medical procedure or term, I can call up a doctor friend. A cop? No problem. Likewise for the legal profession. So why this fixation with young people and the misguided conception that no one other than a young person can write about them? This is patently a misconception."

I couldn't agree more. Shortly after receiving Tracy's sentiments via e-mail, I got a call from one of the great screenwriters of all time, Ernest Lehman. I had faxed Ernie a short note of congratulations after learning about the honorary Oscar he was to receive at the 2001 Academy Awards for his body of magnificent work and he called me to say hello. I shared this with Tracy when I responded to his e-mail, and I also mentioned that agent Ken Sherman (who also spoke in Aspen with me in 2000), had told me that comedy writer/director genius Billy Wilder still goes to the office in Beverly Hills every week. The same Billy Wilder whose *Some Like It Hot* had been selected by the American Film Institute as the greatest comedy movie of all time, in the CBS network special "100 Years . . . 100 Laughs" airing on June 13, 2000, narrated by Drew Barrymore (age 25). The same Billy Wilder who had received the Producers Guild of America "Golden Laurel" award in 2000 as he was inducted into the PGA Hall of Fame for Motion Pictures. The same writer who had given us, in 1999, the marvelous book *Conversations With Wilder* (Knopf), at age 93, working with writer/director Cameron "Almost Famous" Crowe (age 43).

Billy Wilder, all washed-up.

At about the same time my interchange with Messrs. Lehman and Wynn was taking place, the Associated Press reported that Jason Lind, a 13-year-old boy from Torrington, Connecticut, was hospitalized with second- and third-degree burns after mimicking Johnny Knoxville, the creator and host of MTV's highly-rated show *Jackass*. The teen had seen Knoxville put on a fire-resistant suit hung with steaks, then lay across a barbecue while cast mates shot lighter fluid onto the grill to fan the flames.

Ha ha, I forgot to laugh. Programming genius, not. My prediction? The writers win the lawsuit and, hopefully, at least for a little while, the powers that be in American television take a deep breath and grow up.

THE TYPE OF PEOPLE TELEVISION REALLY WANTS

The writing/directing/producing team of Martin Kunert and Eric Manes have done very well in the last couple of years. Their latest success is the sale to CBS of a pilot of *HRT*, a one-hour drama akin to *West Wing* or *ER*, but based around the FBI's Hostage Rescue Team. Their TV show, *Fear* had been airing on MTV since February 2000. They are executive producers of *HRT* with Mark Johnson (*Rain Man*, *What Lies Beneath*).

I first met Martin on the newsgroup misc.writing.screenplays. He has a slightly different view of American culture, having immigrated here from Poland at an early age, after spending a year in England. He's in his mid-30s now. He and Eric met in film school at New York University (NYU). Since they came to Los Angeles with such a hardscrabble New York mentality, I wondered if they still found it hard breaking into the business?

Martin: Extremely. We were doing commercials and music videos, and every single step was extremely difficult. It's a misconception that you get a break and then it's easy coasting, hanging out in restaurants, collecting Oscars.

Eric: You have to work hard for your second break, and your third break, too. It's so easy to fall off the face of the Earth in people's minds.

Kunert and Manes met while pledging a fraternity at NYU and have been friends and business partners ever since. They went through tough times in L.A., at one point being so broke they had to split Ramen noodles for lunch.

Martin: We made a living any way we could. A few years after we got here, we built a postproduction facility, a small place in a house a block away from the El Coyote Mexican restaurant. It was the first computer-based postproduction facility for indie producers. We got a write-up in *American Cinematographer*.

Eric: We got tired of doing anything but shows and movies to make a living. After about six months with that facility, we decided we wouldn't make money in any other way but the business. We panicked later about that decision, but it forced us to concentrate on what we really wanted to do. That's how we got the movie *Campfire Tales* off the ground. We also produced a film called *Lowball* in New York. We put our backs against the wall and we made it.

From what they were telling me, it seemed that they had not ever had that significant "big break" that so many Hollywood hopefuls go looking for. I wondered if their sale of the major feature *Hindenburg* to producer Arnold Kopelson was one?

Martin: It's hard to say what is a big break. Selling *Hindenburg* was a huge break, but selling *Campfire Tales* was also a break.

Eric: You still have to immediately create another project. You don't just make it happen, you make it happen over and over.

Martin: People have to realize that 90 percent of the stuff they come up with will not work out. If you just rely on one project, it most likely will never happen. It might be the tenth one that makes you the money you want. Our agent had some ammunition once we did *Campfire Tales*. With that as our sample script, we pitched 15 people in five days before selling *Hindenburg*.

Eric: We actually sold *Campfire Tales* before *Scream* was done. We felt it was a no-brainer, that people hadn't a seen movie like that in a long time. We planned it so that it had limited locations, with each story in one location, four places in all.

Martin: We finished it before *Scream* but had some problems with the distribution. The main thing was that we wanted to make a film that was cheap to make. The original structure came from that idea. If we made an anthology we could shoot one story, then try to raise more money and slowly finance the whole film.

Eric: But as it turned out, once we had the script, we got the thing financed all at once.

Naturally, I wanted to know whether, as a production company, they would ever look for outside material, since they both write. They pointed out to me that they write so much of their own material and are continually getting submissions from agents for features and other things.

Martin: There's no way we can write *HRT* all by ourselves. As with most TV shows, we'll have a whole staff. We're the executive producers, the showrunners, so we'll see how many we write.

Eric: We'll also have another veteran showrunner on the show. Plus, working with Mark Johnson is just amazing, incredible. He has impeccable taste. Our agency decided that the best way to sell the show was to work a little backwards. They pitched the networks directly, sold CBS on it, then we interviewed studios and settled on Columbia-TriStar, who had a deal with Mark Johnson.

Martin: We met with other producers, but we liked him. We're really happy he agreed to work with us.

Their agency came to them after their *Fear* was picked up as a series on MTV. They had never imagined jumping to prime time.

Martin: I guess maybe things were just building up, with Eric producing, and the films I directed.

Eric: We actually had another deal in the works, but not on the scale of *HRT*, so we had to go with this one.

With their success in television, I wondered if they would continue to do features and film. Kunert and Manes are a perfect example of the type of creative persons that television loves. They've proven themselves as writers and as a directing/producing team. They can deliver, consistently, a must for working in television. If this is the milieu you desire, it might be wise to emulate their example.

FINDING A DIRECTOR FOR YOUR TV MOVIE

To keep up with what's going on with movie directors, look around the DirectorsWorld area of www.creativeplanet.com. You can opt to receive their DirectorsWorld.com Daily newsletter if you wish. I didn't have to seek out who the Directors Guild of America (DGA) nominated for Best Director of a TV movie—it came to me in this newsletter.

Have you ever heard of Jeff Bleckner, Kirk Browning, or Joseph Sargent? You might recognize Martha Coolidge's name from *Introducing Dorothy Dandridge*, but how about British director Stephen Frears? No? Well then, you wouldn't recognize Martin Pasetta, either. All of these directors could get a television movie made for you, if you could convince them of the worth of your screenplay. Try to keep up with the hot directors—you can't help but benefit.

MORE RESOURCES FOR YOUR TELEVISION CAREER

It's almost mandatory to live in Los Angeles or another television center to be a consistently working TV writer, but these Web sites might help you anyway.

American Film Institute (AFI)

Although the exact details on the Sloan TV Writing Workshop and the Television Writers Workshop offered by AFI were not available at press time, you can find out about them at www.afionline.org. Click on "Training."

Academy of Television Arts & Sciences (ATAS)

Have a look around www.emmys.tv if you're bound for Los Angeles. The prime time Emmy Awards are voted on by the ATAS membership of 26 television peer groups, most of whom reside in southern California. The organization's counterpart in New York is the National Academy of Television Arts & Sciences (NATAS). NATAS administers news and sports Emmys, and via affiliated chapters in major cities awards Emmys for local programming. NATAS and ATAS work closely together on the daytime Emmys. The NATAS site is at www.emmyonline.org.

The Animation World Network

A comprehensive site for those in the animation business at http://awn.com.

Behind the Scenes

Although the International Cinematographer's Guild had a rule for many years banning the taking of personal photographs on motion picture and TV sets, still photos taken exclusively by a union member were allowed. At http://members .nbci.com /erbmovie/index1.htm, you'll find the still photo collection of writer/cameraman Stephen Lodge.

Sitcom Format 101

If you are determined to write for the latest hot situation comedy, you'll need a sample script. At www.deadpan.net/sitcom you can learn "the proper script format for some of the shows you probably want to write."

SoYouWanna sites

A very detailed look at sitcom writing is at www.soyouwanna.com/site/syws/sitcom/sitcomFULL.html. You'll find links to scripts for *The Simpsons*, *Seinfeld*, and a lot of other stuff. At www.soyouwanna.com/site/syws/tvpitch/tvpitchFULL.html *SoYouWanna pitch a TV show?* will tell you what to do, once you've written that script.

Talk Shows

The world's largest and most popular talk show fan Web site really is at www.TvTalk Shows.com.

Tube Talk

Got a true story? A part of the Hollywood Producers Network at hollywoodnetwork .com/TV/tubetalk/board.html, this site is hosted by Emmy award-winning producer David A. Simons.

TVPitch.com

At www.mandalay.com/tvpitch/ask.html you'll find the "Ask Jerry" column in which you can "Meet TV's Showrunners," those writer/producers on whom the prime-time medium depends. It's an online seminar featuring head writers from the upcoming television season hosted by Jerry Rannow. You'll learn what it takes to break in and be a successful writer in Hollywood.

THE OFF SWITCH IS MISSING

As vast as television can seem, it's a small world. Shortly before finishing this book, I attended a wake for Barney McNulty, the guy who invented cue cards in the early days of television. The event was held at the Leonard H. Goldenson Theatre at the Academy of Television Arts & Sciences in North Hollywood. Barney was a NBC page on *The Ed Wynn Show* when he was pressed into service to write out the lines in big letters on big cards. Ed Wynn was the grandfather of the writer Tracy Wynn, mentioned earlier in this chapter. Two years before, I had urged Barney to write an account of his fascinating life and tell the world how he'd saved Bob Hope's life and many other stories, but it didn't get done, and another Hollywood legend passed by unchronicled. It's too bad when we remember the shows, but not the people who made them happen.

Television itself just keeps on rolling. Its appetite is voracious and shows no signs of lessening. You might not win a Nobel Prize writing for "the boob tube," but you might get rich and see more of your scripts made than in any other medium.

The Indispensable Organizations: The Writers Guild of America and the Writers Guild Foundation

Thalberg's quote that the writer is "the only indispensable element in Hollywood . . . and he must never find out" doesn't wash at the Writers Guild of America (WGA), east or west. In fact, many of the benefits that screenwriters take for granted these days might not exist if not for the WGA. Contrary to a myth that the WGA doesn't encourage new writers (because all WGA members aren't working all the time), the organization works continually to help improve conditions for screenwriters worldwide, and to encourage excellence in the craft. For example, in 1998, they gave a $2,500 prize for writing at the third annual Los Angeles Independent Film Festival. They also give the Valentine Davies Award at the Guild's annual award ceremonies to "those who have contributed to the entertainment industry and the community at large and who have brought dignity and honor to writers everywhere."

The Writers Guild has one of the best health plans in any industry, which is another reason any writer who is eligible should not overlook becoming a member. A visit to their Web site offers an easy explanation to benefits and activities. If you want to know the basic rates acceptable for any form of script, find the "Revised Schedule of Minimums" on the WGA west site by clicking the "For Writers" tab at www.wga.org/forwriters_index.html and at the WGA, East site at the "Writers" tab (www.wga east .org/mba).

In 1997, things looked shaky for the Guild, when the WGA west called it quits with the WGA, East and set out on its own to negotiate a separate contract with film and TV producers. (It is not commonly realized that the two guilds are separate unions, formed when the Screen Writers Guild dissolved in 1954.) In January 1998, after six months of arguments, the two factions settled their feud in an agreement approved by a wide margin. In mid-April 1998, WGA members voted to change the way national contracts are ratified, eliminating their long-standing two-thirds rule in favor of a one-writer, one-vote plan. The change in voting structure replaced a structure that had been in place since the 1950's and should do much to make WGA members feel more included in Guild business.

For the last edition of this book I interviewed Dan Petrie Jr., who was then president of the Writers Guild of America, west. He is now the vice president. Much of what he had to say still serves as a blueprint for beginning screenwriters, and clarifies the Writers Guild's role.

ADVICE ON THE WRITERS GUILD

Q: Why does it help if you join the Guild?

A: The Writers Guild exists to advance the interests of screenwriters collectively. By screenwriters I mean writers in television and motion pictures and also emerging media. We do it in a number of ways. One, and most important, is in the most traditional labor union fashion, collective bargaining. We negotiate on writers' behalf with the Alliance of Motion Picture and Television Producers (AMPTP), which negotiates on the studios' and networks' behalf for a minimum basic agreement, and through hard negotiations and strikes over the years since the Guild was founded, the things that writers, even writers who are not members of the Guild, take for granted, are standard parts of the minimum basic agreement. Residuals, a health insurance plan, many, many other things. Minimums, working conditions, the prohibition against speculative writing for producers. Importantly, and controversially, the Writers Guild administers the credits for films and television, so that an arbitration committee of writers decides who the credited writers should be on a given film or television show in the case of a dispute, rather than the producer who might have an interest in giving a credit to a nephew or what have you. The Writers Guild seeks to advance collectively the interests of writers in other ways, such as using the media to keep before the public the idea that movies and television shows are written and not just thought up by actors or directors as they go along. The measure to which writers are sought after and respected and the importance given to spec sales, the headlines in the trades about spec sales, are markers of the collective achievement of screenwriters and television writers in that effort. The degree to which screen and television writers are not respected by the business, by critics, by audience members, by film students who think a director does everything, is a measure of how far we still need to go.

Q: How about the idea that the director is the auteur of a film?

A: While film is a collaborative medium, unfortunately that phrase is sometimes used to mean anybody can collaborate on the script. In truth, movies and television shows are collaborative, but I think that writers and the screenplay play a greater role than is generally acknowledged. We can assert the importance of the writer without denigrating the importance of the director. The best pictures often have wonderful collaborations between writers and directors, and sometimes the same person both writes and directs. The vision of a film is not the director's vision, although the director needs to have a vision. It's not the writer's vision, although the writer does need to have a vision.

It's a collective vision. The Writers Guild does not believe in the vanity credit of a film by so and so because that suggests a sole authorship. We don't object per se to the fact that the director's name is listed twice. It's the form of the credit that is a problem for us. The vanity credit was originally intended for those filmmakers whose names genuinely brought people to the theater, like Alfred Hitchcock. That was expanded because directors would see producers' names as a Blank Blank production and want to be on a par with the producer, with a similar credit. On my first movie I got it, but I'm sorry to say I took it.

Q: How about other writers' guilds? Do you interact with them?

A: There's an international association of writers' guilds. It's an important organization. This is a global business and the writers' guilds of all the countries need to communicate with each other and help each other out.

Q: How tough is it, getting into the Writers Guild?

A: There are so many people interested in writing screenplays, but I think it's disproportionate to the marketplace for screenplays. Here's an analogy. There are about 11,500 members of the Writers Guild west. Let's say that's roughly equivalent to the numbers of the Los Angeles Police Department. Imagine if everybody in the world who wanted to be a policeman, instead of wanting to be a policeman in their local community, wanted to join the LAPD. Not that all the world's screenplay work is in L.A., but you know what I mean. And all our 8,000 WGA members are not working all the time. A lot of writers make their living writing or rewriting films that don't get made. The great majority of our members make their money from television, but of course people who are studying the business tend not to study getting into television; they're writing spec screenplays. In that arena the competition is fierce, which is all the more reason you need to write a great script.

If you're interested in finding out more about the Writers Guild of America, contact:

Writers Guild of America, West

7000 W. Third Street, Los Angeles, CA 90048-4329
323-951-4000, outside Southern California 800-548-4532
Web site: www.wga.org

OR

Writers Guild of America, East

555 West 57th Street, Suite 1230
New York, NY 10019
212-767-7800, Fax: 212-582-1909
www.wgaeast.org

At the very least, I suggest you sign up for the free monthly e-mail newsletters and regularly read their publications. And, as mentioned previously, you'll find their Web sites a treasure trove of information.

The Writers Guild Foundation

After the second edition of this book came out, I got a few e-mails and letters about small errors. As usual, I found the proper information and thanked the correspondent for their attention to detail. One big goof that I made was identifying the "Words Into Pictures" event as a Writers Guild of America production. Writers Guild Foundation Librarian Karen Pedersen wrote to remind me that, in fact, the event was created in 1997 by the Writers Guild Foundation and has been held twice, in 1997 and 1999, and to let me know that the third "Words Into Pictures" will be held in 2002.

How are the organizations different? The Writers Guild Foundation is a 501(c)3 non-profit organization that works in concert with the WGA, but it is primarily an educational entity, not a labor union. The mission of the Foundation is, in part, to encourage excellence in writing; to educate the public concerning the role of the writer in film, television, and radio; and to promote further education and communication within the writing community. For more information about them, the 2002 "Words Into Pictures" event (which is worth the trip to L.A.) or the James R. Webb Memorial Library, contact:

The Writers Guild Foundation

7000 W. Third Street, Los Angeles, CA 90048-4329
(323) 782-4544, Fax: (323) 782-4695

DON'T FORGET YOUR ROOTS

I realized while putting together this chapter for the second edition that I had never given Dan Petrie Jr. a commission on the negotiation he did on my behalf on that first film sale. So I sent him a check for $10, with interest, $26 total. It didn't get me a discount on WGA membership, or even on a subscription to *Written By*, but it pays to remember the folks who help get you there.

Getting on the Hollywood Map

It's not easy to live outside Los Angeles or New York and turn out a winning screenplay before learning how the business works, but it's been done. One thing is certain—it is much, much easier to find someone who loves your script, to network and meet top producers and agents, or even produce a low-budget script if you live in the heart of the world film industry.

YOU'LL NEED A CAR

I wouldn't advise arriving in Los Angeles without a car, as L.A. is a huge sprawl of a city. The recent addition of the subway helps, but its routes are limited, and the year 2000 saw a crippling bus strike. You need reliable transportation to make it to meetings, if you are invited to visit someone at a studio or elsewhere. Production companies can be found in Beverly Hills, nearby Century City, Santa Monica, and all over. After all, there are well over 6,000 listed production companies in most directories. Some of the most important ones, or companies headed by major superstars, are not even listed in some books (and that by design). You must also know the geography, which includes places industry people have meetings.

EATERIES AND OTHER PLACES

My favorite restaurant in Hollywood for the longest time was the Village Cafe (generally called the Beachwood Cafe) in Beachwood Canyon, in the area originally known as Hollywoodland. The Hollywood sign was just up the hill, and when I first started going to the cafe there were still people around who remembered the sign when it read HOLLYWOODLAND. A disappointed starlet jumped to her death off the final D, the community realized there were 13 letters in the name, and the LAND came down. Down the hill on Franklin Avenue, the Hollywood Hills Coffee Shop in the Best Western hotel is equally cozy. Many actors and writers live in the area and eat at both cafes.

Can you walk up to their table or booth and start talking to them? That's usually not a good idea, but some times it works.

Down the hill, on Hollywood Boulevard, is the oldest restaurant in Hollywood, Musso & Frank's. This is a restaurant from a Raymond Chandler dream, with a long bar and a steady procession of Hollywood names at lunchtime. Some of their careers have seen better days, but Musso & Frank's is a must-do when you're new to town, and when the Academy of Motion Pictures Arts & Sciences' new facility at the corner of Hollywood Boulevard and Highland Avenue is completed, expect to see a resurgence of business in this most famous of older Hollywood eateries.

A few miles away, across from Paramount on Melrose Avenue, is a marvelous Mexican restaurant called Lucy's El Adobe. If they're on the lot at Paramount, they'll turn up at Lucy's.

These are all workaday places. The real action takes place in Beverly Hills and Century City. If you can get a good table at Morton's on Melrose on Monday night, you're somebody. Want to court a superstar for your project? Invite them to lunch at The Grill, or The Ivy over on Robertson Boulevard—which was the only place to "do lunch" at one time. Remember the scene in *Get Shorty* where Danny DeVito orders his wacky salad? The Ivy.

WHERE THE STARS COME OUT AT NIGHT

The night life? It's like that line from that Neil Simon script—the stars come out at night. The first time I went to Spago, it was to meet a prominent soap opera star who wanted to star in a play of mine. No one told me about the unspoken dress code. I walked in wearing tight blue jeans and a denim shirt, and promptly got a dirty look from Michael Caine, he dressed to the hilt, who was having dinner with his family. The Spago on Sunset is closed now, but the one in Beverly Hills is just as popular as the original. Places in Beverly Hills are pricey, so be prepared. High prices help keep out the riffraff, you see.

Nightclubs? Here's one way to follow some of that; a lady named Mac Africa promotes musical events for stars who also happen to be musicians, like Dennis Quaid and Jeff Goldblum. To get on her mailing list, contact:

MAC AFRICA

P.O. Box 18784, Encino, CA 91416
818-342-2171
E-mail: macafrica1@earthlink.net

Both the film and television academies and the directors and writers guilds put on events that are open to the public. There's always something going on, something for everyone, and chances are very good you'll run into someone who could help move your project forward. You can use the Web to stay informed about these events. At www.oscars.org you can check Film Academy (in Beverly Hills) events (some are free). The TV Academy (in North Hollywood) site at www.emmys.tv also lists events and attendance requirements.

For clubs and restaurants, try the *Los Angeles Times* site at www.latimes.com. Look under the Calendar Live area and you'll find a searchable "Venue" section that you can tailor to your needs. The alternative newspaper, the *L.A. Weekly*, offers similar options on its site at www.laweekly.com, including a "Best of L.A." area.

I mention these online possibilities as a way to help plan an extended visit to Los Angeles. Try to give it at least six months.

Despite the setbacks I've endured, I love the City of the Angels. Where else would I get a thrill like the one I had on a sidewalk near Nate & Al's Deli in Beverly Hills when Fred Astaire said good morning to me, or when I was having dinner with my family one night at the Magic Castle in the Hollywood Hills and Danny DeVito stopped by our table, posing as the maitre d', and asked my mother how she liked her dinner? She didn't recognize him, but everyone else at the table did, and it was a magic moment that made us all laugh. After hours one night, I ran into Nic Cage at Canter's Deli on Fairfax Avenue in West Hollywood, and told him he was going to be a huge star. All I'd seen him in at the time was *Valley Girl*, but he had superstar written all over him. That type of thing isn't unusual when you live in Hollywood.

WEDNESDAY MORNING HAPPENINGS

There's even something for conservatives—the side of the political spectrum that supposedly doesn't exist in showbiz. (Fact: Over 40 percent of Hollywood entertainment business political donations in the 2000 Presidential election went to Republicans.) The Wednesday Morning Club, chaired by writer/director Lionel Chetwynd and a division of the Center for the Study of Popular Culture, puts on bimonthly events that are always entertaining, whether or not you share their political views. For more information, contact:

WEDNESDAY MORNING CLUB
9911 W. Pico Boulevard, Suite 1290, Los Angeles, CA 90035
310-843-3699, Fax: 310-843-3692
Web site: www.cspc.org/wmc

THE COMPETITION ROUTE TO SUCCESS

Once you've completed your screenplay, if you don't find someone immediately interested in buying it, there are several screenwriting competitions and workshops that might help boost your career. You'll find a long list of them at www.moviebytes.com

(with complete information) but in my humble estimation, only a few carry a lot of weight with film and television executives, and those are the ones I'll list here.

If I were starting out as a screenwriter today, I would only enter competitions that would offer me the highest chance of: (a) getting recognition from Hollywood people who matter; and (b) putting me in touch with successful people who could mentor me and propel my career to "regularly working screenwriter" status.

Most competitions outside the L.A. area won't do that. While doing research as a staff writer for the UPN children's series "Algo's Factory," I came across Mike Sherlock, who won the Charleston screenwriting competition for his script *King of the Air*, a dramatization of the first cross-country airplane flight by aviation pioneer Cal Rogers. Mike discovered that having won his prize didn't seem to mean all that much to the Hollywood producers he contacted. I read his screenplay, liked it, and recommended it to a producer who had just finished a film with John Travolta (avid flyer Travolta is a fan of Cal Rogers). Nothing happened.

Another reader of my books won a screenplay competition put on by a major national magazine for writers. She arrived in Los Angeles hoping to get an agent and a deal. She got neither. It was a decent script, but I knew as soon as I read it that it wouldn't have much of a chance except as a light TV movie. The people running the competition were ignorant of Hollywood commerciality.

A subscriber to my newsletter, Canadian screenwriter Michael C. McPherson, after winning the Prelude2Cinema contest (www.prelude2cinema.com), told me that all he received was a certificate worth framing and a check for $200 for his winning screenplay *Against Their Will*. The contest was designed to find a screenplay that could be digitally filmed. *Against Their Will* is a story of a family dealing with a deranged and aged neighbor. One of the proprietors of the contest told him: "I have to admit that after reading your script, it became the benchmark for judging the other scripts by." The movie still has not been filmed.

All the above experiences illustrate why I never tried to enter screenplays contests when I first started writing scripts. I wanted to be paid. When a contest is truly geared toward what will sell in Hollywood, however, the winner gets a different reception. I remind you that Pauline B. Jones' script *I Love Luci, When I Don't Want to Kill Her*, a winner in the Jack Stanley "First Draft" competition in which I was a judge, was quickly snapped up for production. (For more information on this contest, which may have ceased, contact:

JACK R. STANLEY, PH.D., CHAIR
Communication Department
The University of Texas–Pan American, Edinburg, TX 78539
956-381-3583
E-mail: jacks@panam.edu
Web site: www.panam.edu/dept /comm/Faculty/Jacks.html

Now here's a list of competitions that I feel will lead to the quickest screenwriting success, if you win, or sometimes if you simply place. I list them in alphabetical order, not according to any imagined rank within the industry or personal preference.

Carl Sautter Memorial Scriptwriting Competition for Film and Television

There are three divisions: Features/MOW's, Half-Hour Television, and One-Hour Television. You must be a current paid-up member of The Scriptwriters Network. Dozens of industry pros read the winning scripts. Contact:

>   Bob Corcoran, Competition Coordinator
>   Scriptwriters Network , 11684 Ventura Boulevard, #508, Studio City, CA
>   91604
>   323-848-9477
>   Web site: scriptwritersnetwork.com

Chesterfield Writer's Film Project

The Chesterfield competition was begun in 1990 under the auspices of Steven Spielberg and Amblin Entertainment. In 2001, the Writer's Film Project fellowship program is being sponsored by Paramount Pictures. The great thing about this contest is that the winners get living expenses while participating in the 12-month program, during which they write two feature-length screenplays guided by professional screenwriters. Chesterfield also intends to produce the best of each program's work, paying no less than WGA minimums. For information, contact:

ED RUGOFF, THE CHESTERFIELD FILM COMPANY

>   Writer's Film Project, Box 544, 1158 26th Street, Santa Monica, CA
>   90403
>   213-683-3977
>   E-mail: info@chesterfield-co.com
>   Web site: www.chesterfield-co.com

Disney Fellowships

Now a dozen years old, this studio contest seeks "up to eight writers to work full-time developing their craft at Walt Disney Pictures and Television and at ABC Entertainment." No previous experience is necessary, and a $34,000 salary is provided for one year. Fellows chosen from outside of the L.A. area are provided with round-trip airfare and a month's accommodations. Writers with WGA credits are also eligible for this program, but they should apply directly through the Guild's Employment Access

Department at (323) 782-4648. You can't apply to both programs; submit an application to *either* the TV *or* Features area. You must also be United States employment eligible. The fellowship is full-time, with a year-long contract. You cannot continue other employment or schooling during the fellowship period. Watch the fine print. If you are selected, any material written by you prior to the term of the program and currently controlled and/or owned by you must be disclosed in writing and Disney and ABC will have an "Exclusive First Look" at such material. Also, all material written by you during the term of the Fellowship Program will be owned by Disney or ABC. For more information, contact:

FELLOWSHIP PROGRAM ADMINISTRATOR

Walt Disney Studios/ABC Writers Fellowship, 500 South Buena Vista
  Street, Burbank, CA 91521-0705
818-560-6894
Web site: www.abcnewtalent.disney.com

Final Draft Big Break Screenwriting Competition

The first prize winner of this contest wins $5,000 and is flown to Los Angeles to meet with an agent. From there, the winner meets with studio executives. The 1999 winner, *Dawg* by Ken Hastings, began production November 13, 2000, starring Denis Leary and Elizabeth Hurley, produced by Gold Circle Films. Contact:

FINAL DRAFT

16000 Ventura Boulevard, Suite 800, Encino, CA 91436
818-995-8995, Fax: 818-995-4422
Web site: www.finaldraft.com (click on "Screenplay Competition")

Heart of Film

A part of the Austin Film Festival, the Heart of Film Screenwriters Conference, held in the capital of Texas each October, has the buoyant spirit of the Lone Star heart, and scripts discovered there get taken very seriously. You can drink long-necked beers with the 100 or so influential writers, directors, producers, studio executives, and actors who hang out after-hours at the bar of the Driskill Hotel, too. Like me, the folks running this are from Texas and congenital name-droppers. You might meet Robert Altman, Shane Black, James L. Brooks, Sandra Bullock (who lives there), Joel and Ethan Coen, Matthew McConaughey (who reportedly plays bongos naked and lives there), Oliver Stone, or Robert Towne. Contact:

AUSTIN FILM FESTIVAL

Heart of Film Screenplay Competition, 1604 Nueces Street, Austin, TX
   78701
512-478-4795, 800-310-FEST, Fax: 512-478-6205
Web site: www.austinfilmfestival.com/screenplay.

Don and Gee Nicholl Fellowships in Screenwriting

This important Hollywood competition selects five entrants to receive a $25,000 fellowship to sustain them for a year while writing. The ultimate honor in filmmaking is to win an Academy Award, and this international competition is housed at the Academy of Motion Picture Arts & Sciences. It's open to screenwriters who have not earned more than $5,000 writing for film or television. Entry scripts must must have been written originally in English and be the original work of a sole author or of exactly two collaborative authors. Up to five fellowships are awarded each year. You don't have to complete a screenplay during your fellowship, and if you get a paying job during your tenure, the fellowship is suspended until you are ready to resume. Fellowships may not be held concurrently with other fellowships or similar awards. You canould, however, participate in the Sundance Workshops. Nicholl Program Coordinator Greg Beal works hard to keep people informed of alumni success. Contact:

NICHOLL FELLOWSHIPS IN SCREENWRITING AT THE ACADEMY FOUNDATION

8949 Wilshire Boulevard, Beverly Hills, CA 90211-1972
310-247-3000
E-mail: nicholl@oscars.org
Web site: www.oscars.org

Nickelodeon Productions, Fellowship Program

If you want to write for kids, this program is designed to find writers to work full-time at Nickelodeon/Nick Jr. They espouse a "commitment to encouraging meaningful participation from culturally and ethnically diverse new writers" and want writers to have some work experience in child development. Contact:

NICKELODEON PRODUCTIONS, FELLOWSHIP PROGRAM

2600 Colorado Avenue, 2nd Floor, Los Angeles, CA 90404
310-752-8880
Web site: www.fellowshipprogram.nick.com

People's Pilot Competition

The brainchild of writer/producer Larry Brody, this competition is unique in that they initially only want your idea for a television series. The readers are members of Brody Productions or the Shapiro-Lichtman Agency, and the idea is to sell the winning concept to television in the next selling season. First prize is a Writers Guild of America, west-sanctioned development deal. No script is necessary at the contest stage, just your idea. Contact:

BRODY PRODUCTIONS

Cloud Creek Ranch, 422 West Carlisle Road, Westlake Village, CA 91361
E-mail: lbrody@tvwriter.com
Web site: www.tvwriter.com/peoplespilot

Slamdance Screenplay Competition

This competition culminates every January in Park City, Utah, simultaneous with the Sundance Film Festival. Steven Soderbergh, currently the fave director of major Hollywood stars, is a Slamdance alum. Winners of the contest receive cash prizes, software, and introductions to development companies and agencies. Really. The 1997 first place winner, *Chinaware-Fragile* by Christine Desmet, Robert Shill, and Peggy Williams, was optioned by New Line Cinema. The 1998 first place winner, Kate Alfieri, signed with ICM. One thing particularly cool about this one is that writers can call in for coverage on their submissions. Contact:

SLAMDANCE

5526 Hollywood Boulevard, Los Angeles, CA 90028
323-466-1786, Fax: 323-466-1784
E-mail: mail@slamdance.com
Web site: www.slamdance.com

Sundance Screenwriters Lab

A part of the Feature Film Program, a year-round series of workshops and events, the Screenwriters Lab is a twice-yearly workshop that gives emerging screenwriters the opportunity to work intensively on feature film scripts with help from established screenwriters. Participating writers have problem-solving story sessions and one-on-one dialogues for improving future drafts. Darren Aronofsky's *Requiem for a Dream* and Kimberly Peirce's *Boys Don't Cry* came out of this program. Supposedly open to any resident of the United States, the general consensus is that you have to know somebody to get accepted. David Ayer, for example, was recommended by Wesley Strick. However, it really works, "the search is for original, compelling, human stories that reflect the independent vision of the writer or writer/director." The Institute provides airline travel, accommodations, and food for one person per project. Contact:

SUNDANCE INSTITUTE
8857 West Olympic Boulevard, Beverly Hills, CA 90211
310-360-1981, Fax: 310-360-1969
E-mail: featurefilmprogram@sundance.org
Web site: www.sundance.org

USC-Cosby Guy Hanks and Marvin Miller Screenwriting Program

Established by Drs. Bill and Camille Cosby in 1993 in honor of Camille's father, Guy Alexander Hanks, and Bill's producer, Marvin Miller, the 15-week intensive workshop was designed to both assist writers in the completion of a film or television script and "to deepen the participants' appreciation for and comprehension of African American history and culture." Up to 15 participants are chosen for the two-evenings-a-week program. You cannot enter the program if you have been previously hired as a professional television or film writer, but the workshop "is not suitable for novice writers." For more information, contact:

USC SCHOOL OF CINEMA–TELEVISION
850 West 34th Street GT100, Los Angeles, CA 90089-2211
213-740-8194
Web site: www-cntv.usc.edu/cosby.html

Warner Brothers Writers Workshop

This workshop, 25 years old in 2001, is a 10-week training program in the half-hour comedy form, meaning situation comedies (sitcoms). Participants are guided through "the staff writing experience from pitching through table readings to final drafts." The information sheet states: "In years past, as many as half of our participants have been hired as staff writers at Warner Brothers and other studios." Selection is based on your sample script of a half-hour comedy that aired the year before. *Warning*: If selected, you have to pay (was $495, may change). Submission cutoff is in October of each year and the workshop begins at the end of February. For details, contact:

JACK GILBERT
Warner Bros. Writers Workshop, 300 Television Plaza, Burbank,
    CA 91505
818-954-7906
E-mail: Sitcomwksp@aol.com

Final Tips and Other Bizarre Information

The really successful writers (who may or may not be the most talented) that I have known move to Los Angeles. They take courses at UCLA, USC, the American Film Institute and other schools. They attend seminars. They find out where "industry" people hang out, and go there. They continually work to perfect their craft.

Once you understand the real-life map of Hollywood, the next step is to get yourself on the industry map of Hollywood and not remain a complete unknown. The way to do that is to: (1) make friends and be a friend; and (2) display trustworthiness, dependability, patience, and talent, in that order. Please understand, though, the competition is everywhere.

Many times, the Los Angeles–based contributors to the newsgroup misc.writing. screenplays have held impromptu get-togethers, usually at Jerry's Deli in West Hollywood. Some members will drive down from northern California; one couple even flew in from Washington, D.C. But there's a story from an L.A.–based member, Dena Jo Kanner, that I wanted to share with you.

"I pulled into a Starbucks parking lot, only to be greeted by a homeless person, offering to wash my windshield. Well, the last thing in the world I want is a homeless person washing my clean windshield with newspaper, so I told him no, but gave him a buck, anyway. I then reached into my car and pulled out a screenplay I was reading.

" 'Oh,' said the homeless man, 'you wrote a screenplay.'

" 'No,' I said. 'My friend did. I'm reading it for him.'

"Whereupon the man informed me, 'You'll know in 10 pages.' "

"Only in L.A.! It just about blew me away, hearing this homeless person telling me I'd know if the screenplay was any good in the first 10 pages! I guess everyone in Los Angeles really is writing a screenplay."

Hollywood from the Outside

As I've said before, Hollywood is a state of mind these days. Moviegoers see big studio films that could have been made in England, Italy, Germany, Australia or Hong Kong and may not know the difference. The good news for American writers is that the world film industry is open to scripts from outside their borders. This is particularly true in Germany, whose viewership market is second only to North America.

Since I have readers all over the world, and since I wanted to offer American writers some alternate ideas in the case of a writers' strike, I thought that, in this edition, I would add a short chapter about foreign possibilities and perspectives.

CANADA: HOLLYWOOD NORTH, OR ITS OWN UNIQUE WORLD?

Unless you've been living in Antarctica, you probably know that a large number of television shows and films distributed by American studios and networks are made in Canada. The last time I checked, 50 or so features were made in Toronto and Montreal in the summer 2000. The Montreal World Film Festival (see www.ffm-montreal.org/en) screened 360 films from 55 countries during its latest 10-day summer festival. 2001 will mark the festival's 25th year. In 2000, the only U.S. film in competition was Kenneth Lonergan's *You Can Count on Me*, based on a play by the director (which might tell you something about the kind of films they favor). Festival spokesperson Henry Welsh said that Montreal has a tradition of favoring art over commerce and world cinema over Hollywood, and that around 300 agents and buyers come from all over the world to market their films in Montreal.

Montreal also became the first festival to include a special section devoted to feature films made using new digital technologies. In fact, the president of the festival, Softimage Inc. founder Daniel Langlois, set up a company, Media Principia, and produced an all-digital film with Bob Krupinski. Montreal's Ex Centris cinema and new media complex, built at a cost of $25 million by Daniel Langlois, has three cinemas that show movies on standard 16mm or 35mm projectors, in 3-D immersion or in digital high definition. If you're not familiar with Softimage, it's the software used to create 3-D effects in movies like *Titanic* and *Jurassic Park*. According to press releases, Ex Centris "was built ahead of the curve because digital technologies have reduced budgets and increased the number of software and computer tools in the hands of do-it-yourself filmmakers."

The Toronto International Film Festival (see www.e.bell.ca/filmfest) celebrated its own 25th anniversary in 2000, opening its summer event with the world premiere of 10 original short films by Canadian directors who "have figured largely at the festival since its inception in 1975." According to the *Hollywood Reporter*, David Cronenberg, Atom Egoyan, Mike Jones, Guy Maddin, Patricia Rozema, and Anne Wheeler were among the directors who showcased short works of about four minutes each. The films aired in June on the Movie Network in Canada as part of a one-hour special. The Toronto festival also has a Screenwriter Mentorship Programme designed "to assist up to 90 screenwriters with their writing skills through one-on-one or workshop mentoring." You don't have to be Canadian. For details see www.e.bell.ca/filmfest/cinematheque/smpguidelines.htm.

If your script gets filmed in Canada, you'll hear about "Canadian content," which has to do with Canadian federal tax incentives instituted in 1996 that allow for rebates of up to 25 percent of labor costs, and can cover as much as 12 percent of a film's total budget. A certain number of key people in the production must originate from Canada, and that often includes a writer. So if your screenplay suddenly needs rewriting by a Canadian screenwriter, that might explain why. The scheme gives productions filmed in Canada an average tax break of $100,000 or more. Now do you understand why they filmed *The X-Files* in Canada for so long?

In June 2000, a survey released at the Showbiz Expo in Los Angeles, conducted by Stephen Katz, an Oscar-winning sound designer, found that more than a third of the 161 films shot in North America in 1999 were filmed in Canada. This was one reason the L.A.–based Film and Television Action Committee (www.ftac.net) began protesting at conventions.

The same month, however, a study by UCLA economic researchers, as reported in London's *Financial Times*, indicated that overall employment in Hollywood during the first quarter of 2000 was 4 percent ahead of the 1999 figure. The study further noted that over the previous decade, Canada's film production by foreign companies grew by 11,500 jobs, while Hollywood jobs more than doubled. It's hard to tell which claim is right. Also in June 2000, Disney announced the closure of Walt Disney Animation Canada, resulting in the loss of 200 Canadian jobs in Toronto and Vancouver. In February, however, it was announced that revenue from Vancouver, British Columbia's film and television production industry reached $1 billion (US $680 million) in 1999, up 20 percent over 1998, making British Columbia the third-largest production center in North America.

One might think such revenue would make Canadian government officials friendlier toward films and TV shows from Hollywood, but the opposite is true. In January

2000, Canada's TV regulator banned all Hollywood movies from being shown in prime time on Canadian Broadcasting Corp. stations. The CBC was required to remove all Hollywood pictures from the prime time schedules of both CBC and the French-language Radio Canada network within three years so that more homegrown Canuck films and foreign movies could be shown in prime time. Was that backlash or retaliation? In July 2000, the Canadian Independent Film Caucus, a group representing independent filmmakers, claimed that for the past two years Canadian news and documentary crews from Toronto and Vancouver were held up at the border, with some denied entry.

I recently read a story about some screenwriters being stopped at the Canadian border. They told the guard they were American filmmakers and were waved on through with a smile. I couldn't help but think that Californian politicians should consider legislating rebates on budgets like those in Canada.

A survey released by PriceWaterhouseCoopers in November 2000 found that Canada was the world's most "wired" country. According to the survey, 48.2 percent of Canadians surf the Internet, going online for an average of 5.1 hours per week. In comparison, 43 percent of Americans, 38 percent of Australians, and 26 percent of Europeans spent time on the Web. To find out more about what goes on in Canada, check these sites:

Canadian Lawyer Index—www.canlaw.com

CBC's Online Arts & Entertainment—www.infoculture.cbc.ca

Collection of Web Links to Canadian Film Festivals—www.cs.cmu.edu/Unofficial/ Canadiana/CA-filmfests.html

Monster Home—Supposedly, the first feature-length movie created specifically for the Web, at www.monsterhome.com

Société des Auteurs de Radio, Télévision et Cinéma (French language screenwriters in Canada)—www.sartec.qc.ca

The Writers Guild of Canada and the Canadian Screenwriters Collection Society— www.writersguildofcanada.com

IN JOLLY OLDE ENGLAND

Usenet, home to newsgroups like misc.writing.screenplays, is not renowned for gentility and civility, so I became intrigued when I kept seeing regular polite, helpful posts of FAQs (Frequently Asked Questions) about the Internet from Charlie Harris in England. I learned he was an accomplished screenwriter and budding director and found him to be as enthusiastic as myself about using cyberspace to forward screenwriting and film. Here's what he had to say about his career and the Internet.

"I started as a projectionist and worked my way through the cutting rooms (freelance for BBC, etc.) to directing and writing documentaries, TV drama and theatre, and writing feature scripts for production companies in the U.K. and continental Europe. My debut cinema feature as director is a quirky dark film called *Paradise Grove* (www.filmsite.co.uk/paradisegrove).

"In the early 80s, I and group of fellow writers set up the London Screenwriters Workshop, which was the only (and is still one of very few) organizations teaching writing in this country. Now renamed Screenwriters Workshop, our events are regularly attended by writers from all over the country. I still run seminars on screenwriting for SW and at the London International Film School. And for fun I also maintain the Internet Search FAQ Web site at www.purefiction.com/pages/res1.htm."

Charlie's influences with regard to screenplay structure came from surprising places.

"I've read everything I could get my hands on, interrogated friends and neighbours if they went to seminars I hadn't been to, watched (and still watch) films all the time and read as many scripts as I can find. And it's all been important. (Even if some of the screenwriting books I've seen have been significantly flaky.) But my greatest influences have been football matches (soccer to you). Nothing can beat them for tension and variety.

"Other influences are *Alternative Scriptwriting* by Dancyger and Rush; *The Uses of Enchantment* by Bruno Bettelheim (wonderful and thought-provoking); *How to Write a Movie in 21 Days* by Viki King (don't laugh, it's good fun and takes some of the po-faced seriousness out of the craft); anything by Linda Seger, and Nathalie Goldberg; Hitchcock, Hawkes, Sergio Leone, Truffaut, Morecombe and Wise, Kurasawa, The Marx Brothers, and haiku."

Lately, I've noticed that recent English and European films like *The Full Monty* and *Billy Elliot* have had increasing influence on American moviemakers. I asked Charlie to comment.

"It has been said that a typical American film has one act where the hero is stuck and two acts where he tries do something about it (and succeeds), whereas a typical British film has two and a half acts where the hero is stuck and half an act where he tries to do something about it (and fails)! More seriously, differences in structure seem related more to the genre or subject of the film than to the country of origin.

"What I notice is that American films tend to be much quicker to establish the essentials and move into story, whether mainstream or indie. Indeed, it's noticeable that when I show examples of character development from U.S. movies, I often find myself showing the title sequence! Two clips that I like to use are the openings of *Tender Mercies* written by Horton Foote and directed by Bruce Beresford, and John Sayles' *Passion Fish*. Neither are exactly fast-moving films in the conventional sense, but both have firmly established the situation and the basics of their central characters by the time the final title has faded off the screen, allowing the story to get under way with minimum fuss. European films (I include British here) tend to be more indulgent; however, there are excellent examples of exceptions to this rule."

So many aspiring screenwriters and development people I meet seem locked into the established norms of American screenplay structure, so I asked Charlie about his seminars on different structures and why he put them together.

"In my seminars I examine the established rules and discuss how they can be used to strengthen a film, and how sometimes you need to know how to break them. We look at how films have broken the rules in the past and why they did it. It's not difficult to find examples because, as I say, every film is forced to break at least some of them. It would probably be impossible to make a film which kept every single one of them! But as a writer you need to know when you have to change your story to fit the rules, and when you must break the rules in order to make a point, but you also have to know how to do it without destroying the script in the process."

Charlie had a lot more to say, but I'll let you explore his Web site to check in on his evolving theories. I will say, however, that he opened my eyes to how differently Europeans can see film.

Shortly after the second edition of this book was published, I started looking into possibilities in foreign markets, and my first stop was England. Maybe that's because I loved Hitchcock movies and made a deal to do an update of his *39 Steps*, or because I loved Monty Python movies and TV shows like *Fawlty Towers*. I grew even more interested when I wrote an article about selling to Hollywood for the magazine of the Writers Guild of Great Britain (see www.writers.org.uk/guild/Home or contact 430 Edgware Road, London W2 1EH, Phone: +44 0171723-8074, Fax: +44 171-706-2413, E-mail: postie@wggb.demon.co.uk). Nearly half a century old, this union seems more collegial than their American counterparts, and I've always found communications with officers of the Guild like Gregory Evans to be thoroughly enjoyable. When I asked Greg about the state of the British film industry, he was candid about why we didn't get more quality films like *Chicken Run* and *Billy Elliot*.

"The real problem here is scripts," Greg told me. "There just aren't enough good ones. That's what all the producers say, from David Puttenham to the smallest independent. There are good reasons for that which have nothing to do with the quality of British writers. Until very recently we haven't had a proper film industry, just a few jobbing producers. This means it's almost impossible to sustain a living writing for the movies over here. So experienced writers like me, who might want to write screenplays, work in television instead. This may change with the setting up of Film Council, which has a lot of cash (several million pounds) from the National Lottery to spend exclusively on script development (some will go to writers, some will be spent on training, some on script editors)."

The British film and television establishment is working hard to solve such problems. In early 1999, BBC Worldwide, the commercial arm of the British Broadcasting Company, announced that they planned to invest more than $64 million in home-produced feature films. In August 2000, BBC director general Greg Dyke announced that an extra £480 million ($768 million) would be spent on BBC programming over the next two years.

U.K. film attendance reached a 26-year high in 2000, with approximately 143 million movie tickets sold, but some Brits weren't too happy with certain American movies. Audiences were upset by Mel Gibson's *The Patriot*, whose main villain, Colonel William Tavington, leader of Britain's Green Dragoons, shoots a child in one scene, then rounds up screaming villagers, locks them in a church, and torches them alive. Added insults came from *U-571*, which had Americans capturing the German Enigma coding machine, enabling the Allies to break Nazi communications. In actuality, the Brits made the capture in 1941, before the United States entered World War II.

Most U.K. writers do better with traditionally American subjects. Stephen Soderbergh won the Best Director Oscar for *Traffic* in 2000, but some people feel the BBC version, "Traffik" written by Simon Moore, was better. The *Traffic* script is very close to Moore's in many ways, with some scenes word for word the same. Despite such annoyances, most companies in the U.K. are open to outside writers, even Americans.

If you're interested in television and radio programs made by the BBC, see www.bbc.co.uk/writersroom. At the bottom of the page, you'll see a link to the screenplay formats they use.

You might enjoy writing with U.K. writers. I've collaborated with a team in England and a screenwriter in Ireland on separate projects and been happy with the results (although we haven't sold the projects yet). A great number of competent U.K. writers have turned up on the misc.writing.screenplays newsgroup, all with aspirations of writing for Hollywood. I've kept my U.K. friends happy in any way, particularly if I can supply them with 8.5 x 11 paper, which is hard to find there. (They use A4 paper, in case you've never seen a European script. If you want to know what a normal U.K. screenplay looks like, surf over to http://freespace.virgin.net/a.dalla_rosa/U.K. script.htm.)

To learn more about how screenwriting works in the United Kingdom, study the *Writer's Handbook 2001*, the *PACT Guide*, published by the Producer's Association for Cinema & TV, *The Writers and Artists Handbook*, *The Guardian Media Guide*, and the *BFI (British Film Institute) Handbook*. You can find all those books and the U.K. equivalent of this book, *How to Make Money Screenwriting* by Julian Friedmann, at www.amazon.co.uk or at the Screenwriters Store Ltd. (www.screenwritersstore.co.uk). You can also find information on the Screenwriters Store site about the new *U.K. Scriptwriters* magazine established by Friedmann and published six times a year by C21 Media.

"As an agent representing scriptwriters," he says on the site, "I am aware of the problems professional writers face in getting their ideas heard, their spec scripts optioned, then rarely seeing them go into production. Despite the millions of pounds spent annually on development in this country, the earnings from the films and programmes are relatively modes. . . . Over the last 10 years I have taught scriptwriters, script editors, and producers in both the U.K. and on the Continent. I established PILOTS for the EU MEDIA programme, where teams of writers and script editors were trained by working with them over six months on a pilot and bible for a long-running series. . . . There are possibly as many as 10,000 film scripts doing the rounds in the

U.K. at any one time. Last year just over 100 movies were made in the U.K. Unlike Hollywood, it is difficult to live off options in the U.K. They simply are not large enough."

If you're *really* serious about U.K. screenwriting, I've been told that the London College of Printing, so named because it was founded over a hundred years ago and rose to fame as the center for print training in the U.K., is the place to study. One of my readers is a happy graduate. The school has a Media School involving film, journalism, and photography, "all of which are now bigger and more significant than the print aspects of the college" according to Phil Parker, Course Director in Screenwriting. The M.A. program accepts 24 students a year. Students do not have to be U.K. residents. They also offer a B.A. Film and Video undergraduate course, which takes approximately 35 students a year and is a three-year, full-time course. Mr. Parker tells me that "the European film production sector is on a big expansion at the moment, and people are gearing up to compete at all levels with U.S. studio output." For more information, contact:

> Phil Parker, Course Director
> M.A. Screenwriting, London College of Printing, Back Hill, Clerkenwell,
>   London, England, EC1R 5EN
> +44 (0) 20-7514-6853
> www.lcp.linst.ac.uk

If you'd like to take an English vacation and a workshop at the same time, check out The Screenwriters Workshop at www.lsw.org.uk, formerly known as The London Screenwriters' Workshop. It's the country's only charity devoted to the promotion of new screenwriters and is run by and for writers.

You might also surf over to the BBC Education Learning Zone at www.bbc .co.uk/education/lzone/master/links.shtml. You'll find some links to American schools there, I'm happy to say. (Hey, we're not all bad.)

The big U.K. event that brings North American, European, and international film and TV people together each year is the five-day London Screenings, a pre-MIFED (the Milan, Italy fest) jamboree. If you don't know what that's all about, take a look at www.londonmifed.com. Part of the London Screenings is the Raindance Film Festival, which targets international film acquisition executives and attracts an eclectic audience of leading U.K. industry professionals. Who might you meet? Perhaps someone from Ardent Productions, the independent production company headed by Prince Edward (known to the U.K. film industry as Edward Wessex, thank you).

I'm certain that we'll be hearing a lot from U.K. writers and filmmakers in the next few years. They're working on the cutting edge. In October 2000, TVIndustry.com Daily (www.TVIndustry.com) reported that broadband communications company NTL and Universal Studios Networks had formed a joint venture to launch a contemporary library movie channel in the United Kingdom called The Studio, accessible via the Internet by all computer platforms, airing for 18 hours per day, seven days per week, with more than 1,000 movies available. It's the kind of thing I predict will dominate the U.S. market in coming years.

Even traditional English houses are getting into the broadband and Internet act. Legendary British movie house Hammer Films—whose movie style was emulated in Tim Burton's *Sleepy Hollow*—was bought in 2000 by a team of investors that included advertising guru Charles Saatchi, British Film Commission chairman Larry Chrisfield, and former Warner Music U.K. chairman Rob Dickens. The first stage of the new marketing plan was to develop a distribution business via a presence on the Internet. Stages two and three would establish more traditional channels, with the planned production of two to three low-budget mainstream horror feature films and a six to 12 part TV series a year starting in 2001.

Whether you're using the Net as advised by Charlie Harris or looking into more cutting-edge applications, there are a number of great Web resources for learning about U.K. matters:

Breaking Down the Door of the U.K. Market—An article by a working U.K. screenwriter at www.screentalk.org/art027.htm.

DV World—A magazine covering anything and everything to do with digital video on all levels, at www.dvworld.co.uk.

London Town—The city's official site at www.londontown.com.

Mandy.com Film/TV Jobs—Jobs all over the world, including the United States, from a U.K.-based site, at www.mandy.com. Click on "Jobs."

The Probert Encyclopaedia—An encyclopedia aimed at journalists and researchers (free) at www.probert-encyclopaedia.co.uk.

U.K. Scriptwriter's Network—A free service for scriptwriters and those looking for scriptwriters at www.darkin.demon.co.uk.

THE GERMAN FACTOR

In late October 2000, Variety reported that German production company KC Medien was investing almost $500 million in alliances with French-owned Pathe and Peter Guber's Mandalay Entertainment, meaning they would cofinance 20 films through year 2003. KC Medien had previously backed productions like *Austin Powers* and some other films that didn't do as well. A month later, German video distributor Splendid Medien signed a theatrical distribution deal with 20th Century Fox International that gave Fox all German-speaking theatrical and pay TV rights to Splendid product for the next two years (including Steven Soderbergh's *Traffic*). Earlier in the year, The Canton Co. signed a five-year coproduction joint venture with German indie giant Senator Entertainment to do four to six films a year with an average budget of $50 to $80 million.

Joe Roth, who left Disney to start his own Revolution Studios, has a six-year arrangement for distribution through Germany's Senator for 36 pictures. Kopelson Entertainment, a Fox-based production company, has a deal for Munich-based Intertainment to fund $500 million over five years, in exchange for a minimum of 10 films.

And that's what it's all about with Hollywood and Germany. Money. The German entertainment industry makes a lot of money, and it spends a lot of money. That's the perfect candidate for a Hollywood marriage.

Fortunately for American screenwriters, English-language products have a much better chance of global success. When German films make it in the American market, they're an anomaly, like Tom Tykwer's *Run, Lola, Run* and (almost 20 years ago now) Wolfgang Petersen's *Das Boot*. Like Petersen, director Tykwer and his company, X-Filme, are now doing business with Miramax Films, but the catch is, they're bringing their own money to finance the $11 million-plus budgeted *Heaven*. In February 2000, L.A.–based Intermedia acquired the U.S. remake rights to *Alles Bob!* (Everything Bob!), a German-language comedy released by Helkon in Germany to rave reviews during the summer of 1999 for Ridley Scott and Tony Scott's Scott Free Productions. Such an acquisition has been very rare, however.

In July 2000, German production and distribution company IN-motion acquired 76 percent of Los Angeles–based Myriad Pictures for $4 million. The Frankfurt-based company had only gone public on the German stock market the month before. There's plenty of money from Germany, and the German market is very strong for North American film and TV suppliers, largely due to government-backed production incentives akin to those in Canada, as well as German tax shelters. If a show can qualify as a "European production," it's much more likely to get financed. Outside the U.S., Germany is the largest market for TV distributors, who make it a point to know which American stars are hot in Germany and Europe. (For example, David "Baywatch" Hasselhoff is a superstar there, in music as well as television.) Because the German film market is so healthy, it's not uncommon for American screenwriters to sell scripts to German production companies, which are then translated into German and shot in German. Sometimes, the screenwriter can retain the English movie rights. This is why producers like Andreas Grünberg (www.gruenbergfilm.com/credtits.htm), who says he is *always* looking for scripts, post on American newsgroups and chat boards looking for product. Gruenberg wants adventure, action/suspense thrillers (only with female leads), romantic comedies, teensploitation, and family drama, all thematically transferable to Germany/Europe for his company and others. If you have anything like that, see www.gruenbergfilm.com/kontakt.htm.

New Mexico–based writer Peggy Bechko, through Gruenburg, sold an option to a family-oriented screenplay to Studio Hamburg Letterbox Filmproduktion GmbH in Hamburg, Germany after responding to a posting on the Hollywood Litsales Writers and Screenplays wanted page (www.hollywoodlitsales.com). Like other Americans working with the German market, Peggy had to learn the double taxation that takes place in this type of situation, with money coming out on both sides of the Atlantic. All that's necessary to deal with it is to mail the Internal Revenue Service a "relief from double taxation form" and Americans only pay taxes once.

Your best bet to break into the German market is to: (a) look for postings like the one mentioned above; (b) find a U.S. company with German ties; (c) meet a writer who is already selling to the market; or (d) get in touch with a German-based agent or a U.S. agent who sells there.

You might also look into Script House, Germany's first script development agency. They offer consulting services and are apparently successful, having worked on projects like *Sonnenallee*, the winner of the 1999 German Script Award. Look over what they offer at www.scripthouse.de or contact them at:

SCRIPT HOUSE

Rosenthaler Strasse 34/35, D-10178 Berlin
030-283 902 46, Fax: 030 - 283 902 47
E-mail: info@scripthouse.de

Meanwhile, you might be interested in the following Web sites to learn more about the German market. Although they're mostly in German, you can always use AltaVista's translation page at http://babelfish.altavista.com/translate.dyn to sort through a block of text or an entire Web page.

Export-Union des Deutschen Films (ExU)—The official trade association for the promotion of the export of German films at www.german-cinema.de/about/index.html.

German Film / Film in Deutschland—A marvelous page of German film links (in English) by professor Sabine Schmidt of Rhodes College at http://schmidt.for-lang.rhodes.edu/home.html.

IG Medien—A union for anyone working in the German media at www.igmedien.de.

VDD (Verband deutscher Drehbuchautoren / Association of German Screenwriters)—A professional organization for screenwriters, not technically a union, located at www.drehbuchautoren.de.

EUROPA, EUROPA

The good news for screenwriters is that European cinema attendance has been strong for over a decade. In January 2001, Eurostat, the statistical arm of the European Union, reported that box office receipts went up by 80 percent between 1990 and 1998, reaching ECU 4.3 billion in 1998, with a 40 percent jump in the number of tickets sold to 800 million. France accounted for more than 20 percent of all cinema admissions in 1998 (117 million tickets). Next was Germany (149 million), Italy (118.5 million), and the U.K. (115.5 million). Ireland had the highest rate of cinema attendance per capita, with an average of 3.4 admissions per person in 1998 (and Ireland has been a favorite of Hollywood lately, with coproductions, tax breaks galore, and no income tax on writers and artists).

Those kind of figures explain why, in December 2000, the European Union governments announced they would contribute 1 billion euros ($850 million) to a new fund for film and television projects by companies in member states, a fund for "audiovisual" projects, to be administered by the European Investment Bank. The catch is, MEDIA Plus, the European Union group responsible for development, production, and promotion of European film, changed its guidelines so that they would provide funding only for slates of films, not individual projects. To receive funding consideration from MEDIA Plus, European production companies must submit a development slate of three or more films. What this means to you is that you need to submit scripts intended for Europe only to companies that you know have working arrangements with European companies. How do you figure that out? Well, read the trades. Remember, the *Hollywood Reporter* has a direct link to Europe's big entertainment Web site from its home page.

Another possibility is an event that occurs each year during the Berlin Film Festival. The European Pitch Point is designed for "professional scriptwriters to present their ideas for screenplays intended for cinema release or TV movies to a select international audience consisting of high-ranking producers and commissioning editors." A dozen writers are selected by a jury of film professionals. Though it's aimed at European screenwriters, I haven't seen anything that says non-Europeans are ineligible. For more information, see www.pitchpoint.org/EuropeanPitchPoint.

The creme de la creme of screenwriting recognition in Europe is Equinoxe, the workshops headed by actress Jeanne Moreau with SACEM (Société des Auteurs, Compositeurs et éditeurs de Musique) and the Franco-American Cultural Fund, founded in 1993 by Noelle Deschamps and French pay TV giant Canal Plus. Equinoxe offers writing and producing workshops twice a year at the beautiful Chateau Beychevelle in France's Medoc region. It is affiliated with CISAC, the International Confederation of Societies of Authors and Composers, a nonprofit, nongovernmental organization "embracing 180 societies representing creators in 95 countries." Like Sundance, you'll have to know someone to be involved in this one, but what's life without goals? Meanwhile, here are some other sites that might aid your European ambitions. For an overview, contact:

Angelika Schouler
SACEM, Conseiller du Président du Directoire, Equinoxe, 4 Square du
    Roule, 75008 Paris
+33 1 47 15 41 06, Fax: +33 1 47 15 41 32
Email: angelika.schouler@sacem.fr
Web site: www.sacem.org/english/internat/equinoxeateliers2000ang.html

Danske Dramatikeres Forbund—The Danish screenwriters union at www.dramatiker.dk.

European Film Academy—Home of the European Film Awards and more at www.europeanfilmacademy.org.

EuroScreenwriters—A nonprofit site with a database of European screenwriters and links at www.euroscreenwriters.tsx.org.

Euroscript Workshop—A week-long intensive script workshop in France, only open to European writers; see www.euroscript.co.uk.

Euro VR—A virtual reality exploration of places in Europe using QuickTime VR Panoramas at www.eurovr.com/panoramas.htm .

Scrittori Associati di Cinema e Televisione Italiani (SACT)—Italian film and TV writers (site in Italian) at www.sact.it.

THE BEST INTERNATIONAL SCREENWRITING COMPETITION

The Hartley-Merrill Prize began in 1989 after Dina Merrill and Ted Hartley attended the Soviet-American Film Summit in Moscow in the midst of perestroika. They felt compelled to do something for writers there, so they established a screenwriting competition with a cash award of $10,000. It is now administered by Debbie Vandermeulen, who works with the ministers of culture in 17 countries to find great scripts: Argentina, Bosnia, Bulgaria, Croatia, Cuba, the Czech Republic, Estonia, Hungary, Mexico, New Zealand, Poland, Republic of Georgia, Romania, Russia, Serbia, Slovakia, and South Africa. If your country, or the country of a friend is not on the list, please know that any country can get involved; Hartley-Merrill is constantly growing. Competitions held in the individual countries usually get between 100 and 125 entries. The winning screenplays are translated into English if necessary and forwarded to Los Angeles, where an international jury picks the top three selections.

The awards are announced at the annual Cannes Film Festival, with a gala in Los Angeles in June. The grand prize winner is invited to be a part of the Sundance Writers Lab and their airfare and accommodations are paid. First prize is $3,000, with second prize $1,500; this is in addition to the money they win in their home country, which is an average of $5,000. To be eligible, a writer cannot have had more than one feature film made as a writer, although they can have more than one of other film credits. The American judges are people like Alan Ball (*American Beauty*), writer/director/producer Frank R. Pierson, and script rewrite guru Linda Seger.

One of the goals of the competition is to set standards and formats for writers worldwide, which alone is a noble goal. The competition is perhaps the most successful of them all in terms of winners being produced. Twenty-five out of the 33 winners have had their scripts made into films, and Irakly Kvirikadze, the first Hartley-Merrill Grand Prize in 1990, was nominated for the Best Foreign Oscar in 1997, for his film *Les Mille et une recettes du cuisinier amoureux (A Chef in Love)*. For more information, contact:

HARTLEY-MERRILL PRIZE

1875 Century Park East, Suite 2140, Los Angeles, CA 90067
310-277-0707, Fax: 310-226-2490
E-mail: hartleymerrillprize@yahoo.com
Web site: www.hartleymerrillprize.com

LE FESTIVAL INTERNATIONAL DU FILM DE CANNES

Still the sexiest film festival in the world, the Cannes Film Festival (www.festival cannes.fr) is held every May in this beautiful seaside resort in France. Everyone wants to go there, everyone wants to be seen there, and only a few can afford a room. That much you knew. What you may not know is that the center of American activity at the festival is The American Pavilion (see www.ampav.com). After the Writers Guild of America scored a success with their *Screenplay Coffeehouse* at the Sundance Film Festival in 1996, they were invited to be a part of the pavilion. Okay, it's not the same as walking arm-in-arm with Laura Linney into the Palme d'Or ceremony, but it's something. And lest we forget, it was a digitally-made film that won the Golden Palm in 2000 (Lars von Trier's *Dancer in the Dark*). There's hope for everyone at Cannes, even screenwriters. And just in case you're interested, under the "Archives" tab at the Cannes site is a search engine to look up anything in the history of the festival.

EL MUNDO GIGANTE (THE GIANT WORLD)

It amazes me every time I get an e-mail from someone in another country who has purchased one of my books and wants more information about Hollywood. I have friends on all continents. One of them, Jose Levy in Buenos Aires, contacted me about selling the English rights to *El Guarante*, an intriguing miniseries that was the most successful in the history of his country. So far, I've helped him select an agent (CAA) and work his way through offers for the English version, and I've also steered producers his way. My pay? Some nice wine and a funny friend. Jose is also one of Argentina's big publishers, specializing in computer manuals and magazines in Spanish (see www.tectimes.com).

It's amazing who I hear from, like Simon de Waal, an award-winning Dutch screenwriter who explained to me why, when Mike van Diem accepted the 1997 Oscar for his *Karakter (Character)* for Best Foreign Picture, he thanked Jean van de Velde and Rolf Koot in his speech. Dutch film officials were going to send *All Stars* instead, written and directed by van de Velde and produced by Koot. Van de Velde and Koot thought that van Diem's film was better and would stand a much better chance of winning. So they withdrew, and it won. Show me an American director and producer like that!

If you embark on an international career, make friends first. Toward that end, here are some Web sites from more cyber-friends.

Australia's Production Book—Contact information for everyone in film and TV in "Oz" at www.b4bfilmtv.com/prodbook.asp.

Australian Film Festival—For the Australian Film Institute awards (equivalent of the Oscars) at http://cinemedia.net/AFI.

Australian Writers Guild—Pro organization for writers of film, television, radio, theatre, video and new media at www.awg.com.au.

Melbourne Writers' Network—Writers in Melbourne and Victoria, Australia at http://clubs.yahoo.com/clubs/melbournewritersnetwork.

New Zealand Writers—A great site with opportunities for writers around the world at www.nzwriters.co.nz.

New Zealand Writers Guild—A nonprofit association for pro writers at www.nzwritersguild.org.nz/about/about.html.

Golden Harvest Entertainment—The most well-known entertainment company in Asia, at www.goldenharvest.com.

CONNECT Magazine—For anyone interested in "Bollywood," India's Hollywood, by my friend Nyay Bhushan at www.connectmagazine.com.

Claddagh Films Limited—An independent film and TV production company in Galway, Ireland at www.claddagh.ie (with great links).

Merlin Film Group Ltd.—"Ireland's Leading Film Financiers" headed by noted director John Boorman at www.merlinfilms.com.

Italian Writers—The first Web site on Italian writers (in Italian, of course) at www.sceneggiatori.com.

Transmediale—A festival about "digital technologies in present-day society" at www.transmediale.de/01/en/diy.htm.

Companies in Film—A collection of links and e-mail addresses to top Scandinavian film companies at www.filmbyen.com.

Creative Film Management—A well-equipped South African company for African film production, at www.astraweb.co.za/cfm.

South African Writer's Network—Writing jobs and "resources for writers in every genre" at www.futureshock.co.za.

LEARNING THE WORLD MARKET

Smart producers study the world market. They know where they can get production deals. They get information on what movies have done well worldwide, and it's often surprising. For example, Mel Gibson's breakthrough role, *Mad Max*, made $100 million worldwide yet barely got noticed in U.S. theaters.

Swiss-based accounting firm KPMG International (www.kmpg.com), in 1997, began publishing a taxation guide to film and TV financing in world countries, and it became an industry bible of sorts on which countries offer the best incentives and tax breaks for producers. These days, you can keep up with that kind of information on their Web site. Another useful site is WorldTax at www.paradine.com/worldtax/mainframe.html, which has links to pages that introduce the tax system of countries around the world.

You say you're a screenwriter, not a world-hopping producer? Well, guess what? Many smart, rich producers were screenwriters only, until they learned how the world of cinema really works. There are people all over the world waiting to team up with you to get film projects made. I hope this chapter helps you find them.

Joining the Digital Revolution

Hollywood Reality 101—If you're "only" a screenwriter, you can make a nice living. Nevertheless, unless you become a filmmaker you won't fully understand how Hollywood works. If you do become a filmmaker, your life will change forever. I saw it happen with Michael Rymer, who went from being an unsold writer when I first met him to directing his feature, *Angel Baby*, on a shoestring in Australia. The last time I checked, he was directing Anne Rice's *Queen of the Damned* and having quite a nice time.

I've also known writers who became TV show executives and producers, like an old friend named Paul Haggis who received the Valentine Davies award from the WGA in 2001. He learned how the business worked, not just how screenplays work. TV shows, like feature films, need to come in on budget, you see. TV executives don't turn them over to someone who doesn't know how to take a show all the way through postproduction.

Which brings us to the digital filmmaking revolution. Now, for under $10,000, you can start from scratch and buy a computer and monitor and a digital camera that will enable you to make and edit a feature-length digital movie. More and more, being a filmmaker is an affordable prospect. If you didn't see *The Blair Witch Project* or haven't followed this revolution, you might be surprised to know that Spike Lee says he used a $1,200 consumer video camera to shoot his feature *Bamboozled*.

How can you get in on this? I'll provide a few hints; it's something I'm pursuing myself.

AN EDITOR'S POINT OF VIEW

I've been around Hollywood long enough to know that many a film gets saved in the editing room and that a skilled editor can assemble odd footage into a work of art. If you start off making a movie with an editor's point of view, you're better off, and it will save you money.

Norman Hollyn is the author of *The Film Editing Room Handbook: How to Manage the Near Chaos of the Cutting Room* (Lone Eagle) (with digital editing covered, by the way). He teaches a class at USC and has worked on projects as diverse as the *Wild Palms* miniseries, the film *Mr. Destiny*, and the TV series *The Equalizer*. As a music editor, he worked on films like *The Cotton Club* and *Fame*. Here's a conversation we had about editing:

Skip: What do you learn as a writer when you go through the process of editing a movie?

Norman: First, let me say something that I tell students in my USC classes. The processes of writing and editing are almost the same. Editors and writers deal with the same issues—character arc, storytelling, suspense, pacing, etc. Editing, as I say again and again, is rewriting. Having said that, we need to delve a bit deeper into how those similarities get translated from the printed page to the silver screen. Story construction is the hardest thing to learn without actually making a movie, putting it up on the rack and seeing what falls off the axles. There are elements of story that *don't* need to be told because it can all be done in performance and nuance, and there are points that absolutely *cannot be omitted*. Filmmaking is the process of guiding an audience to feel a movie in a way that you, as a filmmaker, want them to feel. Leave out one crucial detail ("that character is the other character's sister," or "he actually saw him fall on the ice"), and you let the audience write their own movie—for better or for worse. Tell the audience too much and you have them way ahead of you, without anything to do except think of tomorrow's laundry list.

What the writer can learn during the editing process is what he or she already should know—storytelling. However, much as the writer needs to learn how to write a script to sell it, the writer should also know how the *rewriting* of a movie (for that is what editing essentially is) can tell a story in this nonwritten medium. Editing, rather than production, is the best way to learn this.

Skip: What's the quickest way to learn editing basics that can help you write better scripts?

Norman: Know the right questions to ask. Once you know that, any observant, clever, and smart writer can figure out most of what he or she likes by looking at tons of movies and asking those questions while watching them. The physical aspects of editing are easy—how does this director build suspense? When does he/she use dialogue overlaps, reaction shots, silence? How does it feel when you cut out of a shot in the middle of a dolly? These questions are the technical building blocks of editing and observing other films is the best way to know what he or she likes. However, you need to know what questions to ask first. The other thing for the observant writer to notice is how scenes are constructed. Get hold of some shooting scripts and compare them to final films. On *Heathers*, we rearranged the structure of the middle part of the film. Simply noticing these things leads to questions of "why?" That's a fruitful place to begin learning.

Is there a quick way? Not really. But you certainly don't need to know how to edit in order to write well. What the writer really needs to pay attention to is how things change from script to screen. Occasionally, the director's commentary tracks on DVDs are good sources for this type of information.

Skip: Should a screenwriter attempt to write things in a script that are usually the concern of an editor? For example, should you write a closeup?

Norman: Deciding whether to use something like a closeup or not is the very cornerstone of what editing really is all about. Making the decisions on how to effectively guide an audience through a script, after you figure out just what is important in the script, is the core of what I teach in my editing classes. To that end, I always read a script many times to figure out what the writer had in mind. What are the major beats of any scene? Where do characters or situations change? What is the subtext of any given moment, of any given scene, of any given sequence? If the writer needs to write "closeup" in order to convey that sense, then I'd say, sure, put it in.

Unless the writer is also the director, however, I rarely have any use for indications like that in regards to style or pace. And, along those lines, just what does "SMASH CUT TO" mean at the end of a scene? My advice is not to even bother with those sorts of directions. We'll figure out how to transition from one scene to another in the editing room, thank you very much.

Skip: Do you think it's wise to try and shoot and edit your own short film to learn the process? If so, where would you advise a writer to start?

Norman: This is really a two-part question. The first part is really "is it wise to cut your own material?" My answer to that would be, no. You need the dialectic of another person to get a real sense of what can help shape a scene. That goes ten-fold if you've never actually made a film before. I'd say, make the film and get someone to work with in the editing room. You don't want to be bothered with all of the technical nonsense. You just want to sit and argue about the piece.

The second part of the question is "As long as you can't afford an editor, should you shoot and edit your own short film?" The answer to that is, of course. It's always better to have hands-on experience than observational. You might be able to learn a nice chunk if a director friend of yours lets you sit in on every day of his or her shoot and every day of his or her editing process. But you'll never truly internalize the how and why of creating matching eyelines until you do it wrong and then find you can't cut it together well in the editing room. You never really and truly find out how to shoot material that you can build towards a climax by watching someone else do it. Filmmaking has too many variables for that. And, of course, since the making of a film is really a date with a series of compromises, you'll never know the feeling of giving something up, until you're forced to do *against your will*. At the very least, you should try and coerce an editor friend to go over shot lists with you before shooting, and try and spend some time on the set with you. Shooting a movie isn't pretty, but it's a lot less pretty in the editing room if you don't do it right to start with.

Skip: What did you learn the first time you edited a film that you didn't know before you started?

Norman: That editing a film is almost as complicated as shooting a film. That without a strong grasp on what you want each scene to do, within the context of what you want the film to do, you're going to be lost in the editing process.

The next thing I learned is to let the footage talk to you. Despite what is written on the page, magic happens when an actor performs in front of camera that has film rolling through it. You can't plan for that and you need to be open to change. But change only works when you make sure that it fits within the film as a whole. So, once again, we're back to having a firm grasp on the film's logline, its inner core.

Skip: Assuming you have written scripts, did becoming a successful editor change the way you looked at a script?

Norman: It's made my scripts leaner because I've learned that you don't have to explain everything. You need to be clear on what the intent of every scene is, and you need to be clear on what you hope to get out of every beat. But that doesn't need to come from description. The other things that I've learned I mentioned earlier; some things are necessary and many things aren't. Relationships are important (this includes characters' relationship to each other and to their environment), character names are important (it's best when they come up naturally in the dialogue relatively early on in the film), and location is important.

Skip: What have you learned about students that you could pass on to my readers to make them better students of moviemaking?

Norman: An interesting question. I've learned that a student's two main jobs are to be open to anything and to question everything. Editing is, like writing, such a personal trip that it's important that you learn how you really feel about something and why. To go back to an earlier example—I've worked with directors who couldn't imagine cutting out of a moving camera, and I've worked with those who can't understand why you wouldn't. I tell my students to watch a lot of movies, try a lot of different edits for each scene they cut, and ask themselves what they like and don't like about each one. They don't even have to ask themselves "why"; all they need to do is see if they like something. Do they like jump cutting? If so, when? Do they like music starting on a scene cut, or slightly earlier or later than a scene cut? Do they like scenes where the editor or director has cut from a big wide shot to a close-up? And then they need to ask themselves what each of those scenes was trying to do. They need to question what I say as well as what they say. They need to develop a series of "sense memories" (to use the acting term popularized by proponents of The Method) to help them to remember what it felt like when a particular event happened on screen. Good students are good at doing that. They'll keep pushing until shut off.

Editing is, as anyone will care to tell you, more complex on a nuts-and-bolts level, than repairing your computer's internal hard drive. It takes most assistants five to 10 years to build up a body of knowledge that will guide them through the process safely.

Anticipating problems is what you need to learn if you're going to cut your own film. That's why I wrote my book—to give both aspiring and accomplished editing room personnel a heads-up on what dangers can be down the line if they don't know what they're getting into.

WHICH HARDWARE? WHICH SOFTWARE?

When you're preparing your script to shoot, one software is the de facto industry standard. Movie Magic Budgeting and Movie Magic Scheduling (see www.moviemagicproducer.com) has for some time been selling for only $99 with a one-year subscription, with all upgrades free during your subscription period. Everyone I know in production uses this software to create budgets/checklists.

Another standard of the business is StoryBoard Quick (see www.powerproduction .com), which will help you draft out scenes if you don't have the ability to draw like Robert Redford. It's available for both Mac and Windows and can be very effective in presentations in selling investors on investing in your film. I highly recommend it.

If you have an older camera, you might need Director's Cut, a device that allows you to import source material originally recorded on VHS, Hi8, or other analog format tapes to any Macintosh equipped with FireWire. It can also import content from live TV, cable, DVD, you name it, via S-Video or composite video. It works automatically with both iMovie2 and Final Cut Pro. See http://sabre.forest.net/powerrinc-24 /index.cfm.

The article "Digital Video 101: Behind the Curtain" at www.creativepro.com /story/feature/6672.html?origin=story is a great "multi-part primer on joining the DV revolution." My favorite book for beginning video filmmakers is *Digital Guerrilla Video: A Grassroots Guide to the Revolution* by Avi Hoffer (Miller Freeman Books). It comes with a CD and will tell you things that you'll never learn in traditional seminars. I first learned of Avi when I read about a documentary he made on the Amazon, editing as he went with a digital camera and an Apple PowerBook.

If you want a fantastic filmmaking education from the comfort of your computer desk, spend less than $100 and get a three-CD program called *How to Make Your Movie: an interactive film school* by Rajko Grlic (see www.interactivefilmschool.com or call them at 800-516-9361). It works with both Mac and Windows, and comes with a Production Notebook that is an education in itself. You'll see why Robert Nickson, a professor of film at NYU Tisch School of the Arts, said it is "a brilliant way to learn filmmaking because it allows you to practice without spending a fortune."

As you get more into digital filmmaking you'll start learning about digital 24-frame progressive (24P) cameras like the Sony/Panavision HDW-F900. 24P became the "Holy Grail" of the digiterati after George Lucas announced he would be using it to shoot his next *Star Wars* installment. TV series have been using it for some time, and rumors about it falling short have drifted through Hollywood, but I've found them to be untrue. As an example, it was reported that the 24P shooting of the Paramount Television series *Diagnosis Murder* was a "near disaster" by a technician at Laser Pacific. Since I happened to know the executive producer of the show, I asked him about it. He said the technician didn't know what he was talking about and that they had had no problems. (The Alliance Atlantis series, *Gene Roddenberry's Earth: Final Conflict* was the first episodic television production to use 24P as an alternative to 35mm film.)

A 24P will probably be too expensive for you to rent, so you might consider a Canon XL-1 or GL-1 (which Apple offers on their Web site). The flip-out LCD screens on the GL-1s are great for showing what is being shot, and they offer a Frame Movie mode (but make sure you experiment with Frame Movie before using it a lot).

I'm generally a big fan of Sony equipment (www.sony.com), so I looked there first when considering the next most important equipment for shooting digital, a multi-format digital videocassette recorder. The Sony DSR-11 DVCAM deck is a wow. It plays and records both NTSC (US standard) and PAL (European standard) from both DV and DVCAM-sized in either mini or standard tape with an i.LINK (IEEE-1394, FireWire) interface. It also comes equipped with a wireless remote control, and some have predicted it will become the new standard deck in DV packages.

The next thing you'll need is a "shotgun" microphone. The Sony 908 is a stereo mike good at short range (8 to 10 feet), even in a noisy environment, for less than $100. You can use it with an extension cable for handheld work or on a boom.

If you plan to record and add ambient sounds or voice dubs after filming and you can't afford a deck/mic package like I've mentioned, take a look at the Olympus DS-150 Digital Voice Recorder (www.olympus.com). It's a fantastic piece of equipment that records 160 minutes of high-quality sound and is barely bigger than a cigarette lighter. Even better, it comes with the IBM ViaVoice (for PC) software. If you get tired of typing your scripts, just load the software and pretty soon you'll have the computer typing out the screenplay you've dictated. All you'll have to do is edit! I absolutely love this recorder package.

I try to adopt the crawl before you walk or run approach with a new area of study, which is why (since I like Mac more than PCs) I've gotten started with iMovie2, an inexpensive software that comes free with newer Apple computers. New PCs have similar software, mostly meant (like iMovie2) for editing of home videos. The desktop Sony VAIOs, for example, come with software that converts digital video to MPEG and captures DV, as long as you don't let the hard disk get too fragmented. If you're inclined to follow my lead about Macs and iMovie, pick up a copy of *iMovie2: The Missing Manual* by David Pogue (Pogue Press/O'Reilly). It's a basic education in videomaking and, like every other book by Pogue, amazingly comprehensive. By chapter 16, you're into the big leagues with a discussion about Final Cut Pro (www.apple.com), Premiere (www.adobe.com), and EditDV (www.digitalorigin.com), the video editing programs that cost $500 to $1,000 and are meant for serious filmmakers. (He doesn't cover MediaStudio Pro, which is also a fine program, details at www.ulead.com.)

David Pogue told me, and I tend to agree, that you could probably edit an entire video feature with iMovie2. If you use the program, you should also check out Slick Transitions and Effects, inexpensive iMovie2 add-ons, at www.geethree.com. It gives you capabilities that much more expensive programs offer.

You may be asking yourself why I like Mac computers so much. Basically, they're easier and still preferred in Hollywood, QuickTime is becoming the cross-platform preferred format for delivery of shorts (like movie trailers) on the Internet, and the excellent Sorensen Video2 QuickTime software (www.sorensen.com) offers better compression than other products and lets you place your own "watermark" on your footage to trademark or protect video from unauthorized use, among other things.

Let me offer some examples of the Mac preference in Hollywood. When Showtime Networks needed to build Storage Area Networks (SANs) to help assemble station-break videos, known as "interstitial material," to keep from continuing to have to manually chase down every needed piece of videotape, they used four Mac workstations for editors, a fifth machine to add and remove material from the SAN, a sixth unit to perform nightly backups, and a seventh to test new software. And when it became obvious that you could edit a feature film on a desktop Mac with Final Cut Pro, the first two to go through that process were at Showtime. In October 2000, the American Film Institute (AFI) installed a state-of-the-art post-production and asset management facility at its Los Angeles–based campus. The facility was built to allow fellows at the AFI Conservatory, the Directing Workshop for Women and other production-based programs to edit their films. The software selected was the Avid 1000XL Media Composer 10.0, running on Macintosh G4s. If you want more information on complete high-end Mac-based systems, including cameras and audio decks, take a look at www.promax .com or call 800-977-6629.

There isn't room in this book to cover everything necessary to get someone started with video editing, but the software mentioned above is a good start. Just try to get a computer with a Firewire port; the 1394 connection is now a standard.

Once you figure out what system works for you and you move into more serious software editing applications, if you want to feel like you're in the big time, take a look at Commotion Pro from Pinnacle Systems (www.pinnaclesys.com). It's available for both Mac and Windows and includes over 75 filters for amazing creative effects like pixel-accurate motion blur, which is instantly previewable on a Firewire device (like my PowerBook). Don't know what "motion blur" is? Think about the pod racers in the last *Star Wars* movie. Refining animations like that, with support for higher-end systems like Media100, is why this $2,000 program is worth every penny.

No matter what I've said about any of the hardware and software here, what matters is simply that you use whatever it takes to get your script up on a screen. At the Hollywood

Film Festival 2000, the winner of the Best Digital Feature was *The Poor and Hungry,* written and directed by Craig Brewer in Memphis, Tennessee. Shot on two consumer digital cameras with the black and white button pushed in to get a grainy b/w look, the whole thing was done, top to bottom, for only $20,000.

GET THE LIGHT RIGHT

The low-budget films that I've seen that fell short usually had two areas of shortcoming if the script, directing, and acting were decent: (1) sound; and (2) lighting. I've given you some ideas for getting quality sound. Now here are some thoughts about getting the light right.

Maurice Jordan is the "Head Honcho" of a cool Web site called Reel Butter (http://reelbutter.homestead.com/index.html). He's also a professional lighting technician. His first advice to any beginning filmmaker is to have some pieces of equipment to help control the light, like a big fill board.

"It's a 4 foot by 8 foot piece of foam-filled card with black on one side and white on the other," he told me. "You can have a few mirrored tiles to bounce light, too. Blocking and adding light is what you try to do any way you can, quick and cheaply. If you want to shoot with light as is, your picture is not going to look very Hollywood. A lot of people start out wanting their films to look Hollywood slick, but shooting on digi with a low or no budget is not going to get you a slick look. So don't really try.

"Lowel makes basic lighting kits that are fairly cheap, and you can rent some of the smaller kits from a local rental house or a local college. Some people I know have gone to Home Depot and bought floodlights and shot with those. If you plan on shooting on digital to transfer to film, that will be more complex and you will have to do a bit more research. If you are going to keep it on video, then you should shoot using a good video monitor if you can. Get an education about it. The book I got when I first got into filmmaking was *Set Lighting Technician's Handbook* by Harry C. Box. *Matters of Light and Depth* by Ross Lowell is about the art of lighting and is quite humorous. Two Web sites I've found helpful are http://digitalidiots.com and www.tapehousedigitalfilm.com.

"If you can afford it, hire a DP (Director of Photography). They will usually find the lighting personnel. Also, a lot of DPs have their own lights, which can be a way to save some money. But the bottom line is, you want someone you can work with, someone you believe in."

John Jackman is the author of the video, "Basic Lighting for DV," which can be ordered online from www.greatdv.com/lighting. The tape covers all the basics in a visual manner, which works well even for beginners. Like Maurice Jordan, he is also a fan of Ross Lowell's *Matters of Light and Depth*. Additionally, he runs the "Craft of Lighting" forum at www.dv.com and offers lighting tips at www.greatdv.com.

"I would avoid using an on-camera light as primary illumination," he advised me. "It will look flat like a news shot. An on-cam light can be excellent for fill, however, in many situations. The primary problems are what you always run into without designed lighting—overhead lights creating ugly shadows on faces, overblown contrast between shadowed areas and light sources. The main problem is excessive contrast with light sources (windows or lamps) that come into the scene. If the lamps used in the scene are bright enough to really illuminate the subjects, they will 'blow out' if shown onscreen. It is possible to arrange shots and lights carefully to keep lamps out of shots but close enough in to illuminate the subjects. Position subjects to be illuminated by light from windows, but do not show the window in the shot. If a window must be in a shot, knock down the light a bit with window gel or black organza. Reflectors are also very handy at evening out contrasty lighting."

There is no easy answer to the question of lighting kits. He also recommends Lowels, and suggests that for greatest flexibility, the kit should include a focusing hard light and a soft light. He suggested that local film commission directories or a directory like www.mandy.com will have listings of DPs who often also are lighting designers. The people who set up the lights, known as gaffers, "are also excellent lighting designers," he said, "though not always. Some just set up lights and aren't too creative!

"Lighting is tremendously important in the look and feel of the image," he told me. "It is often overlooked (like good audio) with truly pedestrian results. If you want to create great images, they must be well and creatively lit! Or, as one wag put it, 'Without lighting your picture is just black!' "

ONCE YOUR FILM IS DONE

Once you have a film ready for exhibition, you'll probably hit the road to film festivals. They've become so important to Hollywood that the Academy Foundation of the Academy of Motion Picture Arts & Sciences in 2000 announced a Film Festival Fund established by the Academy's Board of Governors. The Chicago International Film Festival, the New York Film Festival, the Telluride Film Festival, and the New York International Children's Film Festival were recipients. Lucky for you, some excellent references on existing festivals are available. My favorite is from Chris Gore of Film Threat Weekly (www.filmthreat.com). *The Ultimate Film Festival Survival Guide* is available at the site or you can call (800) 404-4484.

Another fine book is the *International Film Festival Guide*, 3rd edition, edited by Shael Stolberg (Hushion House).

If you're inclined to visit an online film festival, the Yahoo! Internet Life Online Film Festival is the best. Director Mike Figgis premiered his digital movie *Time Code* there. It's a yearly event backed by traditional movie companies like New Line and Mandalay and short film "giants" like iFilm and AtomFilms. The *Hollywood Reporter* and the *New York Times* are cosponsors.

There are thousands of festivals, both virtual and real. I'll leave it at that, and suggest you read the books.

WHERE IT'S ALL GOING

It's a general conclusion in Hollywood that high-speed digital film delivery will one day be the standard. As of this writing, however, only three million Americans had broadband capability that allowed simultaneous wireless, streaming, broadcast simultaneously, mostly in L.A. and New York. That tells me it's inevitable for the rest of the country, but I decided to ask an expert. Beth Kennedy is Exec VP, Business Development, Worldwide for JumpCut's Los Angeles Convergent Media Studios. She has been a senior executive at MCA, Inc., Universal Television, Universal Pictures, and Universal Studios. She served as Los Angeles' first "Film Czar," and has consulted for and produced convergent media projects for clients including Disney, Microsoft, AOL, TNT, General Motors, FilmFestivals.com, and Women in Film.

I asked her first if she thought that quality digital features will get buried in an avalanche of digital filmmaking.

"I would love to be able to say that quality will rise to the top regardless of the medium or distribution platform," Beth said, "but I'm afraid that the proliferation of devices and platforms is going to exacerbate the difficulties in marketing and promoting any film, digital or traditional. That said, there are a number of guerrilla and viral marketing approaches filmmakers can take to target the audience for their film, develop a following, have their audience become evangelists for the project and coordinate and consolidate marketing and promotions, which can reduce the costs and extend the reach.

"More than 90 percent of PCs have Flash animation capability (www.shockwave .com), and short videos can be viewed at www.atomfilms.com or www.ifilm.com. Soon, we'll be able to download full-length feature movies from a variety of sites (Blockbuster, as well as studio-owned sites) instead of trudging to the video store. The marriage between Time Warner and AOL made everyone sit up and pay attention; AOL Plus will escalate the competition in broadband.

"There are a number of independent companies creating original content, and some say they're the cutting edge and the studios are behind the curve. Venture capitalists have financed start-ups to create, produce, and distribute streaming video content for all digital platforms, but many of these have folded. Nevertheless, anyone with a Pentium Processor and a DSL (digital subscriber line) connection can serve thousands of pages a second; they can multicast and distribute to high-speed wireless technologies. Within a few years, the current distribution system won't be recognizable.

[Editors note: On September 26, 2000, ShowBizData.com reported that Zhone Communications now had networking gear that could simultaneously handle telephone, Internet, cable and broadcast TV, and wireless services. Zhone raised $500 million from private investors to build the Broadband Access Node (BAN), which *Business Week* called "the Holy Grail of digital convergence."]

Like me, Beth does not feel that the digital revolution signals the end of traditional Hollywood distribution channels.

"The entertainment industry has always experienced and survived the introduction of new technologies," she said. "The advent of television changed the movie business forever. It changed the economics, the nature and the structure of the business, the politics and leverage between studios, distribution outlets, talent, and unions. It also changed consumer behavior, as did home video, CD-ROMs, and PCs. What's important to remember is that technological change also brings opportunities, both creatively and expanding distribution. IFilmPro, ReelPlay, and others have videos available to download on the Net. New companies announce their entry daily. CinemaNow (funded by Microsoft, Blockbuster, and Kipco, and majority-owned by Lions Gate Entertainment) is an on-demand, pay-per-view library, which includes Internet distribution rights to films from Lions Gate, Trimark Pictures, Tai Seng, Allied Artists, and Salvation. They launched the pay-per-view service with the Internet debut of the Russell Crowe film, *Heaven's Burning.* It is a great marketing device for producers and buyers of films, but my home PC would seriously bog down if I tried to download a video online. My PC just isn't fast enough yet and doesn't have the memory capacity to handle downloads of major movies.

"Two studio initiatives, which will offer digital downloading services are expected to launch in 2001, and in the near future, your TV will be equipped with PC functionalities and you'll be able to point-and-click to select a movie to download, at a minimal fee, and save the trip to the video store. You'll also be able to order that toy or product while watching its commercial (or from a clickable product placement in the film) and have it bill your credit card. From the beginning, the Internet has been the first simultaneous global communications platform; day and date openings are now possible, if not practical technically due to bandwidth limitations. However, the bulk of the growth has taken place in the U.S., and the American character of Web content is impossible to overlook. If you look closely at the numbers, the Internet's demographics are shifting and the technology makes it feasible, economical, practical, and even necessary to develop multiple language and cultural 'customized' versions.

"By 2005, the Computer Industry Almanac estimates that the U.S. share of Internet users will drop to 29 percent. AOL, Yahoo, and other major companies already have foreign language affiliates or country specific sites. The challenge for the creative community then becomes, how will the move to an increasingly global and multicultural audience change content? I believe it will increase the opportunities for 'made-for-Internet-download' movies, targeting niche audiences, which aren't economically feasible for a major studio theatrical distribution, but will be tremendously profitable when offered to a global audience."

HOLLYWOOD JUMPS ON THE BANDWAGON

Everyone in Hollywood is not embracing films on the Net. In June 2000, the Oscar Academy modified the rules for the 73rd Awards so that a film cannot appear on the

Internet before its theatrical release and be eligible for an Oscar. I expect that will change before long, because the Coen Brothers, Roger Corman, Faye Dunaway, Ethan Hawke, Jennifer Jason Leigh, and directors Barry Levinson, Robert Redford, Stephen Soderbergh, and Betty Thomas are only a few of the people who believe in and are involved in a digital future. Even Steven Spielberg got into the act, forming a partnership with toymaker Lego to create a digital moviemaking kit that lets children create and edit their own films. Director Gus Van Sant has said this about digital video: "Quality-wise, it's the same using digital devices and desktop movie applications. That's the huge revolution really. It's making the industry more accessible to people who have previously been shut out."

There are reasons for the revolution. George Lucas said that shooting *Star Wars: Episode II* with digital cameras vastly speeded up the production pace, allowing sets to be torn down immediately after shooting is completed rather than having to wait until dailies are screened the next day. "We are in the digital age now," Lucas he told the *New York Times* after the completion of photography, "and trying to hold onto an old-fashioned technology that's cumbersome and expensive—you just can't do it." The cost of videotape stock for the film, he said, was about $15,000 versus the $2.5 million he would have spent on film stock and processing.

Lest anyone doubt digital distribution, on November 14, 2000, the feature *Bounce*, starring Ben Affleck, played entirely in digital format at the AMC Empire 25 theater in New York's Times Square. The Miramax Films screening was done in partnership with Boeing, AMC Theatres, Texas Instruments, and The Walt Disney Company, delivered via satellite and projected digitally. Disney Senior VP of New Technology Bob Lambert gave a presentation on the future of digital cinema technology at the event.

Of course, digital delivery has been with us for some time. In May 1999, a never-before-released feature, *Dead Broke* starring Paul Sorvino, was broadcast over the Internet via "streaming" at www.ifilm.net. That November, at www.newblood.net viewers could see, in three-minute episodes, *NewBlood* a film about young vampires in London's clubland *only* distributed on the Net. The theaters were next. In August 2000, Texas Instruments announced that more than one million moviegoers had seen all-digital feature films projected by the company's DLP Cinema technology, on 31 screens worldwide. The same month, an online independent survey conducted by ShowBiz Data, Inc., and FilmIT revealed that the majority of individuals who indicated they were employed in the entertainment industry (62 percent) had confidence that full-length feature films would be delivered successfully via the Internet within 12 to 24 months.

PUT UP YOUR SHORTS: RESOURCES FOR GETTING NOTICED

In the busy world of screenwriting, it's generally held that if you can't interest someone in your script in the first 10 pages, they probably won't buy it. Let's extrapolate a similar logic to digital films. If you can't win an award at a film festival or a high-profile national contest like Project Greenlight (see www.projectgreenlight.com), the best way to get noticed as a digital filmmaker is via shorts ported to the Net.

Essential Software

Remember the chapter on building your own Web site? If you choose to build your own site for the purpose of heavy content like short films, I suggest the Dreamweaver Fireworks Studio from Macromedia, which gives you more control of Web graphics and code than any other program. It's the Lamborghini Countach of this kind of software. The next step is The Flash Freehand Studio by Macromedia, which is the choice of over half a million Webmasters worldwide. Think of the best sites with the coolest movement that you know; chances are they've been produced with Flash. If you see animation on a great site, you're guaranteed it's Flash. See www.macromedia.com for more details.

Next, you'll need software to convert the short films for viewing on the Web. My favorite (and the cheapest) is QuickTime Pro (www.apple.com). You might also consider the excellent RealProducer from Real Networks (www.real.com), which is still the industry leader, or software which outputs to Microsoft's Windows Media Player (www.microsoft.com). If you don't want to field e-mail complaints, it might be wise to acquire all of them.

Ample Information and Expos Galore

To keep up with the digital and computer world, some select reading will keep you informed. My favorite magazine of this type is *Videomaker* (www.videomaker.com), which offers a free monthly e-mail newsletter for video production enthusiasts. Next is DV.com (www.dv.com), which has a great newsletter and several online forums that you'll find useful. Both of these magazines put on excellent video expositions.

Newsgroup Resources

When you get serious about making your own movie, subscribe to the newsgroups rec.video.desktop and rec.arts.movies.production. In the former, you'll find real people actually using the hardware and software you have questions about. In the latter, you'll find questions more general to the actual making of movies. Both groups are highly trafficked.

Web Sites You Need

Although www.atomfilms.com and www.ifilm.com are the short film leaders, here are some other helpful sites.

2-pop, The Digital Filmmaker's Resource Site—Overseen by Ralph Fairweather, who first joined the DV Revolution in 1969, this site at www.2-pop.com rocks. It's a part of the creativePLANET (www.creativeplanet.com) network of Web sites, which include:

- http://CinematographyWorld.com—The Cinematography Community
- http://DesignInMotion.com—The Motion Design Community
- http://DirectorsWorld.com—The Directing Community
- http://EditorsNet.com—The Film and Video Editing Community
- http://MovieMagicProducer.com—The Production Solution Site
- http://PostIndustry.com—The Post Production Community
- http://VFXPro.com—The Visual Effects Community

AFCI/Association of Film Commissioners International—At www.afci.org is a truly global resource for production and a network of worldwide film liaison professionals.

Digital Talkies—This ambitious alternative cinema site at www.digitaltalkies.com is based in India.

Eveo—QuickTime movies "that convey the unique creative visions of independent filmmakers from around the world" at www.eveo.com.

Hypnotic—An indie studio within the structure of Universal Studios, this company seeks out emerging filmmakers and incubates them. Details at http://reelshort.com.

Motion Picture Player Association—The MPPA is a nonprofit organization whose programs include a Guerrilla Filmmaking Series. Surf to www.motionpicture player.com (warning, heavy Flash intro).

New Venue—One of my personal favorites at www.newvenue.com, with a FlickTips page that every aspiring filmmaker should read.

Nibblebox—Founded by former NBC executive David Bartis, www.nibblebox.com aims to incubate college filmmaking talent.

Pixies—The "Oscars of the Internet," named after the term "pixel," with real-life black tie awards, at www.pixieawards.org.

QuickTime Film—A page of links provided by Apple to sites using QuickTime software, at www.apple.com/quicktime/qtv/film.

RESFEST Digital Film Festival—A showcase of the best of digital filmmaking, touring major U.S. cities. See www.resfest.com.

Shockwave—The number-one site for very entertaining Flash animations, at www.shockwave.com, with a free Flash player download.

Short Film Festivals—A short film festival list offered by the Oscar Academy, at www3.oscars.org/73academyawards/rules_shortfest.html.

StudentReel—Broadcast your work online here using QuickTime, absolutely free (not just for students), www.studentreel.com.

GETTING YOUR FILM FUNDED

On January 14, 2001, Marion Hart wrote in the *New York Times* that short films were back in a way we had not seen since the 1970s, thanks to the Net. Almost a month later, David Shaw in the *Los Angeles Times* wrote that cyberspace was taking the "sneak" out of sneak previews. "Studios," Shaw said, "say the Internet explosion allows screening reports, gossip, and misinformation to surge virtually unchecked, potentially killing a movie even before it's released."

That's impact. Still, all the information in this chapter can be daunting to the aspiring screenwriter turned filmmaker, and the big question might be, "Where do I get the money for all this hardware, software, and filming?" See Ethan Ramos' Film Investment Incubator at http://members.ebay.com/aboutme/ethanramos. Another site that will help is Film Arts Foundation's Info Pages, an adjunct to their magazine, *Release Print*. The pages include grants, funding, jobs, calls for entries, and other opportunities at www.filmarts.org/infopages.html. The University Film and Video Association site at www.ufva.org offers a student grant program also. If you're a student at NYU Tisch School of the Arts, The Royal College of Art in London, the UCLA School of Theater, Film and Television, or the USC School of Cinema-Television, you may be eligible for a Sapient Digital Media Scholarship Program, awarded annually; ask at your school or find details at www.sapient.com.

If you're not a student but are a U.S. resident, here's some great news. The Small Business Administration (SBA) is now granting entertainment industry-related loans. You need 20 percent of your budget in cash/credit to qualify for a loan guarantee of the remaining 80 percent, and you'll have to demonstrate that you have distribution for your completed movie, but everything else you'll need is explained on their Web site, including how to draw up a business plan that will work. The SBA guarantees bank loans of as much as $750,000 to small business start-ups. The L.A. office's first approved film came in April 2000 to the film production company Gristle Inc. The office grants about $750 million in loan guarantees to 2,700 businesses a year. Take a look around www.sbaonline.sba.gov for complete details.

MUSIC TO YOUR EARS

Because of concerns about piracy during digital transmission of movies, don't be surprised at some point in the future to see independent filmmakers creating their own DVDs and selling them via Web sites, a sort of latter-day mail order movie business. This type of possibility is one reason why Apple now ships a "SuperDrive equipped" Power Mac G4 computer in their upper-end models. The Pioneer-made SuperDrive combines CD and DVD reading and recording capabilities and ships with Apple's iDVD authoring software, which allows users to create interactive presentations on

DVD media using a simple drag-and-drop interface. Apple also offers consumers DVD Studio Pro, a $995 DVD-authoring program.

If you make a movie and are musically-inclined enough to do a soundtrack album as well, you might be stuck when it comes to pressing your own CDs if you don't have the right equipment. If you're a Mac user, selling your own soundtrack is definitely do-able; you can get your own recording studio going for less than $800, thanks to Tascam, the company that started the home recording studio revolution. Their 14-inch-wide USB-ready mixing console, the US-428, requires no internal card, and is portable enough to run with an iBook or PowerBook (see www.tascam.com). You'll need MIDI or audio software to take advantage of the US-428, but ProTools Free from www.digidesign.com is a free download.

When it comes to something like burning my own discs to sell, I want something reliable, so as usual I look to companies that have not let me down in the past. The Predator CD-RW drive from Iomega (www.iomega.com) is compatible with both Macs and PCs and has a top-loading design similar to portable CD players (meaning you're less likely to improperly insert a disc). With four hot-swappable connections—USB 1.1, FireWire, PCMCIA, and USB 2.0—and a stunning software suite, it seems like the best bet to me for backing up my computer, writing music CDs, etc.

I wanted to discuss my ideas about selling self-created soundtracks of a digital movie, so I contacted Gwen Riley, VP of Music at Artisan Entertainment, the innovative folks who brought us *The Blair Witch Project*. My first question was whether you should even worry about trying to put together your own soundtrack, the way the makers of the Hollywood Digital Film festival winner *The Poor and Hungry* had done.

"Not unless you have a great stand-alone record," Gwen said, "although you could consider digital online distribution if the movie was going the same route via the Internet. If you have a particularly enticing movie, some record labels would probably want to get involved and if this was the case, might be willing to help finance some of the music licensing costs for the project up front in exchange for distribution rights. Artisan is unique in that it launched a soundtrack label that is not exclusively designed for Artisan projects. Flash Cut Records was established in 1999 to distribute specialized soundtracks for cutting-edge films with distribution. We can provide marketing and production consultation for soundtracks as well as distribution through one of our relationships. I always encourage everyone to take risks and go with the creative choice for scoring, etc."

And if someone wants to find a company to put together a soundtrack for their film, I wondered, where would they start? She gave me a list:

1. Screen the film for all labels and publishers, particularly those whose catalog is being utilized in the picture.

2. Search for key placement of a potential lead single that will be timely for the release of the picture so you have a showcase spot to offer a potential label.

3. Research the labels that are out there, focus pitch efforts on those having a roster that is most appropriate for the creative direction of the picture.

4. Start early on in the process. If you can secure a label deal early in the game (you typically need to have a distributor for the picture), you may be able to present your director with a full catalog of options early on in post, thus saving precious time making replacements once they get settled on particular tracks that may fall out of the picture."

And does a hit film like *The Blair Witch Project* affect soundtrack sales?

"There is no correlation," Gwen told me. "You need hit songs on the record. The soundtrack market has been oversaturated. The labels have been burned on their investments in high-risk albums tied to uncertain box office results. That's why filmmakers are beginning to find alternative modes of distribution that do not rely upon traditional methods of theatrical marketing, which is what created the demand for soundtrack in the first place."

If you think you might have a worthwhile soundtrack with your movie, you can reach Gwen Riley and learn more about Flash Cut Records by contacting:

ARTISAN ENTERTAINMENT

2700 Colorado Avenue, 2nd Floor, Santa Monica, CA 90404
310-255-3919, Fax: 310-255-3840
Web site: www.artisanent.com

FINAL TOUCHES

Whatever route you use to get your movie known to the world, sooner or later you'll hear opinions about getting a "film look" out of your digital movie. It's doable, via a somewhat mysterious post-production process known as Magic Bullet, which was created at the cutting edge San Francisco production house, called The Orphanage. The chief technology officer of the firm is Stuart Maschwitz, who was once the supervising visual effects artist at George Lucas' Industrial Light and Magic. At the 2001 Sundance Film Festival, a number of features and shorts made use of the Magic Bullet technology, which might tell you something about how good it is. At the Hollywood Film Festival in the summer of 2000, the one name I heard over and over was The Orphanage. The fees for Magic Bullet vary according to how heavily The Orphanage gets involved. They start at $85.00 per finished minute, or $7,650 for a 90-minute film. The editing software they prefer is Final Cut Pro. Contact them at:

THE PRESIDIO

39 Mesa Street, Suite 102-B, Bldg. 39, San Francisco, CA 94129
415-561-2570
Web site: http://theorphanage.com (you'll need Flash to view the site).

Moving from screenwriting to digital filmmaking is a big step, but I'm convinced that anyone with two licks of sense can do it. Doing it right requires a lot of study, trial and error, and going with what works before trying to reinvent the reel. I hope this chapter has spurred you to "Action!"

Things I Can't Do Without

This book is designed to help anyone in the world with a computer and modem write scripts and market them effectively from their location. In the last book, because so many people had asked me about the equipment I use, both hardware and software, and how I went about my business, I tried to include everything and be all things to everyone.

Not this time. It's impossible.

Since the last edition, I've given up doing "Business Edge," the biweekly business computing column for *ComputorEdge* magazine. I'm still a software and hardware geek, though, so I've begun doing reviews and articles for The Writer's Store. Because of that, in some instances I need to remain neutral. So, if you want to know whether I prefer Final Draft or Screenwriter 2000 script formatting software, you won't get it here. (I use both, one on the desktop, one on the laptop.) In this chapter, I'm just going to talk about companies and products that I love and believe might help you, computerwise. If you have any comments or questions, e-mail me at skip_press@excite.com or skippress@earthlink.net. If neither address works, I've probably posted a new one with an Internet location engine like www.four11.com.

NETWORKING BEGINS AT HOME

I still have my 6400/180 Performa and have upgraded it to G3 speed with a Sonnet card that has worked flawlessly (see www.sonnettech.com). We've also added a Windows computer from Compaq that has been great (www.compaq.com) and a G3 Apple PowerBook (www.apple.com). The desktops and the PowerBook are linked via an Ethernet network with add-on internal cards manufactured by Farallon (www.farallon.com), which were stunningly simple to set up. I would recommend Farallon to anyone. If you need to link PCs and Mac like we do, my highest recommendation goes to a software product I used to network the PC and Macs in minutes called PC MACLAN from Miramar Systems (www.miramarsys.com). If you want to see how simple it can be, have a look at www.homepcnetwork.com/pcmacp1ovr.htm. You can use this software to log onto your home network from anywhere worldwide via the Internet.

If you don't have a high-speed Internet connection such as DSL or cable, you'll discover something once you put one up—your computer(s) will get "pinged" repeatedly by hacker robots that look for computers all over the Internet that they can mess with. To combat that, I've used two products that I like very much. Both are PC products because that's where most of the attacks take place. The first is BlackICE Defender, which combines both firewall and intrusion detection technologies for those who have high-speed Internet connections or dial-up Internet access. It blocks inbound connections but also adds an advanced intrusion detection system. If an intrusion occurs, it immediately blocks out hackers. Take a look at www.netice.com.

If you have a Mac, I haven't seen a product from Symantec yet that I didn't like. Their Internet protection products for both Mac and PC also provide Norton AntiVirus protection and the ability to kill those popup ads that Geocities and others display. See www.symantec.com and click on Products or visit your local computer store.

KEEPING COMPATIBLE

In the last book I mentioned being a big fan of VirtualPC from Connectix (www.connectix.com) which allowed me to run software for Windows, DOS, IBM OS/2 and NeXT OPENSTEP on my PowerMac. I'm using version 4.0 covering up to Windows2000 now, and it works about twice as fast as the last version. I have, however, found another program worth mentioning that does the same thing for a lot less money. You can download Blue Label PowerEmulator from www.lismoresoft.com. It's a powerful and easy to use PC emulator for Mac and updates are free.

If you grew up on Macs but are now using a PC and miss some Mac things, I can recommend Executor from www.ardi.com, which makes it possible to port many applications to 80-by-86 platforms, with each program running as a native application, not as emulated software. There are limitations to the programs you can run using Executor, but ARDI has a searchable compatibility database on the site.

One product I absolutely cannot do without is MacLinkPlus from DataViz (www.dataviz.com). The PC Exchange application that comes with Apple computers allows my Mac to read any disk, PC or Mac, and format any disk, PC or Mac, but it doesn't let me read any file. MacLinkPlus handles this in spades, and allows me to translate my newsletters to any file format necessary. The company also makes software for PC to Mac file conversions.

If you need to read Mac files on your PC on a regular basis, you might also have a look at MacDrive 2000 at www.media4.com/products, which *Macworld* magazine called "The preferred Mac-disk-mounting utility." MacDrive is simple and seamless as advertised and it helps keep things compatible in our two-platform office.

PDF IT AND PROTECT IT

When people write me with worries about their screenplays getting stolen if they send someone a Word file or other format, I tell them that if they had their screenplay in PDF form, it's much less likely to happen. The problem is, a PDF file is normally created in Adobe Acrobat, a somewhat expensive program. A very inexpensive alternative can be downloaded from www.jwwalker.com/pages/pdf.html. PrintToPDF works within any Mac program. It's not as powerful as Acrobat, but it's only $20. You will need Acrobat Reader 3.0 or later to view the created PDFs (free at www.adobe.com/products /acrobat/readstep.html). And here's something even better; translations are available in other languages, and though there's no Windows version, PrintToPDF's creator, James Walker, has links to similar PC programs right there on his home page.

STAY TUNED AND STAY SANE

These days I use Norton Systemworks to keep my Macs tuned up and Norton Utilities on the PC. Systemworks is the best software buy on the market in my opinion because the Mac version includes Norton Anti-Virus as well as a product from Aladdin (www.alladinsys.com) called Spring Cleaning, which performs miraculous tune-ups on my Macs, and Retrospect Express (www.dantz.com) which is the best Mac utility for backing up files storable media. The PC version includes Norton CleanSweep, which lets you quickly remove Internet build-up, Norton Ghost for cloning your hard drive via a back up, and WinFax to let you send and receive faxes on your PC. Don't find yourself working on a screenplay and lose it in a crash, unable to recover the file; I'm warning you right now.

AND SPEAKING OF ALL THAT READING

To get ahead as a writer, you often have to do a lot of reading. If you find that you're not reading as fast as you'd like, have a look at the AceReader program from StepWare, Inc. at www.acereader.com. Billed as "a Productivity and Self-Improvement Educational reading tool" of which "everyone from high powered executives to children just learning to read in grade school can benefit," this one truly will help you read faster both on and off the computer, with better comprehension, and if you have kids it will help them, too. Highly recommended.

WHY I NEVER RETYPE OLD SCRIPTS

In the last edition I mentioned how much I used a cheap UMAX scanner to scan all sorts of material, including old scripts and other writing, and how TextBridge Pro from

ScanSoft (www.textbridge.com) got almost every single character right, showed me words it found questionable, and allowed me to fix them on the spot. I still haven't gotten all my old material scanned in for rewriting, but I've tested TextBridge Pro Millennium (the PC version), which works with color scanners, and it's even better. The only thing I've found that compares to TextBridge Pro Millennium is OmniPage Pro (see www.caere.com) which also scans with color and includes software that can turn your documents into hyperlinked HTML pages immediately for publishing on the Web.

SOMETHING TO WATCH YOUR PS AND QS PERFECTLY

Universally, at every Hollywood conference I've ever attended, the biggest gripe from script readers other than bad writing is bad spelling and grammar. As someone who has taught in several universities and a number of online places, it's a complaint of mine as well. If you're using Word and find that it's dictionaries are a little lacking (I do), take a look at SpellCatcher from Casady & Greene (www.casadyg.com). It's available for both Mac and PCs and is amazingly powerful, with multilingual dictionaries on the CD and others available for downloading from the Web site. You can also import customized words (like those oddball Hollywood terms). I advise Mac users to also take a look at Grammarian—you'll never misuse their, there and they're again, and it can speak errors and suggestions if you wish, using over 150 built-in rules. Short of having an electronic *Elements of Style* (Strunk & White) book looking over your shoulder, you can't beat this program.

I'VE GOT MAIL; IN FACT, I'VE GOT THE BEST MAIL

For text-only e-mail that keeps evil, virus-filled attachments from jumping out at you when you open a message, it's hard to beat Claris E-mailer, but that program is no longer developed. That's why I switched to Eudora Pro, which supports HTML (you can see the graphics etc.) and is the #1 Internet e-mail application. With PGP encryption (I rarely use it, but I love having it available) and a jillion other features, it's easy to see why this program has won over 70 industry awards. Eudora is compatible across all platforms (even Linux and Palm) and now comes in three different modes: Sponsored (free, but you have ads pop up for you to read); Paid (no advertising); and Light (no ads, but fewer features). And if you're inclined to "flame" someone, the program will even caution you with an "emotion monitor" called MoodWatch. Details at www.eudora.com.

CLEANING UP WEB RESEARCH AND E-MAIL TEXT

One tool that saves me a lot of time is TextCleaner. If you've downloaded an article from the Web and don't want to spend a long time cleaning it up in your word process-

ing program, you need this software. TextCleaner performs a lot of timesaving operations, including turning three periods into an ellipsis, making curly quote marks out of
straight ones, and converting multiple spaces to a single space. It can automatically
recognize and retain styles, style guides and font designations from Web pages as well.
It will automatically remove e-mail quote symbols (>). If you do heavy Internet research
like I do, and you're on a Mac, surf over to www.studio405.com/textcleaner/.

ALL THOSE MOVIES, ALL THOSE APPLICATIONS

In the last edition, I mentioned how I'm often on the Web for hours every day, doing
research, sending and receiving e-mail, reading posts on newsgroups. And, being one
of those people who likes to have something going on in the background while I'm
working, at the time I was using RealNetworks RealPlayer with preset Net radio channels and to watch streaming video. I'm up to RealPlayer 8 Plus now (download at
www.real.com), and it's a tremendous improvement, but I also have QuickTime Pro
(www.apple.com/quicktime), very cool, and Windows MediaPlayer (www.microsoft
.com), quite nice. Why all three? Because I have to. If you want to watch trailers and
short films on the Net, you'll need all three as well.

MY FAVORITE SOFTWARE TOOL

Have you ever been reading something from a Web site and wanted to save a portion of
the text but not the whole thing? Or in any application, for that matter. If you have a
Mac, get Net-Print 8.2 by surfing to this Web site and downloading at: www93.pair
.com/johnmoe. If you have any questions, contact the product creator, johnmoe
@kagi.com. With this application, all you do is highlight text in any application and
print it or save it (and only the text you want). You can also take multiple chunks of
text and print them on the same sheet of paper or save them in the same file. It can also
include the URL where it came from, the title of the page, and the date it was downloaded. The application is also set up to print labels for Zip disks and CDs. This share-
ware costs $10 and is cheap at that price.

HOLLYWOOD'S (AND THE WORLD'S) BEST DATABASE PROGRAM

When I start making my next film, my database of choice is FileMaker Pro. Fox Feature
Productions used it to implement an asset tracking system for the $200 million epic *Ti-
tanic*. All of the production's assets, including props, sets, and costumes were successfully managed by a FileMaker Pro database. Cost of the software? At the time, $212,
with tax. Rod Henson, IT developer for Fox Feature Production said he "chose File-
Maker Pro for the job because it allowed us to rapidly implement a sound tracking system, make the information readily available and input thousands of assets, including

digital images." They used FileMaker because it is a fully relational database that ac-commodates both PC and Mac users.

Now, with version 5.0, users get Instant Web Publishing. That's why so many indus-try database companies use the program. Whether you're working on a desktop or with a workgroup, FileMaker shuts down the competition like Spiderman shutting down the Green Goblin, only much more quickly. And if you're addicted to your Palm Pilot like my wife and I are, you're covered via the FileMaker Mobile program for Palm OS. It's the first integrated database for Windows, Mac and Palm, which is another reason why more people use this software in Hollywood than any other database. I wish everyone used it — they'd get a much larger and comprehensive *Writer's Guide to Hollywood* if I could send them a FileMaker file. Contact: FileMaker, Inc. at (800) 544-8554 or read all about it at www.filemaker.com.

Also, if you want to do mass mailings for any reason, you might take a look at EZ PostNET 5.1 from Life $ucess Institute, which delivers postal bar code capabilities to FileMaker Pro users. It consists of native FileMaker Pro files and a USPS approved PostNET bar code font. Using PostNET bar codes you'll get more reliable and faster mail delivery, with substantial savings in postage. Read all about it at www.lifesuc-cess.org.

WHY YOU SHOULD CONSIDER SCREENWRITING SOFTWARE

I used an old Underwood portable to type my first two scripts. After winning money on a game show, I bought a new IBM Selectric II and retired for a year to become a pro-fessional writer. I thought that Selectric was as good as it could get. Years later, when I acquired a used IBM DisplayWriter word processor, I was stunned at how much of a difference it made in my writing. How could it get any better?

Then I got my first computer, a PC, and discovered that for once I didn't mind *rewriting* a screenplay. I was satisfied with WordPerfect, then Microsoft Word, for a long time. When I switched to a Power Macintosh, I used ClarisWorks because it came with the computer. When I wrote a script, I used a mere word processor, never thinking there might be a program designed specifically for screenwriting. Oh, what I missed. During the writing of the first edition of this book, I finally got up to speed on the amazing screenwriting software available and will never be satisfied with a word processor again. In addition, I learned about software that coaches writers and pro-grams that put you fully in touch with Hollywood.

PRODUCTION REVISION USE OF SOFTWARE

Once a script goes into production, it is often revised on a daily basis. Thus it is manda-tory that it be stored on electronic media. And they don't print out a new script each time. To keep track of which pages are old and which are new, different colored papers are used. Here's an example from the final draft of the Warner Brothers' film *Assassins*, script by Brian Helgeland, based on a screenplay by Larry and Andy Wachowski:

Rev. 4/03/95 (Blue)	Rev. 5/11/95 (Salmon)
Rev. 4/11/95 (Pink)	Rev. 5/17/95 (Cherry)
Rev. 4/13/95 (Yellow)	Rev. 6/01/95 (Tan)
Rev. 4/26/95 (Green)	Rev. 6/21/95 (White)
Rev. 5/03/95 (Goldenrod)	Rev. 7/03/95 (Pink)
Rev. 5/09/95 (Buff)	

Sure, they had enough money to send it to a typist, but what if they'd been on location, with no typist available? Some scripts, such as the Eddie Murphy's remake of *The Nutty Professor*, are rewritten on the set. Can you imagine doing this kind of redrafting without having the original stored on a hard disk or diskette?

These days, if your script isn't written on Final Draft (www.finaldraft.com), Screenwriter 2000 (www.screenplaysystems.com) or Scriptware (www.scriptware.com), if a production company buys your work they'll scan it in and turn it into a file of one of those programs. As I mentioned earlier, now that I'm doing reviews for the Writers Store, I simply refer people to the Web sites to download and try the programs, or to www.writersstore.com to read reviews there.

Inexpensive and Free Options

Problematically, many beginning screenwriters don't have a lot of money to spend on software, and the programs mentioned above can tend to be expensive, if you think $100 or more is pricey. That's why many people use standard word processing programs and develop macros to automate some of the repeated keystrokes. Fortunately, there are many freeware macros available on the Web, for all types of programs. Here are some places to look, but if they've disappeared by the time you check, don't complain to me. After all, they're free.

Bunch o' Templates—At www.communicator.com/swsoftin.html for all sorts of programs, even AmiPro, as well as reviews of some expensive stuff, courtesy of Rich Wilson.

Writers Software Ranked—Jim Miller is the Webmaster of this site: www.angelfire .com/ny/writesoftware. He has "software for writing of all sorts . . ." He also welcomes suggestions of any other software that might assist writers.

Making a Great First Impression

I hope by this far in the book you know what a "pitch" is and you're even considering doing one for a producer or development person. If you're basically an actor at heart, or just a great storyteller, you're ahead of the game. If you could use some visual aids to get your point across, though, here's some software that might help. PresenterActive is a simple Mac program that lets you drag and drop pictures and movies into a presentation frame, add transitions and sound effects and manipulate the presentation any way you wish. Any picture media supported by Quicktime 4.0 or higher will work, and you can add text to slides, transition sounds and background music. You can even use QuickTime Export and save the presentation as a QuickTime movie, which you can then e-mail as an attachment. Of course, you could do much the same thing with Microsoft PowerPoint or Macromedia Flash, but this one's much easier. Take a look at www.gluon.com for more information. If you make a $5 or higher donation to the charity of your choice—the Gluon folks call it Chareware—they'll send you the enhanced version of PresenterActive (which you can also purchase).

PowerMovie from www.beatware.com is even more powerful. You'll need Power-Point, which is not a problem for Windows users with Microsoft Office. It offers hundreds of customizable templates and amazing effects, including 3D animations and 3D text that you can fade, spin or swoop. You can blend objects and create effects that look like they came from the much more expensive Macromedia Flash. If you're inclined to deliver a visually aided pitch to help sell your screenplay and you have a Windows laptop, I highly recommend this one.

And while we're on a PowerPoint tack, if you're skilled enough with that software to build presentations and you find the Microsoft presentation backgrounds lacking, have a look at the excellent and affordable Powerbacks CD at www.powerbacks.com. My wife and I found it very impressive when we were writing a book on PowerPoint.

SHOULD YOU NEED A MENTOR

If you're new to screenwriting, or if you've written a script and aren't satisfied with it, you might consider hiring a coach. Instead of the script consultants mentioned in a previous chapter, I'm talking about the computer variety, mentoring and outlining programs specifically designed for writers and screenwriters.

Collaborator

In the first edition of this book, I was a big fan of the software program called Collaborator purely because a trio of working writers put it together. A lot of philosophy went into the program, starting with Aristotle's Six Elements of Drama: plot, character, thought, diction, music, and spectacle. The creators of the program also relied on the theories of Lajos Egri. Collaborator is once again available, at www.collaborator.com. I'm still a fan, and Bryn Dane (bryn.collaborator@juno.com) tells me that my readers can save $10 U.S. on the regular price of Collaborator and also save 5 percent on the writer services mentioned on the site. (Only one discount of any kind may be applied per purchase). Just mention the special code—SKIP10.

Dramatica

The creation of Melanie Anne Phillips and Chris Huntley of Screenplay Systems, Inc., Dramatica is akin to a full-year college course. I attended some classes that Huntley gave on Dramatica and can say that they back up their software more thoroughly than any other mentoring program. Although you won't find Joseph Campbell's name in the index, I found many instances of the Campbell influence in Dramatica originally, but Huntley and company keep honing the software so much I can't keep up with it all. I would recommend it specifically to young writers who have no idea whatsoever about workable story structure. Although I wasn't a huge fan of the original Dramatica, positive reviews have greatly increased since. Read all about it at www.dramatica.com.

FictionMaster and WritePro

Although technically not a screenwriting program, I highly recommend Sol Stein's FictionMaster if you want to write masterful dialogue. Stein is a prize-winning playwright produced on Broadway, an anthologized poet, the author of many novels and nonfiction books such as the highly regarded *Stein on Writing*, and the writer of numerous screenplays and TV dramas. The University of California at Irvine presented him with the Distinguished Instructor Award for 1992 in a competition with 552 other teachers. His twelve-week Dialogue for Writers class at UC Irvine was the first college class on dialogue of its kind. Stein's award-winning WritePro was the only program of its kind selected by the Book-of-the-Month Club (and also featured by the Literary Guild). Stein says that by the time you finish using the Dialogue Doctor module of FictionMaster for the first time, "you will know more about dialogue than ninety percent of published writers." I tend to agree, and let me shut up. Take a look at his fine work and boost your writing with a visit to www.writepro.com .

Plots Unlimited

One of the most successful writers in television, Tom Sawyer, is also the creator of this program. Having met Tom Sawyer before he created Plots Unlimited, I know he's a very accomplished writer—one of the writer/producers of *Murder, She Wrote* and the author of scores of other works. You'll get more plot twists from this program than any other, partly because Sawyer has used so many in his years of success. Plots Unlimited allows you to work on a story from any point in the story. Personally, I've rarely been out of story ideas, but that's me. If you're coming up short, see www.ashleywilde.com.

StoryCraft

Designed by TV writer/literary scholar John Jarvis and author/historian Irwin M. Berent, StoryCraft Writers Software is user-friendly, award-winning software that guides writers through a story using The Jarvis Method, which is the accepted standard among university writing programs. This program is a complete course in fiction writing, and a writer's tool for developing story ideas, building characters and their unique worlds, and writing stories using workable structure from millennia of storytelling. It's cheaper if you download it, so see www.writerspage.com/software.htm.

Write a Blockbuster

Write a Blockbuster 4.0 is a virtual screenwriting school, and a great one at that. One caveat—you need plenty of available memory whether using the PC or Mac version. While Blockbuster 4.0's new interface works smoothly and easily, it is built to be used in conjunction with Netscape Navigator and takes up a lot of space on your hard drive. Truby offers 32 story examples with thorough analysis of films like *Star Wars*, *Forrest Gump*, and *Home Alone*. He analyzes with the keen eye of a teacher who understands storytelling *and* screenwriters. See www.truby.com or call Truby's Writers Studio at 800-338-7829 for details.

OUTLINING YOUR WAY TO A BETTER SCREENPLAY

Some people don't have any trouble working out the initial plot points of a screenplay story; it's just the fine points that they have to labor over. Others don't have a clue about how to draft out a plot. Some new software (since the last edition) can help if you have trouble with that. One is from *StoryView* from Screenplay Systems, the developers of Dramatica and Movie Magic Screenwriter 2000. It allow writers to visually outline and develop their stories using a timeline, which might not sound like much until you see it working onscreen. It's actually very difficult to describe until you see it. "The way StoryView displays text could not have been accomplished in software four years ago. The processors weren't fast enough." That's a quote from Stephen Greenfield, President of Screenplay Systems, a working screenwriter who demonstrated the software to me. One of the truly great things about is the "story map" feature, which allows you to print out your plot on as many pieces of paper as you want. If you know what you're doing in creating a presentation for a screenplay pitch, you could come up with some very effective presentation boards using StoryView. Read more about it at www.screenplaysystems.com and demo it; you'll see why it's hard to describe without thorough examination.

The biggest competitor to StoryView is another Windows-only product, *Power-Structure*, an outlining tool created by the makers of Scriptthing, the script formatting program that was bought by Screenplay Systems and renamed Screenwriter2000. Reviewer Thomas Kane preferred PowerStructure because it assisted him without overwhelming, was simple to use and even simpler to learn. Like him, I found Power-Structure a bit looser in feel and more customizable. It's excellent in helping work out obstacles for the protagonist and keeping track of characters to set up rhythms of their appearances. But I can't say I would recommend either of them over the other. Take a look at www.write-brain.com .

There are many other similar programs out there, some of which I've reported on in previous editions, but I have a new favorite that has a big head start on all of them. *Inspiration* is its name, and students and professional writers around the world have been using it for some time now to develop ideas and organize thinking. It offers two routes to plot inspiration—a diagramming view and an outline—which work together to integrate concepts and information into more easily comprehensible form. Granted, you might be able to do the same thing with doodles and scribbles on Post-Its stuck to a large blank wall, but beginners often need a little hand-holding through a creation process. If you find a Web page that is helpful in researching your subject, for example, the Inspiration software will create a hyperlink to refer back to the Web site later with a simple click. There is a spellchecker and the program is available for both Mac and Windows, too. Inspiration is the recipient of numerous awards, including the Best Educational Software (BESSIE). Got a kid who wants to write? Call (800) 877-4292 or visit www.inspiration.com.

A FAVE FOR MY BABY, AND ONE MORE FOR THE ROAD

Before I could afford a laptop, I used a small word processor called an AlphaSmart Pro while writing on the road. Compatible with both Macs and PCs, it would hold almost an entire screenplay in eight separate files, with an easy upload to the computer. Since then, the company has built the AlphaSmart 3000 Laptop WordProcessor, and it's tremendous. It holds 100 pages of single-spaced text and will run for up to 700 hours on three AAA batteries. The keyboard is full-size and it even has a 70,000-word spellchecker and cut and paste capability. It will print to most printers and upload to most PCs and Macs. (The 3000IR model features infrared wireless transmission.) It's in the $200 range. For more info, see www.smartinput.com or call (800) 366-8323.

STORING AND SHARING IN STYLE

Like most computer users, I've become enamored of reading and writing my own CDs. It's the cheapest and most permanent storage available, once you've paid for a CD-RW (read/write) drive, and I promise you that the first time you hear a CD of MP3s you've burned yourself, you'll be permanently hooked. Of course, I long for the day when I can burn a DVD of a movie I've made as easily, but that day is a little more time down the line.

I have two drives that are on my highly recommended list, from different manufacturers. If you want a USB drive, you won't find one more slick-looking or killer dependable than the Predator from Iomega. For PC or Mac, it takes only minutes to set up and will use both CD-R (recordable) and CD-RW discs. The software in the package includes MusicMatch Jukebox for both platforms as well as photo manipulation software and backup programs with which you can "burn" your CDs. If you have a digital camera, you'll be amazed at how many $10 Zip disks you don't have to buy to store all those location shots and family picnic portfolios. In case you didn't know, CDs can be rewritten hundreds of times and last forever. And because it's from Iomega, I'm pretty sure the equipment will last just about that long, too. It's a beautiful thing, and it makes my friends jealous, to boot.

If you're making a movie and running from place to place with a laptop computer with a IEEE 1394 "Firewire" connection, I would seriously consider the industrial-strength Que! Fire from QPS Professional Solutions (www.qps-inc.com or call 714-692-3588). Built for Macs or PCs, it's heftier than the Predator, but it comes with its own silky black carrying case that will inspire a few oohs and aahs on a movie set. The unit is "burn-proof" so that you don't turn discs into "coasters" in fast write mode and you can multi-task if you use it with a PC. CDs created with it can be read on any CD-ROM or DVD-ROM drive. How much can you store on it? The equivalent of 486 floppy disks. I was new to Que before I tried this one, but now I'm utterly sold.

PLACES TO SHOP IN THE REAL WORLD AND ONLINE

In the last edition, I directed readers to Robert Koster's Starcomp at www.starcomp.net and Charles Baik's East Coast–based www.scriptdude.com. While those places are still in business, there's really only one industry leader—the Writers' Computer Store.

If you want to compare prices on any of the software mentioned in this chapter, and a lot more stuff that I didn't have the room or inclination to mention, just know that writers throughout California are devoted to The Writers' Computer Store, where you can get the answer to just about any question related to writing and computers. They offer software, books on screenplays, novels, crime scenes, and book proposals, directories of writing conferences, agents, producers, markets for your work, and much more. All with the best prices and customer service anywhere. Contact them at:

THE WRITERS' COMPUTER STORE
2040 Westwood Boulevard, Los Angeles, CA 90025
800-272-8927, 310-441-5151 for international callers
   Fax: 310-441-0944,
E-mail: sales@writersstore.com
Web site: http://writersstore.com

COMPUTING AND HOLLYWOOD

On December 13, 2000 talk show host Rosie O'Donnell gave every member of her audience a copy of iMovie 2 and an Apple Pro Optical Mouse. That's one example of how much stars like Macs. If you watch closely, you'll see Apple products are all over TV shows, so it's not just me. But here's another reason it's my computer of choice—because it's so much more secure to attack, different branches of the military are using Mac servers to combat hacker-spies and data-destroying viruses. After all, the last time I checked there were less than 40 Mac-specific viruses floating around cyberspace.

And with the new GeForce3 GPU (graphical processing unit) in the new high-end Apple G4s, which have more than 57 million transistors and the ability to perform more than 800 billion operations per second and 76 billion floating point operations per second (FLOPS), well, I'm sold. In a keynote address Apple CEO Steve Jobs gave just before the completion of this book, he said: "The first film Pixar ever made, 15 years ago was called *Luxo, Jr.* We made it using a Cray supercomputer and it took three hours for each frame to compute the graphics. Since there are 24 frames per second, that meant it took more than 75 hours per second to compute the graphics. Well, with the GeForce3 on a Power Mac, we can do that same operation in real-time today."

On November 23, 2000 a *Washington Post* article posed the question, "Should you purchase a computer that runs Microsoft Windows or Apple's Mac OS?" The author concluded that Macs might crash more often than PCs, but they last a lot longer. He's right. I've been using my Performa through three editions and almost six years of this book, with very few problems and through a number of upgrades.

The truth is, however, no one in Hollywood cares what kind of computer or software you use. All they care about if you're a screenwriter is what they read on the page. Nevertheless, if you can dazzle them with a software-driven presentation or a piece of equipment, it helps. Everything that helps sell you and your story is worthwhile in Hollywood, as long as it's legal. In this chapter I simply wanted to give you some ideas about things that I love that might help.

Now let's see your screenplay on screen. I hope I love it. And you'll be able to afford any kind of computer you want.

See You at
the Movies

The great films show us the Family of Man, in all its glories and warts, shortcomings and triumphs, tragedies and comedies, confusions and transformations. Writing the three editions of this book were some of the hardest tasks I ever had, not because it was difficult to make contacts or that I didn't know anything about selling screenplays when I began. It was hard because I, like thousands of writers before me, have had a love/hate relationship with Hollywood.

As I complete this edition, a Hollywood writers' strike has been averted, but the directors' and actors' unions have also threatened to walk the picket lines in defiance of the major Hollywood studios and TV network executives. When the Writers Guild first began meetings on January 22, 2001, prospects didn't look good, and the meetings were only scheduled to last two weeks. After all, studios and networks had been making contingency plans for a writer walkout, producing and stockpiling more TV shows and films to hedge their bets in case of a strike.

This left me in a difficult place because the agent, director, and producer listings in the next part of this book needed to be as accurate as possible. What if there were an extended strike and the smaller companies that are friendlier to beginning screenwriters went bankrupt and disappeared? Then I would have half a book that could be virtually worthless.

Naturally, my publisher didn't understand, which is to be expected, because most people who don't live and work around Hollywood simply don't understand it, no matter how much they try to act like they do. Finally, I convinced an editor of the logic of my arguments, and we waited to see how the talks worked out. Then that editor left the company, and I was back to square one.

So I decided to simply do the best I could, and to urge you to not depend on the exact accuracy of the addresses and phone numbers in this book. Even in a nonstrike time, people move around constantly. Offices move. People leave companies, even people at the top.

That's why you need to subscribe to a database like baseline.com, hcdonline.com, inhollywood.com, showbizdata.com, or filmtracker.com. Electronic databases can be updated hourly; my book has to be done a year in advance. Of course, the database companies could go out of business, but I doubt all of them will.

I write these books because I like movies. I like them a lot, whether I ever get to write the great ones or not. I'm glad to do anything I can to help people write good movies. After the first edition of the book came out, I heard from writers all over the world, some successful, some just starting out. What has been most heartwarming is when I find out that my advice has helped someone get ahead. Here's an example.

Jeremy Cohen wrote to say that he was a 24-year-old screenwriter, a spring 1997 honors graduate of New York University (BFA, Cinema Studies). "I began writing screenplays, poorly, in the spring of 1995." he told me in an e-mail. "I slowly improved, as I wrote, rewrote, and read screenwriting manuals. In February 1997, I picked up a copy of your *Writer's Guide* book, which really got the ball rolling for me. Basically, with the help of the book (mentioning it in a query letter), I got one of my scripts into the door at Anasazi Productions, Ted Danson's now-defunct company (they won an Emmy for *Miss Evers' Boys*). Danson's VP and right-hand man, Peter Stelzer, read the script pretty much by chance, loved it, and wanted to cut a deal with me. Anyhow, with an Emmy-winning producer in my corner (so to speak), I managed to get my latest screenplay, an admittedly absurd, overwritten 'popcorn' thriller, read by Pat Faulstich at Broder-Kurland-Webb-Uffner, one of the most highly-regarded talent/literary agencies in the biz. One of the agents at Broder read my *Bull Run,* and although he had problems with it, I guess he was intrigued by the writing, and wanted to see more from me. Needless to say, I was stunned; hey, I had a decent shot at being signed by one of the biggies! Thank you again."

I'm glad I was able to help. I met many fine people when first writing this book and plenty since as I have traveled the U.S. speaking on panels and making media appearances.

After my *Complete Idiot's Guide to Screenwriting* came out, I've heard from even more people, and now I'm about to start teaching an online screenwriting course for Education To Go, Inc. (see www.ed2go.com) that will put me in touch with students in almost 1,000 colleges and universities across the continent. It's a wonderful prospect.

None of this, however, is why I came to the decision that I loved Hollywood a lot more than I hated it. It wasn't a movie that did it, either. One day, as I was struggling to complete the second edition (these books are always a struggle and not really worth it, financially), I read a quote from Mencius, a Chinese philosopher. I found the following lines on his birthday, May 18th, in the *Wall Street Journal*:

> Heaven, when it is about to place a great responsibility on a man, always first tests his resolution, wears out his sinews and bones with toil, exposes his body to starvation, subjects him to extreme poverty, frustrates his efforts so as to stimulate his mind, toughens his nature and makes good his deficiencies. Men for the most

part can mend their ways only after they make mistakes. Only when they are frustrated in mind and in their deliberations can they stand up anew. Only when their intentions become visible on their countenances and audible in their voices can they be understood by others. As a rule, a state without law-abiding families and trustworthy Gentlemen on the one hand, and, on the other, without the threat of external aggression, will perish. Only then do we realize that anxiety and distress lead to life and that ease and comfort end in death."

Mencius, Book VI Kao Tzu, Part II, 15

By thoroughly studying Hollywood and learning what is necessary to succeed as a screenwriter, my false illusions have, over the years, fallen by the wayside. I emerged from a cave, as in Plato's allegory. I was liberated, but I still had a lot to learn. If I didn't conquer the world outside the cave, with all the resources I could now access, there was no one to fault but myself. I was reminded of what Joseph Campbell said, at the close of *The Hero with a Thousand Faces*:

It is not society that is to guide and save the creative hero, but precisely the reverse. And so every one of us shares the supreme ordeal—carries the cross of the redeemer—not in the bright moments of his tribe's great victories, but in the silences of his personal despair.

I wish you great victories in your writing, and hope I cause you no despair.
See you at the movies. I hope you write a great one.

PART TWO

All About Agents, Lawyers, and Managers

Agent Listings

There exists a Hollywood "Catch 22." You need an agent for most big producers to take you seriously, but agents want writers with a track record. One day, I realized that most agents in town would talk to me if I had a director or producer of note interested in something I'd written. I learned to contact producers first, who would listen to my query and if they liked it, generally say "Have your agent send it over." Then I'd call an agent and say "So and so wants to see my script." Voila! I had an agent, at least for that transaction. It's called "hip pocketing" in the business.

Next, I learned the power of a query letter. I wrote good queries and got in a lot of doors. I learned to wait for a response to my material, and let them call me. I'm willing to wait for months. A "how did you like it?" phone call is intrusive and demands immediate attention. Back then, I used regular post office letters to query because some people don't like getting unannounced faxes. Because of legal access reasons, some will even shut off the fax as it comes in if they don't recognize the sender. Mailed letters can be answered at the addressee's leisure, and the same goes for e-mail.

I would advise that you call first, if you can't e-mail. Despite the fact that I have readers around the world, I still advise doing this because if you "connect" with someone on the phone, they'll remember when your letter comes in. They might even tell you to send the script, and they'll look for it.

In 2001, with an impending strike, you might find that a lot of people have time on their hands to read and will more readily respond to inquiries. The problem is, with a strike, many of the smaller agencies and managers may go out of business. For that reason, I'm listing herein larger companies more likely to be in business strike or no strike. This type of company is perhaps less likely to respond to queries, but that was the way it had to be.

The very best way to get an agent is to be introduced by someone who knows that agent. If that happens, you should remember to be on your best behavior. Master screenwriter Ernest Lehman once referred me to his agent, Phil Gersh, but Phil wasn't a big fan of the script I sent him. That was back in the days when I was filled with the conceit that everyone should like everything I wrote. I wasn't rude about the rejection, though. I realized that merely being referred by a writer as great as Ernie was a boon in itself. If I didn't become a client of the Gersh Agency, so be it.

I've seen a lot of young writers and/or new writers have trouble with agents, producers, directors, and publishers because they could not simply realize that everyone has an opinion and no one is the final word on a written work. Perhaps your writing isn't up to commercial quality yet. On the other hand, maybe the agent had a bad day when they read part of your script before rejecting it. Or perhaps they simply don't like the kind of material you've written, or your particular take on it. You simply have to keep going. Somewhere along the way, if you keep improving your craft (and social skills, if necessary), you will find someone who will share your passion. There are no hidden secrets. For screenwriters, there is only one magic phrase to open the gates of Hollywood: *Great script!*

There are many places to find names and contact information for agents. The Writers Guild publishes and puts on their Web site a list of agents signatory to the Guild, meaning those who subscribe to Guild policies. Some agents have told me they would prefer not to be on the Guild list and have asked to be taken off with no luck, but that probably has more to do with mere clerical administration than anything else.

Are agents reluctant to hear from new screenwriters as is commonly believed? I've always found that, if you do your homework, write a decent script, and pay attention to details like using card stock covers on three-hole punched scripts secured by two brass brads, most agencies will give you at least a cursory read. They'll read you more than once if you show promise.

Lou Grantt, editor and publisher of the *Hollywood Scriptwriter*, agrees. Every August, the *Scriptwriter* devotes an entire issue to the results of a survey of WGA agents in Los Angeles and New York. When agents are asked if they are open to submissions, Lou reports, nearly all of them are.

As an experiment, I listed some entertainment lawyers in the last edition. Now I'm listing only one, because I know him and respect him. As of this writing, I don't have an agent. I have an entertainment attorney, Bruce Grakal, who looks over my contracts (I usually make my own deals). He charges 5 percent of what I make, and it's a good working relationship. I haven't found a production company yet who wouldn't take a script sent in by a lawyer in lieu of a manager or agent. For legal reasons, they want a "paper trail" of correspondence, and an attorney provides that.

Remember, there are legal differences between agents and managers in the State of California. Agents go through a legal certification process to be able to charge commissions for people they represent. They can negotiate deals (as can lawyers). Managers can legally only "tout" a writer, and when they get a commission it must be received as an advisor and/or consultant. Legitimate agents are also registered with guilds they work with, e.g., "WGA-signatory."

If you find discrepancies in any of the information herein, please understand that this book was prepared many months in advance of publication, and people in show business change jobs and addresses *all the time*. I *strongly* suggest you subscribe to an online database like www.filmtracker.com, www.hcdonline.com, inhollywood.com, or www.showbizdata.com for day-to-day addresses and contact info, but *only* when you are ready to market your script. Most of them have free trials, which could help you considerably.

If you send an e-mail to skippress@earthlink.net or skip_press@excite.com, I'll be happy to inform you of any news I might have about listing changes. I'll also answer one free question on any topic you want and will put you on my free monthly e-mail newsletter list if you wish.

May your first or your next sale be a big one, and if someone in this book helps you sell a script, I hope you'll send me two tickets to the premiere of your movie!

HARRIS TULCHIN & ASSOCIATES

11377 W. Olympic Boulevard, 2nd Floor, Los Angeles, CA 90064
310-914-7900
Fax: 310-914-7927
E-mail: EntEsquire@aol.com or EntEsquire@medialawyer.com
Web site: www.medialawyer.com

As a producer, Harris Tulchin has been involved with films like *Mona Must Die* and *To Sleep with Anger*. His Web site offers a Contract of the Month and much free information. Harris Tulchin & Associates is an international entertainment and multimedia law firm created to provide cost effective expertise and timely professional service to its clients in the motion picture, television, music, and multimedia ("Joe Cartoon" on the Internet is a client). Tulchin is a veteran entertainment attorney who has served as counsel for Cinema Group, KCET Television, United Artists, MGM Television, and others. As a private practitioner, his clients have included Sony, Ed Pressman, Ice Cube, Sid Caesar, Showtime, Cineville/HBO, Ed Annunziata (Sega Interactive), John Kricfalusi (*Ren & Stimpy*), and numerous independent producers, writers, directors, and actors. The firm has international affiliates in London, Melbourne, Paris, Rome, and other cities.

And now, to the agents and managers . . .

ABOVE THE LINE AGENCY

9200 Sunset Boulevard, Suite 804, W. Hollywood, CA 90069
310-859-6115
Fax: 310-859-6119

Rima Bauer Greer, Agent

Bruce Bartlett, Office Manager & Story Editor

Rima Greer tells new writers to have two or three scripts to show, not just one. She doesn't mind discussing where she's sent your script. Greer once ran the literary department of the Writers & Artists Agency, so she knows the territory. She has some very good clients, so if you get lucky enough to sign up with her, your career could be well on its way. She's sold scripts like *Milk Money* and *Prime Mates* (which became *Dunston Checks In*).

Contact: Bruce Bartlett with a one to two-page synopsis.

ACME TALENT & LITERARY

6310 San Vicente Boulevard, Suite 520, Los Angeles, CA 90048
323-954-2263
Fax: 323-658-6599
E-mail: amiejc@aol.com

Lisa Lindo Lieblein, Agent/CEO

Amie Castaldo, Literary Agent

Acme has done very well with the writers they've represented, particularly when Nicholas Staff was onboard. They've made deals for "unknowns" like selling an unpublished book manuscript for mid–six figures to Bette Midler's production company, All Girl. They sold some projects purely on a pitch. For new, talented writers, this small agency might be a decent bet.

Contact: Lisa or **Amie** for current needs.

AEI-ATCHITY ENTERTAINMENT INTL.

510 S. Fairfax Avenue, Los Angeles, CA 90036
323-932-0407
Fax: 323-932-0321
Web site: www.aeionline.com

Ken Atchity, President

Chi-Li Wong, Vice President

Vincent Atchity, Manager

Brenna Lui, Director of Development

AEI-Atchity is a literary management and film production company with over 20 films sold or produced for television, video, and theater, their latest being *American Dream* to Columbia Pictures and *Life, or Something Like It* (written by the very hot writer/director/producer John Scott Shepard, who has a blind script deal with producer Scott Rudin and a writing deal with Twentieth Century Fox Television). AEI represents scripts, novels, and nonfiction (true stories), setting up both film production and publication. Prior to show business, Ken Atchity was a professor of comparative literature at Occidental College for 17 years. AEI says they want heroic true stories, action scripts with well-developed characters. They accept scripts without referrals after an initial query.

Contact: Kenneth Atchity, Chi-Li Wong, or **Brenna Lui.**

AGENCY FOR THE PERFORMING ARTS (APA)

9000 Sunset Boulevard, Los Angeles, CA 90069
310-273-0744
Fax: 310-888-4242

New York office:
888 7th Avenue, New York, NY 10106
212-582-1500
Fax: 212-245-1647

With tons of agents on both coasts, major acting talents like Rutger Hauer and writers like Rod Lurie, this agency might be appealing if you write not only screenplays but books and plays as well (like me). They usually require a reference from someone they represent. The most notable big sale (or should I call it a franchise?) in recent times has been *Scary Movie*, which became something called *Scream* (maybe you've heard of it, or the second one, or . . .). They like relationship scripts, too.

Contact: Query for current needs and submission policies.

ANONYMOUS CONTENT MANAGEMENT/ ANONYMOUS ENTERTAINMENT

8522 National Boulevard, Suite 101, Culver City, CA 90232
310-558-3667
Fax: 310-558-4212

Scott Bankston, Manager

Lenny Bekerman, Manager

Steve Golin, Manager

David Kanter, Manager

Larry Kennar, Manager

A management and production company with a first-look deal with USA Films, this company represents clients as diverse as rapper Snoop Doggy Dogg, actress Kate Capshaw, writers like Tom Benedek (*Cocoon*) and Hampton Fancher (*Blade Runner*), and Neil Labute, a writer/director/producer. You're not likely to get taken seriously here without a referral from an existing client.

Contact: Company for current needs and submission policies.

THE ARTISTS AGENCY

10000 Santa Monica Boulevard, Los Angeles, CA 90067
310-277-7779
Fax: 310-785-9336

Mickey Freiberg

Michael Livingston

The Artists Agency was begun by long-time veterans, many of whom have left in recent years. "Unknown" writers might have a hard time getting signed here, but they will consider queries.

Contact: Query for current needs and submission policies.

BAUMGARTEN/PROPHET ENTERTAINMENT

1640 S. Sepulveda #218, Los Angeles, CA 90025
310-996-1885
Fax: 310-996-1892

Craig Baumgarten, Producer

Jessica Berlinski, Manager

Adam Merims, Producer

Melissa Prophet, Producer/Manager

Shawn Minton, Assistant

Ruth Vesler, Assistant

A management/production company, they represent bright young writers like Matthew Bright and Takashi Bufford and produce movies like *Love Stinks* and *Universal Soldier: The Return*. They also seem to be a good bet for student interns; in an ad they placed on iFilmPro.com, they said that interns in the last two semesters have either been hired full-time or referred to full-time positions.

Contact: The Company for current needs.

BENDER-SPINK MANAGEMENT & PRODUCTION

1149 N. Poinsettia Place, West Hollywood, CA 90046
323-845-1645 (Jim Valdes)
Fax 323-512-5347
E-mail: info@benderspink.com
Web site: www.benderspink.com

Chris Bender, Partner

J. C. Spink, Partner

Charlie Gogolak, Manager

Nicole Harb, Manager

Marc Hernandez, Manager

Roy Lee, Manager of New Media

Brian Spink, Manager

Jim Valdes, Development

Bender-Spink are some of the hottest manager/producers in the business. While at Zide Entertainment, Bender and Spink set up over 20 projects including *American Pie*. With growing success, they've added industry veterans who will listen to what you have to offer and make things happen if they like what they hear. I'm still amazed by a deal they got for the makers of a short film in 2000. Bender-Spink accepts query letters for screenplays, shorts, and feature films of all genres. Submit a five-sentence synopsis for each project you wish them to consider by e-mail or fax.

Contact: Jim Valdes and as indicated above.

BONDESEN MANAGEMENT

9350 Wilshire Boulevard, Suite 316, Beverly Hills, CA 90212
310-274-4003
Fax: 310-274-4599
E-mail: info@bondesen.net
Web site: www.bondesen.net

Mikkel Bondesen, Manager

Originally from Denmark, Mikkel Bondesen came to the U.S. for the American Film Institute's Producer Program and got into literary management in 1999. He's done very well in a short time, arranging deals like Phoenix Pictures' $400,000 against $700,000 buy for *Basic* by James Vanderbilt, a thriller set in a military camp. For an extensive look at what he offers, see his Web site.

Contact: Mikkel Bondesen, preferably as outlined on the site.

BRODER KURLAND WEBB UFFNER

9242 Beverly Boulevard, Suite 200, Beverly Hills, CA 90210
310-281-3400
Fax: 310-276-3207
E-mail (for routing): postmaster@bkwu.com

Bob Broder, Partner

Norman Kurland, Partner

Beth Uffner, Partner

Elliot Webb, Partner

Literary Agents: Ted Chervin, Pat Faulstich, Emile Gladstone, Ronda Gomez-Quinones, Bruce Kaufman, Gayla Nethercott, Terry Norton-Wright, Daniel Rabinow, Chris Silbermann, Justin Silvera, Paul Allan Smith, Christoph von Goetz

At one point, this writer-heavy agency experimented with finding scripts from the Net via www.screenplaysubmissions.com. As of January 21, 2000, they stopped accepting new registrants and closed their site, referring inquiries to info@screen playsubmission.com. They continually make impressive spec sales, more often than not by Emile Gladstone. Example from March 2000: *Dog Catcher* by Joe Jarvis and Greg Coolidge, about college guys kicked out of their frat house who disguise themselves as girls to join the "ugly" sorority. Walt Disney bought it for $200,000 against $400,000.

Contact: Agency for current needs and submission requirements.

DON BUCHWALD & ASSOCIATES

6500 Wilshire Boulevard, Suite 2200, Los Angeles, CA 90048
323-655-7400
Fax: 323-655-7470

Tim Angle, President (West Coast)

Debbie Deuble, Literary Agent

Nick Holly, Literary Agent

Hank Metzger, Literary Agent

Neil Stearns, Literary Agent

John Ufland, Literary Agent

New York office:
10 E. 44th Street, New York, NY 10017
212-867-1200
Fax: 212-972-3209

Don Buchwald, Owner

Susan Calogerakis, Agent

Rachel Sheedy, Agent

Don Buchwald's most visible client is radio show host Howard Stern. The L.A. office has done well by new screenwriters like Gary Goldstein; 20th Century Fox and Davis Entertainment paid six figures for Goldstein's *Manhattan Transfer*, the writer's first major sale. John Ufland (who also sold *Waves*) has a reputation for efficiency and congeniality. His recent sales include *Shoot the Moon* to Atlantic Streamline and *Change of Course* to Hearst. He and Debbie Deuble were formerly partners at L.A. Premiere Artists.

Contact: Query the agency for current needs.

THE CALLAMARO LITERARY AGENCY

427 N. Canon Drive, Suite 202, Beverly Hills, CA 90210
310-274-6783
Fax: 310-274-6536

Lisa Callamaro, Agent

A writer-friendly agency with a small number of happy clients that comes highly recommended to me by knowledgeable development folks.

Contact: Lisa Callamaro for current needs.

CIRCLE OF CONFUSION

666 5th Avenue, Suite 303, New York, NY 10103
212-527-7579
Fax: 781-997-0521
E-mail: circleltd@aol.com

Lawrence Mattis, Manager

Rajeev Agarwal, Manager

Jon Sherman, Assistant

Representing people like the Wachowski brothers (*The Matrix*), Lawrence Mattis' company is particularly good for New York–based and science-fiction-oriented writer/directors. A notable sale in 2000 was to Intermedia, who optioned rights to first-time screenwriter Dwayne Smith's comedy spec script "Joe's Last Chance" for mid-six figures. (Dwayne is interviewed in this book.) They accept queries and are interested in all sorts of writing.

Contact: Lawrence Mattis for current needs.

CORALIE JR. THEATRICAL AGENCY

4789 Vineland Avenue, Suite 100, North Hollywood, CA 91602
818-766-9501
Fax: 818-766-7059
E-mail: coraliejr@earthlink.net

Coralie Jr., Owner-Agent

Gary Dean, Agent/Literary

Although she is known for her representation of young people and celebrity look-alikes, Coralie Jr. also represents writers, usually those just starting out in their careers. Gary Dean wants scripts that are classic in nature, all genres, all types. Send him something original, "written from the heart and not about other movies you've seen." And make sure it has card stock covers; people send him things without covers sometimes.

Contact: Gary Dean for current needs and submission policy.

CREATIVE ARTISTS AGENCY (CAA)

9830 Wilshire Boulevard, Beverly Hills, CA 90212
310-288-4545
Fax: 310-288-4800

MAJOR AGENCY, INDIVIDUAL AGENTS NOT LISTED. It is very unlikely anyone there will take on a new writer without a personal recommendation from someone already represented by the agency. There are, however, always caveats. For example, I saw David Tenzer, a television agent at CAA, say at the Hollywood Film Festival that he is not adverse to finding new clients, and he was helping sell a project of a foreign friend of mine at the time, so I knew that was true. The friend, however, had produced a major miniseries in his home country. This once top agency in town is now on an equal par with ICM and William Morris. From its beginning in 1975, when Michael Ovitz, Bill Haber, and Ron Meyer left the William Morris Agency with Rowland Perkins and Michael Rosenfield to form Creative Artists, there was a maverick quality to CAA. The agency's screenwriting clients remain some of the best.

Contact: The agency (if you must) for submission policy. It's almost guaranteed that if you sell something big and are listed in the trades, you'll hear from someone at CAA.

DIVERSE TALENT GROUP

8899 Beverly Boulevard, Suite 510, Los Angeles, CA 90048
310-271-1414
Fax: 310-205-3981

Michael Lewis, Literary Agent-Partner

Sheryl Peterson, Literary Agent-Partner

Susan Sussman, Literary Agent-Partner

Craig Minor, Literary Agent

Amanda Brammall, Assistant Agent

Mary Rickard, Assistant to Ms. Peterson & Mr. Lewis

I was happy to learn that Michael Lewis was at this agency; he's a genial Englishman who represents writer/director Michael Rymer and at one time seemed to be the de facto agent of choice for any writer from the U.K. and the Commonwealth who arrived in Los Angeles. This agency does it all in features and television.

Contact: Amanda Brammall for current needs. They have a Web site coming, but it wasn't up at press time.

ENDEAVOR

9701 Wilshire Boulevard, 10th Floor, Beverly Hills, CA 90212
310-248-2000
Fax: 310-248-2020

MAJOR AGENCY, INDIVIDUAL AGENTS NOT LISTED. It is very unlikely anyone there will take on a new writer without a personal recommendation from someone already represented by the agency. Ronald L. Brassfield posted on the misc.writing .screenplays group that he queried an agent at Endeavor, only to have his query returned with a letter saying they were returning his material because they did not accept unsolicited submissions. Although the wording of the letter suggested he had sent them a script, he'd only sent a query. Brassfield called and was told that basically anything they receive in the mail that they are not expecting is considered unsolicited, including a cold query letter. They've sold scripts like *The Cable Guy* and *Vicious*. Most Endeavor writers are action-oriented but not all. When Sid and Marty Krofft had several studios chasing after a feature version of the Krofft's *H. R. Pufnstuf* kids' TV show, they hired Endeavor clients Scott Alexander and Larry Karaszewski (*People vs. Larry Flynt*) to produce. Endeavor agents come from strong backgrounds. Whatever their criterion is on finding talent, it's pretty certain they're doing something right.

Contact: The agency for submission policy.

THE FIELD-CECH-MURPHY AGENCY

12725 Ventura Boulevard, Suite D, Studio City, CA, 91604
818-980-2001
Fax: 818-980-0754

Judy Cech, Principal

Maggie Field, Principal

David Murphy, Principal

This agency has represented new writers, both in features and television and placed new writers on TV writing staffs. They prefer sophisticated scripts over high concepts. They also have done particularly well working with new women writers. Unfortunately, at the time of this book they were only taking on new clients via referrals from people who know the principals.

Contact: Agency for current needs.

GALLAGHER LITERARY MANAGEMENT

8160 Manitoba Street, Suite 309, Los Angeles, CA 90293
310-822-2070
E-mail: DealmakerX@aol.com
Web site: www.robgallagher.freeservers.com

Rob Gallagher, Head of Literary

Jim Fernald, VP of Development

Formerly a literary manager and Head of Literary for Cyd LeVin & Associates (Luke Perry, etc.), Head of Literary for Messina-Baker (Tim Allen, Drew Carey, Janeane Garofalo, etc.), Gallagher has agented for Major Clients Agency and APA, as well as serving as VP of Acquisitions & Development for Ivy Entertainment. Prior to showbiz, he was a military intelligence agent in Europe during the Cold War. He works with "a select list of talented and prolific screenwriters and directors" and takes out a lot of material, and knows tons of development executives. He also has "about 30 other associates who provide development notes." He's looking for original and high-concept completed scripts to sell and/or produce, and prides himself in his unorthodox "guerrilla warfare" methods of finding material before it reaches Hollywood, which he has done primarily by using the Internet. Pitch only completed specs to him in *only* the following format via his e-mail address *only* (no attachments): Title; Genre; Author, Phone number; Logline; 50-word synopsis; Similar films. He will only reply to pitches he is interested in, within a week.

Contact: Only as described above.

GRAHAM AGENCY

311 W. 43rd Street, New York, NY 10036
212-489-7730
Fax: 212-489-7731

Earl Graham, Owner-Agent

Earl Graham has done well with playwrights who adapt their works for film like Ernest Thompson with the magnificent *On Golden Pond*. Graham reps screenwriters and playwrights only, and the edge goes to playwright. He once had half a hundred clients, but that's been winnowed down in recent years. Because he's been around for so long, Graham probably won't sign you as a new client, but there's always a chance.

Contact: Earl Graham with a query letter and SASE.

HART LITERARY MANAGEMENT

3541 Olive Street, Santa Ynez, CA 93460
Phone and fax: (805) 686-7912
E-mail: tibicen@silcom.com
Web site: www. hartliteray.com

Susan Hart, Agent

I met Susan Hart at the first Hollywood Film Festival, where she had a table with a wicker basket filled with scripts from her clients. She was a literary manager then. Now she's a WGA signatory agent. One writer asked me about her via e-mail and I told him that I expected her to sell some things (just a hunch), and that she would likely give him the concentrated attention that you might not get from other agents for "new" writers. His reply: "Boy, you weren't kidding! I signed on with Susan last week and already she has strong interest in two of my scripts, one as a potential Disney MOW, and the other as a vehicle for a big C&W star who shall remain nameless in case it falls through . . . what an ego boost!!" She has since sold or set up several properties and become licensed as an agent. To see what she likes (mostly all genres), have a look at her Website.

Contact: Susan Hart. Query first via e-mail or fax or hard copy. No release necessary. SASE for mailed reply.

HOFFLUND/POLONE MANAGEMENT & PRODUCTION

9615 Brighton Way, Beverly Hills, CA 90210
310-859-1971
Fax: 310-859-7250

Judy Hofflund, Partner

Gavin Polone, Partner

Gavin Polone was formerly a partner with United Talent Agency and had a big fight with them when he left. Polone is a "hobby" actor; for example, he played Eric Idle's agent in *Burn Hollywood Burn*. He and Judy Hofflund have produced several films like *8MM* and *Stir of Echoes*, while repping top on-camera talent and writers like David Koepp and Andrew Kevin Walker. They generally work with established writers, so don't get your hopes too high.

Contact: The company for current needs and submission policies.

IFA TALENT AGENCY

8730 Sunset Boulevard, Los Angeles, CA 90069
310-659-5522
Fax: 310-659-3344

Agents: Ilene Feldman, David Lillard, Wendy Murphey, Joe Vance

Judd Landon, Head of Literary

Judd Landon came over from the William Morris Agency to head literary for this small agency, which has a strong talent base. Landon's mandate was to acquire new material for IFA clients and to actively approach signing writers and directors. Landon worked at Morris for five years in their independent film division, where he secured financing for independent films like *Plan B* for New Regency (starring Diane Keaton) and *Free Money* (starring Marlon Brando). Landon might be more open to new writers than other agencies with a distinguished reputation like this one. Just don't ask who their talent clients are.

Contact: Judd Landon for current needs and submission policies.

INTERNATIONAL CREATIVE MANAGEMENT (ICM)

8942 Wilshire Boulevard, Beverly Hills, CA 90211
310-550-4000
Fax: 310-550-4100

New York office:
40 West 57th Street, New York, NY 10019
212-556-5600
Fax: 212-556-5665

MAJOR AGENCY, INDIVIDUAL AGENTS NOT LISTED. It is very unlikely that either the L.A. or N.Y. office will take on a new writer without a personal recommendation from someone already represented.

This was the first big agency I ever came in contact with. Jack Gilardi, who took my writing under his wing then, represented Jeff Bridges at the time and for years afterward. A great number of major stars are with this agency (particularly actresses), so if you're calling the Screen Actors Guild to find out who represents that actor you want to get your script to, chances are good you'll wind up talking to an agent at ICM. Jeff Berg, the head of the agency, is probably the one who got the big money for books ball rolling, when he locked himself in his office for three days and sold Peter Benchley's *The Island* for a then unbelievable $3 million. Nick Reed, head of Motion Pictures/Literary, is a genial English chap who favors playwrights and complains that most of them can't also write a good screenplay. If you can do both, he might talk to you.

Contact: The agency (if you must) for submission policy. It's almost guaranteed that if you sell something big and are listed in the trades, you'll hear from someone at ICM.

LAYA GELFF AGENCY

16133 Ventura Boulevard, Suite 700, Encino, CA 91436
818-713-2610

Laya Gelff, Owner

Laya Gelff is only interested in TV movies and action-adventure features. To be considered here, send in a query letter with a synopsis describing your project. If you send in the script without querying, it'll just come back marked "Return to Sender." And don't forget the SASE if you want your material returned. She has less than a dozen overall clients, and prefers referrals.

Contact: Laya Gelff, as described.

THE GERSH AGENCY

232 N. Canon Drive, Beverly Hills, CA 90210
310-274-6611
Fax: 310-274-3923

Phil Gersh, Founder

David Gersh, Head of Literary

Joe Gatta, Motion Picture Literary

Jennifer Stevenson, Literary Agent

New York office:
130 West 42nd Street, 24th Floor, New York, NY 10036
212-997-1818
Fax: 212-391-8459

Mike Lubin, Head of Motion Picture Literary

Although they don't always get the big splash publicity of other large agencies, The Gersh Agency has both coasts covered and long-time clients like screenwriting legend Ernest Lehman (*Sound of Music*, *North by Northwest*) if that gives you any idea. Phil Gersh has made this a family business as well. His son David heads the literary department. The Los Angeles office does not differentiate between agents, which is to say the agents represent what they want. The agents listed here are only those who pertain to writers (there are many more). As with most large agencies, you'll be better off getting referred from one of their clients.

Contact: Either office for current needs and submission policies.

INDUSTRY ENTERTAINMENT

955 S. Carrilo Drive, 3rd Floor, Los Angeles, CA 90048
323-954-9000
Fax: 323-954-9009
Web site: www.industryent.com (under construction at press time)

Keith Addis, Chairman

Nick Wechsler, Chairman (Production)

Gregg Apirian, Manager (New Media)

Tucker Carney, Manager (New Media)

Guymon Casady, Manager (Literary)

Marc Evans, Producer/Director of Development

Margaret Riley, Manager (Literary)

Susan Solomon, Manager (Literary)

A massive management/production company once known as Addis-Wechsler, Industry has a "first look" production and discretionary deal with New Line Cinema through 2001. Only personnel of interest to writers are listed, but they handle major talent like Richard Dreyfuss, Jack Lemmon, Sting, Sela Ward, and James Woods. Writers and writer/directors they manage include Callie Khouri, Barry Levinson, and Billy Bob Thornton. As a production company they skew toward more eclectic fare like *Quills* and *15 Minutes* but they are also attracted to more commercial properties like a remake of the Jerry Lewis movie *Cinderfella*. Just don't mention Michael Ovitz here—Rick Yorn and Julie Silverman left Industry to join Artists Management Group, taking clients like Leonardo DiCaprio.

Contact: Managers, but you'll probably need a referral.

LESLIE B. KALLEN AGENCY & SEMINARS

15303 Ventura Boulevard #90, Sherman Oaks, CA 91403
800-755-2785, 818-906-2785
Fax: 818-906-8931
E-mail: kallengroup@earthlink.net
Web site: www.lesliekallen.com

Leslie B. Kallen, Agent

Leslie B. Kallen used to tell audiences when she gave seminars that she loves new writers, and she's done well by them, with several award-winners on her roster. Alone and in conjunction with professor Richard Walter, she has delivered seminars throughout North America. (Having personally appeared with her at one venue, I vouch that she knows her business.) Kallen is signatory with the WGA and runs a successful boutique agency. She's looking for "a great story well told." She does a lot of script reading, and is always looking for a good one, either Movie of the Week or feature film. She doesn't want any episodic or sitcom scripts, and no poetry or children's novels. Her partner in New York is Frank Weimann of The Literary Group International.

Contact: Leslie Kallen.

KAPLAN/PERRONE ENTERTAINMENT

3815 Hughes Avenue, 3rd Floor, Culver City, CA 90232
310-841-4338
Fax: 310-204-2713

Aaron Kaplan, Manager/Producer

Sean Perrone, Manager/Producer

A slightly off the Hollywood radar management/production company, Kaplan/Perrone has a "first look" production deal with Escape Artists and writing clients like Ryne Douglas Pearson of *Mercury Rising* fame. I'm told they're a company to watch.

Contact: Either principal for current needs.

KAPLAN-STAHLER-GUMER AGENCY

8383 Wilshire Boulevard, Suite 923, Beverly Hills, CA 90211-2408
323-653-4483
E-mail: bgumer@ksgagency.com (Robert Gumer)

Mitch Kaplan, Principal-Literary

Elliot Stahler, Principal-Literary

Robert Gumer, Principal-Literary

PLEASE NOTE: Kaplan-Stahler has many working writers in episodic television. Think TV, Emmy. Don't send a feature here or a TV movie. These guys want writers who can write an hour episode or a half-hour episode of existing series. No, they don't want to see your brilliant new series idea, the pilot of which you've already written. They want great episodic writers. They do sell some spec screenplays, though, like *Why Can't I Be Audrey Hepburn?*

Contact: Robert Gumer with a query letter, mail or e-mail (notice their fax isn't listed). Send a summary of your writing background and a synopsis (a paragraph or two) of your sample script.

JON KLANE AGENCY

120 El Camino Drive, Suite 112, Beverly Hills, CA 90212
310-278-0178
Fax: 310-278-0179

Jon Klane, President

Dave Klane, Agent

Representing almost 30 quality writers like Lewis John Carlino (*The Great Santini*) and Ebbe Roe Smith (*Falling Down*), this is an excellent boutique agency that is writer-friendly. You'd be lucky to have them on your side.

Contact: Agency for current needs.

MAJOR CLIENTS AGENCY

345 N. Maple Drive, Suite 395, Beverly Hills, CA 90210
310-205-5000
Fax: 310-205-5099

Partners: Jeffrey A. Benson, Ian Greenstein, Michael Margules, Stephen L. Rose, Richard A. Weston

Agents: Ken Greenblatt, D. Scott Henderson, So Yun Kim, Michael van Dyck

One of the few agencies located in Beverly Hills, Major Clients is an amalgamation of agents from other agencies. The partners learned the business in executive ranks at major entertainment companies and have upwards of a hundred clients. Major Clients has a good literary department, with good screenwriters like Karen McCullah Lutz of *10 Things I Hate About You* fame.

Contact: The agency for current needs and submission policies.

METROPOLITAN TALENT AGENCY

4526 Wilshire Boulevard, Los Angeles, CA 90010
323-857-4500
Fax: 323-857-4599

Christopher Barrett, Owner & President

Dan Baron, Literary

Bradley Glenn, Literary (his fax 323-857-4526)

Jeff Okin, Talent/Literary

Garth Pappas, Talent/Literary

Chris Barrett has a long history of "boutique" agency talent representation. He formed Metropolitan with other agents who are no longer there. Metropolitan represents actors, directors, producers, and writers. Their talent list includes Andrew Dice Clay, Harry Hamlin, and Kim Wayans. Only agents who handle literary clients are listed here. Metropolitan agents have sold scripts like *The Pearl*, *Ronin,* and *The Stars Fell on Henrietta*. Dan Baron reps writers like Gabriel Casseus, who wrote the remake of *Bedazzled*. Jeff Okin's numerous clients include writer/director Jean Claude Lamarre (*Higher Ed*), and with Garth Pappas, J. Max Burnett (*Possums*). Bradley Glenn reportedly sold *The Courier* for more than $1 million for Michael Brandt and Derek Haas (new writers at the time) and isn't afraid to take on other undiscovered scribes when they have excellent material.

Contact: Agents listed above for current needs.

ORIGINAL ARTISTS

9465 Wilshire Boulevard, Suite 840, Beverly Hills, CA 90212
310-275-6765

Jordan Bayer, Agent

Matt Leipzig, Agent

Chris Prince, Agent

Representing writing teams like Nick Falacci and Cheryl Heuton (both regular visitors to the misc.writing.screenplays newsgroup) and solo acts like Gavin Scott (*Small Soldiers*) and the brilliant Martin Hynes (*George Lucas in Love*), this is a small but good writer-friendly agency. They set up Hynes' *Honest Abe* pitch that Disney bought and they keep their writers working.

Contact: Agents listed above for current needs.

PARADIGM, A TALENT & LITERARY AGENCY

10100 Santa Monica Boulevard, Los Angeles, CA 90067
310-277-4400
Fax: 310-277-7820

New York office:
200 West 57th Street, Suite 900, New York, N.Y 10019
212-246-1030
Fax: 212-246-1521

Sam Gores, Partner (N.Y.)

Stuart Robinson, Partner (L.A.)

Jim Hess, Agent (L.A.)

Pat Quinn, Agent (Head, Television Movies, L.A.)

Nate Quan, Agent (Television, L.A.)

Mark Ross, Agent (L.A.)

Lucy Stille, Agent (L.A.)

Valarie Phillips, Agent (L.A.)

Paradigm has well over 100 clients that include a lot of top actors like Andy Garcia, Laurence Fishburne, Randy Quaid, and Harry Shearer. They rarely take on anyone un-introduced, but given their success, it might be worth a try. Stuart Robinson and Jim Hess represent John Sayles, while Lucy Stille is agent for a number of writers including David Aaron Cohen (*The Devil's Own*) and Shana Larsen (*200 Cigarettes*). Valarie Phillips has the very hot John Scott Shepard (*Life, or Something Like It*), and Pat Quinn knows as much about TV as anyone in town (formerly with Metropolitan, she teaches at UCLA as well, and is a great person to know).

Contact: Pick one of the **agents** listed and plead your case.

LYNN PLESHETTE AGENCY

2700 N. Beachwood Drive, Los Angeles, CA 90068
213-465-0428
Fax: 213-465-6073

Lynn Pleshette, Owner

Michael Cendejas, Agent

Lynn Pleshette says a talented screenwriter will get ahead no matter what, as long as they stick out the turndowns, simply because there is such a dearth of good scripts. Headquartered in beautiful Beachwood Canyon, she's only interested in features and TV movies, so if you have a good one and are looking for someone who might believe in your talent, this agency could be it. One of Pleshette's best sales was *The Truman Show* (the Jim Carrey starrer). She represents a small but quality group of writers like Sam Montgomery (*Breakdown, U-571*).

Contact: Story Department with a query. Due to the large volume of letters received, they only respond by phone if interested.

PMA LITERARY & FILM MANAGEMENT, INC.

45 West 21st Street, Sixth Floor, New York, NY 10010
212-929-1222
Fax: 212-206-0238
E-mail: info@pmalitfilm.com, queries to queries@pmalitfilm.com
Web site: www.pmalitfilm.com

Peter Miller, President

Delin Cormeny, VP & Director of Development

Kate Garrick, Development Associate

Nora Pitiger, Development Associate

After Peter Miller became a father, his crisscross flights between Los Angeles and New York slowed down. Selling both books and screenplays (some high-profile projects), Miller has maintained a presence on both the East and West Coasts. They've sold a number of TV movies. He actively looks for new writers in the fiction, nonfiction and screenplay categories. Miller likes to attach himself as a producer on projects, which can be a hindrance in the minds of some production companies, but he doesn't insist on it. He is also the author of *Get Published! Get Produced!* Delin Comeny (whom I met on a panel at the Aspen Summer Words writers festival) was in film development in Los Angeles before working with Miller in N.Y. She surprised me by saying they had sold two *treatments* for writers in recent times. Though she doesn't know just why, Delin is also adept at selling books for African American authors.

Contact: Query anyone mentioned above by mail, fax or e-mail.

PREFERRED ARTISTS

16633 Ventura Boulevard, Suite 1421, Encino, CA 91436
818-990-0305
Fax: 818-990-2736

Brad Rosenfeld, Agent

Roger Strull, Agent

Lew Weitzman, Agent

Paul Weitzman, Agent

Here's where you'll need a great query letter, but the good news is you can send in a complete script with it, rather than waiting for them to ask for it. That's what they told me originally; recently I've been told they sometimes change their minds about unsolicited submissions. So call and find out. Preferred Artists openly states that it is interested in minority writers, so if that describes you, you're in luck. (Unsold screenwriters are not considered a minority.) TV or feature, episodic or TV movie, drama or comedy, they'll look at it if they love the query. They have some notable sales; Roger Strull epresents quality writers like Patrick Sheane Duncan (*Courage Under Fire* and *Mr. Holland's Opus*).

Contact: Agents listed above.

THE ROTHMAN AGENCY

9465 Wilshire Boulevard, Suite 840, Beverly Hills, CA 90212
310-247-9898
Fax: 310-247-9888

Jim Rothman, Agent

Robb Rothman, Agent

Dan Brecher, Agent

Dennis Kim, Agent

Kevin Plunkett, Agent (Features)

Keith Prince, Agent

This small but effective agency has some excellent feature writers like Kerry Ehrin (*Inspector Gadget* and *Mr. Wrong*), but you should think of this agency as a little William Morris, television division. If you have a great sample script and you can tell these folks about it in a very entertaining manner, they might respond. Mike Scully from *The Simpsons* cold-called Jim Rothman. Probably, though, you'll need a track record that this agency will recognize or need to be referred by someone in the business that they know, meaning a studio executive, a development executive, or one of their clients. They mostly don't have time to develop new careers.

Contact: One of the agents if you fit the criteria mentioned.

SANFORD/GROSS & ASSOCIATES

1015 Gayley Avenue, Suite 301, Los Angeles, CA 90024
310-208-2100

Brad Gross, Partner

Geoffrey Sanford, Partner

Rogers Hartmann, Agent

A strong boutique that split off from a larger one. Handling writers and directors, they represent excellent writer/directors like Michael Radford, Bruce Joel Rubin, and Ron Shelton. These are thoughtful, congenial agents very adept at selling specs for new writers; if they rep you, you can't go wrong.

Contact: Brad Gross for current needs.

JACK SCAGNETTI AGENCY

5118 Vineland Avenue, Suite 102, North Hollywood, CA 91601
818-762-3871

Jack Scagnetti, Owner

Sandra Kern, Agent

Devin Schaffer, Agent

Scagnetti is a Hollywood veteran who has operated out of the San Fernando Valley for a long time. He handles just about everything but don't send him any TV shows. TV movies? Okay. Features? Sure. Even novels, but no TV episodes. If you want an agent who faxes 10 things a minute and cruises the Internet, this might not be the place, but according to FilmTracker.com, Scagnetti does have an interesting client named George Lucas. Maybe you've heard of him.

Contact: Jack Scagnetti, who likes a query letter and synopsis.

SHAPIRO-LICHTMAN

8827 Beverly Boulevard, Suite C, Los Angeles, CA 90048
310-859-8877
Fax: 310-859-7153

Mark Lichtman, Owner

Marty Shapiro, Owner

Susanna Adams, Assistant

Agents: Christine Foster, Budd Moss, Peggy Patrick, Laura Rhodes, Bob Shapiro, Susan Salkow Shapiro, Lisa Sullivan

This agency represents real quality writers. For example, David Webb Peoples, who wrote *Unforgiven*, that won an Oscar for Clint Eastwood. In addition, they have William Kelley (*Witness*), W. D. Richter (*Brubaker*), and Harlan Ellison. Shapiro and Lichtman have known each other for three decades. Whether it's a TV or feature client, they have a reputation for treating writers right. The agency represents people other than writers as well. The list above is all the agents, but not all of them rep writers. If you want a good, trustable agency, this could be it, whether you write TV (any type), features or even interactive.

Contact: The agency for current needs and submission policy.

THE IRV SHECHTER COMPANY

9300 Wilshire Boulevard, Beverly Hills, CA 90212
310-278-8070
Fax: 310-278-6058

Irv Schechter, Founder

Debbee Klein, Vice President

Don Klein, Vice President

Agents: Frank Balkin, Below the Line/Literary; **John Goldsmith,** Animation & Literary (Head of Animation); **Ms. Boyd Hancock,** Below the Line/Literary; **Josh Schecther,** Literary

Irv Shechter spent a decade and a half at William Morris before opening his own agency. Other agents at the agency have been at the business since college or even high school, and as you might have guessed, his family is in the business. In the past, this agency has handled every kind of writer, including Saturday morning TV (not many agencies handle animation writers). There are a lot of writers represented by this agency, so don't hold your breath about getting them to sign you; if it happens, though, you'll be well taken care of—the partners will see to that.

Contact: This agency works by referral only but you might give it a try if you're intent on writing for animation.

TAVEL ENTERTAINMENT

9171 Wilshire Boulevard, Suite 406, Beverly Hills, CA 90210
310-278-6700
Fax: 310-278-6770

Connie Tavel, President

Vanessa Livingston, Manager

Vera Mihailovich, Manager

Chris Ridenhour, Manager

Plato Wang, Manager

As a production company, they have credits like *Urban Legend*. As managers, they have actors like Nick Nolte. Connie Tavel's other company is Hunt-Tavel Productions, in partnership with a very talented actress named Helen Hunt. They're writer-friendly and hot, but you can't just mail in an unsolicited submission. You have to love a company where someone named Plato works, but they're very discriminating about what and whom they'll take on.

Contact: Managers listed above for current needs.

UNITED TALENT AGENCY (UTA)

9560 Wilshire Boulevard, 5th Floor, Beverly Hills, CA 90212
310-273-6700
Fax: 310-247-1111

James Berkus, Chairman

Jeremy Zimmer, Partner, Head of Motion Pictures/Literary

Peter Benedek, Partner-Agent

Agents: Dan Aloni, Elena Barry, Blair Belcher, Marty Bowen, Jason Burnes, Andrew Cannava, Howard Cohen, Shana Eddy, Charlie Ferraro, Richard Green, Chris Harbert, David Harbert, David Kramer, John Lesher, Hayden Meyer, Sue Naegle, Howard Sanders, Cynthia Shelton-Droke, Liz Ziemka

The talent this agency represents sounds like a Who's Who of Hollywood, with talents like Jeff Bridges, Drew Carey, Jim Carrey, Johnny Depp, Calista Flockhart, Harrison Ford, Danny Glover, Elizabeth Hurley, Christopher Lambert, Madonna, Ben Stiller, and Charlize Theron. They also represent major producers like Kathleen Kennedy and major directors like Barry Levinson.

In the writer/plus department they're amazing. Get a deep breath, then read a few examples–Dan Aloni is the agent for Tom Shadyac (*Liar Liar*), Barbara Dreyfus reps a number of writers including the magical Malia Scotch Marmo (*The Polar Express* and *Hook*), Blair Belcher's clients include Curtis Hanson (*L.A. Confidential*), Peter Benedeck has M. Night Shyamalan (*The Sixth Sense*), Marty Bowen has Charlie Kaufman (*Being John Malkovich*), Andrew Cannava has Alan Ball (*American Beauty*), Howard Cohen reps Chris Noonan (*Babe*), David Kramer has John Stockwell (*Top Gun*), John Lesher handles Paul Thomas Anderson (*Boogie Nights*), Hayden Meyer reps Daryl Quarles (*Big Momma's House*), and Howard Sanders represents author Nicholas Sparks (*The Notebook* and *A Walk to Remember*).

In the last edition I wrote how Andrew Cannava got Universal Pictures to pay $750,000 against more than $1 million for Jeff Nathanson's spec script *Rodolfo*, to be produced for Imagine Entertainment by Brian Grazer. (Okay, so Nathanson wasn't a newbie; he wrote *Rush Hour* and other films.) That project about an illegal immigrant in the United States who tries to get deported when his sister dies back home and eventually becomes a hero hasn't made it to the screen, but Nathanson made it to the bank. Writers at this agency are Oscar and Emmy winners and multi-million dollar stars, so if by some chance you get signed by UTA, it can most definitely make your career.

Contact: Query the agency for current needs and submission policies. Chances are very good you'll need a reference to get taken seriously at UTA, but why not give it a shot?

WILLIAM MORRIS AGENCY

151 El Camino Drive, Beverly Hills, CA 90212
310-859-4000
Fax: 310-859-4462

Norman Brokaw, Chairman Emeritus

Walter Zifkin, Chief Executive Officer

Jim Wiatt, President/Co-Chief Executive Officer

Jerry Katzman, President

Cassian Elwes, Packaging/Film, Co-Head WMA International

Hylda Queally, Senior VP/Co-Head WMA International

Sam Haskell, Head of Television Worldwide

David Wirtschafter, Executive VP/Head of Motion Pictures Worldwide

Mike Simpson, Executive VP/Co-Head Motion Pictures Worldwide

Robert Stein, Co-Head Motion Pictures Worldwide

Rob Carlson, Head of Literary & Talent

Alicia Gordon, VP, West Coast Literary (agordon@icmtalent.com)

Lewis Henderson, Head of New Media

New York office:
1325 Avenue of the Americas, New York, NY 10019
212-586-5100
Fax: 212-246-3583

Alan Kannof, Chief Operating Officer & ExecutiveVP

George Lane, Head of East Coast Motion Picture Division

Bill Contardi, Motion Pictures/Literary (wac@wma.com)

London office:
52-53 Poland Street, London, England W1S 7LX
+44-20-7534-6800

Stephanie Cabot, Managing Director

Founded in 1898, the William Morris Agency is the largest and oldest talent and literary agency in the world. The official statement of the agency, which is run by an 11-member board, is that they "are a prestigious family of experts dedicated to helping clients pursue their goals in motion pictures, television, music, theater, literature, personal appearances, commercials, and new media." William Morris has approximately 3,000 clients worldwide. The last time I checked, the L.A. office had 12 business affairs personnel (in-house lawyers) and one full-time PR person onboard.

In the last edition I said: "Of all the major agencies, William Morris is probably the most progressive." I stand by that. When no other major agency cared, William Morris formed a division to foster low-budget, independent filmmakers. They are similarly aggressive and innovative in new media.

The people listed in the offices above are generally not people who would deal with new writers, but at least you'll know who runs the show in each place and in what areas. Note that I've listed e-mails for Alicia Gordon and Bill Contardi above. As far as I know, Alicia does not mind a short, polite e-mail inquiry. I know Bill from a panel I chaired at Book Expo America on which he appeared; he told me much the same, but please realize that he handles film rights to books for smaller agencies around the country, so keep your message short and sweet.

As far as WMA agents in Los Angeles go, I feel Alan Gasmer is still probably the hottest spec script salesman in town and Deborah Blackwell is about the same in television. (This agency has always been and still is the most influential with regard to television.) Does this mean you can contact them and get them to answer the phone? Probably not. You should follow the William Morris submission policy given below. As with all major agencies, you're much better off being referred by a William Morris client.

Contact: William Morris has the following rules. "We do not consider unsolicited manuscripts or telephone queries, and request that all written queries be accompanied by SASE. A proper query letter consists of a description of your project, a synopsis/outline if available, and biographical information." (Naturally, with e-mail you won't need the SASE.)

THE WRIGHT CONCEPT

1811 W. Burbank Boulevard, Suite 201, Burbank, CA 91506
818-954-8943
Fax: 818-954-9370
E-mail: mwright@wrightconcept.com
Web site: www.wrightconcept.com

Marcie Wright, Owner

Steven Dowd, Assistant

Marcie Wright has run a small agency but a good one for years. She originally concentrated on television but branched out to sell about half TV and half feature films. She's been in the same location for over a decade, in beautiful downtown Burbank close to the Warners and Universal TV machines. The one thing she won't have anything to do with is unsolicited material, so stop licking those stamps right now. If you want to mail, fax, or e-mail her a query letter stating what you and your property are all about, that's okay, but if it's delivered by Uncle Sam, you'd better have an SASE enclosed or you might not hear back. Marcie's Web site, updated weekly, highlights her clients and their successes. Be sure to check out the very interesting bit on Harold Bell Wright.

Contact: Marcie Wright, as described above.

WRITERS & ARTISTS

924 Westwood Boulevard, Suite 900, Los Angeles, CA 90024
310-824-6300
Fax: 310-824-6343

Norman Aladjem, CEO

Marti Blumenthal, Partner

Joan Scott, Partner

Jim Stein, Head of Literary

Rick Berg, Literary Agent

Rich Freeman, Literary Agent

Dave Phillips, Literary Agent

New York office:
19 West 44th Street, Suite 1000, New York, NY 10036
212-391-1112
Fax: 212-398-9877

Stephen Small, Head of Film, TV, and Talent

Angela Chang, Literary

While they represent top talent like Anne Archer, Jennifer Beals, Lolita Davidovitch, James Gandolfini, Reginald Hudlin, Denis Leary, Mario van Peebles, and Gene Wilder, only the literary agents of this agency are listed here, and they sell a lot of scripts as the biggest agencies. *Wrestling Ernest Hemingway* was one of my favorites, and *The Rock* was great, too. Of course, I'm a fan of any agency with the aesthetic sense to call itself Writers and Artists. One particularly good reason for a new screenwriter to sign with this agency is that a large percentage of their clients are directors as well as writers. For example, Marti Blumenthal represents now novelist Stephen J. Cannell, who was once a television institution. Rich Freeman handles Daryl Ponicsan (*The Enemy Within*), Joan Scott agents Luis Valdez (*La Bamba* and *Zoot Suit*) and Jim Stein handles writer/director Eric Schaeffer (*If Lucy Fell*).

Recent arrival Dave Phillips was interviewed in a previous edition of this book. In August 2000, he sold the romantic comedy *Closers* to Dimension Films, with a reported $1 million payday to screenwriters Monica Johnson and Josh Stolberg when photography begins, with Penelope Spheeris directing. Writers & Artists can be a first-time screenwriter's dream. The agency previously got Columbia Pictures to pay $650,000 against $1 million for the *Keeping the Faith* romantic drama by Stuart Blumberg. The script was Blumberg's first screenplay; he'd previously written for television's *Mad TV*. Michael Stipanich brokered the deal. Think they like romantic screenplays?

In January 2001, after five years at United Talent Agency, talent agent Steve Small joined Writers & Artists as head of the talent, overseeing talent agents working both the Los Angeles and New York offices. UTA talent agent Ryan Martin joined him, bringing along clients like Dean Cain and Denis Leary. About the same time, literary agent Angela Chang moved from Gersh Agency in L.A. to Writers & Artists in New York. Given the bulking up of the past year, expect even better things from Writers & Artists.

Contact: The agency for current needs. A referral would help.

ZIDE/PERRY ENTERTAINMENT

9100 Wilshire Boulevard, Suite 615 East, Beverly Hills, CA 90212
310-887-2999
Fax: 310-887-2995
E-mail: inzide@inzide.com
Web site: www.inzide.com

Warren Zide, Manager

Craig Perry, Producer

Sheila Hanahan, VP Production & Development

Jennifer Frankel, Manager

Steve Freedman, Manager

Bob Sobhani, Story Editor

Zach Tann, Executive (Internet)

Zide/Perry is both a management company and a production company. If they sell a script, they take a 10 percent commission. If they produce the project, your 10 percent will be returned once the film is funded. They've produced *American Pie*, *Final Destination*, and *The Big Hit*, among others. They look for good writing "with very commercial material." In July 2000, Paramount paid low-six against mid-six figures for *The Flip Side*, a pitch by Zide/Perry-repped screenwriter Emily Baer. In October 2000, Paramount paid $600,000 against $1 million for an untitled 27-page thriller treatment from Chap Taylor about a jewel thief whose wife is taken hostage. Their Web site covers their submission guidelines in detail, offers a free newsletter, and has industry interviews and much more.

Contact: Managers and **Story Editor** above, but it's best to submit to them via the Web (instructions in full on the site).

PART THREE

All About Producers and Directors

Producer and Director Listings

A great movie rarely happens without a script, yet often the director takes credit for the entire effort with the "a film by" credit. No film would ever get made unless someone produced it, however, and that's a tough job. Producers are the real powers in Hollywood and have been ever since the studio system changed to a more independent structure. Can you schmooze talent? Can you raise money for whimsical dreams? Are you willing to spend a couple of years of your life on a single sheaf of paper around 120 pages thick? Then you could be a producer.

The hottest person in Hollywood is the writer/producer, particularly in television. To get to Multi-Millionaire City, become a television writer, get a hit series, and retire for life in five years. Of course, then you'll want to produce films, and then after you've won your Oscar, maybe you'll run for office.

I've consistently found working producers to be very engaging, ever ready to share information, and willing to hear from writers anywhere in the world. Their main gripes are that some writers who contact them do not know the basics of the screenwriting craft and are not patient in waiting to hear a response to their submission.

In compiling the producers, I've tried to find the most responsive people possible whom I also think will still be in business if there were an industry-stopping strike. I mostly list company heads and people who might directly interact with writers.

So good luck, and good writing.

40 ACRES & A MULE FILMWORKS, INC.

75 S. Elliot Place, Third Floor, Brooklyn, NY 11217
718-624-2974
Fax: 718-330-0117

L.A. office:
8899 Beverly Boulevard, Suite 401, Los Angeles, CA 90048
310-276-2116
Fax: 310-276-2164
E-mail: gjs40acres@aol.com
Web site: www.40acres.com

Spike Lee, Chairman

Gregory Sneed, COO

Sam Kitt, President (Los Angeles)

Andre Hereford, Director of Development (New York)

Arlene Gibbs, Creative Executive (Los Angeles)

Steve Lee, Creative Executive (Los Angeles)

Spike Lee put black filmmaking back on the map when *She's Gotta Have It* came out. He won't take no for an answer. When *Malcolm X* was in trouble, he got on the phone to Bill Cosby and Oprah Winfrey and raised the extra cash. The company has branched out with a very successful documentary, *The Original Kings of Comedy,* and a movie of the week. Ever the innovator, Lee has made three shorts exclusively for the Web and his last feature, *Bamboozled*, was shot on a $1,200 consumer video camera. They usually do their own projects, but they'll listen to anything interesting.

Contact: Andre Hereford, Arlene Gibbs, or **Steve Lee**.

ADAM KLINE PRODUCTIONS

c/o Lions Gate Entertainment, 4553 Glencoe Avenue, Suite 200, Marina Del Rey, CA
   90292
310-314-2000
Fax: 310-314-9557
E-mail: arkpix@aol.com

Adam Kline, President

Lyn Monroy, Story Editor

The former Executive VP of Production at TransAtlantic Enterprises, an independent production company responsible for Oliver Stone's *Heaven and Earth*, Adam Kline produced the film *Shadow of Doubt*, a political thriller for Largo Entertainment with Melanie Griffith and Tom Berenger that aired on HBO. He has also set up several comic books at studios as features and/or television series including a Dark Horse comic book entitled "John Dynamite" and a DC comic entitled "Ms. Tree." In 2001, he signed an overall producer deal at Lions Gate Entertainment and relocated to the studio.

Contact: Adam Kline, who is always aggressively looking for good scripts. The way he evaluates unknown screenwriters is by having them send, by mail, e-mail, or fax a five- to seven-sentence summary of a property. He likes "commercial, mainstream material."

ALAN SACKS PRODUCTIONS, INC.

11684 Ventura Boulevard #809, Studio City, CA 91604
818-752-6999
Fax: 818-752-6985
E-mail: asacks@pacbell.net

Alan Sacks, Producer

Teena Portier, Assistant

Alan Sacks goes all the way back to *Welcome Back Kotter,* the TV series that launched John Travolta toward superstardom. His eclectic resume includes *Lizard Woman* and *Cowboy Poetry Gathering* (a celebration of 10 years of cowboy poets). He's now the Chair of Media Arts at Los Angeles Valley College and currently developing full two-year programs to train students for jobs in entertainment industry in broadcasting (radio and television), cinema, and new digital media. It's the best deal in town for learning digital filmmaking. Los Angeles Valley College is at 5800 Fulton Avenue, Van Nuys, CA 91401-4096, 818-781-1200. Currently working on *Welcome Back Kotter: The Movie* (he created the series), he's looking for anything "totally cool" or "cutting edge." *The Color of Friendship*, a 2000 TV movie, was a multi-award winner, including the Emmy for Outstanding Children's Program.

Contact: Alan Sacks. Query before sending a screenplay.

ALLIANCE ATLANTIS MOTION PICTURE GROUP

808 Wilshire Boulevard, 3rd & 4th Floor, Santa Monica, CA 90401
310-899-8000
Fax: 310-899-8100
Web site: www.allianceatlantis.com

Toronto office:
121 Bloor Street East, Suite 800, Toronto, Ontario M4W 3M5, Canada
416-967-1174
Fax: 416-967-0971

Peter Sussman, President

Mark A. Horowitz, President

Seaton McLean, President of Motion Picture Production

Marcus Forby, VP of Le Monde Entertainment

Melissa Amer, Manager of Acquisitions & Development

Ted East, Sr. VP of Production & Development

Charlotte Mickie, Sr. VP of Acquisitions & Development

Jan Nathanson, Director of Acquisitions & Development

Damion Nurse, Acquisitions Coordinator

Karen Tohana, Submissions & Development Coordinator

This is a massive company, operating mostly in Canada, but notice they have two floors in Los Angeles. They like actors' movies that others might not risk, like Ed Harris' *Pollock* and the shown first in digital *Bounce* with Ben Affleck and Gwyneth Paltrow. Le Monde Entertainment tends to like erotic thrillers like *Zebra Lounge*, and the TV arm has projects in the pipeline like Eric Garcia's *Anonymous Rex* series and *The Dragonriders of Pern*. Use this e-mail scheme to contact them: firstname.lastname@allianceatlantis.com.

Contact: Karen Tohana, others as necessary.

ALPHAVILLE

5555 Melrose Avenue, DeMille Bldg., 2nd Floor, Hollywood, CA 90038-3197
323-956-4803
Fax: 323-862-1616
E-mail: firstname@aville.com

Caldecot "Cotty" Chubb, Producer/President

Sean Daniel, Producer

Jim Jacks, Producer

Jennifer Moyer, Director of Development

Rebecca Nelson, Producer's Assistant

Alphaville is pure entertainment. They got a remake of the 1932 *The Mummy* done so well it became a huge hit and led to an immediate sequel. They're remaking *The Bride of Frankenstein*, too. If it really moves, they like it. Housed at Paramount, they got the studio to buy Christopher Thornton's action pitch "Suburban Bounty," to produce with MTV Films. It's about a 25-year-old man who brings to the bounty-hunting business the passionate physical energy he puts into snowboarding. Alphaville also teamed with MTV on the comedy feature *Pootie Tang* with Chris Rock. They love comedy, producing *Rat Race*, director Jerry Zucker's return to comedy directing, and signing top sitcom stars Ray Romano and Kevin James to a feature project. If you have something that a young male audience would love, this is the place. Note the e-mail scheme. For example, Rebecca Nelson would be rebecca@aville.com.

Contact: Jennifer Moyer for current needs.

AMEN RA FILMS

9460 Wilshire Boulevard, Suite 400, Beverly Hills, CA 90212
310-246-6510
Fax: 310-550-1932

Wesley Snipes, Actor/Producer

Kimiko Fox, President

Victor McGauley, Sr. VP

Julian Zolkin, Creative Executive

This stable, growing company is now also into management, with actors like Vincent D'Onofrio on their roster. When I checked with them shortly before finishing this book, they had four films in production. They like action properties like *Fast Flash to Bang Time* and the *Blade* movies, but properties don't have to be for Wesley Snipes. For example (one of my favorites of that year), the company's TriStar's film, *The Big Hit* starring Mark Wahlberg and Lou Diamond Phillips, co-produced with Zide-Perry Films and executive produced by Terrence Chang and John Woo. They also go for intellectual fare; I've spoken with Victor McCauley about James Baldwin properties. They're open to anything good, and quite pleasant to deal with.

Contact: Julian Zolkin for current needs.

AMERICAN ZOETROPE

916 Kearny Street, San Francisco, CA 94133
415-788-7500
Fax: 415-989-7910

L.A. office:
310-899-8000
Web site: www.zoetrope.com

Francis Ford Coppola, Writer/Director/Producer

Linda Reisman, Head of Production

Bobby Rock, VP

Avde Soichet, Creative Executive (L.A. Office)

Tara McCann, Head of Television (L.A. Office)

Thanks to a co-financing/distribution deal with VCL Film + Medien AG, American Zoetrope expects to turn out 10 films with budgets of $10 million each during the next two years. MGM receives a 25 percent distribution fee and is handling domestic distribution through its United Artists banner. Your best bet with them is to go through the development process on their Web site; after all, they optioned a couple of scripts that way (see the "Lightning in a Bottle" chapter). What do they like? It's as eclectic as Coppola himself, who has an eco-friendly resort in Belize and is always trying something new. He gets involved with old friends like Robert Duvall's *Assassination Tango*, and you probably saw *Bram Stoker's Dracula* and *The Godfather* movies. This multi-award winner (including the Directors Guild of America's highest honor, the D. W. Griffith Award) isn't a bad winemaker, either.

Contact: Avde Soichet for TV needs and **Bobby Rock** via the SF office and the Web site for features.

APOSTLE PICTURES

1697 Broadway, Suite 300, New York, NY 10019
212-541-4323
Fax: 212-541-4330
E-mail: apostlepix@aol.com

Denis Leary, Actor/Director/Producer

Jim Serpico, President

Tom Sellitti, Producer

Bartow Church, Assistant to Jim Serpico

Denis Leary's writing and acting in *Two If By Sea* with Sandra Bullock was not a success, nor was *The Dumbo Drop* with Ray Liotta and Danny Glover, which may explain why he signed on for his own ABC TV series (*The Job*) in 2001. Nevertheless, the company has a first-look production deal with Dreamworks SKG, and the former "Angriest Man in America" is starring with Elizabeth Hurley in *Dawg*, screenplay by Ken Hastings, produced by Gold Circle Films, the 1999 winner of the Final Draft screenplay competition. Speaking of which, Leary's feature connections might help turn his TV sitcom into a hit; in the March 21, 2001 episode, his pals in the precinct compete for an assignment to a harassment case involving Elizabeth Hurley.

Contact: Bartow Church for current needs.

ART OF WAR

Sony Pictures Entertainment, 10202 West Washington Boulevard, Lean Bldg. 333, Culver City, CA 90232
310-280-7410
Fax: 310-280-2198

Marc Schmuger, President

Mark Ross, Creative Executive

David Baird, Director of Development

Christi Boyens, Office Manager

A company founded by a former Columbia marketing executive, Art of War develops project in all genres, from broad comedies to dark thrillers. They mostly work with established writers who can sell them a pitch or develop something from one of Schmuger's own ideas, but producer/master pitchman Robert Kosberg helped Irving Belateche (a director profiled in the last edition of this book) and Webb Millsaps sell a pitch called "Time Killers," about a modern-day cop who finds himself up against a serial killer from the future. The company got Columbia to pay six figures for the pitch "What Men Want Most," a comedy about sports widows, from writer Scott Fifer and producer Stephanie Epstein. If you hook up with a producer like Kosberg and have a major feature type project, this could be an interesting place to go.

Contact: David Baird about current needs.

AVENUE ENTERTAINMENT GROUP

11111 Santa Monica Boulevard, Suite 2110, Los Angeles, CA 90025
310-996-6800
Fax: 310-473-4376
Web site: www.avepix.com

Cary Brokaw, Chairman, CEO

J. J. Jamieson, President of Television

Sheri Halfon, Sr. VP, CFO

Geoff Goodman, Office Manager

With motion pictures to its credit like *Short Cuts, The Player*, and Gus van Sant's *Drugstore Cowboy*, Avenue has a three year, non-exclusive deal with Intermedia, which funds all development expenses and co-finances production costs. J. J. Jamieson was formerly director of miniseries and motion pictures for television at NBC and the company's TV movie production has been quite respectable of late (see Web site for details). Strong, quirky, artful movies are their cup of tea. No, Cary Brokaw is not related to NBC news anchor Tom Brokaw.

Contact: Cary Brokaw at cbrokaw@avepix.com or **Geoff Goodman** at ggoodman @avepix.com for current needs.

BALTIMORE/SPRING CREEK PICTURES

4000 Warner Boulevard Building 76, Room 8, Burbank, CA 91522
818-954-1210
Fax: 818-954-2737
Web site: www.Levinson.com

Barry Levinson, Director/Writer/Producer

Paula Weinstein, Producer/CEO

Robin Forman, Executive VP

Leonard Amato, Executive VP

Derek Dauchy, VP

Vanessa Coifman, VP of Development

Jacqueline Cruz, Asst. to Vanessa Coifman, *Jcruzbsc@aol.com*

Robyn Snyder, Director of Development

Naketha Mattocks, Story Editor

Andrew Lear, Development Assistant

Barry Levinson first made his mark with *Diner,* which spawned the career of a dozen major film stars. With such films as *Avalon, Bugsy, Tin Men,* and *Quiz Show*, *Analyze This*, and *The Perfect Storm* to his credit, as well as the TV series *Homicide, Life on the Street* (in partnership with Tom Fontana), Levinson is a major Hollywood player. Paula Weinstein is a 20-plus-year industry veteran who has worked with virtually every major studio and as a talent agent with William Morris had clients like Jane Fonda and Donald Sutherland. She's been a production executive at Warner Brothers, 20th Century Fox, The Ladd Company, and United Artists.

Contact: Development people or **Story Editor** above.

BANDEIRA ENTERTAINMENT

8447 Wilshire Boulevard, Suite 212, Beverly Hills, CA 90211
323-866-3535
Fax: 323-866-3599

Beau Flynn, Producer

Tripp Vinson, Senior Executive for Development & Production

Christine Johnson, Director of Development

With political comedy projects in the pipeline like *Advance Man* and *American Heroes*, they're not afraid of subjects that often fail onscreen. They also tend to like romantic comedies like *The Love Letter*, which starred Steven Spielberg's wife Kate Capshaw. (The company has a first-look production deal with Dreamworks SKG.) And they also have upcoming *Date School*, about a New York service that critiques dating skills for clients. It's based on an article in *Mademoiselle* and will star Ben Stiller. Dramas aren't a problem either, particularly those with social commentary like *Requiem for a Dream* (about addiction), which won an Oscar nod for Ellyn Burstyn, and *Tigerland*, about a rebellious U.S. Army recruit in the 1970s. Tripp Vinson was VP production at Artists Production Group, the production arm of Artists Management Group, before coming to Bandeira. They intend to expand their menu to thrillers and action fare, so don't judge them solely on what they've done in the past.

Contact: Christine Johnson (but they have a lot going on).

BEACON COMMUNICATIONS

120 Broadway Suite 200, Santa Monica, CA 90401
310-260-7000
Fax: 310-260-7050
E-mail: info@beaconpictures.com

Armyan Bernstein, Chairman

Marc Abraham, President

Suzann Ellis, Sr. VP of Development & Production

Caitlin Scanlon, VP of Development

Steve Asbell, Director of Development

Megan Weiss, Creative Executive

Got a political thriller or spy story? Beacon's *Air Force One* earned more than $320 million worldwide. They grabbed Michael Beckner's spec *Spy Game* for Doug Wick (Red Wagon) to produce, and were behind *Thirteen Days*, about the 1962 Cuban missile crisis. They love the struggle of good and evil, having starred Arnold Schwarzenegger to duel with the Devil in *End of Days*. Beacon is one of those unique companies that provides their own financing, usually from foreign sources, and greenlight their own films. They have more spy movies in the pipeline like *Wild Bill Donovan* (who ran the OSS, precursor of the CIA, in WWII) and the political thriller *Shadow Government* with Jonathan "U-571" Mostow.

Contact: Development people or **Creative Executive** above.

BERG/SACCANI ENTERTAINMENT

7421 Beverly Boulevard, Suite 4, Los Angeles, CA 90036
323-930-9935
Fax: 323-930-9934
E-mail: info@berg-saccani.com
Web site: www.berg-saccani.com

Jon Berg, Partner

Damien Saccani, Partner

Dave Donegan, Head of Interactive

A management production company handling some of the actors of Allison Ander's *Gas, Food and Lodging*, producers Berg and Saccani have a film in development with MGM and a first-look deal with Universal. They have a relationship with Neal Moritz of Original Film and tend to like crime and thriller projects. They also have done Web sites for major Hollywood companies and so understand that world very well, too. They might be a good bet for a hot new writer who likes the crime/thriller genre.

Contact: Either partner.

BILL MELENDEZ PRODUCTIONS

13400 Riverside Drive, Suite 201, Sherman Oaks, CA 91423
818-382-7382
Fax: 818-382-7377
E-mail: stdolmo@aol.com

Bill Melendez, President

Sandy Arnold, Head of Production

Leo Moran, Creative Director

Evert Brown, Creative Director

Joanna Colletto, Office Manager

When you've done all the *Peanuts* TV specials and videos, who needs anything else? Bill Melendez was the perfect choice to bring the *Peanuts* characters to the world, but his *Frosty Returns* wasn't bad either. Mr. Melendez is in his eighties now, but if you have a spectacular animation project with whimsical good-naturedness that could be a "franchise" hit, you might check with this company.

Contact: Joanna Colletto for current needs.

BLUE WOLF PRODUCTIONS

725 Arizona Avenue, Suite 202, Santa Monica, CA 90401
310-451-8890
Fax: 310-451-4886

Robin Williams, Actor/Producer

Marsha Garces Williams, Producer

Cyndi Margolis, Executive Assistant

This small company owned by Robin Williams and his wife had a major hit with *Mrs. Doubtfire*, which came from a book Marsha Williams discovered. Williams wanted to do a project of mine, but two years remaining on his *Mork & Mindy* TV series contract precluded him from getting involved at the time. Williams played with the Comedy Store Players in Los Angeles every Monday night then and was easily approached about projects. Maybe you'll get luckier than I did. With things in the pipeline like *The Interpreter*, about an average Joe who lands a job as an interpreter during tense, globally important international situations and screws them up, and the starring role in the Liberace biopic, he's looking at comedy first these days. Blue Wolf has a first-look production deal with Walt Disney Pictures.

Contact: Cyndi Margolis for current submission policy and needs.

BOZ PRODUCTIONS

1632 N. Sierra Bonita Avenue, Los Angeles, CA 90046
323-876-3232
Fax: 213-876-3231
E-mail: boz51@aol.com (Bo Zenga) or jmmonarch@aol.com (Jeff Monarch)

Bo Zenga, Writer, Director, Producer

Jeff Monarch, Director of Development

Steve Dandois, Story Editor (direct line 323-876-4870)

Bo Zenga had a banner year in 1997, when he sold a dozen pitches to major studios. He's aggressive; he got Emilio Estevez onboard his *Time Jumpers*, then they took it to Estevez' old buddy Tom Cruise, who signed on to an instant studio deal. Then Cruise backed out, but Zenga almost immediately set the deal up with Dreamworks SKG. In February 1999, he set up "Last Summer I Screamed Because Friday the 13th Fell on Halloween," which became Dimension Films' *Scary Movie*, which took in over $40 million at the box office the first weekend. Then, however, Zenga (executive producer on the film) sued Brillstein-Grey Entertainment, saying the company cheated him out of credit and fees. The suit was unresolved as we went to press. Zenga will listen to a pitch from just about anyone, so feel free to tell him what you have to offer.

Contact: Bo Zenga or **Jeff Monarch** with query.

BREAKING IN PRODUCTIONS

433 North Camden Drive, Suite 600, Beverly Hills, CA 90210
310-288-1881
Fax: 310-288-0257
E-mail: tohollywood@hollywoodnetwork.com
Web site: http://hollywoodnetwork.com

Carlos de Abreu, President/Producer

Janice Pennington de Abreu, Producer

The Hollywood Network is one of the largest World Wide Web entertainment business sites in existence, featuring over 80 Hollywood experts, from agents to producers to script consultants. Breaking In Productions is an offshoot of the Hollywood Network's "Christopher Columbus Discovery Awards," which takes in scripts by new writers. Winners of the competition are presented to major players and agents in Hollywood. Carlos and Janice are the co-founders of the Hollywood Film Festival. Now that Janice Pennington has left her long-time role on TV's *The Price is Right*, she will devote more time to producing. They like classy projects with an international flair and can get a script to anyone in Hollywood who matters.

Contact: Carlos de Abreu for current projects and needs.

BUTCHERS RUN FILMS

8978 Norma Place, West Hollywood. CA 90069
310-246-4630
Fax: 310-246-1033

Robert Duvall, Actor/Producer

Rob Carliner, Producer/Manager

Adam Prince, Director of Development

To get *The Apostle* made, Robert Duvall wrote a check for $4 million. Rob Carliner produced. They sold it to USA/October for $5 million and that's all they made on it. That takes guts. Adam Prince, Director of Development, directed their latest film, *Assassination Tango*, which they shot in New York and Argentina. The budget is $8 to $10 million. They did it with American Zoetrope and United Artists. Prince came on-board after winning an award from USC and writing something they believed in. Agents regularly call Rob Carliner to try to sign Duvall, who lives on a farm in Virginia and doesn't have a regular agent, but since Duvall is agency-independent, they can bypass packaging and call the director of the film. Their criteria for material is "as long as it's good." Rob Carliner only reads three pages before he knows whether something is good or not. They have a soft spot for Westerns, particularly with totally different characters, something not seen before. They want just a standard format script, no extra cute touches. They are *not* only looking for stuff for Robert Duvall to star in.

Contact: Rob Carliner.

C-2 PICTURES

2308 Broadway, Santa Monica, CA 90404
310-315-6069
Fax: 310-828-0443

Mario Kassar, Partner

Andrew Vajna, Partner

Joel B. Michaels, President/Production

James Middleton, Senior Vice President

Gabrielle Benson, Director/Development

At one time, this team was riding as high as anyone, when they had a company called Carolco. Later came Cinergi, and now C-2. In October 2000, Hollywood learned that they were teaming with German-backed Intermedia Films teamed to co-produce and finance both *Terminator 3* and *Basic Instinct 2*. With Arnold Schwarzenegger committed to return for *T-3* and Sharon Stone onboard the *Basic Instinct* sequel, it seemed possible that the glory days had a chance of returning. Another project in the pipeline is a loose remake of *I Spy*, the old TV series that made Bill Cosby a TV star. Just don't expect Sylvester Stallone to show up for another segment of *Rambo*. Maybe you have something that could be a power-packed thriller franchise like Kassar and Vajna know how to produce so well, that isn't a remake or sequel?

Contact: Gabrielle Benson for current needs.

THE CANTON COMPANY

Warner Bros., 4000 Warner Boulevard, Building 81, Suite 200, Burbank, CA 91522
818-954-2130
Fax: 818-954-2967

Mark Canton, President

Nathan Kahane, Vice President

Anna DeRoy, Producer

John Goldstone, Creative Executive

Michael Gordon, Assistant to Producer

Scott Coleman, Assistant

With a multi-year deal at Warners, Canton has also formed a joint production and financing venture with Senator (a big German company). If you want to know what kind of films Mark Canton likes, surf over to www.imdb.com and look him up. He used to run a studio. *Red Planet* and *Get Carter* (with Sylvester Stallone) were disappointments, and sometimes I can't figure Mark Canton out. For example, in November 2000, he spent six figures to option the rights to Lou Cannon's *New York Times* magazine article "One Bad Cop" about the L.A. Police Department Rampart division scandal, despite the fact that Dave Ayer's very similar *Training Day* was already scheduled to be distributed by Warners. In the pipeline are a massive number of projects including epics like *Alexander the Great* and *Troy* and a movie about singer Enrico Caruso. Think high profile, big stars, with international appeal.

Contact: John Goldstone for current needs.

CAPELLA FILMS, INC.

9242 Beverly Boulevard, Beverly Hills, CA 90210-3710
310-247-4700
Fax: 310-247-4701

Andreas Lindstroem, Chairman

Alessandra McAliley, Executive Vice President

Andrew Milner, President of Capella International

Rolf Deyhle, President

David Korda, President of Production & Development

Bridget Hedison, VP of Development

Capella International is a German-backed company with a taste for spy films. In 1996 they acquired international rights to *Austin Powers*. On a more modest budget was *Provocateur*, a spy thriller with action TV star Nick Mancuso. Capella Intl., the sales division of Capella Films, bought worldwide rights (excluding Scandinavia and Russia) to the $7.5 million Swedish action drama *Commander Hamilton*. If you have something suitable for a European co-production, you might consider this company. In the pipeline at press time was *Santiago*, about a futuristic bounty hunter, and *C.O.D.*, about a real-life detective who rescues children kidnapped in child custody battles.

Contact: Bridget Hedison for current needs.

CAPPA PRODUCTIONS

445 Park Avenue, New York, NY 10022
212-906-8800
Fax: 212-906-8891

L.A. office: 818-560-7805

Martin Scorsese, Producer/Director

Barbara De Fina, Producer

Shira Levin, Director of Development

Sonja Grunden, Creative Executive (L.A., DeFina/Cappa Prods.)

Don't assume this famous director is unreceptive to new writers. He's unpredictable. Just when you think he'll make mob movies forever, out he comes with *The Age of Innocence*. And when *The Gangs of New York* is in the pipeline, the company gives us *You Can Count on Me*. The company has a first look deal with Walt Disney/Touchstone Pictures, and that's where you'll find the Los Angeles office. Look for a remake of Kurosawa's *The Seven Samurai*, but it probably won't be a Western like *The Magnificent Seven*. And another Italian movie, only this time it's a biography of the house of Gucci. What do they want? With Scorsese it should be obvious. Passion. In any way they're involved, epic, classic, even if it's a "small" movie like *You Can Count on Me*, which was the 2000 Sundance Grand Jury Prizewinner and garnered an Oscar nomination for the always-fascinating Laura Linney.

Contact: Shira Levin or **Sonja Grunden**.

CARSEY-WERNER-MANDABACH

4024 Radford Avenue, Building 3, Studio City, CA 91604
818-760-5598
Fax: 818-760-6259

Marcy Carsey, Partner

Tom Werner, Partner

Caryn Mandabach, Partner

Kathy Busby, Vice President of Development

Eric Berg, Director of Development

Don't get the idea this is a small company because I've only listed a few names. They've had franchise hit sitcoms like *Cybill, Grace Under Fire, Roseanne, 3rd Rock from the Sun,* and the drama hit *Profiler.* The principals of the company were multimillionaires long ago, with *The Cosby Show,* and Bill Cosby's new show with them on CBS was also a success. Getting onboard a successful Carsey-Werner show is an E-ticket to the big bucks. Many of their things in development I mentioned in the last edition haven't come to fruit, like the sitcom deal with Alan Spencer, best known for *Sledge Hammer!* and their feature remake of *The Incredible Mr. Limpet* with director Norman Jewison. Vice chairman and CEO Stuart Glickman left, and Caryn Mandabach was promoted to full partner. *That '70s Show* is their latest hit, and they do have a features division, so why not?

Contact: Eric Berg; you might have little chance without an agent, but it's worth a call.

CASTLE ROCK ENTERTAINMENT

335 North Maple Drive, Suite 135, Beverly Hills, CA 90210
310-285-2300
Fax: 310-285-2435
Web site: www.castle-rock.warnerbros.com

Alan Horn, Chairman, CEO

Martin Shafer, President, Castle Rock Pictures, Inc.

Liz Glotzer, President, Feature Production

Steven Rabiner, Senior VP of Production, Castle Rock Pictures

Glenn Padnick, President, Castle Rock TV

Robin Green, Senior VP, Castle Rock TV

Rob Reiner, Director/Producer

Andrew Scheinman, Director/Producer

Pam Singleton, Sr. Creative Manager

Gaylyn Fraiche, Creative Executive

Brady Thomas, Creative Executive

John Surre, Development Assistant

What started as a film production company for actor/director Rob Reiner grew into a major organization. With hits like *A Few Good Men, In the Line of Fire,* and *Seinfeld,* there's a lot of money there. I loved their *Mickey Blue Eyes,* with Hugh Grant and James Caan, but it didn't eat up the box office. The same goes for *Miss Congeniality,* starring Sandra Bullock, but as a general rule I like just about all Castle Rock films. They're approachable; one executive has a particular kind of screenplay he'd like to see, but I'm keeping that one for myself!

Contact: Development assistant or **creative execs.**

CENTROPOLIS FILM PRODUCTIONS, INC.

10202 W. Washington Boulevard, Astaire Bldg., Culver City, CA 90232
310-244-4300
Fax: 310-244-4360
E-mail: devlin@centropolis.com
Web site: www.centropolis.com

Roland Emmerich, Director/Writer/Producer

Dean Devlin, Producer/Writer

Ute Emmerich, Partner (Roland is her brother)

William Fay, President

Jennifer Lew, Asst. to President (jeniferl@centropolis.com)

Peter Winther, Senior VP of Development

Marc Roskin, VP of Development

Originally from Stuttgart, Germany, Roland Emmerich, son of one of Europe's largest manufacturers of gardening equipment, grew up wanting to manufacture movies. When he teamed up with Dean Devlin to do *Stargate,* they began adding to the success that began with the Jean-Claude van Damme hit *Universal Soldier* (which Devlin wrote).

Then came the megahit *Independence Day*, and in early 1998, the company moved to Sony Pictures Entertainment with an amazing 10-picture deal. They founded Centropolis Streamline to make lower budget films and have done OK in television with *Stargate SG-1*. They also have a special effects company. They're somewhat open to new writers, I've learned, and their Web site is top-notch.

Contact: Development people mentioned above.

CHESLER/PERLMUTTER PRODUCTIONS

1045 Gayley Avenue, Suite 200, Los Angeles, CA 90024
310-443-9650
Fax: 310-443-9524
E-mail: chesperl@aol.com

Lewis B. Chesler, Chairman & Executive Producer

David Perlmutter, Chairman

Stephen Ujlaki, President

Kevin Commins, VP of Development

Meredith Freeman, Creative Executive

Chesler/Perlmutter has done a number of films for HBO including *Valentine's Day* with Randy Quaid. They've also sold a number of things to UPN and done sci-fi features with Alliance Atlantis Communications. They specialize in producing material, which is either Canadian content or Canadian-European co-production, meaning that writers must either be Canadian or holders of EEC passports. Their features are usually in the $2 to $5 million range, for cable and broadcast television, as well as series, and they're also now producing family films, especially those revolving around animals. They also want thrillers, mysteries, and sci-fi and prefer the story take place in the United States No period, historical, horror, or comedies, and their budget range is $2 to $7 million.

Contact: Kevin Commins by e-mailing a logline ONLY.

CHICK FLICKS

116 N. Robertson Boulevard, Los Angeles, CA 90048
310-854-5811
Fax: 310-854-1824

Sara Risher, President

Janis Chaskin, Executive VP

Michele Brennan, Creative Executive

The title of the company says it all. With an in-house development and production deal with New Line Cinema, they're into making movies women like. Sara Risher was co-executive producer of Wes Craven's *New Nightmare* and executive producer of *Wide Sargasso Sea*; she knows how to raise money to make films. With things in the pipeline like *Neurotica* (a female journalist imagines cheating on her husband while writing about extramarital affairs) and *Tales Not Be Told* (a woman falls for a mysterious man and fights to win him away from an evil woman), they like edgy material. Interestingly enough, most of the things they have in development were written by men.

Contact: Michele Brennan for current needs.

CODIKOW FILMS

8899 Beverly Boulevard, Suite 719, Los Angeles, CA 90048
310-246-9388
Fax: 310-246-9877
E-mail: pitch@codikowfilms.com
Web site: www.codikowfilms.com

Stacy Codikow, Producer/Writer

Sherri James, VP of Development

John Orlando, Creative Executive

Kevin Vermilion, Assistant to Stacy Codikow

A graduate of the University of Southern California's School of Cinema, Stacy Codikow has produced a number of feature films, an Emmy-award-winning television series, and written a lot for television. Her first feature, produced at age 24, won the American Film Institute's Award for Best Feature. Her *Under the Hula Moon* was picked as Best Feature at the Worldfest Charleston International Film Festival, after premiering at Cannes. Lately she's been writing a lot for television, and was selected as one of 10 to participate in the AFI Writers Workshop with Chris Carter, but she still maintains a staff and is looking for properties. The great thing about Stacy is that she's helped a number of people get started in this business by working on staff with her. You can read all about it on her busy Web site. At press time she was looking for a romantic comedy.

Contact: Sherri James.

COLOMBY/KEATON

2110 Main Street, Suite 302, Santa Monica, CA 90405
310-399-8881
Fax: 310-392-1323

Harry Colomby, Partner

Michael Keaton, Partner

Jennifer Keohane, Producer

Helen Baines, Story Editor

Ford Oelman, Creative Associate

Harry Colomby was co-producer of the 1983 Michael Keaton hit *Mr. Mom*, so their relationship goes back a long way. As a production company, their forgettable *Body Shots* (originally titled "Jello Shots") didn't set the world on fire, which might explain why things they have in development mostly have Keaton attached to star. In the pipeline are movies like *Bump in the Night*, a movie with Jerry Bruckheimer about con artists who get the tables turned on them by ghosts (remember *Beetlejuice*?). They also have the female-driven *Play With Fire*, and *Eyes of the Wicked*. All of which should tell you they like movies with an edge.

Contact: Helen Baines for current needs.

COSGROVE-MEURER PRODUCTIONS

4303 West Verdugo Avenue, Burbank, CA 91505
818-843-5600
Fax: 818-843-8585
E-mail: umysteries@aol.com
Web site: www.unsolved.com

John Cosgrove, Chief Executive Officer

Terry Meurer, President

Rebecca Whittington, VP of Development

Joanna Levi, Feature Development

Stuart Schwartz, VP of Reality Development

Michael Sluchan, Director Development

Jennifer Bilovsky, Development Assistant

Responsible for the long-running hit TV series *Unsolved Mysteries,* Cosgrove-Meurer is a stable company with a bent for mystery, having such other credits as *Voice from the Grave: A Friend's Betrayal.* VP of Development Rebecca Whittington came from Once Upon a Time Films, a company that delivers a lot of TV movies, but they're doing feature films now as well. They have things in the pipeline like *Ball in the House,* about a screwed-up teenager trying to straighten out his life, and *Reunion* with MGM, which was inspired by an episode of their TV series.

Contact: Development people mentioned above, depending on what you want to sell them, with a query.

CRUSADER ENTERTAINMENT

132 B Lasky Drive, Beverly Hills, CA 90212
310-248-6360
Fax: 310-248-6370
E-mail: info@crusaderentertainment.com
Web site: www.crusaderentertainment.com

Howard Baldwin, Chief Executive Officer

Karen Baldwin, Executive VP, Creative

Stuart Benjamin, Executive VP

Paul Pompian, Executive VP

William J. Immerman, Executive VP

Jennifer Smith, Executive VP of Television

Nicholas Morton, VP of Development

Craig TenBroeck, Creative Executive, Film

Tom Brainard, Creative Executive, Television

Todd Slater, Creative Executive, Television

Larissa Watson, Creative Assistant

With a three-year first-look distribution deal with Paramount, this company was funded by Philip Anschutz, a Denver billionaire, who has ownership in the L.A. Kings, Staples Center, and L.A. Lakers, as well as lots of movie theaters. The company was known as

Baldwin/Cohen Productions. They have a family films division with fare like *The Rat's Tale*, a reworking of the Cinderella story from the rat's point of view. They're into finding and giving new talent opportunity. It's *that* Baldwin family, with Alec Baldwin producing some of the projects. Their most notable projects to date were *Entropy* by Phil Joanou, a film revolving around the band U2 and *Mystery, Alaska*, which had disappointing box office even though it was written by David E. Kelley and directed by the genius Jay Roach. Oh well, they won't run out of money anytime soon, and they have development potential like nobody's business. Their Web site explains just about everything about them.

Contact: Any **Creative Executive** listed above.

CYPRESS FILMS

The Film Center, 630 Ninth Avenue, Suite 415, New York, NY 10036
212-262-3900
Fax: 212-262-3925
E-mail: lovisa@cypressfilms.com
Web site: www.cypressfilms.com

Joseph Pierson, President, Co-Director

Jon Glascoe, Producer, Co-Director

Peggy Glascoe, Producer, Office Manager

Lovisa Kihlberg, Director of Development

I first came across this company when I stumbled upon the "Making Cherry" site, which chronicled the making of the independent film *Cherry* starring supermodel Shalom Harlow. It was a goofy, fun little movie that you might have seen on cable. Cypress was established in 1987 by Joe Pierson and Jon Glascoe, who have worked in television as well as film. They've created more than 40 hours of programs for TV including the Emmy-winning *Lost in the Barrens* for the Disney Channel. Half a dozen made for cable movies are in their background. Although they're mostly doing their own projects, they're open to queries, and Lovisa Kihlberg is the hands-down "Development Babe" winner of this edition of the *Writer's Guide to Hollywood*. They have a relationship with Alliance Atlantis and things in the pipeline like *Welcome to the Monkey House*, from the short story by Kurt Vonnegut.

Contact: Lovisa Kihlberg with a short query.

DEEP RIVER PRODUCTIONS

100 N. Crescent Drive, Suite 350, Beverly Hills, CA 90210
310-432-1800
Fax: 310-432-1801

David T. Friendly, Producer

Marc Turtletaub, Partner

David Higgins, Senior Executive

Julie Durk, Senior Executive Producer

Creative Executives: Michael McGahey, Missy Pontious, Will Rowbotham

This is a new company with success written all over it. David Friendly was president of Imagine, then president of Davis Entertainment before producing films with Fox 2000, including the Eddie Murphy starrer *Dr. Dolittle* and *Courage Under Fire*. He also produced *Big Momma's House*. Marc Turtletaub is a financier who took his father's money-lending business, the Money Store, public and then sold it in a $2.1 billion deal. Reportedly, Turtletaub's stock was worth around $700 million. He talked with dozens of aspiring partners before settling on Friendly. Julie Durk previously worked with Richard and Lauren Shuler-Donner. This company, with its wealth, can go by their instincts, which has always been the best formula for success in Hollywood. In the pipeline are many projects including: a movie with comedian Steve Harvey, Kyle Long's spec script *The Million Dollar Fan* (his first sale), and (my favorite) a project about the Harlem Globetrotters.

Contact: Michael McGahey or other creative executives.

DI NOVI PICTURES

3110 Main Street, Suite 220, Santa Monica, CA 90405
310-581-1355
Fax: 310-399-0499

Denise DiNovi, Producer

Edward L. McDonnell, President

Alison Greenspan, VP of Development

Marc Wolf, Director of Development

Garrick Dion, Story Editor

Brad Wiss, Story Editor

Amir Yazdi, Development Assistant

Denise DiNovi made a name for herself working with oddball director Tim Burton. She is always looking for good projects which tend to be funny and/or female in theme. Di Novi's first-look deal with Warner Brothers came when Turner Pictures (where she had a deal) merged with the studio. She does romantic movies like the charming *Practical Magic* with Sandra Bullock and *Message in a Bottle*, but she's got a big time fun side, too, with *The Jetsons* also on her plate. In the pipeline are over two dozen projects including a romantic comedy with Kevin Spacey, Danielle Steel's *The Ghost*, and from the Nicholas Spark's best-selling novel, *A Walk to Remember*. Alison Greenspan previously worked with Robert Zemeckis and Marc Wolf worked with Goldie Hawn.

Contact: Marc Wolf or either **story editor** for current needs.

DIMITRI VILLARD PRODUCTIONS

8721 Santa Monica Boulevard, Suite 100, Los Angeles, CA 90069-4511
310-229-4545
Fax: 310-854-6044
E-mail: dvillard@loop.com

Dimitri Villard, President

Susan Danforth, Development

Dimitri Villard averaged almost a film a year for a while: *Timewalker* (Concorde, 1982) and *Death of an Angel* (Fox, 1984), then he wrote and produced *Once Bitten* (Goldwyn, 1985), starring Jim Carrey. That comedy vampire film was not the hit some expected, and it would be another decade before Carrey hit his stride, but Villard continued with *Flight of the Navigator* (Disney, 1986). Some of his films after that are ones you probably never heard of: *Purgatory* (New Star, 1987); *Frankenstein General Hospital* (New Star, 1988); *Hide and Go Shriek* (New Star, 1988); and *Easy Wheels* (Fries Entertainment, 1989). In 1996 Villard's big project was *In Love and War* for New Line, directed by Oscar winner Richard Attenborough, starring Sandra Bullock and Chris O'Donnell as the young Ernest Hemingway. Not a hit, but he's still making films, with things like *Out of Time* by William Stadiem in the pipeline (Stadiem wrote the Dolph Lundgren film *Pentathlon*).

Contact: Susan Danforth. They're especially interested in science fiction, historical drama, and comedy.

DISTANT HORIZON

8282 Sunset Boulevard, Suite A, Los Angeles, CA 90046
323-848-4140
Fax: 323-848-4144
E-mail: distanth@ix.netcom.com

Anant Singh, President

Brian Cox, Producer

Jennifer Ivory, Production Coordinator

Sanjeev Singh, Acquisitions Executive

With such credits as *Cry, The Beloved Country* and *Sarafina!* behind them, Distant Horizon is as much distribution as production, their most recent success being *The Dish* from Australia. They do have project in the pipeline, though, movies with a cause like *One Just Man*, about a prosecutor's experience in the New York legal system (from the James Mills book) and more set in South Africa like *The Long Run* (about a marathon runner) and *Mr. Bones* (set against a golf tournament but about reading witch doctors' bones).

Contact: Query **Sanjeev Singh** via mail, fax, or e-mail.

RONA EDWARDS ENTERTAINMENT

264 S. La Cienega Boulevard, Suite 1052, Beverly Hills, CA 90211
323-466-3013
Fax: 323-467-1258

Rona Edwards, Producer/Manager

Interviewed in this book, Rona Edwards has a long history in Hollywood and contacts with everyone who matters, as well as the ability to sell in Europe. She teaches a course at UCLA Extension about breaking into the business as well. She ran Port Street Films for TV star John Larroquette and was Vice President of Creative Affairs for producer Michael Phillips before going into business for herself. Her most recent producing credits were *Out of Sync*, one of VH-1's "Movies That Rock," which was written by her client, Eric Williams, and *Der Mörder Meiner Mutter* (The Murderer of My Mother) for German television. She's very discriminating, and basically looks for solid, no-nonsense, commercial writers whose work she can set up.

Contact: Rona Edwards with a short query.

EGG PICTURES

5555 Melrose Avenue, Jerry Lewis Building Annex, Los Angeles, CA 90038
323-956-8400
Fax: 323-862-1414

Jodie Foster, Actor/Director/Producer

Meg LeFauve, President

Lisa Buono, VP

Lorielle Evelyn Mallue, Director of Development

Academy-Award-winner Jodie Foster is one of the few successful child actors who made a transition to an adult career, and what a career. A Yale graduate and recipient of the Douglas Sirk Award for exceptional achievement at the Hamburg Film Festival, Foster enjoys intellectual material and character-driven films. Her staff is loyal and gets promoted; Meg LeFauve was once VP and Lisa Buono was previously story editor. They're more open to material than they used to be. Meg LeFauve has lectured at the Learning Annex and taken pitches from attendees at the event and she showed up for UCLA's Pitchfest (she's an instructor in the Independent Producer's Program). On their slate is the female-centered modern-day Western *One Hundred Years On*, the Depression-era *Flora Plum*, and possibly a biopic about Hitler's favorite filmmaker, Leni "Triumph of the Will" Riefenstahl. You'll need an agent or lawyer to get them to look at a project, however.

Contact: Have your agent or lawyer contact **Lorielle Evelyn Mallue** to explain the project before forwarding it to Egg.

ESCAPE ARTISTS

Sony Pictures, 10202 West Washington Boulevard, Lean Building 333, Culver City,
    CA 90232
310-244-8833
Fax: 310-244-2151
E-mail: scheme firstname_name@spe.sony.com
Web site: www.hollywoodlitsales.com

David Alper, CEO & Partner

Steve Tisch, Producer

Todd Black, Producer

Jason Blumenthal, Producer

Chrissy Blumenthal, VP of Development

Howard Meibach, Director of Internet Literary Acquisitions

Erica Kane, Story Editor, phone: 310-244-5053

Sharyn Steele, Development Assistant

Lindsay Willen, Development Assistant

This is complicated. Black & Blu Entertainment (Todd Black and the Blumenthals) merged with the Steve Tisch Company and Summit Entertainment to form Escape Artists. Summit, however, remains a separate company. I'll let Howard Meibach explain it to you: "The people behind such films as *Forrest Gump, I Know What You Did Last Summer, Risky Business, Donnie Brasco,* and *Wild Things,* have joined us to help turn your stories into movies." As you can see, Meibach is listed above. Suffice it to say these folks are among the most receptive and Internet-active in the biz. They have projects coming up like the high-budget *Bermuda Triangle.*

Contact: Via **Hollywood Lit Sales** or development or story people.

ESPARZA-KATZ ENTERTAINMENT

8899 Beverly Boulevard, Suite 506, Los Angeles, CA 90048
310-281-3770
Fax: 310-281-3777
E-mail (general): esparzakatz@msn.com

Moctesuma Esparza, Producer/Director—cocte@ix.netcom.com

Robert Katz, Producer—robertk@earthlink.net

Legiah Villalobos, VP of Creative Affairs

Greg Gomez, Director of Development

Robert Katz and the award-winning writer/director/producer Moctesuma Esparza formed their company in 1984, and though there were some lean years, they've been on a roll for over a decade. *Gettysburg* is perhaps TNT's biggest success story, and their feature film *Selena* made a star out of Jennifer Lopez. As always, they have a ton of projects in the pipeline including biopics of Bobby Darin, Timothy Leary, and rock guru Bill Graham, but as you know from the interview with Bob Katz in this book, they're open to anything that has "a great story, good writing, and compelling characters, done in a unique and different way."

Contact: Anyone listed above with a short description of what you have available. Describe full projects (no treatments) only.

EVOLUTION ENTERTAINMENT

7720 Sunset Boulevard, Los Angeles, CA 90046
323-850-3232
Fax: 323-850-0521

Mark Burg, Partner

Oren Koules, Partner

Andrew Weitz, Agent

Managers: Doug Draizin, Stephen Gates, Kristof Guy, Paul Nichols

As a management company, these folks manage talent you know like Peter Falk, Farrah Fawcett, Janine Turner, and Kari Wuhrer. Films in their production slate include the comedy *Tour Guide*, to be directed by actor Daniel Stern, and *Love Comes to the Executioner*, a quirky romance revolving around a prison executioner who falls in love in his scheduled-to-die brother's incarcerated ex-girlfriend (whew), with Sandra Bullock involved. Then there's second generation Hollywood director Nick Cassavetes' *Going After Cacciato*, about a military deserter pursued by his unit, based on a novel by Tim O'Brien. Think about films that appeal to people in their twenties, like *Monster Truck*, about a disgraced NASCAR driver who goes into monster truck racing. Oren Koules and Stephen Gates set up the comedy spec project for clients David Capper and Kevin Lipski, and will executive produce it. Note that Andrew Weitz is an agent—management/production companies like this need one because of California agenting laws.

Contact: Anyone listed above.

FACE PRODUCTIONS

335 N. Maple Drive, Suite 175, Beverly Hills, CA 90210
310-285-2300
Fax: 310-285-2386

Billy Crystal, President

Samantha Sprecher, VP of Development

Annette Mathews, Story Editor

With a first-look production deal with Castle Rock and a talent like Billy Crystal at the helm, the company is riding high with upcoming films like *America's Sweethearts* with Julia Roberts in which Crystal plays a frantic PR flack (the project was picked up in turnaround by Revolution Studios). They also have one coming in which Crystal plays an uncouth NYPD detective forced to team up with a female detective from Scotland Yard. If either one is as great as *Analyze This*, I'm there. If you have a script in which Billy Crystal could also star, this is the place. If you talk to him, ask him if he has a copy of the 25th anniversary of the Improv comedy club, which he hosted. I'm in the opening!

Contact: Samantha Sprecher or **Annette Mathews.**

FAIR DINKUM PRODUCTIONS

c/o MGM, 2500 Broadway Street, Bldg. E-5, Suite #5018, Santa Monica, CA 90404
310-586-8471
Fax: 310-586-8469

Henry Winkler, Actor/Director/Producer

Troy Wright, Executive Assistant to Producer

Henry Winkler was working as a waiter at the Great American Food and Beverage Company in Los Angeles before he put on a black leather jacket and started showing Richie Cunningham the meaning of life on *Happy Days*. Imagine that—getting an order of burgers and fries delivered by the Fonz. Winkler's come a long way since, directing such feature films like *Cop and a Half* and creating such hit TV shows like *MacGyver*. There are all sorts of odd facts about Winkler. He wrote for TV's *The Partridge Family*, for example, and he even executive produced a Western—*Dead Man's Gun*, a trilogy of Western anthology stories for Showtime. I was glad to see him acting again in Adam Sandler's *Water Boy*. Winkler always has something interesting coming up, like his "Pure Imagination" series of short live-action movies with Sesame Workshop. If you want to see what he likes, just look at what he's done.

Contact: Troy Wright for current needs.

FARRELL/MINOFF PRODUCTIONS

14011 Ventura Boulevard, Suite 401, Sherman Oaks, CA 91423
818-789-5766
Fax: 818-789-7459

Mike Farrell, Actor, Producer, Director

Marvin Minoff, Producer

Though he's mostly been involved recently with his role on the highly successful *Providence*, Mike Farrell does have some upcoming projects with Marvin Minoff including *In Silence*, about a woman who grows up with deaf parents and a project with Showtime. Farrell is a heavy human rights activist, and sometimes his script tastes reflect that. His first feature film with producer Marvin Minoff was the critically-acclaimed *Dominick & Eugene,* and their *Patch Adams* with Robin Williams was a noble effort as well. Marvin Minoff spent 15 years with major agencies such as William Morris and IFA (now ICM), rising to become VP of the motion picture department before leaving the agency business in 1974. He co-produced the historic Nixon interviews with David Frost and was responsible for James Michener's *Dynasty,* which starred Harrison Ford, Amy Irving, Sarah Miles, and Stacy Keach. Minoff is also responsible for a long list of television specials, including the Guinness Book of World Records specials.

Contact: Marvin Minoff. He and Farrell do their own reading and will consider anything that is well-written.

FINE LINE FEATURES

116 North Robertson, Los Angeles, CA 90048
310-854-5811
Fax: 310-659-1453
Web site: www.flf.com

New York office:
888 7th Avenue, New York, NY 10106
212-649-4800
Fax: 212-956-1942

Mark Ordesky, President of the New Line Cinema

Steven Friedlander, Executive VP (L.A.)

Rachael Horovitz, Senior VP of Production & Acquisition (N.Y.)

Meredith Finn, Director of East Coast Acquisition & Production (N.Y.)

Arianna Bocco, VP of Acquisition & Production (L.A.)

Alexandra Rossi, Director of European Acquisitions (N.Y.)

Marshall Lewy, Creative Executive (L.A.)

Michael Macari, Creative Executive (L.A.)

Joe Revitte, Creative Executive (N.Y.)

Sharifa Johka, Story Editor (L.A.)

Meredith Finn, Story Editor (L.A.)

J. J. Lousberg, Story Editor (L.A.)

A division of New Line, Fine Line brings us daring features that often offend mainstream sensibilities like David Cronenberg's controversial *Crash*, but they also provide hilarious comedies like *State & Main* and wildly different films such as *Dancer in the Dark*. With so many movies on their distribution and development slate, you might think they wouldn't listen to a lone writer, but I saw one of their creative executives say, at the 2000 Hollywood Film Festival, that he would listen to any interesting query (Los Angeles office), without even so much as a release form. Of course, personnel change like the wind in Hollywood, so don't hold me to that if they tell you something different. To see what they have coming up, visit the Web site and click on the "Slate" button.

Contact: Any creative executive or story editor listed. If you hear "We don't accept unsolicited projects," don't say "But Skip Press said . . ." If you get that response, you're better off finding a company who works with them regularly, particularly a company headed by actors they like.

FLOWER FILMS

9220 W. Sunset Boulevard, Suite 309, Los Angeles, CA 90069
310-285-0200
Fax: 310-285-0827
E-mail: daisyfilm@aol.com
Web site: www.flowerfilms.com

Drew Barrymore, Partner

Nancy Juvonen, Partner

Linda McDonough, Director of Development

Okay, I admit it. I am in love with Drew Barrymore, but don't tell her because I'm married and too old for her and it would make Tom Green (her fiancé) sad if he knew. I think she's not only a doll but a very smart filmmaker who managed to make the *Charlie's Angels* remake into a profit machine when "everyone" thought it would tank. The company has a two-year, first-look production deal with Columbia Pictures. Things on the burner include the teenage romance *Donnie Darko* and *Entering Esphesus*, from a novel by Daphne Athas about how three sisters lives change when they move to a rural Southern town, as well as (my favorite, I think), a remake of the Jane Fonda starrer, *Barbarella*. And let's not forget, *So Love Returns*, an adaptation of a 1958 Robert Nathan novel "about a man whose world is shattered by the death of his wife, until a magical woman from the sea appears to help him and his children heal," which is apparently a serious, non-comic role. They're open to projects (mostly only potentially starring Drew) and I hope I get there before you do.

Contact: Linda McDonough, who is now also their new media whiz.

FOUNTAINBRIDGE FILMS

10202 W. Washington Boulevard, Crawford Building, Culver City, CA 90232
310-244-8080
Fax: 310-244-8484

Sean Connery, Actor/Producer

Rhonda Tollefson, President/Producer

Lynnette Ramirez, Creative Executive

Joyce Tollefson, Office Manager

Joanna Butan, Executive Assistant

On the Sony lot with a first-look deal and with a second-look deal at Intermedia, Fountainbridge has the world wired, but why not, with Sean Connery at the helm? Lest you think they're flooded with great projects, however, let me clue you in: Lynnette Ramirez was taking pitches at the PitchFest of the Hollywood Film Festival that I ran in 2000. In their pipeline is a remake of the classic *The Ghost and Mrs. Muir*, along with an untitled golf movie and a number of other films that might not necessarily star Connery, like one about my ancestor, Mary Queen of Scots. Although I still haven't seen *Finding Forrester,* Connery is just about my favorite actor (maybe I like Eastwood better) and the one I'd most like to play golf with (I can beat you, Scotsman!).

Contact: Lynnette Ramirez for current needs.

FURTHUR FILMS

100 Universal City Plaza Bldg. 507 #4E, Universal City, CA 91608
818-777-6700
Fax: 818-866-1278

New York office: 825 8th Avenue, 30th Floor, New York, NY 10019
212-333-1421
Fax: 212-333-8163

Michael Douglas, Actor/Producer

Lisa Bellomo, Senior VP of Production

Marcy Drogin, Senior VP of Production (N.Y.)

James LaVigne, Creative Executive

I wrote a book about Michael Douglas and his father, and I received an offer on one of my properties from Michael once (the producer who took it to him blew the deal for me, but that's a story for a former book). I didn't stand a chance once Douglas bought *Romancing the Stone*, and now it looks like he's back in a romantic comedy mood, with projects on the slate like *As Told To*, about a successful NBA coach who hires a ghostwriter to write a book and falls in love with her, and *Mr. Big in Littleville*, about a businessman who turns around the fortunes of a small town and finds love in the process. Several of the projects in development are set up with Allison Segan, rumored to become the head of his company at one point, who produced the forthcoming romcom *One Night at McCool's*, about how a one night stand wreaked havoc on a man's life. Sorry, I don't know why they spell it "Furthur."

Contact: James LaVigne for current needs and submission policies.

GEORGE STREET PICTURES

3815 Hughes Avenue, Suite 3, Culver City, CA 90232
310-841-4361
Fax: 310-204-6310

Bing Howenstein, President

Scott Nocas, VP

Chris O'Donnell, Principal

P. J. Byrne, Director of Development

Brenna Parks, Executive Assistant

When they were based at Warner Bros., their romantic comedy *The Bachelor* didn't burn up the box office, but I thought it was pretty clever of the writer to recycle a silent film into the screenplay. Renee Zellweger as the love interest about a man who must marry within 24 hours to become eligible for a $120 million inheritance? Made sense to me. The "Y2K" thriller pitch they bought from Stu Zicherman didn't stop the world, either, but this is a good company receptive to writers, and Chris O'Donnell is a fine actor. Coming up from them are a diverse slate of projects including: *The Rook*, about a doctor and a convict who coerces him into criminal activity, *The Triangle*, a movie of the week, and *Get Me to Frank by 35*, about a single mom torn between the father of her son and another man.

Contact: P. J. Byrne. (Note: There was a georgestreet.com registered at press time, but I'm not sure they own it.)

THE GOATSINGERS

179 Franklin Street, Sixth Floor, New York, NY 10013
212-966-3045
Fax: 212-966-4362

Peggy Gormley, Partner

Harvey Keitel, Partner

Dennis O'Sullivan, Executive Assistant

Harvey Keitel, God bless him, is always so interesting to watch onscreen. He's gotten me through the worst pieces of dreck like *The Piano* (so shoot me, I hated it). Plus he's always been fantastic about helping new writer/directors get started, like that guy Tarantino with *Reservoir Dogs* (which I loved). Now, with an exclusive first-look deal with German independent giant Kinowelt Medien, Goatsingers has the financing to develop and produce "art house fare" starring Keitel. An example cited by Kinowelt Co-CEO Rainer Koelmel when they announced the deal was the Sundance winner *Three Seasons* (1999), in which Keitel starred and Tony Bui directed. One of my readers, Peggy Bechko, reported that she highly enjoyed trying to sell Peggy Gormley a screenplay. Upcoming is an adaptation of William Shakespeare's *The Merchant of Venice*. I can't wait to see how Keitel handles the "pound of flesh."

Contact: Peggy Gormley and tell her what you have.

GONE FISHIN' PRODUCTIONS

3000 West Olympic Boulevard Building 2, Suite 1509, Santa Monica, CA 90405
310-315-4737
Fax: 310-315-4715

Casey Silver, Producer

Chris Salvaterra, Executive Vice President

Paul Brehme, Director of Development

Former Universal Pictures chairman and CEO Casey Silver set up Gone Fishin' in October 1999. The company has a first-look deal with Universal and plenty of funds for development. They spent six figures of that money in August 2000 when they bought Steven Christopher Young's pitch "Hell on Wheels," a broad comedy set in the world of demolition derby. Silver will produce. In November, they paid a similar price for the comedy spec script "Good and Dead," written by first-time screenwriter John Killoran, about a guy who fakes his own death to get away from his overbearing girlfriend. (Killoran is managed by Bondesen Management, listed in this book.) With other projects in the pipeline like *The Party Professional* (about a party animal at a university) and *Welcome to America (a.k.a. Village People)* you might think they only like young male wild comedies, except the latter is a drama with director Jim Sheridan and not about the disco group of the 70s at all. They have more than one project with Sheridan, as a matter of fact. It's a smart company you'd do well to work with.

Contact: Paul Brehme for current needs.

GOOD MACHINE

417 Canal Street, Fourth Floor, New York, NY 10013
212-343-9230 and 212-229-1046
Fax: 212-343-9645
E-mail: scheme of firstinitiallastame@goodmachine.com
  (e.g., dlinde@goodmachine.com) or info@goodmachine.com
Web site; www.goodmachine.com

Ted Hope, Co-Founder

James Schamus, Co-Founder

David Linde, Partner

Noreen Ward, Senior VP/Head of Operations

Anthony Bregman, Senior VP of Production

Ross Katz, Director of Production

Amy Kaufman, Senior VP Acquisitions & Co-Production

Anne Carey, VP of Development

Cielo Cerezo, Story Editor

There simply isn't a classier company in the business as their *Crouching Tiger, Hidden Dragon* showed us with Oscar nominations. In March 2001, they signed an exclusive multi-year, first-look production deal with Miramax Films. With impeccable taste, they've recently been behind films like *The Tao of Steve*, *The Brothers McMullen*, and the previous Ang Lee film, *The Ice Storm*. Upcoming films are *One Night at McCool's* with Michael Douglas and *Berlin Diaries*, a World War II love story from Ang Lee, starring Nicole Kidman as a Russian princess.

Contact: Anne Carey or **Cielo Cerezo**.

GRADE A ENTERTAINMENT

368 N. La Cienega Boulevard, Los Angeles, CA 90048
E-mail: GradeAProd@aol.com

Andy Cohen, President

Grade A Entertainment began in June 1996 as a production and development company for film and television. Company president Andy Cohen has held numerous executive positions at busy production companies, such as Norman Lear's Act III Productions and David Permut's Permut Presentations. Cohen was also Senior VP of Orr & Cruickshank Productions (*Three Men and a Baby, Father of the Bride*). He's been involved in the sale and/or production of over 25 projects. Cohen's recent credits include co-producer of Warner Brother's *It Takes Two*, associate producer of Touchstone Pictures' *Captain Ron*, and a movie for the Disney Channel. He is also very involved with the Maui Writers Conference. Since the first edition of this book, Cohen was able to sell a screenplay from a writer he first contacted via the Internet, and he takes query letters by e-mail *only*.

Contact: Andy Cohen, who says, "I'm a salesman to the studios and, as such, I am looking for good, commercial, castable fare. I sell a lot of comedies, romantic comedies, and family films, but I also like thrillers and action pieces. Right now, I read all letters and submissions. Send a query letter first describing the project and its characters. If I want to read the screenplay after that, I must have a signed release."

GREENESTREET PRODUCTIONS

9 Desbrosses Street 2nd Floor, New York, NY 10013
212-343-1049
Fax: 212-343-0774
E-mail: general@gstreet.com
Web site: www.gstreet.com

Fisher Stevens, Partner

John Penotti, Partner

Bradley Yonover, Partner

Debbie Johnson, General Manager

Andrew Marcus, Project Coordinator

Jamie Gordon, Director of Development

Courtney Potts, Development Executive

Matthew H. Rowland, Producer (L.A.)

Fisher Stevens was a founding member of the off-off-Broadway theater group Naked Angels. The company's *Illuminata* starring John Turturro and Susan Sarandon was about a playwright, and so was *Pinero*, starring Benjamin Bratt (Julia Roberts' boyfriend) as Latino writer Miguel Pinero. Their *In the Bedroom* was the winner of the Special Jury Prize at Sundance 2001. It was distributed by Miramax, with whom they have a deal. This company is all about theater background, independent film, New York liberal intelligentsia, actor-based productions. You can find a clear statement of their "manifesto" as a company on their Web site.

Contact: Development people above. The e-mail scheme is firstinitiallastname@ gstreet.com (example, djohnson@gstreet.com).

THE HENSON COMPANY

1416 N. LaBrea Avenue, Hollywood, CA 90028
323-802-1500
Fax: 323-802-1835 and 323-960-4096

Lisa Henson, President

Brian Henson, Producer

Juliet Blake, President of Television

Ruth Ann Caruso, VP of Television

Robert Valois, Director of Development

A lot has changed at the house that Jim Henson and Kermit the Frog built since the last edition. They still have offices in New York and London, but in February of 2000 the German company EM-TV acquired the Jim Henson Company and the Muppets for $680 million in stock and cash. That hasn't changed the focus of their fare, only vastly increased their development pool. They're still working on *Neverwhere*, based on Neil Gaiman's fantasy-adventure novel about a businessman who finds a mysterious world beneath the streets of London. They have other fantastical projects in the chute like *King of the Elves* about a group of elves fighting the Troll King who elect a normal American as their king, and *Time Dogs* about a robot dog and a human dog travelling through time to find their master. And of course they also have a number of things upcoming for television and . . . did you guess? Another Muppet movie.

Contact: Rob Valois for current needs.

HORSESHOE BAY PRODUCTIONS

500 S. Buena Vista Street Animation 1G, Burbank, CA 91521
818-560-3229
Fax: 818-848-6832

Gary Foster, Producer

Mark Steven Johnson, Writer/Producer/Director

Julia Dray, President

Eric Baiers, Director of Development 818-560-4635

Jim Braden, Creative Associate

Amberwren Briskey-Cohen, Creative Associate

Brian Olson, Creative Associate

Karen Peterkin, Creative Associate

Renee Foresman, Creative Associate

When former Lorimar founder Lee Rich started Eagle Point Productions with Gary Foster, they were the first producers to sign a first-look, non-exclusive deal with Mandalay Entertainment on the Sony Pictures lot. When Lorimar was riding high, chairman and CEO Lee Rich was one of the most influential people in Hollywood. Then

Lee Rich left for Paramount Network TV to develop TV series and telefilms. Now with a production deal with Walt Disney/Touchstone Pictures and hits as *Sleepless in Seattle* and *Tin Cup* behind them, Horseshoe Bay is a formidable force. Okay, so their Sidney Lumet remake of *Gloria* starring Sharon Stone wasn't a hit, but their upcoming remake of the old *Father Knows Best* TV show should do quite well, and so should their remake of the Jerry Lewis classic *The Bellboy*, this time starring Jackie Chan.

Contact: Eric Baiers or **Creative Associates** for current needs.

ICON ENTERTAINMENT

5555 Melrose Avenue, Wilder Building, 2nd Floor, Los Angeles, CA 90038
323-956-2100
Fax: 323-862-2121

Mel Gibson, Actor/Director/Producer

Bruce Davey, Chairman

Karen Glasser, President of Features

Kevin Lake, VP of Features

Jim Lemley, President of Television

Eveleen Bandy, VP of Television

Catherine Loerke, Director of Development

What can you say? It's Mel Gibson. *Mad Max, Lethal Weapon,* and the Academy-Award-winning *Braveheart*. He's *The Patriot*, he's *What Women Want*. He has two dozen kids or something. He makes TV movies about the Three Stooges just because he loves them. He says what he wants. In October 2000, he told the press, "I thought it was as boring as a dog's ass," in reference to Wim Wenders' *The Million Dollar Hotel*, in which Gibson stars and his company helped produce. It'll probably be a hit; it's got Gibson. What a guy—he spent three months putting together a video to distribute to school kids explaining his feature version of *Hamlet*. My friend Gary Finlan worked on the video, and told me that Gibson and Bruce Davey dropped everything at a crucial time to sit in the parking lot and read a hot script that was on the auction block. Got one?

Contact: Catherine Loerke. Submission through any agent or lawyer is okay.

IFC PRODUCTIONS

1111 Stewart Avenue, Bethpage, NY 11714
516-803-4511
Fax: 516-803-4506
Web site: www.ictv.com

Jonathan Sehring, President

Caroline Kaplan, VP of Production & Development

Alison Bourke, Production, Development & Film Acquisitions

This is *not* a production company where you can submit scripts. If, however, you intend to write screenplays and film them yourself, this is one of the first places you should look for help in financing and distribution. IFC Productions is a division of the Independent Film Channel and affiliated with the Bravo Channel. It provides financing for filmmakers and has critically acclaimed theatrical releases to its credit like John Sayles' *Men with Guns* and Kimberly Peirce's *Boys Don't Cry*, the movie in which Hilary Swank earned a best actress Oscar. Karyn Kusama's *Girlfight*, winner of the Grand Jury Prize for Best Feature and Best Director for Kusama at the Sundance Film Festival, owes its budget to IFC. Their InDigEnt (Independent Digital Entertainment) initiative, created by director Gary Winick (*The Tic Code*), John Sloss and IFC Productions, was launched in 2000 to allow great digital movies to be made cheaply, giving actors like Campbell Scott and Ethan Hawke a chance to direct their first films, and to allow the entire crew to equally share the profits. I absolutely love this operation.

Contact: Caroline Kaplan when you've studied the site and are ready to make a movie.

IGNITE ENTERTAINMENT

6762-B Lexington Avenue, Los Angeles, CA 90038
323-860-0565
Fax: 323-860-0575

Marc Butan, President

Scott Bernstein, Senior VP

Noah Rosen, Manager

John Sacchi, Director of Development

You might have seen some of the products of this management and production company. *But I'm a Cheerleader*, about teenagers sent to a rehabilitation camp to "cure" suspected homosexual tendencies was interesting, even though it didn't make much at the box office. *Desert Blue* with Christina Ricci and *The Suburbans* with Ben Stiller are other examples of the quirky comedies Ignite has produced. They represent writers like Brent Boyd, whose romantic comedy spec "Love Simple" is set up with Avenue Pictures, and John Heffernan, whose *Snakes on a Plane* should be interesting. Do you write wacky comedies? Got teen and young professional content in your script? This could be the place.

Contact: John Sacchi about current needs.

IMAGEMOVERS (ALSO DARK CASTLE ENTERTAINMENT)

100 Universal City Plaza, Bldg. 484, Universal City, CA 91608
818-733-8313
Fax: 818-733-8333
Web site: www.imagemovers.com

Robert Zemeckis, Writer/Producer/Director

Jack Rapke, Producer

Steve Starkey, Producer

Bennett Schneir, Creative Executive

Jennifer Perini, Head of Creative Affairs

Steven Cotliar, Story Editor & Assistant to Bennett Schneir

Andrew Goodman, Story Editor & Assistant to Jack Rapke

2000 was quite a year for this Oscar winner (for *Forrest Gump*). The man who brought us *Romancing the Stone*, *Who Framed Roger Rabbit?* and the *Back to the Future* films formed Dark Castle Entertainment with mega-producer Joel Silver and picked up Mark Hanlon's spec script "Chimera," a mystery at sea, as their first project. With Dark Castle at Warners and Imagemovers at Universal, the latter with a first-look deal at DreamWorks, Zemeckis and company are busy. Zemeckis also got the American Cinema Editors (ACE) Golden Eddie Filmmaker of the Year Award. And in March 2001, the Robert Zemeckis Center for Digital Arts was opened at his alma mater, USC. The 35,000-square-foot facility was billed as the first fully digital facility at any U.S. film school. In development? A ton of stuff, but they're always looking.

Contact: Story Editors. You may have to dial the main number and listen to a directory of names to get the proper number.

JERSEY FILMS

10351 Santa Monica Boulevard, Suite 200, Los Angeles, CA 90025
310-203-1000
Fax: 310-203-1010
Web site: www.jerseyfilms.com

Danny DeVito, Co-Chairman/Actor/Director/Producer

Michael Shamberg, Co-Chairman

Stacey Sher, President/Partner

Adrienne Biddle, Creative Executive

Sindy Lin, Story Editor

When Danny DeVito was just starting out as a director, back when he was a star of Jim Brooks' great sitcom *Taxi* and lived down the hill from actor Raymond Burr, a mutual friend of ours (producer James Nelson) gave DeVito a script of mine called *Street Song*. At the time, I was trying to get the funds to make the movie with actress Sandahl Bergman. DeVito liked the script, but said he didn't have time to work with me to fix it. He sure doesn't have time now! Jersey is a very active company and comes up with great projects on a regular basis like *Erin Brockovich* and *The Caveman's Valentine*. Jersey Television has also taken off, with its first sale in late 2000. They have almost 50 things in development, including *Honey West* (from the old TV series starring Anne Francis) and *Bandstand (a.k.a. American Bandstand)*. Hey, maybe DeVito's waxing nostalgic? I'd still love to work with him.

Contact: Sindy Lin for current needs and submission procedures. The e-mail scheme is firstname.lastname@jerseyfilms.com.

KAREEM PRODUCTIONS

5458 Wilshire Boulevard, Los Angeles, CA 90036
310-201-7960
E-mail: hbroda@aol.com

Kareem Abdul-Jabbar, President

Freddy Jellin, Producer

Lorin Pullman, Vice President

Hanna Brada, Creative Executive

When the first edition was being written, the Laker Hall of Famer wasn't interested in receiving scripts and wouldn't take anything unsolicited. With the second edition, he'd lost the two executives he had with him, but said he would look at properties. Being a big fan, I was just thrilled to have him in the book. Now he has new people, with no announced projects, but don't be surprised if you saw a film about *A Season on the Reservation: My Sojourn with the White Mountain Apache*, a book by Kareem about his amazing true story of coaching some high school Native Americans for a year. The great one is still at the head of the class.

Contact: Query **Hanna Brada** for current needs.

KENNEDY-MARSHALL COMPANY

1351 Fourth Street, Fourth Floor, Santa Monica, CA 90404
310-656-8400
Fax: 310-656-8430

Kathleen Kennedy, Producer

Frank Marshall, Producer/Director

Zanne Devine, President/Producer

Mark Ross, VP of Development

Nancy Covello, Story Editor

John Tantillo, Development Assistant

These are the producers whom Steven Spielberg relied on for years at Amblin. They've continued with some productions for kids of all ages like *The Indian in the Cupboard* (the latter script written by *E.T.* screenwriter Melissa Mathiesen, whose husband used to be Harrison Ford), which my kids loved, and Frank Marshall produced the mega-hit *The Sixth Sense.* They've always been receptive to and ready to cultivate promising new talent, and helped start the Chesterfield screenwriting competition. Projects in the pipeline include the Warner Bros.' action drama *Expendables* with Marshall directing, about a group of maximum-security prison inmates who perform high-risk deep-sea dives, and a film based on "Over the Edge," an article about some people taken prisoner by Muslim fundamentalists.

Contact: Nancy Covello for submission policy and current needs.

KILLER FILMS

380 Lafayette Street #302, New York, NY 10003
212-473-3950
Fax: 212-473-6152
E-mail: killer@killerfilms.com
Web site: www.killerfilms.com

Christine Vachon, Producer

Laird Adamson, Executive

Pamela Koffler, Producer

Daniel Wagner, Production Coordinator

Brad Simpson, Head of Development

Jocelyn Hayes, Story Editor

This very busy company has over two dozen projects in development and knowing them, most of the movies will get made. They're an in-your-face New York–based indie production company with a first-look TV deal with HBO. They're responsible for films like *Boys Don't Cry* and *I Shot Andy Warhol*. They're all over the board with what they like, from dark comedies to psychological horror-thrillers, and even a 1940 love affair between filmmaker Orson Welles and the great singer Billie Holiday. The office is in a loft on Lafayette Street in Greenwich Village—if that doesn't explain them to you, I can't help you. Look for Robin Williams in their urban psychological thriller *One Hour Photo*, done with Fox Searchlight, and the controversial *Hedwig and the Angry Inch*. If you have something "wack" that actors would love, set in an urban environment, this is probably the place for you.

Contact: Jocelyn Hayes, and you're on your own.

KOPELSON ENTERTAINMENT

2121 Avenue of the Stars, Suite 1400, Los Angeles, CA 90067
310-369-7500
Fax: 310-369-7501

Arnold Kopelson, Chairman/CEO

Anne Kopelson, Co-Chairperson

Matthew Gross, Executive VP

Nana Greenwald, President of Creative Affairs

Mark Stein, Creative Executive

Lara Wood, Story Coordinator

Matt Sullivan, Story Editor, e-mail matthews@fox.com

With almost 50 projects in development and a discretionary deal with Fox soon to end, Kopelson Entertainment may be at Paramount by the time you read this. They're bringing financing with them from the Munich-based Intertainment AG, which will allow the Kopelsons to produce a minimum of 10 films over five years with an average budget of $50 million. (They didn't get a single green light when at Fox.) The Kopelsons were hitmakers with *The Fugitive* with Harrison Ford, as they were with *Seven* with Morgan Freeman and Brad Pitt, *Falling Down* with Michael Douglas, and the Academy Award-winning *Platoon*. Arnold Kopelson received the Motion Picture Showmanship Award from Publicists Guild of America for his "extraordinary showmanship, which helped his films reach a combined gross of $1.25 billion." Expect that figure to rise dramatically in the next year or so.

Contact: Matt Sullivan for current needs and submission policy.

ROBERT KOSBERG PRODUCTIONS

c/o Merv Griffin Entertainment, 9860 Wilshire Boulevard, Beverly Hills, CA 90210
310-385-3165
Fax: 310-385-3162
Web site: www.moviepitch.com

Robert Kosberg, Producer

Kira Mason, VP of Development

Here's the deal. Robert Kosberg doesn't write. He doesn't do e-mail. I'm not sure he even physically produces movies. He pitches. He sells things. He helps get properties on the screen. He has a CD that he sells via his Web site that explains the process, but he also posts what he's looking for there. He will absolutely not get back to you unless he thinks you have something he can sell. There is really no one else in Hollywood who operates the way he does. He was behind *12 Monkeys* and has things in the pipeline like an update of *The Hardy Boys*, which he's doing in conjunction with Ben Stiller's Red Hour Films.

Contact: Robert Kosberg however you choose.

THE LADD COMPANY

9465 Wilshire Boulevard, Suite 910, Beverly Hills, CA 90210
310-777-2060
Fax: 310-777-2061

Alan Ladd Jr., President

Kelliann Ladd, Producer

Elisabeth M. Robinson, Producer

Natalia Chydzik, Creative Executive

Peter Bisanz, Creative Executive

Great entertainment of all kinds is what this company is about. *Chariots of Fire* and *The Brady Bunch* are very different from *Blade Runner*, and so are the *Police Academy* movies. What do you do when you grow up watching your Dad be a big movie star? Alan Ladd Jr. has run production companies and studios and is spoken of fondly around town as "Laddie." Kelliann Ladd has a smart eye for movies and often appears on panels to talk to writers (in fact, I've been on one with her). They have almost 20 projects in the pipeline including *The Flower Net*, from a book about an American detective who falls in love with a Chinese government detective; it takes place in both California and China. Good news for writers is that it was bought on the basis of only 40 pages and an outline.

Contact: Either **Creative Executive** for current needs and submission policy.

LANGLEY PRODUCTIONS

2225 Colorado Avenue, Santa Monica, CA 90404
310-449-5300
Fax: 310-449-5330

John Langley, President, Producer/Writer/Director

Douglas Waterman, Supervising Producer

Elie Cohn, Producer, Features

Murray Jordan, Producer, TV

Anthony Carr, President of New Media

Karen Hori, VP of TV

If you call and they put you on hold, you'll hear "Bad boys, bad boys, whatcha gonna do?" That's because John Langley created Fox's long-running reality series *Cops*. He formed Langley Productions in 1995 to create, acquire, and produce TV series and features. The film unit is headed by Elie Cohn, who produced Martin Scorcese's *Search and Destroy* and worked on *Raging Bull, Colors,* and *Rocky.* If you have a script you want them to see, contact Elie Cohn. If TV's your aim. . . .

Contact: Karen Hori and tell her what you have.

LANSDOWN FILMS

2425 Olympic Boulevard, Suite 4060W, Santa Monica, CA 90404
310-247-7343
Fax: 310-247-7325

Jonathan Lynn, Director

Lia Bassin, Director of Development

Ilana Gutman, Assistant

Jonathan Lynn makes features films—funny feature films like *My Cousin Vinny,* the movie that made Marisa Tomei a star and got her an Academy Award. If you thought *The Distinguished Gentleman* was a pretty good film, or *Sgt. Bilko* with Steve Martin, then you share Lynn's comic sensibilities. You might have even liked *The Whole Nine Yards.* A TV version of *My Cousin Vinny* will be coming to us soon, courtesy of Jersey Films and CBS, and in the feature pipeline is the comic *Guam Goes to the Moon* and *Baker Street,* based on a true story of a London bank heist in the 1970s. Lynn is managed by Judy Hofflund of Hofflund-Polone.

Contact: Query **Lia Bassin** for current needs.

LANDSCAPE ENTERTAINMENT

12400 Wilshire Boulevard, Suite 1200, Los Angeles, CA 90025
310-447-7500
Fax: 310-447-7501

Robert Cooper, Partner

Michael Birnbaum, Partner

David R. Ginsburg, President/CEO

Nick LaTerza, Executive VP

Marc Rosen, Sr. VP

Barbara Bloom, VP of Television

Judy Ranan, Head of TV

Jeff Wachtel, Head of Internet Division

Steve Rubenstein, Director of Development

Peter Sullivan, Story Editor

Canadian TV producer CTV joined forces with Robert Cooper (former DreamWorks production chief and before that, president of TriStar Pictures) to form Landscape. Cooper helped bring the Oscar-winning *American Beauty* to DreamWorks. Set up primarily for TV, the company has a first-look deal with NBC to develop a minimum of three miniseries. With over $30 million in Canadian money backing the venture, Cooper quickly brought in former Alliance Atlantis Communications Motion Picture Group president David R. Ginsburg, who was formerly Cooper's partner at Citadel Entertainment, where they produced more than 50 films, including *Gia*. Citadel became a division of Alliance Atlantis in 1997. Marc Rosen joined the company from Lynda Obst Productions.

In the pipeline is a movie based on Nicholas Christopher's novel *Veronica*, also a *Matrix*-type love story, and a time-travel romantic comedy based on two novellas by sci-fi author Harry Turtledove. The company's first Internet project, "C-Scam," was written by Larry "M.A.S.H." Gelbart. The movie division is adapting four of Gregory McDonald's "Flynn" mystery novels, and the TV division has a movie about church bombings in the American South. In short, the company is cutting-edge, covers a lot of bases, and knows the media "landscape" as well as anyone.

Contact: Steve Rubenstein or **Peter Sullivan.**

LICHT-MUELLER PRODUCTIONS

132-A S. Lasky Drive, Suite 200, Beverly Hills, CA 90210
310-205-5500
Fax: 310-205-5590
Web site: www.licht-mueller.com

Andrew Licht, Producer

Jeffrey Mueller, Producer

Doug Hammond, Development

Here's the info from their Web site (edited slightly by me): "Licht/Mueller Film Corporation producers Andrew Licht and Jeffrey A. Mueller have produced six motion pictures (two of which debuted number one at the U.S. box office) grossing a total of over $500 million in world-wide box office, all with the unusual distinction of being written by first-time, unproduced screenwriters who include: Darren Star (*Sex in the City*), Ted Elliot, Terry Rossio (*Aladdin*), and Neil Tolkin (*Richie Rich*). Licht and Mueller have an instinct for discovering young talented writers and directors and an ability to sculpt and focus their talents, developing successful motion pictures with potent concepts, solid stories, and high entertainment values." Those movies include *Waterworld, Little Monsters,* and *The Cable Guy.* Read an interview with Licht at www.inzide.com /index.cfm?id=17 .

Contact: See the requirements on the Web site, then get in touch with **Doug Hammond** at doug@licht-mueller.com or lichtmueller@hotmail.com.

LION ROCK PRODUCTIONS

2450 Broadway Street, Suite E-590, Santa Monica, CA 90404
310-449-3205
Fax: 310-449-3512

John Woo, Director/Producer

Terence Chang, Producer

Caroline Macaulay, Senior VP

Suzanne Zizzi, VP of Television

Annie Hughes, Creative Executive

Lori Tilkin, Creative Executive, New Media

Todd Weinger, Development Associate

Laurance Walsh, Executive Assistant

John Woo. Need I say more? Three-year, first-look film and television deal with MGM. He brought his Hong Kong cinema legend to Hollywood and revolutionized action movies with *Hard Target, Broken Arrow, Face-Off,* and *Mission: Impossible 2.* The name of the company comes from a Hong Kong mountain peak, which is where Woo and Chang are from. They will take faxed queries, and any writer wanting information is welcome to call. Scripts don't have to be the kind Woo would direct. For example, *Windtalkers* is one they have coming out, about Navajo code talkers during World War

II. But they also have some of the same good stuff, like *Bulletproof Monk*, with Chow Yun-fat of *Crouching Tiger, Hidden Dragon*.

Contact: Creative and **development** people mentioned. E-mail scheme is firstinitial lastname@mgm.com (ex: ltilkin@mgm.com).

LIONS GATE FILMS

4553 Glencoe Avenue, Suite 200, Marina Del Rey, CA 90292
310-314-2000
Fax: 310-392-0252
Television Office: 323-692-7300

New York Office:
561 Broadway Suite 12B, New York, NY 10012
212-966-4670
Fax: 212-966-2544
Web site: www.lionsgatefilms.com

Jon Feltheimer, CEO

Joe Drake, President of International

Joanna Brinen, Director of Television

Karoline Kuelzer, Head of TV Movies & Minis Development

Kate Pretrosky, Director of Development (L.A.)

Sarah Lash, Director of Acquisitions & Development (N.Y.)

Don't let the small amount of people listed above fool you. Those are just the names you need to know; Lions Gate Entertainment is massive. Recently, they've been moving the company more and more to Los Angeles, which began when Jon Feltheimer became their West Coast–based CEO and they acquired Santa Monica–based Trimark Holdings. Lions Gate's headquarters may remain in Vancouver, but they're more and more a Hollywood company. They have a $200 million revolving credit fund from Chase Manhattan and tons more money from other international sources. Their projects are too numerous to mention; see the Web site. They're open to hearing from you. When I was looking for financing for a script of mine, I got an immediate, friendly e-mail response from Sarah Lash.

Contact: Development people listed. E-mail scheme is firstinitiallastname@ lgecorp.com (ex.: slash@lgecorp.com).

SI LITVINOFF PRODUCTIONS

2825 Woodstock Road, Los Angeles, CA 90046
323-848-6907
Fax: 323-848-6908

Si Litvinoff, Producer

Paul Madden, Creative Affairs

Si Litvinoff has been a producer, coproducer, and/or executive producer on some daring films. Stanley Kubrick's *Clockwork Orange,* Nicholas Roeg's *The Man Who Fell to Earth* (mostly cast from Litvinoff's personal phone book), Roeg's *Walkabout,* and Francis Simon's *The Queen* come to mind immediately. He has also been heavily involved in music, producing "The Glastonbury Faire" (the Woodstock of England) and Broadway, off-Broadway, and London musicals. A former lawyer, Litvinoff entered motion picture production in 1967. Along the way, he has also represented over 100 theatrical productions and dozens of top artists. The classic *Writers in Revolt* anthology is dedicated to Litvinoff. His clients have included the famous and infamous: Andy Warhol, Terry Southern, Timothy Leary, Quincy Jones, Lou Reed, and the Billie Holliday Foundation, among many others.

Contact: Paul Madden. Si Litvinoff is always looking for "originality, real intelligence, underlying social significance, real emotion."

LIVEPLANET

1201 W. 5th Street, L.A. Center Studios, Los Angeles, CA 90017
213-534-3100
Fax: 213-534-3101
E-mail: info@liveplanet.com
Web site: www.liveplanet.com

Ben Affleck, Actor/Writer/Producer

Matt Damon, Actor/Writer/Producer

Chris Moore, Producer

Jeff Balis, Producer

Kent Kubena, VP of Development

Derek Milosavljevic, Creative Executive

This company was formed by a merger of Chris Moore's Supermega Productions and Matt Damon and Ben Affleck's Pearl Street Productions. They have a first-look production deal with Miramax, but that doesn't always mean a green light even for actors like these—Miramax decided they had too many World War II projects, so one with Matt and Ben, based on a true story, got dumped. They're an ambitious company with big plans for what they call "integrated media," new entertainment experiences that break down the barriers. Their Project Greenlight, a screenwriting contest that resulted in a million bucks for the winner to make his film, was a big success along this line. The winner was Pete Jones' *Stolen Summer*, about an 8-year-old Irish Catholic boy struggling to get his cancer-stricken 7-year-old Jewish friend into Heaven.

Contact: Kent Kubena, who is a great guy, very bright and eager to find top-notch writers.

LOGO ENTERTAINMENT

1888 Century Park East Suite 1900, Los Angeles, CA 90067
310-276-6700
E-mail: logoent@earthlink.net

Louis Gossett Jr., Executive Producer/Actor

Dennis Considine, Executive Producer

Laurie Ferneau, Executive Asstistant & Development

Logo Entertainment was created in 1990 as an independent production company to showcase the talents of Louis Gossett Jr. Gossett is best known for his Oscar-winning performance as Sergeant Foley in *An Officer and a Gentleman,* and his Emmy-winning role as Fiddler in the historic TV miniseries *Roots*. The company produced *Run for the Dream: The Gail Devers Story,* a Showtime original film, and with Kushner-Locke they coproduced the TV movies *Carolina Skeleton* and *Father & Son* (both for NBC). Their Showtime film, *Inside,* dealt with the treatment of political prisoners in South Africa during apartheid. This type of social concern reflects the kind of project Gossett likes. Their TV movie *The Color of Love: Jacey's Story* received high acclaim in 2000.

Contact: Laurie Ferneau for current needs.

LONGFELLOW PICTURES

145 Hudson Street, 9th Floor, New York, NY 10013
212-431-5550
Fax: 212-431-5822
E-mail: longfellow@mindspring.com

Sidney Kimmel, Chairman

Andrew Karsch, Producer/President

Jane Garnett, Director of Development

Carolina Herrera, Story Editor

Amy Wood, Story Editor

Longfellow Pictures was founded in 1988 by Andrew S. Karsch and William R. Hearst III. Since then, Karsch has produced films like *The Prince of Tides* and *Princess Caraboo* and Warren Beatty's *Town and Country*. Longfellow Pictures' chairman Sidney Kimmel is a New York–based industrialist. The company's *Famous*, starring Mira Sorvino, was done in conjunction with GreeneStreet Films. *The Perfect You* was also a coproduction.

Contact: Story editor or **development people** with a query letter. They prefer a synopsis (half a page to a page in length). If they like it, they will request the script. They generally like "mind-provoking films in any number of genres."

MAD CHANCE PRODUCTIONS

4000 Warner Boulevard, Bungalow 3, Burbank, CA 91522
818-954-3803
Fax: 818-954-3447
General e-mail: madchance@sprintmail.com

Andrew Lazar, Producer

Jody Hedien, Producer

Far Shariat, Director of Creative Affairs

Doug Davison, Director of Development

Sean Wicks, Creative Assistant

With credits like *Space Cowboys* and the upcoming *Panic* about the last two years of Robert F. Kennedy's life, Mad Chance has a very exciting short history and future. They're even into animation, like the live-action/animated comedy feature *Cats and Dogs*. Personally, I'm looking forward to their feature version of *Get Smart*. They buy wild spec scripts like *Smoking Is Good for You*—when a tobacco farmer buries his son under a crop, his cigarettes actually cure cancer. My kind of company!

Contact: Anyone but the producers. The general e-mail scheme is firstname.lastname@warnerbros.com (for example, andrew.lazar@warnerbros.com).

MALPASO PRODUCTIONS

4000 Warner Boulevard, Building 81, Burbank, CA 91522-0001
818-954-2567
Fax: 818-954-4803

Clint Eastwood, Producer, Actor, Director

Melissa Rooker, Director of Development

In 1998, my favorite actor got the Producers Guild of America's David O. Selznick Lifetime Achievement Award in theatrical motion pictures. In 2001, he received the Akira Kurosawa Award for lifetime achievement in film directing at the San Francisco International Film Festival. I've generally loved every one of his movies, including the Academy-Award-winning *Unforgiven* and even *The Bridges of Madison County.* Eastwood loves books about like he loves jazz; in March 2001 he picked up Dennis Lehane's bestselling novel *Mystic River* to produce and direct. And don't forget, his *True Crime* was based on a book as well.

Contact: Melissa Rooker. It's very likely you'll need a top agent to deliver that script for you, but if you have a book. . . .

MANDALAY ENTERTAINMENT

5555 Melrose Avenue, Lewis Building, Los Angeles, CA 90038
323-956-2400
Fax: 323-862-2266

Peter Guber, Chairman

Paul Schaeffer, Vice Chairman

Ori Marmur, Executive VP of Production

Scott Sanders, President of Series Television

Don't let the small number of people listed fool you. When Peter Guber and Lions Gate Entertainment (a big investor) announced they would move the company from Sony in a five-year deal with Paramount and produce 20 pictures in the deal. That got changed to three pictures per year, and now with the input of German money, their slate has been expanded to nine pictures a year. Their *Deep End of the Ocean* didn't do so well, but *The Score*, about an older cat burglar (with Marlon Brando, Robert DeNiro, Edward Norton, and Angela Bassett) sure sounds good. Don't assume that just because they're huge you won't be heard. Reader Ethan Campbell told me in July 1999 that with the assistance of my book, he queried 68 different production companies and directors and was rejected by all but Mandalay. Ryan Johnson, Ori Marmur's assistant, sent him a release form and he submitted his script. They didn't buy it, but they replied that his script "has good heart and is a good story."

MANIFEST FILM COMPANY

1247 Euclid Street, Santa Monica, CA 90404
310-899-5554
Fax: 310-899-5553
E-mail: manifilm@aol.com

Lisa Henson, Producer

Janet Yang, Producer

Naomi Despres, VP

Kevin Kelly, Assistant to Lisa Henson

Josh Cowing, Assistant to Janet Yang

The company's *Zero Effect* with Bill Pullman and Ben Stiller was funny but not groundbreaking, but *People vs. Larry Flynt* stirred some people up. They have things in the pipeline like *Wither*, about three-century old Salem witches. They seem to like female-centered projects—they were behind *The Joy Luck Club*—and another one they're planning is *Other Powers*, the story of feminist pioneer Victoria Woodhull, the first woman Wall Street broker and the first woman to run for President. *High Crimes* reunites Morgan Freeman and Ashley Judd in a story about a female attorney forced to defend a husband accused of committing military crimes under a different identity. And perhaps not least, they're executive producing "Alice," a contemporary pop music version of Lewis Carroll's *Alice's Adventures in Wonderland*, which MTV Films will produce. The project may star Britney Spears.

Contact: Assistants with description of your project.

MATERIAL

4000 Warner Boulevard, Bldg. 139, Room 27, Burbank, CA 91522
818-954-1551
Fax: 818-954-5299
E-mail: material@gte.net

Jorge Saralegui, Producer

Channing Dungey, Executive VP

Percy Zuletta, VP of Development

Alexa Platt, Exec. Assistant

In January 1998, former executive VP of production for 20th Century Fox Jorge Saralegui began a first-look producer deal at Warner Bros. The move was a surprise because Saralegui had been expected to remain at Fox. Films in the pipeline include Anne Rice's *Queen of the Damned* (directed by my friend Michael Rymer) and they have other high profile features coming up like *Showtime,* about a hard-nosed cop forced to team up with a flamboyant rookie who is the star of a reality-based TV show designed to help improve the image of the police department. If that sounds funny, consider the cast: Robert DeNiro, Eddie Murphy, Rene Russo. It's been a while coming, but it's looking like Hitsville at Material.

Contact: Percy Zuletta for current needs.

THE MATTHAU COMPANY

11661 San Vicente Boulevard #609, Los Angeles, CA 90049
310-454-3300

Charles Matthau, President

Michael McDavitt, President of Management Division

Lana Morgan, Director of Creative Affairs

One of the world's greatest actors had a son, who became a very good director. Walter Matthau isn't with us any more, but Charlie is, and that's Hollywood's gain. With movies to his credit like *Grumpier Old Men, Dennis the Menace,* and *Doin' Time on Planet Earth* (which I liked I lot), someone with a funny script would do very well working with this talented director and his company. They're also into management, which could be good for the right writer. They have a few things in development but nothing very high profile, suggesting that they might be looking for a breakthrough property.

Contact: Lana Morgan for current needs.

MBST ENTERTAINMENT
(MORRA/BREZNER/STEINBERG & TENENBAUM)

345 N. Maple Drive, Suite 200, Beverly Hills, CA 90210
310-385-1820
Fax: 310-385-1834

Buddy Morra, Partner

Larry Brezner, Partner

David Steinberg, Partner

Stephen Tenenbaum, Partner

Andrew Tenenbaum, Partner

Mike Marcus, Manager

Jennifer Todhunter, Director of Development

A management and production company with a first-look production deal with Walt Disney/Touchstone Pictures, these guys know funny. The talent they handle have done all right: Billy Crystal, Sid & Marty Kroft, Robin Williams, for example. Films coming out include *Freddy Got Fingered* with Tom Green, about a guy who has to move back in with his parents, but it's not all funny business there. *Cellular* is a thriller about man who gets a distressing call from a woman who has been kidnapped but has no idea where she is; he has to save her life before the battery dies.

Contact: Jennifer Todhunter. When she asks how you found out about them, say "Skip Press, who used to take a playwriting workshop with Buddy's wife Carol, says you're the best!" E-mail scheme is usually firstname@mbst.com (example, Jasmin@mbst.com).

TERENCE MICHAEL PRODUCTIONS, INC.

505 S. Beverly Drive, Suite 131, Beverly Hills, CA 90212
310-201-0700
Fax: 310-201-9854
E-mail: linktm@earthlink.net
Web site: www.terencemichael.com

Terence Michael, Producer-Chairman

John W. Gates, Exec. Vice President

Scott Schultz, VP Creative Affairs

Terence Michael Productions was formed in 1991 to produce independent films. "We rarely work alone," says Terence Michael, "almost always teaming up with other producers. They have formed a partnership with Martin Wiley (producer of *Under Siege II* and *Never Talk to Strangers*) for action films. Their past films have been in the $500,000 to $5 million range and have all been comedies. Wiley's company wants to do more comedies, Michael more action films, thus the collaboration. Michael prides himself on always working with the original writer(s) and often first-time directors. In the pipeline are several comedies, such as *Die Wholesale*, a broad comedy about a Price Club which gets taken hostage on Christmas Eve. Also, *Peroxide Passion* and *It's A Miserable Life*, both quirky comedies in the $1 to 2 million range. He has *Chill Factor* at Warner Brothers, a big *Speed*-like action piece which Morgan Creek is taking over.

Contact: Terence Michael. Pitch first, via query letter or e-mail. He's looking for high concept comedy, thriller, and action with a male lead. He reads everything personally.

MONTAGE ENTERTAINMENT

2118 Wilshire Boulevard #297, Santa Monica, CA 90403-5784
310-966-0222
Fax: 310-966-0223
E-mail: montage.ent@usa.net

David Peters, Producer

Bill Ewart, Producer

James Mercurio, Director of Development

If you like movies like *Mi Vida Loca* and *Gas, Food, Lodging*, this is the place for you. Sharp independent fare with heart, some humor and an edge is what this company is about. Their director of development, Jim Mercurio, is mentioned in the gurus section, so if you want to know what they have coming up and what they're looking for, ask him.

Contact: James Mercurio as listed above or at ssjohny@aol.com.

THE MONTECITO PICTURE COMPANY

1482 East Valley Road, Suite 477, Montecito, CA 93108
805-565-8590
Fax: 805-565-1893

L.A. office:
9465 Wilshire Boulevard, Suite #920, Beverly Hills, CA 90212
310-247-9880
Fax: 310-247-9498

Tom Pollock, Partner

Ivan Reitman, Partner

Joe Medjuck, Producer

Michael Chinich, Development/Casting/Production Executive

Jacqueline Marcus, Director of Development

Felicity Cockram, Assistant to Tom Pollock

Juliet Ward, Assistant to Ivan Reitman

The company in beautiful Santa Barbara has a multi-year, first look production, cofinancing, and distribution deal with Dreamworks. Their *Road Trip* was a surprise hit, and *Evolution* (with Reitman directing) looks to be one as well. Ivan Reitman's films tell you what they like. Upcoming is *My Canadian Girlfriend*, in which a geek becomes very popular at his high school when he claims to have the most beautiful Canadian girlfriend in the world. I spoke to Tom Pollock once when he was running Universal and I was writing for the *Hollywood Reporter* monthly magazine. I said, "Tom . . ." and he interrupted me. "Do I know you?" "Well, no, why?" "Because you called me Tom like you knew me." Pause. "Okay. Um, Mr. Pollock . . ." But they're open to new writers; I know someone who just called him and went in and pitched to Pollock.

Contact: Jackie Marcus or **Michael Chinich.**

MORGAN CREEK PRODUCTIONS

4000 Warner Boulevard, Bldg. 76, Burbank, CA 91522
818-954-4800
Fax: 818-954-4811
Web site: www.morgancreek.com

James G. Robinson, Chairman/CEO

Jonathan Zimbert, President

Joseph Martino, Senior VP of Development

Hilary Galanoy, VP of Development

As a foreign distributor of a great number of popular films, Morgan Creek really knows the international market. They have a domestic distribution deal with Warner Bros. and another deal with Franchise Pictures, and a $200 million revolving line of credit from Chase Manhattan Bank. All of which means they have plenty of money to make upcoming films like *Flying Tigers* (about the famed flyers in the Pacific theater in World War II). With the *Ace Ventura* movies in their background and what could be a surprise hit with a movie about the outlaw Jesse James, this is one of the busiest companies in town, so don't be surprised if you have to jump through some agent hoops to get their attention. They usually like big action "tent pole" summer release movies; when they do "small" movies like *The In Crowd* they don't do as well.

Contact: Hilary Galanoy. The company e-mail scheme is firstinitialoffirstnamelastname@morgancreek.com (Example, Hgalanoy@morgancreek.com).

MOSAIC MEDIA GROUP (WAS ATLAS ENTERTAINMENT)

9169 Sunset Boulevard, Los Angeles, CA 90069
310-724-7350

Allen Shapiro, President

Charles "Chuck" Roven, Producer

Scott Welch, Head of Production

Douglas Segal, Senior VP of Production

Richard Suckle, VP of Production

Atlas was the former company of Dawn Steel, the first woman to run a major studio. Todd Smith left ICM after 20 years to create a management roster of film and television artists for Atlas, which includes working with longtime client Jimmy Smits to jointly develop and produce. The new company was formed when Atlas merged with Gold/Miller and its music arm, Third Rail, to create a new management and film/TV production entity. They have a four-year, first-look, 10 to 12 title coproduction deal with MGM/UA. Behind movies like *City of Angels, Fallen, 12 Monkeys,* and *Three*

Kings, the films they have in the pipeline include the remake of *Rollerball* and the *Scooby Doo* live action feature. Think big star, big feature movies with some thought behind them, and you have it.

Contact: Gloria Fan for current needs.

MR. MUDD PRODUCTIONS

5225 Wilshire Boulevard Suite 604, Los Angeles, CA 90036
323-932-5656
Fax: 323-932-5666

John Malkovich, Producer/Director/Actor

Lianne Halfon, Producer

Russ Smith, Producer

Aileen Argentini, VP of Production

Shannon Clark, Creative Associate

John Malkovich has an international appeal, as evidenced by his company's first-look production deal with and discretionary development funds from Granada Film. What do they like? Basically, properties which delve into turmoil of the human spirit (kind of like roles Malkovich plays so well). They are *not* only looking for things for him, however. Projects in the pipeline include *Ghost World* (in conjunction with Jersey Films) about a loser who hasn't had a date since high school, and *Lost*, a mob story centering on the relationship between a mother and a child, based on a novel by Lucy Wadham. Now there's another aspect to the company—John Malkovich's directorial debut, *The Dancer Upstairs*, was a Spanish production by LolaFilms, and starred heartthrob Javier Bardem. They have a full development slate and develop almost everything in-house.

Contact: Shannon Clark via a short fax describing your project; if she sees something they're interested in, she'll let you know.

MTV FILMS

5555 Melrose Avenue, Modular Bldg. #213, Los Angeles, CA 90038
323-956-8023, 323-862-1386
Web site: www.mtv.com

Van Toffler, President of MTV Productions

David Gale, Senior VP of Production

Momita Seugupta, Director of Production

Maggie Malina, VP of Original Movies for Television

Susan Lewis, Director of Development, 323-956-4291

Gregg Goldin, Story Editor

Lisa Smith, Story Editor (N.Y.), 212-846-4071

Chris Grimley, Development Assistant

Under the Viacom umbrella like the Paramount Studios where they're housed, MTV Films brought out *Beavis and Butthead Do America*, Spike Lee's *The Original Kings of Comedy* documentary, and features like *Kevin and Perry Go Large* and the hilarious *Election*. In the pipeline are equally pop culture strong projects like *Nevermind: The Kurt Cobain Story* and *Fothermuckers* (cute title, yuk, yuk) about a 21-year-old wanting to stop him mom from having an affair. With over two dozen projects in development, no doubt the pollution will continue unabated for some time to come.

Contact: Development or **story people** above, dude.

MUTANT ENEMY, INC.
P.O. Box 900, Beverly Hills, CA 90213-0900
310-579-5180
Fax: 310-579-5380

Joss Whedon, CEO

Tom Plotkin, Creative Executive, 310-579-5181

George Snyder, Director of Development, 310-579-5182

Diego Gutierrez, Asst. to Joss Whedon

They have a deal with Twentieth Century Fox and a big hit feature there named *Buffy the Vampire Slayer*. They're also behind the TV series and its spinoff, *Angel*. So if you're just dying to write for either show, here's where you contact them. They're riding high in TV right now, but remember, they started in features.

Contact: George Snyder.

MACE NEUFELD PRODUCTIONS

10202 W. Washington Boulevard, Jimmy Stewart Bldg. #220, Culver City, CA 90232
310-244-2555
Fax: 310-244-0255

Mace Neufeld, Producer

Elizabeth Kern, Associate Producer

Kel Symons, VP of Development

David Engel, Director of Development

Jeff Kirschenbaum, Creative Executive

Dax Phelan, Story Editor

With Bob Rehme, Mace Neufeld was responsible for movies of major Tom Clancy novels: *A Clear and Present Danger*, *The Hunt for Red October*, and *Patriot Games*. But the pair split up and Mace moved his operations to the Sony lot. Recent projects include *The General's Daughter*, based on the novel by Nelson DeMille, and in the pipeline are a number of similar, tough-edged projects, my favorite being *Concrete Blonde* from the novel by Michael Conolly, with a script from Dan Petrie Jr. If you have a novel or script that Neufeld likes, he'll never give up on it—I saw him say, at the Hollywood Film Festival 2000, that he was going into production with a property he'd been wanting to make for 22 years!

Contact: Jeff Kirschenbaum or **Dax Phelan** for current needs.

NEVER A DULL MOMENT PRODUCTIONS

1406 N. Topanga Canyon Boulevard, Topanga, CA 90290
310-455-1651
Fax: 310-455-1893
E-mail: ndull@aol.com

David N. Gottlieb, Producer, Director

Lisa Hallas Gottlieb, Producer

In business for almost a decade, this husband-and-wife team produces movies for cable and television, features, documentaries, and videos. If you're a parent, you might have seen a video they did for babies and toddlers entitled *Meet Your Animal Friends*. They've also done the movies *Midnight Child* and *Deadly Love* for Lifetime. Generally, they are open to any genre as long as the script is well-written and the characters are intriguing.

Contact: Lisa Hallas Gottlieb, who says, "I prefer to receive query letters with a summary of the script and the credentials of the writer. If I would like to read a script, I will send my own release form, or it could be submitted by an agent or lawyer."

NEVERLAND FILMS, INC.

10323 Santa Monica Boulevard, Suite 106, Los Angeles, CA 90025
310-772-0008
Fax: 310-772-0006
Web site: www.neverlandfilms.com

Al Corley, Partner/Producer

Eugene Musso, Partner/Producer

Bart Rosenblatt, Partner/Producer

From their Web site: "Neverland Films, Inc. is a production company founded by Al Corley, Bart Rosenblatt and Eugene Musso . . . Al Corley began his career in the entertainment industry as an actor, perhaps best known to television audiences for his role of Stephen Carrington in the hit series, 'Dynasty.' When he decided to make his move behind the camera, Corley teamed up with long-time friends Bart Rosenblatt and Gene Musso, whose careers were in business and finance, to form Neverland Films. In addition to their feature films, the Neverland trio has coproduced a full length docudrama about Studio 54 and New York in the late 70s, entitled 'The Last Dance' and produced several original theatrical plays for the New York stage." Their feature credits include *Ring of Fire* starring Kiefer Sutherland, *Drowning Mona* starring Danny DeVito and Bette Midler, *Palmetto* starring Woody Harrelson, and *A Brother's Kiss* with Marisa Tomei.

Contact: Any of the **partners** above.

NEW REGENCY PRODUCTIONS

10201 W. Pico Boulevard, Bldg. 12, Los Angeles, CA 90035
310-369-8300
Fax: 310-969-0470
Web site: www.newregency.com

Arnon Milchan, Producer

David Matalon, President

Sanford Panitch, President of Production

Alexandra Milchan, VP of Acquisitions

Kara Francis, Senior VP of Production

Jason Weiss, Director of Development

Alexa Ort, Story Editor

They had past hits like *Pretty Woman* and *L.A. Confidential*, and that impressed Fox enough to woo them away from Warner Bros. in a 15-year pact made in 1997. With his film financing abilities, Arnon Milchan has been a very influential producer for quite some time. A New Regency "signature" film might have the elements of street wisdom mixed with top-level corporate and/or political shenanigans, with a redemptive human outcome. Their most recent big hit was *Big Momma's House* with Martin Lawrence. The most exciting film they have in the pipeline (at least to me) is *Daredevil*, based on the popular Marvel comic of the same name. This is a big company, so only personnel meaningful to writers are listed above.

Contact: Alexa Ort for current needs and submission policy.

LYNDA OBST PRODUCTIONS

5555 Melrose Avenue Bldg. 210, Hollywood, CA 90038
323-956-8744
Fax: 323-862-2287

Lynda Obst, Producer

Greg Hoffman, Executive VP of Production

Thia Montroy, VP of Development

Do yourself a favor and read Lynda Obst's book *Hello, He Lied* sometime for a real tour of Hollywood business. Obst came from the book world and doesn't take Hollywood too seriously any more, with a home in Austin, Texas, near her friend Sandra Bullock, with whom she did *Hope Floats*. You've probably cried over some of her movies, like *Sleepless in Seattle*, and unless you are a "baby boomer," you probably didn't see her *The 60s* miniseries. Housed on the Paramount lot, the company also has a deal with Lakeshore for smaller, niche films with budgets under $10 million. In the pipeline are films like *American Pastoral* (from a Philip Roth novel, about a daughter who leaves her conservative family to become an anti-war activist) and *How to Lose a Guy in 10 Days*, about a woman jilted at the altar who gets back at men through a series of flings but finds one guy is harder to lose.

Contact: Thia Montroy for current needs.

OLMOS PRODUCTIONS, INC.

Walt Disney Company, 500 S. Buena Vista Street, Mail Code 1803,
    Burbank, CA 91521
818-560-8651
Fax: 818-560-8655
E-mail: olmosproductions@hotmail.com

Edward James Olmos, President/Actor

Nick Athas, Producer (N.Y.)

Javier Varon, Director of Development

From the time he starred in *The Ballad of Gregorio Cortez,* Edward James Olmos has been a crusader both on screen and off. His *American Me* created a mild uproar when some of the personnel involved in the movie died in what some thought were gang-related circumstances that sprang from the subject matter of the movie, but that didn't stop ABC Entertainment from giving him a major production deal to develop series, miniseries, and MOWs. His latest is *The Judge*, a miniseries for NBC about a federal judge wrongfully accused of murder. I will never forget how, the day after the Los Angeles riots following the Rodney King trial, Olmos stepped onto the sidewalk with a broom and led a band of like-minded individuals of all races into the crisis area to begin cleaning up. It's one of the most astonishingly human things I've ever seen in my life. If you have a TV project that is powerfully written and might make a difference, this could be its home.

Contact: Javier Varon (who is also a fine writer and was introduced to Olmos in a roundabout way via myself).

ON STILTS PRODUCTIONS

310-391-6053
E-mail: PStelzer@aol.com

Peter Stelzer, President

Normally, I would not list any producer or production company who only wanted their phone and/or e-mail address listed. I'll make an exception for people I trust, and Peter Stelzer is certainly one of them. Also, I've only heard very good reports from people who have contacted Peter via my book. When I first met him, he was vice president of Ted Danson's Anasazi Productions, the Paramount Studios–based production company that won awards for project like *Miss Evers Boys*: five Emmys, two Cable Aces, one Golden Globe, two Humanitas, the AMA, the NHEA, the NAACP, and the Golden Laurel. The Golden Globe was the only contest where the company didn't win Best Picture. At Anasazi, the stated aim was "to make movies that inspire people to be more loving, ethically aware, and socially responsible." Stelzer is still committed to "life-affirming, or at least intellectually satisfying, stories. Especially heartfelt, character-driven, issue-related projects and high concept children's scripts." He's looking for projects he can launch on television, or make into low-budget movies.

Contact: Peter Stelzer via e-mail with a short description of what you have. If you call, he'll pick up the phone himself. If he likes what you have, he'll ask to see it.

ORIGINAL FILM

2045 S. Barrington Avenue, Los Angeles, CA 90025
310-445-9000
Fax: 310-445-9191

Neal H. Moritz, Producer

Brad Luff, Exec. VP of Production

Heather Zeegan, VP of Production

Mark Rossen, President of Television

Jennifer Tuthill, Director of Feature Development

Brian Gefsky, Director of TV Development

Justin Rosenblatt, Creative Executive

Jennifer Grandy, Manager of TV

Development Assistants: Russ Brown, Amanda Cohen, Evan Cooper, Gretchen Douglass, Joshua Lawson

Their first-look deal at Columbia includes a discretionary fund and gives the company a first dollar gross position on their pictures. Do you write scripts that appeal to teenagers? In recent years they've brought us *I Know What You Did Last Summer*,

Cruel Intentions, and *Saving Silverman.* Mark Rossen was a top agent at ICM before signing on as head of the TV arm, and is as ready to develop as much new talent in TV as they have through features. Short filmmaker? They bought the spec screenplay "Short Hills" from Craig Moss and Steven Schoenburg, who made "Saving Ryan's Privates." In the pipeline are movies like *The Glass House* by Wesley Strick, starring Leelee Sobieski, and *Miss Potter*, a look into the romantic life of children's book author, Beatrix Potter.

Contact: Any **Development Assistant** mentioned above.

OUTLAW PRODUCTIONS

9155 Sunset Boulevard, W. Hollywood, CA 90069
310-777-2000
Fax: 310-777-2010
E-mail: outlaw@outlawfilm.com
Web site: www.outlawfilm.com

Robert Newmyer, Producer

Jeffrey Silver, Producer

Scott Strauss, President of Production

Brad Ley, Creative Executive

Often sexy, always edgy, hip movies, that's these folks. They have a first look production deal with Intermedia which provides Outlaw with a $3 million annual discretionary fund and distribution by Warner Brothers. This means they can option quite a few screenplays. They've been behind films like The *Santa Clause, Don Juan deMarco* (a script everyone in town wanted), and *sex, lies and videotape.* In the pipeline are projects like *Ace in the Hole,* a con vs. con caper about a professional con man blackmailed into helping a Las Vegas casino boss evade an FBI murder investigation.

Contact: Brad Ley for current needs, but you may end up with one of the many unlisted executive assistants.

OUT OF THE BLUE . . . ENTERTAINMENT

10202 W. Washington Boulevard, Astaire Bldg., #1200, Culver City, CA 90232-3195
310-244-7800
Fax: 310-244-1539

Sid Ganis, Producer

David Levine, Executive VP

Mike Johnson, Assistant

Marissa Kamin, Assistant

Alex Siskin, Assistant

They did Adam Sandler's *Big Daddy* and brought us *Deuce Bigalow: Male Gigolo.* They have a project upcoming with Dana Carvey as well as a big screen version of TV's *I Dream of Jeannie.* And a remake of Frank Capra's *Mr. Deeds Goes to Town* with Adam Sandler. In October 2000, they bought the spec script "Pearls Before Swan," a first script from Brent Weindling, a comedy-drama about a likable but stuffy college professor whose uncle bequeaths him a strip club. Weindling's script was a winner in the Diane Thomas UCLA Screenwriting Competition. Sid Ganis is the Vice President of the Academy of Motion Picture Arts and Sciences and was the president of world-wide marketing for Columbia/Tri-Star prior to starting his production company. Think funny and big box office if you want to sell them something.

Contact: Any **assistant** above.

OVERBROOK ENTERTAINMENT

100 Universal City Plaza, Bldg. 489, Universal City, CA 91608-1002
818-777-2224
Fax: 818-866-5440
E-mail: scheme firstname.lastname@psg.unistudios.com

Will Smith, Partner

James Lassiter, Partner

Teddy Zee, President of Motion Picture Division

LaDawn Williams Bailey, General Manager

Motion Picture Executives: Glendon Palmer, Lori Zuker

SoYun Roe, Executive in charge of Development & Production

John Dukakis, Executive VP of Music

David Tochterman, Executive VP of TV

Stacey Matthew, VP of TV

Rashad Liston, Coordinator of Music Videos

By box office totals, who is the number-one star in the world over the past few years? You guessed it—the former Fresh Prince of Bel Air. They're working on a remake of Clint Eastwood's first directorial effort, *Play Misty for Me*, and of course Will Smith is doing the Muhammad Ali biopic. Also in the pipeline is a movie about the Moulin Rouge, which opened in 1955 in Las Vegas and billed itself as the country's first interracial hotel and casino, and a project for Cedric the Entertainer. Teddy Zee was president of Davis Entertainment before coming to Overbrook.

Contact: SoYun Roe. (Note: There is a Web site registered for overbrookentertainment.com but I'm not sure they own it.)

PERMUT PRESENTATIONS

9150 Wilshire Boulevard, Suite 247, Beverly Hills, CA 90212
310-248-2792
Fax: 310-248-2797

David Permut, Producer/President

Steve Longi, VP of Production

Daniel Mitchell, Development Associate

My first encounters with David Permut and how he sold *Dragnet* and *Blind Date* are chronicled in the chapter about loglines and high concepts. David does big movies like *Face-Off* and people who work with him inevitably move on to become successful producers as well. In the pipeline is director Rod Hardy's first feature, the low-budget action-thriller *Route 52* about outsiders stranded overnight and suspected of murder in a small, depressed mountain town. Rod was a successful director in Australia before he emigrated to the United States to direct the miniseries *20,000 Leagues Under the Sea* and the Emmy-nominated *Buffalo Girls*. Permut is also working with writer-director-producer George "Midnight Run" Gallo to do the comedy *Double Take* at Disney. Last but not least, he's teamed up with Massimo Graziosi of Spring International in an international production partnership to do two films with budgets in excess of $100 million. Graziosi was formerly the president of Castle Rock International. As far as receptiveness goes, David Permut and Steve Longi are two of my favorite people in the business, so I hope you sell them something.

Contact: Steve Longi or **Daniel Mitchell.**

PERSISTENT PICTURES

9350 Wilshire Boulevard, Suite 328, Beverly Hills, CA 90212
310-777-1814
Fax: 310-777-1820
Web site: www.persistentpictures.com

Dan Stone, Producer—stone@persistentpictures.com

Matthew Rhodes, Producer—rhodes@persistentpictures.com

Brian Dillingham, Story Editor—mail@persistentpictures.com

Dan Stone formed Persistent Pictures, Inc. in late 1994. Since then, he has optioned a wide range of literary properties, from a coming-of-age drama to the true-life story of one of the largest government corruption cases in U.S. history. They have worked with several established talents: Andrew Chapman *(Iron Man, Sea Wolf, Beethoven III),* Meg Richman *(Wings of an Angel),* Ariel Dorfman *(Death and the Maiden),* and Mark Medoff *(Children of a Lesser God).* They look for "scripts by writers who are passionate about creating works of quality that Persistent Pictures can be proud to be involved with—character-driven scripts that could be submitted to Sundance [the Sundance Film Festival]." Not represented? Don't want to sign a release form? They'll read your script anyway. See the Web site for their latest projects.

Contact: Anyone listed above.

PHASE 1 PRODUCTIONS

3210 Club Drive, Los Angeles, CA 90064
310-842-8401
Fax: 310-280-0415
E-mail: phase1prod@earthlink.net

Joe Wizan, Partner

Don Schneider, Partner

Steve Wizan, President

Dru Ransom, VP of Creative Affairs

With films to its credit like *Kiss the Girls, Dunston Checks In,* and the marvelous *Wrestling Ernest Hemingway* as well as recent releases like *Along Came a Spider*, this company makes great movies whether they be thrillers or comedies, high budget or low. (Hey, my kids loved *Dunston.*) Of course, as long as James Patterson (*Kiss the*

Girls and *Along Came a Spider*) keeps writing great novels, you might be out of luck selling them anything but a comedy. Joe Wizan has been a successful producer for three decades, going all the way back to *Jeremiah Johnson*, which starred Robert Redford.

Contact: Dru Ransom for current needs.

PHOENIX PICTURES

10202 W. Washington Boulevard, Frankovich Bldg., Culver City, CA 90232
310-244-6100
Fax: 310-839-8915

Mike Medavoy, Chairman/CEO

Arnold Messer, President/COO

Matt Bierman, Executive VP of Production

Eric Paquette, Executive VP of Production

Brad Fischer, Director of Development

Mike Medavoy has been a major player in Hollywood for a long time. This might explain the title of his company (a phoenix rises from the ashes to be reborn). His company likes edgy, liberal cause stuff like *The People vs. Larry Flynt*, and the Barbra Streisand film *The Mirror Has Two Faces*. If you get in the door at Phoenix, you probably won't have to worry about your script being too controversial for them. Their television development hasn't delivered what they expected when the last edition of this book came out, which might explain the departure of television VP Marc Lorber. Matt Bierman came to the company from Village Roadshow. Projects in the pipeline include a movie for Showtime and the feature adaptation of a book about Jimmy Lerner, a white-collar executive convicted of voluntary manslaughter, torn from his family, and thrust into a maximum security prison.

Contact: Brad Fischer for current needs and submission policy at (310) 244-6540.

MARC PLATT PRODUCTIONS

100 Universal City Plaza, Bungalow 5184, Universal City, CA 91608
818-777-1122
Fax: 818-866-6353

Marc Platt, Producer

Abby Wolf, President

Development Executives: Sara Cline, Christian McLaughlin, Adam Siegel, Dan Teebor

TV Executives: Kacey Arnold, Moe Jelline, Joey Levy, Gregory Lessans

With serious films like *Legally Blonde*, about a sorority girl dumped by her boyfriend who becomes a lawyer and frees a blonde accused of killing her older, rich husband (based on a novel by Amanda Brown) and not-so-serious movies like *Josey and the Pussycats* to their credit, it might appear that movies that appeal to the female audience is the secret to this company. Except they're also doing *Ghost Soldiers*, about the rescue of 500 American POWs in the Philippines during World War II (which also came from a novel). They may do a remake of the 1973 TV film *The Girl Most Likely* but who knows? They have almost two dozen properties in development, from all sources, including pitches and are interested in theater as well as film and TV.

Contact: Executives listed above.

EDWARD R. PRESSMAN FILM CORPORATION

130 S. El Camino Drive, Beverly Hills, CA 90212
310-271-8383
Fax: 310-271-9497

New York office:
130 W. 57th Street, Suite 3B, New York, NY 10019
212-489-3333
Web site: www.pressman.com

Edward R. Pressman, President

Alessandro Camon, Senior VP of Production

Neil Friedman, Executive VP

Jeff Conner, VP of Publishing, Top Dollar Comics

Erin O'Rourke, VP of Production, Sunflower Productions

The Edward R. Pressman Film Corporation has been a proving ground for directors: Terence Malick's *Badlands,* John Milius' *Conan the Barbarian,* Oliver Stone's *Wall Street,* Alex Proyas' *The Crow,* and Barbet Schroeder's *Reversal of Fortune* are examples. Several Pressman films have received Oscar nominations and Academy Awards. The company's creative focus is "to develop strong relationships with talented directors, writers, and actors early in their careers." If you want to see all the things they are releasing and developing, check out the Web site. They do a lot of dark, even sick stuff like *American Psycho*, from the novel by Brett "Less Than Zero" Easton Ellis. And they are also publishers.

Contact: Erin O'Rourke—e-mail scheme is generally firstname@pressman.com (example: erin@pressman.com).

PROMARK ENTERTAINMENT GROUP

3599 Cahuenga Boulevard West, Third Floor, Los Angeles, CA 90068
323-878-0404
Fax: 323-878-0486
E-mail: promark@promarkgroup.com
Web site: www.promarkgroup.com (site not fully functional at press time)

Conny Lernhag, Chairman (Sweden)

Jonathan Kramer, President

Steve Beswick, Senior VP of Production

Gil Adrienne Wishnick, VP of Creative Affairs & Development

Denise Ballew, VP of Creative Affairs & Acquisitions

Promark Entertainment Group is owned by Promark Konsult, a Swedish corporation. It was formed to produce and acquire theatrical motion pictures and to distribute them in both foreign and domestic (U.S.) markets. Jonathan Kramer had his own company before joining Promark. Steve Beswick has almost two decades of experience in show business. Gil Wishnick was in development at Republic Pictures, Samuel Goldwyn, and United Artists. Since the company is a foreign sales company, they mainly produce action films you might have never heard of (*The Stick-Up*, *One Way Out*, *The Shipment*, etc.) In the pipeline are films like *Starchild*, about an alien coming to Earth to find a fertile woman. (Didn't Gary Shandling already do that?) "Our films are male-oriented, urban in setting, and hopefully smart," says Gil Wishnick. "We try to find projects with a fresh premise, a clever hook, and strong characters."

Contact: Gil Adrienne Wishnick. A short synopsis is preferred.

PROPAGANDA FILMS

1741 N. Ivar Avenue, Hollywood, CA 90028
323-462-6400
Fax: 323-802-7001

New York office:
902 Broadway, Suite 1603, New York, NY 10010
212-982-1700
Fax: 212-982-8700

Rick Hess, President

Trevor Macy, COO

Brian Oliver, VP of Production

Paul Schiff, Producer

Charles Wolford, Exec. Producer, Satellite Films & Music Videos

Colin Hickson, Head of Commercials & Music Videos

Pat Dollard, Head of Management Division

Managers: David Flynn, Rob Gomez, Keith Redmon, Tammy Rosen

Thrillers, weird movies, and very edgy comedies are what Propaganda and their NY affiliate Satellite Films are all about. Maybe you saw *Being John Malkovich* or *Nurse Betty* or Michael Douglas in *The Game*? They have a deal with Constantin Film of Germany and they also do videos and commercials as well as manage. If it's something different, they could be into it, like *Titan*, a property in the pipeline about the myth of Perseus and his journey to save the Princess Andromeda. David Flynn was formerly an agent with ICM. The company manages top directors like directors Spike Jonze and Simon West.

Contact: Any of the **managers** listed above. A number of personnel in the NY office are not listed, so call for info.

PROUD MARY ENTERTAINMENT

433 N. Camden Drive, Suite 600, Beverly Hills, CA 90210
310-288-1886
Fax: 310-288-1801
E-mail: proudmaryent@earthlink.net

Mary L. Aloe, Executive Producer

Todd Waxler, Executive Producer

This company has been involved in a number of films that have attracted international attention. *Full Metal Racket* was nominated for a Golden Palm at the Cannes Film Festival for Best Short Film. This goofy parody starring tennis player Bobby Riggs as a drill sergeant terrorizing 10 year olds on a tennis court was a take-off on the Stanley Kubrick film. A more serious film with a military backdrop was their TV movie *The Princess & the Marine*, about the Middle Eastern princess who ran away with a U.S. marine, which came to them via Tom Colbert's Industry R&D company.

Contact: Either of the principals.

PROVIDENCE ENTERTAINMENT

13801 Ventura Boulevard, Sherman Oaks, CA 91423
818-728-9700
Fax: 818-728-9797
E-mail: cbond@providencefilms.com
Web site: www.providencefilms.com

Victor Vanden Oever, CEO

David Williams, President

Cindy Bond, President of Production

Michael Harpster, President of Marketing

Providence Entertainment had the number-one limited release of 1999 with *The Omega Code*. Other films Providence has distributed include *Hands on a Hard Body*, and *Grizzly Falls* (a great movie that our whole family enjoyed). Cindy Bond also cofounded an international children's film festival, Backyard National Children's Film Festival, which was mentioned in the *Wall Street Journal* and *USA Today* and held at Paramount Studios in November 2000. The festival showcased films made by kids 18 years old and under. LEGO, the toy manufacturer, was the corporate sponsor. In mid-1996, Interstate Batteries Chairman Norm Miller, Anne Miller, and Cindy Bond formed the production entity Norann Entertainment. In early 1999, Norm Miller, Cindy Bond, David Williams (former Chairman of Legacy Releasing, Managing Director Credit Lyonnais, COO Orion Pictures), Michael Harpster (former head of marketing at New Line for 15 years), and Victor Vanden Oever (Benson Music, Wessex Entertainment, Merrill Lynch) formed Providence. To date they have distributed five films, with three additional films slated for release in 2001. Recently, Providence opened a home video division and has plans for a foreign division as well.

Contact: Cindy Bond via fax or e-mail with no more than a one-page synopsis along with a cover letter. If she is interested she will call and request a script, which must then be submitted through an agent or lawyer. She says: "A Providence film is one that would receive a G, PG, or PG-13 rating that has positive values minus gratuitous sex, violence, and profanity. Specifically I am looking for films that will work in our various under-served niche marketplaces: Family, Latino/Hispanic, African American, Christian, Country."

PUNCH PRODUCTIONS

1926 Broadway #305, New York, NY 10023
212-207-8127
Fax: 310-442-4884

L.A. office (a.k.a. Punch 21):
11661 San Vicente Boulevard, Suite 222, Los Angeles, CA 90049
310-442-4880

Dustin Hoffman, Owner

Jay Cohen, Co-Owner (L.A.)

Lee Gottsegen, President

Laura Gherardi, VP of Production

Murray Schisgal, Creative Director

Heather Waterman, VP of Development (L.A.)

Contrary to what some think, this production company doesn't only do projects with Dustin Hoffman. Sure, they were behind *Wag the Dog*, but the principals were also producer on *Boys and Girls* in 2000, and a small "industry" (Hollywood) movie that I absolutely loved called *Swimming with Sharks*. They have almost 20 projects in development, including a biography of famed photographer Alfred Stieglitz and *After You*, based on the Stephen Greenleaf novel *Ditto List*, which seems reminiscent of Hoffman's star turn in *Kramer vs. Kramer*.

Contact: Heather Waterman in the L.A. office for current needs and submission policy.

RADIANT PRODUCTIONS / RED CLIFF PRODUCTIONS

914 Montana Avenue, Second Floor, Santa Monica, CA 90403
310-656-1400
Fax: 310-656-1408
E-mail: merfilms@aol.com

Wolfgang Petersen, Director/Producer

Gail Katz, President/Producer

Samuel Dickerman, Sr. VP

Rosemary Tarquinio, Head of TV

Susan Stein, Director of Development

David Markus, Story Editor

Veronica Becker, Development Assistant

I've been a big fan of Wolfgang Petersen since the day I saw his German language *Das Boot*. Since he's been making films in the U.S., I've only been disappointed once (*Outbreak*). Big action films with big stars is their fare: *Air Force One*, *In the Line of Fire*, and *The Perfect Storm* all were top box office draws. Though they have a number of projects in the development hopper, some don't sound like the normal Petersen film. One example is *Dickey Slaughter, Truant Officer*, about a town conspiracy uncovered in the search for two teenagers, which is a comedy. Others, like *Devil's Teardrop*, based on a novel by Jeffrey Deaver, author of *The Bone Collector*, sound like more of the same great thriller stuff.

Contact: Development people or **Story Editor** for current needs, but you'll probably have little luck without a top agent.

RECORDED PICTURE COMPANY

7001 Melrose Avenue, Los Angeles, CA 90038
323-460-4747
Fax: 323-936-4913

London office:
24 Hanway Street, London W1T 1UH, England
+044-020-7636-2251
Fax: +044-020-7636-2261
E-mail: rpc@recordedpicture.com
Web site: www.recordedpicture.com

Jeremy Thomas, Producer/Chairman

Chris Auty, Managing Director

Hercules Bellville, Director

Giles Gordon, Director (L.A.)

Alexandra Stone, Sr. VP of Development (L.A.)

Some of the company's films have had a similar theme: dissolution. *Naked Lunch,* the hallucinatory ramblings of writer William Burroughs in North Africa, is one, as was *The Sheltering Sky* and *The Last Emperor* (the company's biggest hit). Recorded Picture has not been very active in the U.S. development market of late, but they do maintain an L.A. office and are still doing business here.

Contact: Alexandra Stone with a query.

RED WAGON ENTERTAINMENT

10202 West Washington Boulevard, Hepburn West, Culver City, CA 90232-3195
310-244-4466
Fax: 310-244-1480

Doug Wick, Producer

Lucy Fisher, Producer

Gail Lyon, President

Tara Mark, Creative Executive

Rachel Shane, Creative Executive

David Schreiber, Story Editor

Housed on the lot of Sony Pictures Entertainment, Red Wagon makes major motion pictures with major stars. Douglas Wick learned the film business working with director Alan Pakula and moved up to become associate producer on *Starting Over*. He came up with *Working Girl* as a Cinderella story set on Wall Street, but every major studio passed on it until Twentieth Century Fox took a chance. The film got six Oscar nominations and won five Golden Globes. Following this success, Wick started Red Wagon at Columbia. *Wolf* was the company's first production, followed by *The Craft* (another original Wick concept). Steven Spielberg was going to direct *Memoirs of a Geisha* (adapted from the novel by Arthur Golden) but that project was put on hold.

Now, fresh off a Best Picture Oscar for *Gladiator* and the huge box office of other successes like *Stuart Little*, it's doubtful you can break in here, but if you do you'll be working with the best.

Contact: David Schreiber. Query first with a phone call or fax.

RENAISSANCE PICTURES

100 Universal City Plaza, Bldg. 78, Universal City, CA 91608
818-777-0088
Fax: 818-733-0223

Sam Raimi, Director/Producer

Robert G. Tapert, Executive Producer

Patrick Moran, President of TV

Mike McDonald, Director of Feature Development

Liz Friedman, Director of TV Development

Tamara Dow, Creative Executive

Geoff Martin, Creative Associate

Jeff Cruce, Development Associate

Although he made an early splash with the film *Army of Darkness* and the *Darkman* movies, lately Sam Raimi has been into TV series, as executive producer of *Cleopatra 2525*, *Young Hercules*, *Spy Game* and *Xena: Warrior Princess*. The short-lived but engrossing *American Gothic*, created by former Hardy Boy Shaun Cassidy, was another Renaissance production. If you have something dark and menacing with a sense of justice woven in, you might find a sympathetic ear here—it's worth a try.

Contact: Development and creative people listed.

RHINO ENTERTAINMENT

10635 Santa Monica Boulevard, Second Floor, Los Angeles, CA 90025
310-441-6557
Fax: 310-441-6553
E-mail: Stephen.Nemeth@rhino.com
Web site: www.rhino.com

Stephen Nemeth, Head of Production

The company that started as a record album recycling outfit has been responsible for films like *Valley of the Dolls* and *Why Do Fools Fall in Love* (Frankie Lyman biopic), and *Fear and Loathing in Las Vegas*. If Stephen Nemeth doesn't have a stroke making a biopic about Johnny Rotten of The Sex Pistols, they'll probably continue looking for properties that have that same general pop culture appeal to young audiences as well as baby boomers chic.

Contact: Stephen Nemeth—he'll get back to you immediately.

THE RUDDY MORGAN ORGANIZATION, INC.

9300 Wilshire Boulevard, Suite 508, Beverly Hills, CA 90212
310-271-7698
Fax: 310-278-9978
E-mail: ruddymorgan@earthlink.net

Al Ruddy, Producer

André Morgan, Producer

Louisa Kwan, Creative Affairs Executive

Douglas Nam, Creative Affairs Executive

Yuri England, Executive Assistant

Established in 1984, The Ruddy Morgan Organization (RMO) is a major production company with a long track record in feature films and a large presence in network television. They've also become active in managing Hong Kong directors hoping to be the next John Woo, given their relationship with Raymond Chow's Golden Harvest (Hong Kong's biggest production company). Ruddy and Morgan won the Academy Award for Best Picture *(The Godfather)*, two Golden Globes and Italy's "David of Donatello" award. Their TV successes include the Chuck Norris series *Walker: Texas Ranger* and they were behind the movie *Mr. Magoo*. The most exciting thing in the pipeline is the long-awaited *Atlas Shrugged*, from the novel by Ayn Rand.

Contact: No designated development person, but **André Morgan** has told me he's open to queries. (You might have read Eric Garcia's interview earlier in the book; he broke in at Ruddy-Morgan.)

SCOTT RUDIN PRODUCTIONS

5555 Melrose Avenue, DeMille Building #100, Los Angeles, CA 90038-3197
323-956-4600
Fax: 323-862-0262

New York office:
120 West 45th Street, 10th Floor, New York, NY 10036
212-704-4600
Fax: 212-869-8557

Scott Rudin, Producer

Adam Schroeder, President

Scott Aversano, Senior VP (L.A.)

Angelique Palozzi, Creative Executive

Jose M. Calleja Jr., Co-Director of Development (L.A.)

Carrie Cook, Co-Director of Development (L.A.)

Mark Roybal, Director of Development (N.Y.)

John Delaney, Development Executive (N.Y.)

Melvin Mar, Development Executive (L.A.)

Narges Takesh, Development Assistant (L.A.)

Scott Rudin knows how to pick them, in any genre. Consider *The Addams Family, First Wives Club*, *The Search for Bobby Fischer*, *The Truman Show*, and *Sleepy Hollow*. Rudin is an aggressive producer who has both coasts covered and goes after the best properties around. Note he has *two* directors of development in Los Angeles; he has to, with almost 50 projects in the pipeline. Hint: he loves books. He bought Olivia Goldsmith's *First Wives Club* in manuscript form when no publisher would take it, snatched up *Angela's Ashes*, and is planning on adapting the long-awaited *Stranger in a Strange Land* by Robert Heinlein.

Contact: Any of the **development people** listed.

SARABANDE PRODUCTIONS

530 Wilshire Boulevard, Suite 308, Santa Monica, CA 90401
310-395-4842
Fax: 310-395-7079

Steve Sarabande, Founder

David Manson, President

Arla Sorkin Manson, Executive VP

David Strohmeyer, Director of Development

If you ever saw Nicolas Cage in the marvelous *Birdy* you were looking at something from these folks. They have a deal with Columbia TriStar Television and movies in the pipeline like *Stand-Up Tragedy* with Mickey Rourke, about a priest mentoring an inner-city schoolteacher. Given their past, you can generally count on them liking heartfelt young angst material.

SATURN FILMS

9000 Sunset Boulevard #911, West Hollywood, CA 90069
310-887-0900
Fax: 310-248-2965
Web site: www.saturnfilms.com

Nicolas Cage, CEO/Producer

Norm Golightly, President/Producer

Clarke Anderson, Director of Development

Jen Bosworth, Development Assistant

For a time, this company was active via their Web site, looking for material. Then they got swamped and backed off that stance. Their first film, the bizarre but entertaining *Shadow of the Vampire*, was a tour de force for Willem Dafoe and earned him an Oscar nomination. They have a deal with Intermedia Films and plenty of money to develop, but as *Shadow* illustrates they're not only looking for things in which Cage can star (but he does have this *thing* for vampires). Clarke Anderson is an aspiring writer herself, hailing from North Carolina, and the last time I saw her she said she'd love to find a good Western, but she was open to just about anything.

Contact: Clarke Anderson. There are a number of assistants at the company but she's the one who decides whether the material gets bumped upstairs.

SCOTT FREE PRODUCTIONS

634 N. LaPeer Drive, Los Angeles, CA 90069
310-360-2250
Fax: 310-360-2251

Ridley Scott, Co-Chairman

Tony Scott, Co-Chairman

Lisa Ellzey, President

Zach Schiff-Abrams, VP of Development & Production

Anne Lai, Creative Executive

Rene Brar, Story Editor

Ersin Pertan, Development Assistant

They have a two-year, first-look deal with Jerry Bruckheimer Films and another deal with Intermedia, but after winning the Best Picture Oscar for *Gladiator* in 2001, this company could get a deal anywhere (well, actually, they could before the win). Ridley Scott is simply one of the best directors in the world, which was evident from the time of *Blade Runner* onward. Despite a bit of kerfuffle that arose over the Screen Actors Guild strike of 2000 and the commercials arm of their company, this is a place that likes legendary projects. To provide some examples, some of the things they have in the pipeline are *Captain Kidd*, *Hell's Angels*, and *Tristan and Isolde*. I wish you all the best in selling them a future legend—I wouldn't mind doing so myself!

Contact: Zach Schiff-Abrams (whose former employer was Edward R. Pressman).

SECTION EIGHT

4000 Warner Boulevard, Bldg. 81, Room 117, Burbank, CA 91522
818-954-4840
Fax: 818-954-4860

George Clooney, CEO/Partner

Steven Soderbergh, CEO/Partner

Ben Cosgrove, President

Kevin Field, VP

Amy Cohen, Development Coordinator

Erika Armin, Executive Assistant

This company began when George Clooney twisted producer Jerry Weintraub's arm for a shot at the remake of *Oceans 11*. Every actor in town wanted onboard. Why?

Because Steven Soderbergh was signed on to direct, and if you didn't know why before the 2001 Academy Awards, Mr. Double Nomination and Best Director Winner for *Traffic* probably gave you some idea why, when he said a blessing for anyone who does any creative thing each day. As a company, they did well with the live re-do of the nuclear drama "Fair Safe" (starring Clooney). They have several things in development including the very interesting biopic of Moe Berg called *The Catcher Was a Spy*. You probably don't stand a chance, but the good news is they're receptive to new talent and will listen.

Contact: Amy Cohen and tell her you do something creative every single day and you'd like her to read it.

LLOYD SEGAN COMPANY

1041 N. Formosa Avenue, Pickford Bldg. #208, West Hollywood, CA 90046
323-850-3130
Fax: 323-850-3133

Lloyd Segan, Producer

Stephen Hollocker, VP

Karen White, Director of Development

Many people in Hollywood tried to get a biopic of Jimi Hendrix done, and this company did it. Other movies include *The Boondock Saints* and *The Bachelor*. By the time you read this, *Bones* with Snoop Doggy Dog, about a revengeful ghost, may be released, but not everything they do is hard-edged. In the pipeline is *Just Like a Woman*, a modern-day version of *Alice in Wonderland*. Well, on second thought, it might just be hard-edged, after all. . . .

Contact: Karen White for current needs.

SESAME WORKSHOP
(WAS CHILDREN'S TELEVISION WORKSHOP)

One Lincoln Plaza, 4th Floor, New York, NY 10023
212-595-3456
Fax: 212-875-6175
Web site: www.sesameworkshop.org

Gary Knell, President, CEO

Karen Gruenberg, Executive Vice President

Renee Mascara, Vice President

Michael Loman, Executive Producer, Sesame Street

Nina Elias, Executive Producer, Dragontale

Nancy Steingard, Senior VP, Creative Development

Shortly after unveiling its new name, Sesame Workshop announced a number of new productions, including *Carney's Class* ("think global, act local") with Australia's Southern Star Pacific. Premise? A kindergarten class puts Earth back in order. Then there was *Sponk*, "the first-ever convergent comedy improv game show for kids ages 8 to 12." With television, CD-ROMs, magazines, books, film, and more things than you can count, the folks who brought us over three decades of *Sesame Street* and other award-winning programs are stronger than ever. In the pipeline are the animated "Sagwa, the Chinese Siamese Cat," based on a book by Amy Tan, and "Pure Imagination," a series of short live-action movies from Henry Winkler's Fair Dinkum. Big Bird's house is still going strong.

Contact: Nancy Steingard. Sesame Workshop prefers material from recognized agents of established writers, and preferably writers who have written for children's television.

SEVEN ARTS PICTURES

7080 Hollywood Boulevard, Suite 201, Hollywood, CA 90028
323-464-0225
Fax: 323-464-8305

Peter Hoffman, Chairman

Colleen Camp, Producer/Partner

Neil Canton, Producer/Partner

Susan Hoffman, Producer/Partner

Eric Sandys, President of Production

Kate Hoffman, Creative Executive

Victor Teran, Creative Executive

My favorite film from this company is *Repossessed* with Linda Blair, but then I know Linda. Their highest-profile film recently was *Duets*, about people who travel across the country for karaoke competitions. It starred Huey Lewis and Gwyneth Paltrow. Why them? Well, Gwyneth's father, Bruce Paltrow, directed. In their development bin are films like *Rat Race* and *Interstate 60*, so just don't take them any road movies, unless the script is *really* good. They have a distribution deal with Paramount Pictures

Contact: Either **Creative Executive.**

SFX TOLLIN-ROBBINS

10960 Ventura Boulevard, Second Floor, Studio City, CA 91604
818-766-5004
Fax: 818-766-8488

Michael Tollin, Partner

Brian Robbins, Partner

Chris Castallo, Director of Creative Affairs

Shelley Zimmerman, VP of Development

If you contact this company and find the personnel have changed, don't blame me. First it was Tollin/Robbins, then it was Marquee Tollin/Robbins after a merger with the Marquee Group, and a multi-year deal with Nickelodeon. The company responsible for movie hit *Varsity Blues* works a lot in TV, producing HBO's *Arli$$* for adults and *Kenan and Kel* and *Cousin Skeeter* for the kids watching Nickelodeon. Now the company has been acquired by SFX Broadcasting out of New York, so who knows what the future will bring. In the pipeline are the features *Pay or Play* with Frankie Muniz, about a high school kid whose English paper is stolen and made into a blockbuster movie, and with Keanu Reeves, *Hardball*, about a slacker who loses a bet and has to borrow money from a friend under the condition that he will take over and coach a Little League team in the projects. Sports, kids, TV, movies. I'm sure you have the picture by now. Do you have something to "pitch" to them?

Contact: **Shelley Zimmerman** about your project.

SHORELINE ENTERTAINMENT

1875 Century Park East, Suite 600, Los Angeles, CA 90067
310-551-2060
Fax: 310-201-0729
E-mail: mail@shorelineentertainment.com
Web site: www.shorelineentertainment.com

Morris Ruskin, Co-Principal

Vicky Pike, Co-Principal

Eluana Okilo, Director of Development

Aaron Slater, Executive Assistant

Shoreline Entertainment, Inc., was formed in 1994 by Morris Ruskin and Mary Skinner. The company started out specializing in character-driven independent films; as an example, Ruskin coproduced *Glengarry Glen Ross*. In 2000, they worked with HBO and Lions Gate to do the thrillers, *Asylum* and *Beeper*. The company has been a mainstay at film festivals in recent years, and the most prominent film in their pipeline is *The Man from Elysian Fields* with Andy Garcia and Mick Jagger. They have a full explanation of everything they are and are doing on their Web site.

Contact: Eluana Okilo for current needs.

SILVER LION PICTURES

701 Santa Monica Boulevard, Suite 240, Santa Monica, CA 90401
310-393-9177
Fax: 310-458-9372
Web site: www.silverlionfilms.com

Lance Hool, Producer/Director, lancehool@silverlionfilms.com

Conrad Hool, conradhool@silverlionfilms.com

David Kohner Zuckerman, Director of Development, dkz@silverlionfilms.com

Crocodile Dundee in Los Angeles, who woulda thunk it? These folks did, and they also put Hogan in *Flipper* and did the feature version of *McHale's Navy*. Personally, I liked their nutty basketball flick, *The Air Up There*, too. They have a number of things in development, mostly funny, but they're open to queries about most genres.

Contact: David Kohner Zuckerman with a query letter, via e-mail, fax or ye olde snail mail.

SILVER PICTURES

4000 Warner Boulevard, Bldg. 90, Burbank, CA 91522
818-954-4490
Fax: 818-954-3237

Joel Silver, Chairman

Dan Cracchiolo, President of Production

Susan Levin, VP of Production

Erik Olsen, Creative Executive

Go to the Internet Movie Database (www.imdb.com) and look up Joel Silver, if you don't know who he is. You'll think the company is all about movies, but look again. They did "The First 100 Years: A Celebration of American Movies" TV special. Mostly though, big-budget, high-action films like the one my kids are waiting to see, *Speed Racer*, is what you'll get from Silver. Then of course we have "art" movies like *The Matrix* (just kidding, but it was very artful). Silver worked with Richard Donner on several films and formed a company with him called Decade. The *Lethal Weapon* movies, the *Die Hard* movies . . . get the picture? Give it your best shot.

Contact: Erik Olsen, and good luck.

THE ROBERT SIMONDS COMPANY

100 Universal City Plaza, Bldg. 1320, Penthouse 1A, Universal City, CA 91608-1085
818-777-5445
Fax: 818-866-1404

Robert Simonds, Producer

Tracey Trench, President of Creative Affairs

Joy Gorman, VP of Creative Affairs

Stephanie Pottruck, Creative Assistant

Robert Simonds has been in the major feature comedy business since teaming up with Adam Sandler and producing *Happy Gilmore*, *The Wedding Singer*, *Big Daddy,* and *The Waterboy* (among others). Simonds' *Problem Child* was good for a sequel, even if his big-screen version of the TV series *Leave It to Beaver* wasn't. *Dirty Work* with another "Saturday Night Live" alumni, Norm MacDonald, didn't set the world on fire, but Simonds probably barely noticed. He generally has around three dozen projects in development at any one time, one of which is with another SNL alum, Molly Shannon. And he's also doing a feature version of the TV series *Get Smart*. If you're agentless, you might not have much of a chance with this major comedy player, but if you have something that's really funny, give it a try. Simonds has a first-look agreement with Universal Studios to produce four to five pictures a year.

Contact: Joy Gorman, and be funny!

SMITH ENTERTAINMENT

2818 La Cienega Avenue, Second Floor, Los Angeles, CA 90034
310-815-0300
Fax: 310-815-0822
E-mail: info@smithentertainment.com
Web site: www.smithentertainment.com

Greg Smith, Manager/Producer

Brian Schiffer, Manager/Producer

Edgar Cayago, Junior Manager

This management and production company explains what they're all about on the opening page—a network of relationships based on the appreciation of excellence and professional trust. They cover a lot of territory, managing the careers of a growing number of exciting feature film screenwriters, novelists, directors, and Internet content creators. What is particularly interesting about this company for writers is that they represent a number of up and coming directors like Steve Purcell, who received a Best Concert Film Grammy in 1998 for his work on Alanis Morissette's "Jagged Little Pill" tour. The right script from you, packaged with one of their directors, might transform your career.

Contact: Anyone listed above (but read everything on their Web site first).

SOUTHERN LIGHT (WAS SANDOLLAR PRODUCTIONS)

10202 W. Washington Boulevard, David Lean Bldg. #100, Culver City, CA 90232-3195
310-244-2550
Fax: 310-244-0950

Dolly Parton, Executive Producer/Actress

Helena Hacker Rosenberg, VP of Movies & Series

Edward Acaac, Development Associate

Brian Gibson, Development Associate

For a long time, Dolly Parton had a company with manager/producer Sandy Gallin. They were at Disney then, and ambitious, with a television arm of the company that developed some good projects. Personally, I liked her TV movie *Unlikely Angel* but then, I've been to her theme park, Dollywood. Now that she's regrouped and set up shop at Sony, she has things in development with titles like *Heavens to Betsy* and *Solid*

Gold Cadillac. You can probably guess the kinds of movies they are. The one I hope she gets made, though, is a Mae West biopic. Go, Dolly, go.

Contact: Either **Development Associate,** ya'll.

SOUTH FORK PICTURES/WILDWOOD ENTERPRISES, INC.

1101 Montana Avenue, Suite E, Santa Monica, CA 90403
310-395-7779
Fax: 310-395-2575
E-mail: sfpics@earthlink.net

Robert Redford, Owner

Michael Nozik, President

Leslie Urdang, Producer

Karen Tenkhoff, Producer

Miranda de Pencier, Director of Development

Per Saari, Creative Executive

Linda Davis, Story Editor

In 2000, Robert Redford puzzled some by starting a production company in conjunction with his Sundance Institute. Some folks thought that odd because he already had two production companies. Equally puzzling was the box office disappointment of *The Legend of Bagger Vance* with Will Smith and Matt Damon, but c'est la showbiz. Something tells me that *Wendy and the Lost Boys* with Fox 2000, about a young woman who falls in love with an artist, then becomes torn between him and her male friends, will bring Redford back to familiar territory and larger success. After all, he left his native Santa Monica to travel to Europe and paint before he became a movie superstar. Redford turned down a piece of mine once and did *The Milagro Beanfield War* instead. Nice movie, I knew the star and know the production company, but if he'd done my *Texas Rising,* he would have had a hit. (Are you reading this, Bob?)

Contact: Any of the **Creative/Development/Story** people above.

SOUTHPAW MEDIA GROUP

1250 6th Street, Suite 200, Santa Monica, CA 90401
310-587-3537
Fax: 310-255-4850

Richard B. Lewis, Producer

Gregg Feinberg, President of Production

Rachel Fraizin, VP of Production

Haley Fox, VP of Development

Corey Ackerman, Director of Development

There are a number of people named Richard Lewis in Hollywood, so don't think this one is the comedian Richard Lewis. The head of this company is Richard Barton Lewis, who has a list of credits a mile long that includes *Backdraft, Robin Hood: Prince of Thieves,* and *The Magnificent Seven* TV series (as executive producer). So this means they do both TV and big budget features, right? Right. Projects in the pipeline include *Nailed Right*, a *Diner*-like story set in Brooklyn in the '70s, "on the fringes of the Mob," which might not be big budget but will probably be good, given this company's track record.

Contact: Haley Fox or **Corey Ackerman** for current needs, but only if you're left-handed. (Joke—Southpaw, get it? Okay, bad joke, I'm sure you can do better.)

SPANKY PICTURES

708 Broadway, 9th Floor, New York, NY 10003
212-634-4440

L.A. office:
1041 N. Formosa Avenue, Pickford Bldg., Room 199, W. Hollywood, CA 90046
323-654-3033
Fax: 323-850-2745

Ted Demme, Chairman

Tracy Falco, VP of Development

Jennifer Eatz, Director of Development

Eric Brown, Executive Assistant

Emma Tillinger, Executive Assistant

A music video director who did Bruce Springsteen's moving "Streets of Philadelphia" piece, Ted Demme has also worked with Denis Leary on a number of projects including the feature *The Ref*. He seems to like hard edges and one word titles. There was *Snitch* in 1998 and *Life* in 1999, then *Blow* in 2001, about a young man working with Colombian drug traffickers to smuggle cocaine in the 1970s. In the pipeline are some longer titles:

The Last of Sheila—a remake of the 1973 film about a widower's attempt to discover his wife's murderer—and *Eddie Killed the President*—about two buddies who have to face their inner fears one night. Do you kinda get the idea he likes East Coast subjects?

Contact: Tracy Falco or **Jennifer Eatz,** and be nice!

SPYGLASS ENTERTAINMENT GROUP
(WAS CARAVAN PICTURES)

500 S. Buena Vista Street, Animation Building, 3C, Burbank, CA 91521
818-560-3458
Fax: 818-563-1967

Gary Barber, Co-Chairman & CEO

Roger Birnbaum, Co-Chairman & CEO

Jonathan Glickman, President of Production

Derek Evans, VP of Production

Jeremy Steckler, Creative Executive

Marlena Thomas, Executive Coordinator

Resident on the Disney lot, Spyglass also has a five-year, first-look German and Austrian distribution deal with Constantin Films. In their prior incarnation as Caravan, they brought us *Angels in the Outfield* and *While You Were Sleeping*. They tend to like spiritual subjects. After making the action-comedy *Metro* with Caravan, Eddie Murphy agreed to develop films with them, including *Holy Man*, about a shopping channel program director who puts a spiritualist on the air to save his job. Another film planned was *Prayer*, a film inspired by John Irving's 1989 book *A Prayer for Owen Meany*. Then there was *A Course in Miracles,* about a young Jesuit priest investigating miracles for the Vatican. And let's not forget their relationship with M. Night "Sixth Sense" Shamalayan. They want scripts they can make quickly.

Contact: Jeremy Steckler.

STARGAZER ENTERTAINMENT

11828 La Grange Avenue, Los Angeles, CA 90025
310-479-1200
Fax: 310-473-9166
E-mail: wmrc1@aol.com

Wayne Rogers, Executive Producer

Amy Rogers, Executive Producer

Bill Tannen, Executive Producer

Linda Black, Executive Assistant

Not much has changed with this company since the last edition. *Age Old Friends* and *Perfect Witness* are still their main film credits; they've been doing AMC's "Hollywood Report" series and Charlie Rose Specials. Still, they were actively looking for scripts from new writers when former development executive Marc Bienstock posted that fact on America Online. Think television; that's what they do. You probably remember Wayne Rogers from the *M.A.S.H.* TV series? He's a decent director, too.

Contact: Bill Tannen with a query via mail or fax.

STEAMROLLER PRODUCTIONS, INC.
(WAS SEAGAL/NASSO)

1041 N. Formosa Avenue, Writer's Bldg., Suite 11, W. Hollywood, CA 90046
323-850-2940
Fax: 323-850-2978 and 323-850-2979
E-mail: steamrollerprod@aol.com
Web site: www.stevenseagal.com

Steven Seagal, CEO/Director/Writer/Producer/Actor

Phillip Goldfine, President/COO

Tim Wassberg, Story Editor

Tracy Irvine, Executive Assistant

With the release of *Exit Wounds* the week before the Academy Awards of 2001, Hollywood wondered if Steven Seagal was truly back. It topped the box office, and the answer is a resounding "yes." I've seen all Seagal's movies except *The Glimmer Man* and like most I like him in movies like the *Under Siege* series (number three is in the pipeline as we go to press) and *Above the Law*. Phil Goldfine is an experienced executive always on the lookout for something different, however. He always shows up at the Hollywood Film Festival and will listen to any interesting project.

Contact: Tim Wassberg for current needs.

STORYLINE ENTERTAINMENT

10202 W. Washington Boulevard, Jimmy Stewart Bldg., Suite 206, Culver City, CA
   90232
310-244-3222
Fax: 310-244-0322

Craig Zadan, Producer

Neil Meron, Producer

Dave Mace, VP of Television

A. B. Fischer, VP of Feature Development

Travis Knox, Creative Executive

Lisa J. Roth, Executive Assistant

If you want to do a high-profile TV movie like *The Beach Boys* or *The Three Stooges*, you'd probably think of Craig Zadan first. The company is very good at dealing with formerly-seen material; for example, in the pipeline is a reworking of Ray Bradbury's *Fahrenheit 451*. With *Enchanted*, however, they're moving into features with a film about an animated woman who ventures into the real 3-D world, only her animated true love follows her to bring her back. Of course, Zadan's been there before. He produced Kevin Bacon's breakthrough feature, *Footloose*. They're working on a remake of *The Music Man* for television, as well as a half-hour dramedy called "Jupiter and Mars" for the Fox Family Channel, and some Broadway shows, too. With deals at Columbia TriStar Television and Walt Disney Pictures/Touchstone Pictures, if they like your project they can make it happen—whatever it is!

Contact: Travis Knox for current needs.

SUMMIT ENTERTAINMENT

1630 Stewart Street, Suite 120, Santa Monica, CA 90404
310-309-8400
Fax: 310-828-4132

Patrick Wachsberger, Chief Executive Officer

Bob Hayward, Chief Operating Officer

Dave Garrett, Executive VP

Eric Feig, Head of Production & Acquisitions

Dawn Ebert-Byrnes, Director of Development

One of the partnering companies in Escape Artists, this company has deep ties to foreign markets, where they've distributed films like *Book of Shadows: Blair Witch 2* and *American Pie*, and they've been involved with fascinating films like *The Dish*, *Memento*, and *Insomnia*. Things in the pipeline at press time included *Panic* (an untitled Robert Kennedy project), *The Affair of the Necklace*, starring Hillary Swank, and *The Brothers Grimm*. What does all this mean? That if you have something not quite mainstream, with foreign possibilities and a little different, they might like it.

Contact: Eric Feig or **Dawn Ebert-Byrnes** for current needs.

SUNBOW ENTERTAINMENT

1725 Victory Boulevard , Glendale, CA 91201
818-241-3100
Fax: 818-241-7168

New York office:
100 5th Avenue 3rd Floor, New York, NY 10011
212-886-4900
Fax: 212-366-4242
E-mail: postmaster@sunbowentertainment.com
Web site: www.sunbowentertainment.com

Joe Bacal, Co-Chairman

Tom Griffin, Co-Chairman

C. J. Kettler, President

Carole Weitzman, Senior VP of Production

Nina Hahn, VP of Development

Ken Olshansky, Director of Creative Affairs

In every book I have at least one company listed simply because I like what they do, and this is one. Sunbow specializes in quality family entertainment for the U.S. and international markets and is one of the top distributors of quality family entertainment throughout the world. They've received the following accolades: the Peabody Award, the Ohio State Award, the Action for Children's Television Award (ACT), the Emmy, and awards from the New York International Film and Television Festival. In the past they've done *G.I. Joe*, *The Mask,* and *The Tick.* They're always up to something interesting, so if you're a "family writer" they might want to hear from you.

Contact: Ken Olshansky, but you might need to query or submit through an agent or lawyer.

SUNTAUR/ELSBOY ENTERTAINMENT

1581 N. Crescent Heights Boulevard, Los Angeles, CA 90046
213-656-3800
Fax: 213-656-6311
E-mail: suntaurent@aol.com

Paul Aaron, Writer/Producer/Director

Michael Henry Brown, Writer/Producer

Rick Andreoli, Director of Development

You probably know Suntaur from their 1999 movie *In Too Deep* with Omar Epps and LL Cool J. They're into network TV, cable, theater, and feature films. Michael Henry Brown is the author of numerous plays and wrote the screenplay for *Dead Presidents* (directed by the Hughes Brothers for Caravan Pictures). Paul Aaron, "the youngest theatrical director in Broadway history" (his words), has worked in both film and theater, winning multiple awards for his work, which includes directing *The Miracle Worker,* starring Melissa Gilbert and Patty Duke. In 1996, Paul executive-produced *Grand Avenue* with Robert Redford for HBO. As a team, Brown and Aaron created *Laurel Avenue* for HBO, with Michael writing the screenplay and Paul executive producing. I didn't hear from anyone who contacted them via the second edition who made a deal with them, but they're still in business.

Contact: Rick Andreoli. Query first. If you send a letter, a SASE is appreciated. Requests made by e-mail will be answered once a week.

TAPESTRY FILMS INC.

9328 Civic Center Drive, Beverly Hills, CA 90210
310-275-1191
Fax: 310-275-1266

Peter Abrams, Producer/Partner

Robert L. Levy, Producer/Partner

Jennifer Gibgot, President of Production

Jonathan Komack-Martin, Executive VP

Andrew Panay, VP of Production

Terry Guerin, Director of Literary Affairs (212-496-1000)

Michael K. Eitelman, Creative Executive

Executive Assistants: Michelle Castillo, Jennifer Hilton, Jeremy Martin, Nichole Somers

Although it's been a long time since I've seen him, I've known Peter Abrams since I first started screenwriting, and his fortunes are the same as mine: some not so good, some very good. I loved *Point Break*, didn't like *She's All That*. *The Wedding Planner* was a big hit for them in 2000, but the hotly anticipated *Pay It Forward* with Haley Joel Osment and James Spacey (from a novel) fell flat. When I knew him, Peter Abrams never turned down an opportunity to read a script from a writer he thought had promise. He read several of mine and always had good feedback. Naturally, I lost touch with him just before he hit it big. The company has a Columbia TriStar Television deal, under which they will develop prime time comedy and drama series, and they're very much in the feature business. If Peter buys one from you, tell him I said hello.

Contact: Michael K. Eitelman for current needs.

TIG PRODUCTIONS, INC.

100 Universal City Plaza, Universal City, CA 91608
818-777-2737
Fax: 818-733-5616

Kevin Costner, President/Partner/Producer

Jim Wilson, Partner

Soraya Delawari Dancsecs, Creative Executive

Thirteen Days wasn't exactly a hit, and neither was *3000 Miles to Graceland* (done with Franchise Pictures). Now Kevin Costner has moved from Warner Brothers to Universal, so maybe his fortunes will change. Costner always believes in his projects, although proclaiming that world leaders should all see *Thirteen Days* made him look a bit silly. What's up next? Maybe *Shank*, from a novel by Roderick Anscombe, about a man imprisoned for killing his wife who has an obsessive love affair with the prison nurse, breaks out of jail and . . . well, maybe not, it was a Warners project. But this is where you'll find him.

Contact: Soraya Delawari Dancsecs for current needs.

TRIBECA PRODUCTIONS

375 Greenwich Street, 8th Floor, New York, NY 10013
212-941-4000
Fax: 212-941-4044
E-mail: contactus@tribecafilm.com
Web site: www.tribecafilm.com

Robert De Niro, Partner

Jane Rosenthal, Partner

Hardy Justice, VP of Creative Affairs

Angela Robinson, Creative Executive

Scott Neustadter, Director of Development

Executive Assistants: Kate Feeney, Meghan Lyvers

I think Robert De Niro is a genius. He has a company in a New York neighborhood he loves, and the company makes movies no one expects them to make, like *Thunderheart* with Val Kilmer. When he makes movies they *do* expect him to make, like Chaz Palminteri's *A Bronx Tale,* they're great. In 1996 the company acquired film rights to the Tony-winning Broadway musical *Rent*, so when it comes to the screen you'll know from where. *Wag the Dog, Analyze This, Meet the Parents*—have they been hitting it lately, or what? Oh wait. They did *Rocky & Bullwinkle.* (My kids loved it.) There's a great scene in *Analyze This* where DeNiro the mob boss says "What're we gonna do, put up a Web site?" He did, and it explains all about them. Yo, check it out and tell them about yourself, or fuddegaboudit. They have a deal with Metro-Goldwyn-Mayer and they're gonna make some great movies; maybe you'll write one of them.

Contact: Scott Neustadter or anyone **creative.**

TRILOGY ENTERTAINMENT GROUP

2450 Broadway Street, Penthouse, Suite 675, Santa Monica, CA 90404-3061
310-449-3095
Fax: 310-449-3195

Pen Densham, Founder

John Watson, Founder

Guy McElwaine, Pres./COO/Partner

Mark Stern, President of TV/Partner

Nora O'Brien, VP of Production

Kelly Stuart, Director of Development

Creative Executives in TV: Julie Fitzgerald, Ellen Rand

Rachel Leonard, Executive Assistant

If you like the work of writer/director Pen Densham as much as I do, you'll like Trilogy. The "camera on the arrow" in *Robin Hood* was his. (The producer of that one, Richard B. Lewis, is listed under Southpaw earlier.) This company is a grouping of a lot of very creative people, like Guy McElwaine, who was a top agent for a long time. They have quite a few things in development, including a remake of Ernest Lehman's *Sweet Smell of Success*, a movie about the Flying Tigers of World War II legend, and another from the old *Outer Limits* TV show. Deals with MGM and New Line Television ensure they'll be busy from quite some time.

Contact: Kelly Stuart or, if you have TV in mind, either of the **Creative Executives.**

VALHALLA MOTION PICTURES
(WAS PACIFIC WESTERN PRODUCTIONS)

8530 Wilshire Boulevard, Fourth Floor, Beverly Hills, CA 90211-3122
310-360-8530
Fax: 310-360-8531
E-mail: vmp@valhallamotionpics.com
Web site: www.valhallamotionpics.com

Gale Anne Hurd, CEO/Producer

Barbara Boyle, President

Sig Libowitz, VP of Production

Tracy Mercer, Director of Development

Robin Winston, Story Editor

David Herrera, Development Assistant

Executive Assistants: Tiger Bela, Tim Reid, Denise Hayes-Wouters

Valhalla has a first-look deal with Kinowelt USA that includes discretionary fund and revolving development financing for feature film budgets between $20 to $80 million. The company was formed in 1982; *The Terminator* was their maiden project. Big-budget, big box office movies like *Armageddon* are their style, but their old lower-budget division, No Frills Films, produced fine movies like *The Waterdance*. One of the more interesting projects in their pipeline is *Clockstoppers*, about a young boy and some friends who find dad's time machine and get in a ton of trouble. That fits in with Gale Anne Hurd's claim that she always looks for "character-driven projects in all genres." They are, however, doing *The Hulk*.

Contact: Tracy Mercer. Don't just mail in a script; they have to be interested first, but they show up at Spec Script Marketplace and such venues, so they're always looking for new writers.

VANGUARD FILMS

1230 La Collina Drive, Beverly Hills, CA 90210
310-888-8020
Fax: 310-888-8012
E-mail: vgrdfilm@pacbell.net
Web site: www.vanguardfilms.com

John H. Williams, President/Producer

Eric Bennett, Vice President

Development Executives: Venecia Duran, Rob Moreland

The company has a first-look production deal with Dreamworks SKG through 2003. They distributed *The Hills Have Eyes* but have made several thoughtful and socially-conscious films like *Seven Years in Tibet* and *Sarafina!* Their kidflick *Shrek* could be an animated hit. If you want to know about other things in the pipeline like *Pet Boy* and/or *Rednecks in Space*, take a look at the Web site.

Contact: Either **Development Executive** for current needs.

VILLAGE ROADSHOW PICTURES

3400 Riverside Drive, Suite 900, Burbank, CA 91505
818-260-6000
Fax: 818-260-6001

Bruce Berman, Chairman/CEO

Bernie Goldmann, President of Production

Jordanna Fraiberg, Creative Executive

William Heflin, Story Editor

Executive Assistants: Paul Dy, Suzy Figueroa, Cathleen Hoadley, Rozzana Ramos

Village Roadshow Pictures began as the American production arm of the Australian cinema and entertainment company, Village Roadshow, Ltd., and has often been a launching point for Australian talent moving to the United States. When they landed a big deal with Warner Bros. worth more than $300 million in production, the company really took off. *Analyze This*, *The Matrix*, *Three Kings,* and *Space Cowboys* are films they have partnered with under the deal. The company is packed with many executives who are not listed above, so don't be surprised if you need an agent to get through. Nevertheless, if you have a film, TV show, or animated feature with an international flavor, this might be the place for you.

Contact: William Heflin for current needs and submission policies.

VON ZERNECK-SERTNER FILMS

13425 Ventura Boulevard, # 301, Sherman Oaks, CA 91423
818-789-2766
Fax: 818-789-2768

Frank von Zerneck, Partner

Robert Sertner, Partner

Randy Sutter, VP of Production

Peter Sadowski, VP of Production

Danielle von Zerneck Fearnley, VP of Development

Nancy S. Mouton, Executive Assistant

Christina Barnes, Assistant

This company has Robin Cook's *Virus* as well as his *Invasion*; they generally go after books to develop for television. That doesn't mean they won't look at other things, as they have a long list of credits, but in recent years they've really liked books. When author Trevor Meldal-Johnsen asked me whether he should sell his book *Mistress* to Frank von Zerneck (who liked it very much), I told him to go for it because the TV movie would almost certainly get made. Unfortunately, the deal never happened. If you have a book (published) that you think would make a great TV movie or miniseries, this company might be able to make it happen.

Contact: Query **Danielle von Zerneck Fearnley** for current needs and submission policy.

JERRY WEINTRAUB PRODUCTIONS

4000 Warner Boulevard, Bungalow 1, Burbank, CA 91522-0001
818-954-2500
Fax: 818-954-1399

Jerry Weintraub, Producer

Kimberly Pinkstaff, Assistant to Mr. Weintraub

John Tomko, Senior VP of Development & Production

Jerry Weintraub has a long list of major film credits and is a major feature film producer. His past projects including *Diner,* the *Karate Kid* movies, *Nashville,* and *The Avengers.* Like any other company housed on a major studio lot, don't count on them looking at your project unless it is submitted through an established agent. I have, however, found them very receptive in the past and it never hurts to ask. Most recent projects include the remake of *Oceans 11* with an amazing cast and directed by Steven Soderbergh. Recent acquisitions include a comedy pitch entitled "Fishin' Magician" set in rural Alabama and "Day Trader" about a high school kid who goes nuts with the stock market.

Contact: John Tomko for current needs and submission policies.

YORKTOWN PRODUCTIONS

3000 Olympic Boulevard, Bldg. 2, Suite 2465, Santa Monica, CA 90404
310-264-4155
Fax: 310-264-4167

Norman Jewison, Director/Producer

Dianne Hatlestad, Creative Executive

Liz Broden, Executive Assistant

Norman Jewison is Mr. Movie to Canadians. He's won a lot of awards since he began directing feature films in the 1960s, with hits like *The Cincinnati Kid* (1965) and *In the Heat of the Night* (1967, which won five Academy awards). Many great movies followed, both drama and comedy, my favorite being the hilarious *The Russians Are Coming! The Russians Are Coming!* in 1966. In 1987, Jewison had a smash hit with *Moonstruck*, which won Oscars for Cher as best actress, Olympia Dukakis as best supporting actress, and John Patrick Shanley for best screenplay. In 1986, he established the Canadian Centre for Advanced Films Studies (he is Chair Emeritus). He also helped create and present *InterActive 96*, a "professional development conference/series of workshops to introduce creative artists to the opportunities becoming available in the rapidly evolving world of interactive technology." His most recent hit was *The Hurricane* with Denzel Washington, and in the pipeline is *Dinner With Friends* for HBO Films, based on Donald Marguiles' off-Broadway play that won the Pulitzer Prize in 2000.

Contact: Dianne Hatlestad for current needs.

SAUL ZAENTZ COMPANY

2600 10th Street, Berkeley, CA 94710
510-549-1528
Fax: 510-486-2108

Saul Zaentz, Producer

Saul Zaentz made millions and a few enemies as the owner of Fantasy Records, a company that recorded the superstar group Credence Clearwater Revival in the 1960's. Zaentz backed the film that made Michael Douglas a force in the movie business and made Jack Nicholson a superstar through *One Flew Over the Cuckoo's Nest*. His next project, *Amadeus* was a huge hit and Zaentz' hat was thrust back in the Hollywood ring. Another long lull, then came *The English Patient*. If you have a project that's a quirky look at the unconquerable human spirit, you might check with Zaentz. Zaentz collected a lot of awards after making *The English Patient*. He has won more awards than I can list here, including the Irving Thalberg Oscar.

Contact: Saul Zaentz for current needs.

ZALOOM FILM

1351 Fourth Street, Fourth Floor, Santa Monica, CA 90401
310-656-8400
Fax: 310-656-8430

George Zaloom, Producer

Bruno Fortuna, VP of Development

Robin Goodfellow, Director of Development

If you're a kid, you love these guys. They brought us *Encino Man* and *H-E-Double Hockey Sticks*, as well as the Wonderful World of Disney Telefilm Series. They do TV series, TV movies, and great documentaries like "Frank Capra, An American Legend." The things they have in development are more of the same; if that's your kind of show, give them a shout.

Contact: Development people listed.

THE ZANUCK COMPANY

9465 Wilshire Boulevard, Suite 930, Beverly Hills, CA 90212
310-274-0261
Fax: 310-273-9217
E-mail: zanuckco@aol.com

Richard D. Zanuck, Producer

Lili Fini Zanuck, Producer/Director

Dean Zanuck, VP

Harrison Zanuck, VP

It's a classy family affair, downright Hollywood royalty at this company. Richard Zanuck and his wife, Lili, have made the best of it, with such movies as *Cocoon* and *Driving Miss Daisy*. Other credits include *Jaws, The Sting,* and *The Verdict*. More recently, *Deep Impact*, a coproduction between Paramount and DreamWorks SKG was a hit, and I loved *True Crime* with Clint Eastwood. Their remake of *Planet of the Apes* might not please fans of the original, but I think it will make a lot of money. Big budget, big box office, with an occasional foray into the human condition, that's Zanuck. If you had your screenplay picked up by them, you'd be very fortunate.

Contact: a **Zanuck.**

ZOLLO PRODUCTIONS, INC.

257 West 52nd Street, Second Floor, New York, NY 10019
212-957-1300
Fax: 212-957-1315
E-mail: zpi@aol.com
Web site: www.members.aol.com/zpi/index.html

Frederick Zollo, Producer

Nicholas Paleologos, Producer

Bostic Beard, VP of Creative Affairs

Executive Assistants: Jesse Hove, Jonathan Wexler

Have a look at the Web site—these folks do it all. I'll let you find out for yourself what ZPi, 52nd Street Productions, and Stuart Street Partners are about. Meanwhile, they've been behind classy productions that offer poignant social commentary, films like *Quiz Show*, *Mississippi Burning,* and *Hurly Burly*. They have a deal with Sony Pictures Entertainment and are heavily involved in theater. In short, many possibilities here if you have the right thing.

Contact: Bostic Beard for current needs.

ZUCKER/NETTER PRODUCTIONS

1411 Fifth Street, Suite 402, Santa Monica, CA 90401
310-394-1644
Fax: 310-899-6722

David Zucker, Producer/Director/Writer

Gil Netter, President

Lawrence Grey, VP

Executive Assistants: Mike Ades, Phil Dornfeld

Think: (1) very funny–the *Naked Gun* movies and *Dude, Where's My Car?* (well, okay, stupid, too); (2) very charming–*My Best Friend's Wedding*; or (3) bizarre–the upcoming *Phone Booth*, about a guy who has to stay on a pay phone while outwitting a terrorist. This company has a deal with Fox 2000 and Twentieth Century Fox overall and basically makes whatever strikes their fancy. Their latest acquisition before press time was *Rule #3*, about a business-like hitman who becomes enraged by speeding driver, then infiltrates and terrorizes the life of the guy, who happens to be a wealthy, arrogant heir. Dude, where's your script?

Contact: Anyone listed above, but don't call from a phone booth, and don't mention O. J. Simpson.

Glossary

PLEASE NOTE: *Like any industry, the film and television business has its own verbal and written shorthand, which is in constant flux. Therefore, the terms defined below are not intended to be a complete list of "Hollywoodspeak" but only serve as a primer. They are also geared mostly for terms used regularly in Hollywood, not so much for technical terms used in the writing of scripts.*

"A" Page   A revised page of a script that extends a scene beyond the original page, going onto a second page (i.e. Page 1, 1A, 2, 3, 3A). Normally only used with scripts in production.

Action   The description of the moving pictures within a scene, as opposed to dialogue, which is formatted differently. Action includes sounds which are particularly notable in the scene, such as when a BOMB EXPLODES (important sounds are generally CAPPED).

ad lib   Dialogue made up by characters or actors in real time on a movie set. This term comes from the Latin *ad libitum*, "in accordance with desire."

Against   Used to describe the ultimate potential payday for a writer in a film deal. $300,000 against $750,000 means that the writer is paid $300,000 when the script is finished (through rewrite and polish), and if the movie goes into production, the writer gets an additional $450,000.

Alan Smithee   A fictional name traditionally taken by a writer or director who doesn't want their real name credited on a film because of some disagreement with the final product.

Angle   A notation suggesting a different camera angle within a scene to focus on a particular person or thing. For example, ANGLE ON SHERIFF.

Approved writer   A writer that a television network feels can be trusted to deliver a good script on time without many problems.

Arbitration   A binding committee determination by members of the Writers Guild of America regarding what writers should receive screen credit on a completed film. Open only to WGA members or potential WGA members.

Attached   When name actors and/or a director agreed to make a movie from your script, it is said they are "attached".

Audio/Visual Script   A dual column screenplay with video description on the left and audio and dialogue on the right, used in the production of commercials, documentaries, etc.

Back door pilot   A two-hour TV movie which is a setup for a TV series if ratings on the movie warrant. Not as common these days—a one-hour or 30-minute pilot is usually done instead.

Back end   To get paid on the back end is to receive payment once a movie project is fully funded and/or when profits are realized.

Back story   The background of a main character or events that took place before the main action. Useful for the writer, but rarely of much interest to the audience.

Bankable   A movie star or director, occasionally an author (such as Stephen King or John Grisham) who can get a project financed if their name is attached. When someone bankable is attached, financiers know that a high enough percentage of the public will see the film and that production costs can likely be recouped.

Beat   (1) A high point of a scene in a script that advances the plot; or (2) a parenthetically indicated pause interrupting dialogue which may be indicated by either (a) (beat) or (b) . . . (ellipses).

Beat sheet   A short description of the main events in a screenplay or story. Example with Truman from *The Truman Show*: (1) Truman has breakfast; (2) Truman says hello to neighbors; (3) Truman hears stage light fall to the ground, sees it on ground, and gets very curious about what's really going on.

b.g. (background)   Action occurring behind the main focus of the action, usually designated "in the b.g."

Brad   A brass fastener used to hold a three-hole punched screenplay together; Hollywood people prefer solid brass.

Bump   A troublesome element in a scene or storyline that negatively draws the reader/viewer's attention away from the overall flow of the story.

The Business   The Hollywood moviemaking and television business; more broadly, show business in general.

Button   A term developed in TV writing, particularly sitcoms, referring to a witty line that tops off a scene and transits to the next. James Cameron made copious use of buttons in *Titanic*.

Cable   Any cable television network, like Showtime, or cable television in general.

CGI   Computer-Generated Images, as seen in *Toy Story* or *Dinosaur*, but also applying to computer-aided alterations of filmed scenes as in *The Matrix* and other action films.

Chain lightning twist   A crucial climax scene that causes the viewer to flash back to various points in the screenplay, mentally adding up clues that have been planted that make this climax logical. A good example is the point at the end of *The Sixth Sense* where we realize Bruce Willis' psychiatrist character has been dead all along.

Character   Any personified entity appearing in a screenplay.

Character arc   The progress of the emotional development of main characters during the plot.

Cheat a script   To adjust a word processing or screenplay formatting program so that it compresses the distance between lines on a page, allowing you to compact a script that might be 125 pages or so onto 120 pages or less. 90 to 120 pages is the acceptable length of a single-spaced feature film script, which averages one minute shooting time per page. Not a good idea.

Close Up   A very close camera angle on a character or object.

Committed   Term designating that an actor, director, producer, production company, or studio has agreed to be involved in a project, often legally binding.

Conflict   The heart of drama; someone wants something, and people and things keep getting in the way of them achieving the goal. The obstacles can sometimes be common to both the hero and villain, and the ultimate goal laudable for both parties.

Courier 12 pitch   The preferred font of both U.S. publishers and the Hollywood film industry.

Coverage   The Hollywood producer or development executive who will personally read your script is more the exception than the rule. Usually, a script is given to a reader for a report. The two- to three-page synopsis which the reader produces is called coverage. Coverage stays on file at large production companies and studios, accessible to anyone at the facility for future reference.

Credit   A completed project on which a writer's name appears onscreen. Many screenwriters labor for years, often making a good living writing scripts, before a script is filmed with their name appearing onscreen. Thus it is of primary importance to have a film credit. Battles over credits are fought weekly in WGA arbitrations. Also, the WGA has a point system against which credits are evaluated, with a certain level of points necessary to join. Contact the WGA for more details.

Development   What happens to a script after it is acquired. Since it generally costs so much money to film a script, and since studio executives have to justify their high salaries, scripts are "developed." This basically means that they are rewritten, often many times with several different writers. (Then, if the movie fails, the executive can claim they got the best writers to work on it and should therefore not be blamed.) When the process lasts a long time, it is referred to as "development hell." If a screenwriter is lucky, he or she is allowed to remain on the project as the primary writer, the one with top screen credit. When a project gets the go-ahead to be filmed, the project moves from development into pre-production.

Dialogue   The speeches that take place between characters.

Digital   A film made entirely with a digital camera.

Extension   A note placed directly to the right of the Character name denoting how the character's voice is heard. O.C. is an extension that stands for Off-Camera.

Feature   A film made to be exhibited in movie theaters. The term originated in the early days of film, when cartoons or short films were shown prior to the main feature of the evening. In Hollywood, it is generally more desirable to make a feature than any other type of movie.

f.g.   Action occurring in front of the main focus of the action, usually designated "in the f.g."

Fox   An example of Hollywood shorthand for a studio or network. Fox is Twentieth Century Fox. NBC is often referred to in the trades as "the Peacock," while CBS has been called "the Eye" because its logo resembles a human eye, and "Black Rock" because of the New York building where its headquarters are found. There is no dictionary of such Hollywood terms, but they are used regularly in articles in the trades and should be learned by anyone serious about working in Hollywood.

Flashback   A scene from the past interrupting the action to explain character motivation or reaction to the immediate scene.

Freeze frame   An image on the screen stops, freezes, and becomes a still shot.

Ghost   The inner struggle that torments a main character, usually from some unresolved incident of their past. Also "wound."

Go wide   To send out a script to as many potential buyers as possible, usually on the same day.

Green light   The day every producer lives for is when a project is okayed for production by the person(s) in charge of financing.

The Guild   For actors, there is only one guild, the Screen Actors Guild. For Hollywood writers, there is only one guild, the Writers Guild of America.

Header   An element of a Production Script occupying the same line as the page number; header information includes the date of a revision and the color of the page.

Heat   A buzz on the Hollywood grapevine about a "hot" script, or a project in which some top star or director is interested. Heat can also apply to a person. For example, if Steven Spielberg was interested in a script, there would be heat on it. In fact, it would be white hot.

Helmer   A *Variety* "slanguage" term designating a director.

High concept   A short statement of the basic idea of a movie, which can often be expressed in the title. For example: *Abbott & Costello Meet Frankenstein*.

Hip pocket   A casual relationship with an established agent in which the agent will agree to say they represent you even though you don't have a signed, formal agreement. You will be expected to do all your own marketing, bringing in the agent only when you generate some interest in your property.

Hook   A songwriting term borrowed by Hollywood to describe that thing in a story that catches the attention and keeps you interested.

Indies   Motion pictures financed and produced independently, that is, outside of major studios such as Warner Brothers or Paramount Studios.

Intercut   A script instruction telling the reader that the action moves back and forth between two or more scenes.

It's not for us   Hollywood shorthand for any reason why a producer or production company does not want your script. Don't ask them to explain.

Leave-behind   A one to three page synopsis you may be asked to leave with someone after a pitch meeting.

Let's do lunch   What started off as an innocent phrase is now generally considered to be a sarcastic way of saying "I may never contact you again." Depending on the person, however, it might be a sincere invitation.

Locked pages   A software term for screenplay pages that have been finalized before handing out the script to department heads and others in preparation for production.

Logline   Hollywood's "25 words or less." A sentence (two or three at the most) that summarizes the entire plot of your screenplay.

Master scene script   The scenes of a film without the adornment of scene numbering.

Match cut   A movie transition in which something in the scene following seems to directly match something in the previous scene.

Miniseries   Three hours or more of the same movie, shown on successive nights or weeks on U.S. television networks.

Montage   A device popularized by Sergei Eisenstein, used to show a series of scenes, all related and building to a conclusion.

M.O.S.   A German-born director wanting a scene with no sound told the crew to shoot "mit out sound" and so it has been since.

MOW   A Movie of the Week, a film made primarily for airing on television, although some MOWs are exhibited in theaters outside the United States.

Multimedia   More than one medium at once; scriptwise, this usually refers to CD-ROM games or Internet-based programs.

Notes   Ideas about a property communicated to a writer by a director, producer or film or TV executive, verbally or in writing. "Giving notes" is a regular practice, intended to improve a script in theory. In practice, notes mean absolutely nothing unless the writer agrees with them or will lose control of the project if the notes are not implemented.

O.C.   Abbreviation for Off Camera that denotes the speaker is resident within the scene but not seen by the camera.

One-hour episodic   A television show whose episodes fill a one-hour time slot, week to week.

Opening credits   Onscreen text describing the most important people involved in making a movie, such as the stars.

One-sheet   A one–page description of a property. Also referred to as a "one-pager."

Option   The securing of the rights to a property for a given length of time. Standard practice for an option once included paying 10% of the agreed-upon purchase price, with the balance due when the option was exercised. If the option expires, the writer keeps the money and the property with no commitment to the buyer. For beginning screenwriters, an option often means the producer wants to try to sell the project exclusively for six months to a year or longer, with no money down or a token $1 payment. This is known as a free option. Often, if they don't pay for it, they won't value it, so don't give anyone a free option.

O.S.   Abbreviation for Off Screen; the speaker is not resident within the scene.

Package   To put together the elements necessary to secure financing for a film; basically, a script, a director, and an acceptable star or ensemble. When an agency "packages" and sells a project a studio, it gets an extra percentage for the package.

Page one   To completely rewrite a screenplay from page one.

Pan   What we see when a stationary camera pivots back and forth or up and down.

Parenthetical   An inflection to a speech, also known as a "wryly" because of the propensity to accent a character's speech. Example: JOE (wryly).

Pass   A rejection of your script. "We're going to take a pass" means "We will not buy your script." You may or may not get a more detailed explanation.

Pitch   To describe your story, script or property, with or without visual aids, in hopes it will be bought.

Points   Percentage profit participation. One point equals 1 percent. Gross points are valuable; net points are often worthless.

Polish   In theory, to rewrite a few scenes in a script to improve them. In practice, a writer is often expected to do a complete rewrite of a script for the price of a polish.

Possessory credit   The "A Film By" credit at the opening of a film, reputedly invented by French director Jean-Luc Godard.

Post-production   Turning raw film footage into a movie.

POV   Point of View; a camera angle placed so as to seem as if the camera is in the eyes of a character.

Pre-production   The stage of a film project where the script is finalized and the preparations for filming to begin take place.

Production script   A script in which no more major changes or rewrites are anticipated to occur, which is used for filming.

Property   Any story in any form that might form the basis of a movie, whether it is in the form of a screenplay or not.

Punch up   To improve a script, usually a sitcom, by making the dialogue leaner, more biting, or clever.

Reader   A person who reads screenplays for a production company and writes a report about each as to its potential worth.

Register   Film properties such as treatments and screenplays can be registered with the Writers Guild of America for $20 ($10 for WGA members). Once it is registered, WGA personnel preserve it in case of future legal wranglings over the property.

Release   A legal document you may be asked to sign which absolves the company reading your material from legal liability, should they have already acquired material similar or identical to your property. Check with your lawyer.

Reversal   A place in the plot where progress made is lost. Over 2000 years ago, Aristotle referred to them as "perepetia".

Romcom   Industry shorthand for a romantic comedy, just as situation comedy is shortened to sitcom.

Sample   A script which best represents the quality of your writing.

Scene   Action taking place in one location.

Scene heading   A short description of the location and time of day of a scene, also known as a "slugline."

Screening   The showing of a film for people involved in the movie industry, or for test audiences, done to gauge reactions to the film.

Screenwriter   The most important and most abused person in Hollywood.

Scribe   A *Variety* "slanguage" term designating a writer.

Script   The blueprint of a movie story through visual descriptions, actions of characters and their dialogue.

The set   Any place, either in a studio or on location, where filming takes place.

Set up   (1) To get a project accepted for production at a production company, studio, network or any other entity capable of financing it. (2) The elements in place at the beginning of a story that help set the story in motion. The set up of *Cast Away* might be: a dynamic corporate executive is stranded alone on a desert island.

SFX   An abbreviation for Sound Effects.

Shooting script   The draft of the screenplay that is used to make the movie by the cast and crew. Even then, changes are often made, with the changes designated by different colored pages.

Short   A short film, 30 seconds to several minutes in length, which has a beginning, middle and end; often made these days to showcase a filmmaker's expertise on the World Wide Web.

Shot   What the camera sees.

Showrunner   A writer/producer who runs the show for a television network, the person ultimately responsible for the show getting on the air each week.

Signatory   If a producer or production company is a signatory of the Writers Guild of America, they have signed an agreement to abide by WGA rules. If a new screenwriter sells a script, they cannot necessarily join the WGA unless the entity who purchased the script is a WGA signatory. Contact the WGA for details on who is and is not a signatory.

Sitcom   A situation comedy, a 30-minute (in the United States) show revolving around repeating characters in funny situations.

Slug line   The ALL CAPS text that begins a scene, such as: EXT. MAJOR MOVIE STUDIO—DAY.

Smash cut   A quick or sudden cut from one scene to another.

Soap opera   In the U.S., a (usually daytime) drama so named because they were originally sponsored by laundry detergents.

Spec   A script written speculatively, without being hired or commissioned, on the hope that it can be sold.

Split screen   Different scenes taking place in two or more sections of the screen; the scenes are usually interactive, as in the depiction of a phone conversation.

SPFX   A script abbreviation denoting Special Effects.

Step deal   A payment schedule common to television in which the writer is paid upon completion of each element necessary to a completed screenplay.

Step treatment   A scene by scene description of a screenplay.

Stock shot   A film sequence previously shot and available for purchase from a film library.

Storyboard   A scene by scene roughly-drawn visual outline of the plot of a script.

Storyline   Roughly the same thing as a logline, although you might be allowed more than three sentences to tell the tale.

Straight-to-video   A finished film of which no attempt is made to exhibit it in movie theaters. Rather, it is only sold as a VHS video or DVD.

Super   Abbreviation for "superimpose" meaning the layering of one image on top of another.

Synopsis   Usually, a two- to three-page, double-spaced description of a property.

Tag   A short scene at the end of a movie that usually provides some small feel-good, upbeat addition to the climax.

Tag line   An advertising tease line often seen on movie posters. The tag line of *Brother, Where Art Thou?* by the Coen Brothers was "They have a plan, but not a clue."

Take a meeting   To be interested enough about a property to meet with the writer to discuss it. If a producer says, "Let's take a meeting," take it. If they meet with you more than twice about a project without making a deal, however, they may be violating Writers Guild of America rules. Contact the WGA for details.

Teaser   The normally two to three-minute opening of a TV movie or one-hour episodic TV show that primes the viewers by setting up the story.

Thriller   A fast-paced, high stakes crime story in which the protagonist is increasingly in danger.

Title   Text appearing onscreen to denote a key element of the movie, a change of location or date, or person involved.

The Trades   News periodicals pertaining to the film industry. Most prominent are *The Hollywood Reporter*, *Daily Variety*, and *Variety* (weekly).

Tracking   An analysis of the worthiness of any given project that is floating around Hollywood for purchase at the moment, with information traded back and forth among the various development executives in town.

Trailer   Advertisements for upcoming films, so named because in earlier years they were played after the end of the feature, thus "trailing" it.

Transition   An editing transition within the telling of a film story such as DISSOLVE TO or CUT TO.

Treatment   Technically, a scene-by-scene description of all the action of an entire script, reaching 45 to 50 pages or longer. In common parlance, a treatment is usually five to seven pages long, really little more than a synopsis.

Turnaround   When a script has been developed but for one reason or another will not be put into production by the purchasing party, the writer or production company in control of the project is given the chance to get it produced elsewhere.

TV queue   A supposedly nonexistent list of actors kept by TV networks that track who audiences like or "queue up" to see.

Tweak   To make minor changes to a scene or portion of a script.

URL   Uniform Resource Locator. A term which denotes an address on the World Wide Web. Many Hollywood executives and production companies have URLs printed on their business cards. For example, Skip Press can be found at: http://home.earthlink .net/~skippress/.

V.O.   An abbreviation for Voice Over, denoting that the speaker is not present in the scene but commenting upon it, or that the voice of a speaker in the next scene is heard by the audience.

WGA   The Writers Guild of America, with offices in Los Angeles and New York.

WGA Signatory   An agent, producer or production company that has signed an agreement to abide by existing payment agreements with the Writers Guild of America.

Work a room   To judiciously make yourself known to important industry players at a party or other event.

Wrinkle story   An example of sometimes goofy Hollywood film executive short-hand. When writer David Saperstein first tried to sell his *Cocoon*, a science-fiction story involving mostly senior citizens, one person rejected it because it was "a wrinkle story."

Writers Guild of America   See WGA above.

[**NOTE**: If you think of some terms I've left out (and I'm sure there are plenty), please let me know at skippress@earthlink.net. If you do, it's worth one free question about selling your property to Hollywood.]

Resources

Writing screenplays that sell means you must go to school forever. You have to keep up with trends in arts, literature, and society to stay relevant to the moviegoing audience. So just as much as you watch movies, read scripts, and keep reading. Meanwhile, read books. In addition to all the books already mentioned in previous pages, all the books and periodicals referenced below are those I consider essential reading to understand both the craft of screenwriting and the business of Hollywood. Keep discussing and honing your craft in the midst of your reading and perhaps, one day, a book you've written will be listed below. Or even better, someone will be writing a book about your career.

BOOKS

Aristotle. *Poetics*. New York: Prometheus Books, 1992.

Blacker, Irwin R. *The Elements of Screenwriting: A Guide for Film and Television Writing*. New York: Macmillan, 1988.

Callan, K. *The Script Is Finished, Now What Do I Do?* Chicago: Sweden Press, 1993.

Campbell, Joseph. *The Hero with a Thousand Faces*. Princeton, NJ: Princeton University Press, 1990.

Campbell, Joseph. *The Hero's Journey: Joseph Campbell on his Life and Work*. New York: Harper and Row, 1990.

Campbell, Joseph. *The Masks of God: Occidental Mythology*. New York: Penguin Books, 1991.

Campbell, Joseph. *The Masks of God: Oriental Mythology*. New York: Penguin Books, 1991.

Campbell, Joseph. *The Power of Myth*. New York: Doubleday, 1991.

Cole, Hillis R., Jr. & Haag, Judith H., *The Complete Guide to Standard Script Formats*. Los Angeles: CMC Publishing, 1999.

de Abreu, Carlos, and Howard Jay Smith. *Opening the Doors to Hollywood*. Beverly Hills: Custos Morum Publishers, 1995.

Egri, Lajos. *The Art of Dramatic Writing*. New York: Simon & Schuster, 1972.

Field, Syd. *Screenplay*. New York: Dell, 1984.

Field, Syd. *Selling a Screenplay: The Screenwriter's Guide to Hollywood*. New York: Dell, 1989.

Froug, William. *Screenwriting Tricks of the Trade*. Los Angeles: Silman-James Press, 1993.

Goldman, William. *Adventures in the Screen Trade*. New York: Warner Books, 1989.

Goldman, William. *Which Lie Did I Tell?* New York: Pantheon Books, 2000.

Hague, Michael. *Writing Screenplays That Sell*. New York: McGraw-Hill, 1991.

Hunter, Lew. *Lew Hunter's Screenwriting 434*. New York: Perigee Books, 1994.

King, Viki. *Write a Movie in 21 Days: The Inner Movie Method*. Atlanta: Perennial Library.

Lee, Donna. *Magic Methods of Modern Screenwriting: A Practical Handbook of TV and Movie Scriptwriting*. New York: McGraw Hill Inc./College Custom Series, 1995.

Perret, Gene. *Comedy Writing Step by Step*. Hollywood: Samuel French Trade, 1982.

Phillips, Julia. *You'll Never Eat Lunch in This Town Again*. New York: Signet, 1992.

Polti, George. *Thirty-Six Dramatic Situations*. Boston: The Writer Inc., 1988

Press, Skip. *The Complete Idiot's Guide to Screenwriting*. New York: Alpha Books/ Macmillan, 2000.

Sautter, Carl. *How to Sell Your Screenplay*. New York: New Chapter Press, 1992.

Searle, Judith. *The Literary Enneagram*. Portland, OR: Metamorphous Press, 2001.

Seger, Linda. *Making a Good Script Great*. Los Angeles: Dodd Mead, 1989.

Taussig, H. Arthur. *The Wizard of Oz: Decoding & Decyphering an Archetypal Masterpiece*. Costa Mesa, CA: ATW Publications, 1999.

Trottier, David. *The Screenwriter's Bible*. Los Angeles: Silman-James Press, 1998.

Vogler, Christopher. *The Writer's Journey*. Los Angeles: Michael Wiese Productions, 1992.

Walter, Richard. *Screenwriting: The Art, Craft and Business of Film and Television Writing*. New York: New American Library, 1988.

Wharton, Brooke A. *The Writer Got Screwed (but didn't have to)*. New York: Harper Perennial, 1999.

PERIODICALS

Daily Variety and *Variety*
Forbes
Hollywood Creative Directories
The Hollywood Reporter
SCREENTALK: The International Voice of Screenwriting
Written By (Writer's Guild of America)
Los Angeles Times
The Wall Street Journal

Index